Best wishes to you!
Kathryn Busby Massing
and George

THEN AND NOW

by

KATHRYN BUSBY MASSING

A Grain of Salt

My life is not worth a grain of salt.
And yet—Perhaps it is. Perhaps just one grain.
So, as of the third of April, 1993, I am writing my life history.
Perhaps, just perhaps, someone will find it interesting.

authorHOUSE

1663 LIBERTY DRIVE, SUITE 200
BLOOMINGTON, INDIANA 47403
(800) 839-8640
WWW.AUTHORHOUSE.COM

© 2004 KATHRYN BUSBY MASSING
All Rights Reserved.

No part of this book may be reproduced, stored in a retrieval system, or transmitted by any means without the written permission of the author.

First published by AuthorHouse 10/29/04

ISBN: 1-4184-9198-5 (sc)

Library of Congress Control Number: 2004096155

Printed in the United States of America
Bloomington, Indiana

This book is printed on acid-free paper.

Table of Contents

Dedication viii
Introduction ix
Acknowledgments x

Part One   Growing Up in Middle America 1
Chapter 1 A Bit of Genealogy 1
Chapter 2 Growing Up 9
Chapter 3 Teenage Years 40
Chapter 4 Meeting the Massings 51
Chapter 5 Early Married Life 64
Chapter 6 The War Years 75
Chapter 7 Furlough in Florida 84
Chapter 8 California 91
Chapter 9 Army Life by George-Camp Lee
to Southeast Asia 101
Chapter Ten George Returns 107

Part Two   Married Life in Ohio 110
Chapter 11 Pinecrest, Crystal Lakes, Ohio 110
Chapter 12 Friendships 121
Chapter 13 Birth, Death, and Polio 130
Chapter 14 Matisse and Camping 139
Chapter 15 Florida Again 147
Chapter 16 Our Trip East, and Looking for a New Home ... 154
Chapter 17 Oakhaven and Art 162
Chapter 18 More Art and Fun and a New Home 170
Chapter 19 A Trip to California 184
Chapter 20 Working at the Library 191

Chapter 21 Our Boys 199
Chapter 22 A New Job 206
Chapter 23 My J A G Library 217
Chapter 24 Trips to Florida 227

Part Three Flourishing in Florida 235
Chapter 25 Going to Florida for Good! 235
Chapter 26 Casa Masbu - Return to Naples 244
Chapter 27 Fun with the Kids 259
Chapter 28 An Unfortunate Happening 263
Chapter 29 Our Loss - Death of a Matriarch 277
Chapter 30 Cruising Through the Caribbean 281
Chapter 31 A Little Girl and a New Home 285
Chapter 32 Twenty-Nine Palms North
Fort Myers, Florida 288
Chapter 33 A Bit of Florida 307
Chapter 34 The Middle East 311
Chapter 35 The British Isles 325
Chapter 36 Cote d' Azur 342
Chapter 37 To Germany, Then Back to Paree 348
Chapter 38 Back to London 358
Chapter 39 Ted's Sheds at Southwest Florida Fair 363
Chapter 40 Kid Stuff 367
Chapter 41 The End of Monte's Dream 371
Chapter 42 A Eulogy to Mother Massing 379
Chapter 43 Sanibel and Captiva Islands 386
Chapter 44 Family Fun 396
Chapter 45 Going Home in 1993 410
Chapter 46 Daytona Beach 415

Chapter 47 Washington D. C. and Philadelphia
By George C. Massing Washington D. C. and Environs 419

Chapter 48 Edison Parade, Ridgefarm Reunion,
Disney World and Church 432

Chapter 49 The Last Trip to the North - 1994 439

Chapter 50 Now 452

Chapter 51 Observations 455

Dedication

This book is dedicated to my beloved husband, George Clemens Massing, without whose dedicated help it would not have been written, and to all descendants of the Busby lineage, and allied families, living now, and those yet to come. My love for them all is abounding and forever.

Introduction

Being interested in people (relatives or not), artistic endeavors, travel in the United States (lower forty-eight as the Alaskans call us) and islands, British Isles, Europe, The Holy Land and Egypt, I felt I had to write this book. Traveling throughout the United States and Europe, there was a great deal of genealogy to be garnered.

It was always great to go, but after all, we are Americans, so do have the nesting instinct. Therefore, where I have lived is a wide range from my birthplace of Ridgefarm, Illinois, to Dayton, Ohio, to the fantastic and beautiful land of Florida, with all its lush semi-tropical flora and numerous interesting fauna.

Living now in the most beautiful spot in the world, Fort Myers, and its inviting environs of Southwest Florida, I wanted to share my life, past and present, with everyone. Come with me on a wonderful trip in my world.

This book is about one typical American family that has lived the American dream of life, from genealogy back to 798 A.D. to Now. It tells of the happiness, the joy of living to the present time, full of exploits and happiness and sadness of the world the way it was and is. Why wouldn't everyone be interested in it? It will bring memories to everyone who reads it.

It ends in happiness and security in the knowledge of having lived a full and precious (rewarding) life in this old wonderful world!

Acknowledgments

My husband George converted my hand written manuscript to the computer working laboriously the many hours and days it took, with all the software and computer incompatibilities switching from an Epson Equity 1 to a Gateway computer. With his persistence and a lot of help he finally won the battle.

Joshua and Jenna Massing helped with the typing, and Jenna and Devon Massing helped George get out of computer glitches he got into.

Judy Massing was always available when the going got rough. "Keep writing, she kept saying to me." And when George lost pages in the computer or he couldn't find his backup, or had other problems, she was there to help him out of his dilemma. She also helped him convert data from his former computer, an old Epson Equity I, to his new Gateway, because many problems arose due to incompatibilities between the two computers. Between the two of them, they worked out all the bugs and produced results.

Our son, Lawrence Busby Massing, "Larry" helped prepare the back cover of this book by computer enhancement of a photograph he took for use in the book. He provided advice and assistance, when needed throughout the book editing process..

Robert Raushel, Larry and Judy's German exchange student, thoroughly enjoyed typing several pages on the computer. He wanted to do more, but it was too near his time to leave for Germany. He was soon packing and finishing up his activities and could no longer help with my book.

In extreme cases of needing help, we turned to Kathy Bryce, who is a computer whiz and friend of Judy. She was called only when we were in dire straights and needed professional help.

We sent several chapters of the book manuscript to my nephews wife, Nancy Busby, in Kissimmee, Florida, to correct incompatibilities between the computers. In doing so she backed up data in WordPerfect which required George to enlist the aid of Kathy Horodowich, a manager at the local Gateway Country Store, and her technician Christina, to examine George's Gateway disks and advise what was necessary to get WordPerfect installed on his Gateway.

Gateway's tech staff also spent many hours assisting him with updating his Gateway with a new 40 gigabyte hard drive, new modem, updated Bios, doubled memory, and several other necessary items to complete the book.

Sandy Reis helped George with many of his computer problems and updated my manuscript with backup on floppy disk and compact disk.

In the final stages of the book George has further enlisted the professional aid of Barbara D. Cook, a very knowledgeable person on WordPerfect, to clean up George's many problems with the manuscript and get it ready for publication.

Personally, I think it would have saved time and troubles if I had sat there and typed the whole book. But that isn't the way it is done today. Out goes the typewriter and in comes the computer.

So when there were problems, they were completely foreign to me. They had to be worked out by anyone willing to help.

I thank one and all, including anyone whose name was unintentionally omitted, who helped put this book to rest. It was a challenge to us all, but we survived, and here it is! Read on, Dear Ones, and enjoy!.

Part One
Growing Up in Middle America

Chapter 1
A Bit of Genealogy

My grandmother, Sarah Ann Waddington, was very excited. She was about to arrive at Vermilion Grove, Illinois. She had been riding the huge noisy train for days, coming from her home in Salem, New Jersey, to visit her mother's brother, Uncle Will Vanneman, and his wife Emma.

The train chugged along, finally coming to a stop. Sarah caught up her purse and parasol, and stepped outside. Holding her parasol high above her head and lifting her skirts up, Sarah stepped out the door and down the steps, showing dainty black high buttoned shoes and white ruffled pantalettes.

A young man, my grandfather Parris Mendenhall, and a couple of his friends watched with excitement and growing anticipation, as she ran across the platform to greet her Uncle and Aunt. They enfolded her in their arms with great joy and happiness.

"That's the girl I'm going to marry!" said Parris to his friends. He had never seen a more beautiful woman. Sarah Ann Waddington became Sarah Ann Mendenhall on 19 December, 1877. She was called Sally by her family and close friends.

KATHRYN BUSBY MASSING

The parents of Sarah Ann Waddington were Joshua and Anne Vanneman Waddington who lived on a farm outside of Salem, New Jersey, with a town house in the city of Salem. They were staunch Quakers and were members of the beautiful Friends church in downtown Salem.

Anne's parents were Andrew and Ann Vanneman from Cumberland, New Jersey. Joshua's parents were Aaron and Sarah Keasby Waddington of New Jersey. Aaron's father was Jonathon the third, whose father was Jonathon the second, whose father was Jonathon the first, whose father was William Waddington who came from England in 1695. He purchased 1000 acres of land in Salem County, New Jersey, on Alloways Creek.

Joshua and Anne had seven children: Pauline, Laura, Ernst, Louella, Sarah Ann, Florence and Jennie.

Pauline married Henry Holme, a dairy farmer, who became very well to do. They lived in a very large house in an exclusive area of Baltimore, Maryland.

Laura married and moved to Long Beach California. Ernst was a partner of Pauline's husband and lived in the same neighborhood.

Louella was killed by a trolley street-car in Indianapolis, Indiana, when she was visiting her sister Sally.

Florence and Jennie never married and lived in the large family farm home all of their lives. Even though they were "old maid school teachers" they were beautiful, wonderful great aunts to me.

Aunt Pauline had planned on one of her trips to England to take Grandma to see Waddington Old Hall and Mildenhall Manor, but Aunt Pauline came down with lumbago, and they could not go.

Exciting beautiful silk dresses had been made for Grandma for the trip. She packed them away in a large trunk, as she thought they were too fancy and showy for such a small place as Ridgefarm. Some of the more simple dresses she wore, but the dressier, fancier ones she left packed in the trunk. On rainy days, it was our greatest pleasure to run up to the third floor attic and dress up, and parade around the full sized almost empty attic.

The Mendenhalls trekked westward from Chester County, Pennsylvania, where John Mildenhall and his brother Benjamin, and sister Mary, settled after coming to America from Maridge Hill, Wiltshire, England on the second voyage of William Penn, in 1683.

Parris Mendenhall's immigrant ancestor, John Mildenhall, left England with his brother and sister. John was a farmer, but he helped his brother Benjamin, barn builder, to build a huge barn which has been converted into a beautiful old rustic restaurant in Mendenhall a small village near Chester, Pennsylvania. Today it is called The Mendenhall Inn. It is an excellent restaurant.

When on a trip to Philadelphia in 1992 with forty five church members, we stopped there for a dinner. We were set up in the former loft of the barn by candlelight with elegant appointments. The stuffed sole they served was the first I had ever eaten. I found it to be delicious. The group all agreed this was the highlight of our nine day trip.

In England, the Mildenhalls lived at Mildenhall Manor near the town of Marlborough. The name Mildenhall was changed to Mendenhall after arrival in America. We visited Mildenhall Manor, in 1985 and found it to be a lovely stone and brick manor house, with beautiful grounds and four or five brick houses for their servants and workshops. The present owners invited us to sit on the front porch and have a lovely English tea with them, while we discussed the past. It was the thrill of a lifetime. My roots were here, too! I am so sorry my mother and grandmother could not have been with us. It would have meant so much to them. It meant so much to me to think I was seeing it for them. The immigrant John Mildenhall, married Elizabeth Maris, who, along with her father and mother, had passage on the same ship from England as John. They were married two years later. John and Elizabeth's son, John, married Susannah Pierson. John and Susannah's son, Mordecai, married Charity Beeson, and they migrated to Guilford County, North Carolina, were they remained until their deaths.

Mordecai and Charity's son, Richard, married Jane Thornburgh. They left North Carolina for Ohio with a group of settlers. When traveling through Kentucky, they were attacked by Indians near Lexington. Richard and their little dog were killed. They were buried together. Aaron was one year old at the time of his father's death. His mother continued on to Greene County, Ohio, with the children, where she raised them alone.

Aaron married Lydia Anderson from Nantucket, Massachusetts, and moved to Vermilion County, Illinois, when their son, Richard, was two years old. Richard married Louisa Haworth from Union County, Indiana, and lived on a farm near Vermilion Grove, Illinois. They had two sons Parris, my Grandfather, and James, who was killed in a horse accident when he was eighteen years old.

Parris grew up on the farm and attended old Vermilion Grove Quaker Academy. He then attended Bloomingdale College in Illinois, and Earlham Quaker College in Richmond, Indiana.

Sally had been a school teacher for several years before she was married. Sometimes, she taught young boys who were much taller and larger than she. These awkward young boys attended school when they couldn't work in the fields. In the winter, it was so cold they would come early to school and start a fire in the pot bellied stove, so it would be warm when the younger children and Sally arrived at school.

Six years after their marriage, Parris and Sally had a son Kenneth, who died at the age of thirty one due to a brain hemorrhage. He married Jessie Hacker from Indianapolis, Indiana. They had no children.

Four years later Georgia, my mother, was born to Parris and Sally. She was a beautiful brown eyed girl, although Sally and Parris were both blue eyed.

On her second birthday, she was given a little red wagon. She was so happy with it, and wanted to show it off to her Grandparents. Pulling it behind her down the road to their home two miles away, she finally arrived hot and sweaty. Her Grandpa, Richard, was in the barnyard when he saw her. He said, "What are you doing here? You're too small to be going down the road by yourself!" He hurriedly harnessed the horse to the buggy, and carried her and the little red wagon home.

Georgia attended the Quaker Academy in Vermilion Grove, Illinois. Vermilion Grove was called Peanut because Abe Lincoln bought a bag of peanuts and ate them on the spot, when Abe came there to deliver a speech.

It was a good place to grow up. After Richard died, Louisa lived with Parris and Sally, who took special care of her for ten years. It was a well known fact what a special person Sally was and how good she was with her father and mother-in-law.

Parris sold the farm and they moved to Indianapolis, Indiana, where Georgia attended Butler College to become a teacher and where she also studied fine arts. She became a kindergarten teacher. She recalled, the children would be so hungry they would eat their paste, when they were given some for their projects.

Parris and Sally bought a farm in southern Indiana, in Ripley County, for a summer vacation place.

Georgia had fallen in love with Charles Milton Busby, who was born on a farm four miles east of Ridgefarm, which was three miles south of Vermilion Grove.

Georgia and Milt, as he was called, were my mother and father. One rainy day on the farm Milt could not work in the fields, so he went over to the Mendenhall home in Ripley County, where Georgia was living with her parents at the time. He took her back home with him and they stopped off at Greensburg, Indiana, and were married. Milt rented a buggy after they got off the train in Danville, Illinois, at the livery stable which had belonged to Joseph Clemens Massing, who was the grandfather of George Clemens Massing, my future husband. Milt took Georgia home to his parents house where they stayed.

The next day the wheat was dry enough from the rain for Milt to be back in the fields again threshing the wheat.

Isaac Busby was our immigrant, or at least our first known Busby ancestor in America, born in 1759. (A Busby is a military full dress fur hat, very tall, worn by the Guard at Buckingham Palace and other military functions.) One reference book states that he came to America at an early age, but I can find no proof of that. The first reference confirms that he was a wheelwright by trade, with a wife and children living on a farm in Monroe County, Virginia, which is now a part of West Virginia. His wife was Prudence Tucker, who died in Virginia.

Isaac moved to Wayne County, Indiana, and lived there with his son Isaac Newton, until his death. George and I found his grave in 1983. He was buried in the Busby Cemetery at Pendleton, Indiana, in the middle of a cow pasture surrounded by wheat fields. We had to climb over fences and be careful of the bulls in the pasture, but there

KATHRYN BUSBY MASSING

he was, buried in that grave right below my feet. It was heartwarming to see his grave.

Isaac and Prudence's son, John, married Phoebe Boggess, and they trekked west from Virginia to Indiana and later to Catlin, Illinois, where they lived for several years, after which they moved to Madison County, Iowa, near Winterset, where they settled among beautiful rolling hills. Their home on the top of one of the hills was a stagecoach stop. When we were there in 1982, we could see the huge deep wheel tracks of the stagecoach coming up the hill and stopping in front of their house. The area where they lived had a magnificent view. No wonder they wanted to go west where they certainly found their dream land and home. John and Phoebe were buried at Winterset Cemetery. The eight foot tall narrow gravestone has his inscription on one side and hers on the other.

John and Phoebe's son, Silas Milton Busby, married Mahala Francis Dowers, both of whom were born in Ripley County, Indiana, and were married in Vermilion County, Illinois, and are buried in Crown Hill Cemetery in Ridgefarm, Illinois.

They lived at the end of a long lane, three and a half miles east of Ridgefarm, in a large pretentious two story gray frame home with large posts in front, and a tall round tower room above the roof, which was used as a lookout for Indians in early days. When I was a little girl living a couple of miles through the fields, farther if by road, it was kind of run down but still beautiful. The house, barn, and outbuildings were torn down by Loren (Spud) Spesard, who bought the land.

Silas Milton and Mahala's son, Charles Wilbur, married Rose Ella Jones the daughter of Ira Grover and Ruth Conner Jones. William Jones is our first known Jones ancestor in America. His son, Aaron, was born in New Jersey, in 1782. He married Phoebe Watkins, and they moved westward to Quaker, in Vermillion County, Indiana. They bought land from the government and built a double log cabin.

Their son Ira Grover Jones married Ruth Conner at Newport, Indiana, in 1885. Their children were: Emilene, George, Rose Ella, Jake, Indiana, and Stephen. Ruth died in childbirth having her seventh child. Records show Ruth, Aaron, and Phoebe are all buried at Old Hopewell Cemetery at Quaker Point, Indiana. The Individual grave sites are now impossible to find, due to vandalism, and lack of care in that section of the cemetery.

Two years after Ruth died in childbirth, Ira Grover remarried to a widow, Rhoda Weller Rice, and had four more sons. Their names were: Perle, Frank, Bertie, and James Arthur.

A History of Vermilion County, Illinois, printed in 1903, says Ira Grover Jones was a prominent farmer, farming 3000 acres of land adjoining the Busby land.

They moved to a large, beautiful home at the south side of Ridgefarm on the main north south road, at the entrance to Crown Hill Cemetery, the land for which was donated by him.

Charles Wilbur and Rose Ella Jones Busby, Ira Grover's daughter, had four boys and four girls, three of which died in infancy.

The fourth girl, Maude, died at the age of forty one, leaving a son James and a daughter, Rosella, who became an important part of our lives.

The four sons were Charles Milton, my father, Frank, Edwin, and Roosevelt, all of whom had adjoining farms. Frank moved to Ridgefarm and lived in a beautiful, large home on the east edge of town. Frank and Jesse Mills Busby had four children, Robert, Ruby, Dorothy, and Carl.

Edwin and Nora Glick Busby had two children, Martha and Roger.

Roosevelt and Lois Hutchins Busby had two children, William (Bill) and Wayne. Bill remains living on the same land where Ira Grover and Ruth Conner Jones lived in a large wooden farm house with all their children. A new modern home was built by them, on the site of the old Jones homestead.

Charles Milton Busby, my father, bought land a couple of miles away. He was best known by friends and family as Milt. The Busbys and the Joneses were neighbors, having adjoining farms on the east side of Ridgefarm, where five generations lived, or nearby, within a few miles of one another.

Milt and Georgia had a little girl they named Anna Rose after her two grandmothers, Sally and Rose Ella. The night Anna Rose was born, Doctor Hinshaw came from Chrisman for her birth. She was so tiny and weak she was not expected to survive. Sally kept a fire in the kitchen stove all night, and, keeping the oven door open, kept Anna Rose in the oven. She had made an incubator for her. The doctor, when he came back to see Georgia the next day, said, "I never expected her to live through the night!" Anna Rose grew strong and healthy, and became a great help to Georgia, in raising the other children. Ann, as she was called, was like a second mother to all of us.

The twins came next. Georgia and Milt decided they would name the child after Milt if it were a boy. When they found out they had two boys they named one Charles and one Milton. Their middle names were to be Mendenhall after Georgia's maiden name. When she found out the doctor had not put Mendenhall down as their second name, she was very upset! It was when the twins signed up for the draft in World War II, the omission was discovered.

Then came little Louise. When she was born, the doctor told Georgia she should not have any more children. She was having them too fast, and her health was suffering. Some relatives from Lapel, Indiana, came to visit when Louise was about one year old, bringing their little boy, who had diarrhea. Louise got diarrhea and died just five days before her first birthday. Georgia held the baby in her arms as she died. "I just couldn't put her down!" she said, when reliving that time many years later. Georgia had Mary Ellen twenty-two months after Louise was born, when the doctor told her again, she must not have any more children. In two years she had Catherine, for which I'm glad, or God would have given me to another family. I was the last.

Chapter 2

Growing Up

When the twins were babes in arms, Mother and Dad were visiting Grandpa and Grandma, in their home in Indianapolis. Mother wanted to go shopping at a department store. Dad took her there, but did not want to go inside, so he stood outside the door in the front of the store holding a twin in each arm. It caused quite a stir. Everyone stopped to talk, and wanted a closer look at the beautiful little babies. When Mother came out of the store, there was quite a crowd around Dad and the boys.

Two or three years later, when the family was visiting Grandpa and Grandma in Indianapolis, when they were toddlers the family was on the front porch of their home, "It sure is hot, isn't it?" The neighbor lady yelled across to them from her front porch. "It's hot enough to take all your clothes off!"

Everyone went into the house, leaving the two boys playing on the porch. When Mother returned to the porch, to see how they were getting along, the boys were playing naked.

When the boys were about three years old, they started climbing the windmill in the barnyard at the farm. They were way up, one right behind the other, when Aunt Florence, who was visiting from New Jersey, as she did often, looked down from the house and saw them. She ran out in horror to the windmill. She very quietly talked them back down.

They were into everything, needing constant supervision. Mother always said what one couldn't think of the other one would.

Ann almost made it seem as if they were triplets as she did everything they did. She was walking when they began to crawl. She would get on the floor and crawl with them. As they all grew older she helped Mother raise the twins, as well as the rest of us when we came along. She hovered over all of us all her life wanting only the best for us.

Mother was so ill, when I was born, I was taken to live with my grandparents, Sally and Parris Mendenhall, where I stayed until I was two years old.

"Are you going home with me?" my mother would ask.

I would waddle over to my beloved Grandfather in his black leather chair and say, "Am I going home with Mommy?" "No" he would say. "No" I would turn and say to my mother.

One day after such a conversation, she picked me up and carried me out of the house screaming and carrying on so, all the neighbors heard.

I enjoyed my life on the farm but I was always glad to go back to visit my grandparents. On one such visit a few months later, Mother found me sitting on the stairs with my head on my arms on the step above, crying my heart out. "Why are you crying?" she asked.

Grandpa won't talk to me!" I cried. "I talked to him but he won't talk to me."

Grandpa had died, and was laid out in the parlour. My mother scooped me up into her arms, and explained Grandpa had gone to Heaven.

All my relatives on my mother's side were Quakers. We all went to the Friends Church. The early ones came over from England in the 1680's and 1690's, to escape religious persecution. Several came with the well known Quaker, William Penn, and settled on land bequeathed to him by land grant, by the King of England.

Many migrated south, following the coast, and later to the west, away from Pennsylvania. They settled in and around Ridgefarm and Vermilion Grove, Illinois, where many Quakers were already established. I grew up in this gentle, quiet religion.

THEN AND NOW

I accepted Christ as my Savior, when I was twelve years old, at our Quaker Friends Church in Ridgefarm, during a revival meeting. From then to now, The Lord has been a great part of my life, leading me and helping me be a better person because I know what the reward will be. I know there is a Heaven and I will be there one day. I don't discount the fact that Heaven can also be on this earth. We make our own lives and it can be good or bad. It behooves us to do the best we can, in order that we may have a rich and full life.

All the Quakers I ever knew were the most wonderful people in the world. They were the best, kindest, most thoughtful and loving people I have ever known.

In a recent movie, a man was asked, "How do you know that for a fact?"

"Quakers don't lie!" He said. I was thrilled to hear this, as this is my firm belief, and it always has been. I have never known a Quaker to lie.

Many of my friends were Quakers until I left home at which time I found it difficult to find churches of the Quaker faith.

The gentle way in which a Quaker is raised is still beautiful and rewarding. People think I've forgotten how little we five kids fought but my Mother and Gram would not tolerate fighting. Of all the things about them I remember most was they couldn't abide arguments. Peace at all cost. Of course, there was some sibling rivalry. It was an excellent background for future living that became more and more hectic.

It sometimes makes us seem tactless if we talk too quickly, or cannot think of a softer answer, before blurting out the truth. Much to my chagrin, I've been known to be that way.

"Matthew, Mark, Luke and John, saddle the horse and we'll all get on." My beloved Quaker Gram used to say this to me, when I was trying to remember which book of the bible came next in the new testament. "That's what I was taught, when I was a little girl," she told me several times.

Of course, that was the mode of travel in those days, but it is a memorable way of remembering the first four books of the New Testament. I have never forgotten it. It sort of hangs in there, with me, whenever I need to know.

I have read the bible through five times, as well as studying and considering it. Gram read it through seven times, and knew her bible well.

When Grandpa wanted to move back to the Ridgefarm area, Grandma hated to give up their home in Indianapolis, where they had lived for twelve years, and the farm in Ripley County, Indiana.

"If we could buy Uncle Will's home in Ridgefarm, I would go back to Illinois." She said.

They moved to the large, red brick, Victorian home with wrap around porches, very tall and elegant. It was as much of a home to my brothers and sisters and me, as the farm was out east of town where we lived. The house was situated in the third block on the road going west out of town. There was an iron fence about four feet from the road, across the front of the house. We had to open the gate, to proceed up the sidewalk, passing a huge maple tree.

One would step up onto the porch and enter the house through a tall, narrow, iron decorated door. Immediately to the right was a large ebony, curving, stairway going upstairs. It was great to throw a right leg over the banister starting from the top, building momentum until one whirled around and down, and jumping off the stair rail to the floor. No better ride in the world.

To the left was the entrance to the parlor, and straight ahead about ten or twelve feet, was the door to the living room. In the entrance hall at the right of the living room door was the tall, narrow, clothes rack with a mirror and long curved clothes hooks. At the base of the clothes rack, was a closed hinged box, for the galoshes. The box doubled as a seat, with arms, to sit and pull on galoshes. To the right of it was a tall, decorative, pottery container that held several black umbrellas.

On the opposite side of the living room door is the fireplace with a beautiful carved oak mantel piece, and a mirror. A Seth Thomas clock patented July 30, 1878, which Grandma wound and set every Sunday without fail, stood on the mantel. The clock measured twenty-three inches tall, sixteen inches wide, and four inches thick. Books lined the walls in glassed in bookcases, and a Victorola stood at the end of the bookcases.

Grandma's favorite music, which she played all the time, was by Fritz Chrysler who was a famous violinist of the time.

In the center of the room was a four foot square black wooden table, which held an antique lamp and Grandma's well-used bible. At the right side of the table was Grandpa's huge black leather rocker, which became Grandma's after Grandpa died. On the left side of the table was a big wooden rocker with six inch arm rests, on which we girls would do our school work.

To the left of that rocker was the door to the dining room and straight ahead of the chair was the kitchen door entrance. There was a large wooden table in the center of the kitchen, with eight wooden chairs. To the right of the kitchen door was the large kitchen range, with its top warming oven, and six round stove lids, with the water tank on the right for hot water. The baking oven was on the right side of the fire box. Pressing irons were heated on top of the stove. Detachable wooden handles were clipped on to pick them up to iron clothing.

An outside door led to a partially closed in red brick entrance porch. This was the entrance to which all vagrants would come and ask for food.

One time I opened the door to a hungry man, asking for food. I ran to grandma, who was sitting in her chair, reading her bible.

"There's a man outside, Grandma, asking for food, "What shall I do?"

"What do we have?" she asked.

"All we have is one crust of bread and a little peanut butter," I answered.

"Give it to him!" Gram said, without hesitation.

I went back to the kitchen and fixed him the crust and peanut butter and as I handed it to him, he looked at it with hunger in his eyes.

"Thank you very much I appreciate it" the man said and started eating the bread as he walked down the sidewalk towards the front gate.

Next to the door was a large tall Victorian china and linen cabinet. On the opposite side of the room the wall was covered with built in cabinets, which held pots and pans, food and all other such things.

Opposite the stove was the sink. We had a bucket of water with a dipper in it, from which we all drank. Later we had running water. To the left of the sink was the outside door to the large enclosed back porch, which also enclosed the cement basement steps. On the left side of the kitchen wall cupboards was a door, which led to a bedroom and the bathroom.

To the left of the front entrance was a door, that went into the parlor, where all the beautiful Victorian furniture was. This was the most beautiful room in the house, with its marble fireplace, along the outside wall. Right outside the window was where the porch curved and there was the most pleasant place in the world, the swing. I spent most of my life in that swing, I think. It gave a full view of all the neighbors up and down the street. It was a very quiet street with very little activity, so one's thoughts were developed and enlarged upon with no interruptions. Sometimes my mind goes back there to that swing to get my bearings, even now.

From the parlor one went into the formal dining room through a large open arch. The dining room table would hold twelve people. An outside door went onto the porch from here. A door led to the downstairs guest bedroom and bathroom.

Another door on the right led into the dining room, and, with one or two steps, one went into the kitchen from which the food was prepared to be served in the formal dining room.

There were three large bedrooms upstairs, all furnished with beautiful, dark, antique Victorian furniture. Grandma's bed was made from a walnut tree off her father's farm in New Jersey.

I loved to sleep in Gram's bed. She had a wonderful feather bed on it. I loved to punch it up from its flat size, to a full, fat, fantastic bed, and climb on top. My body would float down and move sideways according to how the feathers had rearranged themselves, when I had fluffed them. It was just like floating on a cloud!

There was a closed in, curving stairway going to a full size, wonderful attic. In the center of the attic was another wooden stairway leading to a hole in the roof which was an Indian lookout.

At the right of Grandma's house was her flower garden, where she grew hundreds of gladioli and peonies, which always produced huge, gorgeous blossoms. People would come through the gate, and buy bunches of the flowers to take to Crown Hill Cemetery every Memorial Day, to use for decorating the graves.

My mother took a lot of the flower bulbs and started a field of flowers at the farm. The first year there were four rows about 200 feet long. They multiplied each year, until it grew to such a large field, that she couldn't cope with them anymore. She let me take the huge bulbs, some of which were five inches in diameter, to all the neighbors, to sell to them.

I don't know whatever happened to the ones I didn't sell because she stopped growing them. Mother always took big containers and jars full of these cut gladiolis and peonies to Crown Hill Cemetery for Memorial Day. Five generations of our relatives are buried there. She put them on all our relatives graves making them the prettiest of all. Some years they were taken out the evening before and other years early in the morning of Memorial Day. I enjoyed helping her with this and talk about our ancestors.

There would be a beautiful ceremony at the rounded center of the cemetery, on Memorial Day, which the whole town attended.

Between Grandma's house and the flower garden were huge overloaded green and purple grapes, that were so prolific in growth they would come through the slats of the arbor, and hang down through the heavy leaves.

At the far end of the flower garden were the raspberry brambles that grew the most luscious, huge, red raspberries I have ever seen or tasted. When I got old enough Grandma would, after the dew each morning, send me out to get some fresh berries for breakfast, when they were in season. Blackberries and gooseberries which grew along the fence were made into pies.

There were several large barns and buildings at the back of Grandma's house. In the back of the house, I used to wash clothes in the summertime. The sun shone brightly, as I filled the round galvanized, three foot wide wash tub and scrubbed with a galvanized and wooden wash board. I would scrub sheets up and down gently against the board, rubbing soap on them first. After they were washed, and rinsed, I took them over to the long clothesline, and hung them in the sun. We had the most beautiful, whitest, best smelling sheets I ever saw. Then, when they were put over Grandma's wonderful feather bed, it was pure pleasure to sink into the fragrantly fresh sheets and float into dreamland.

The large orchard gave us the most delicious, perfect, Jonathon and Grimes Golden apples I have ever eaten. The apples were gathered in the fall and taken to the basement where they were dumped in large, wooden bins all around the wall.

Grimes Goldens, which were so delicious, are a thing of the past, unless one can find an old old tree. Apples have been developed in order to sell, not because they are excellent in taste, as it should be. Grimes Golden can sometimes be found in Illinois and Michigan or Ohio. The apple room smelled so wonderfully fragrant, it was a delight to run downstairs to the far room and gather some apples to eat of an evening in front of the fireplace in the living room.

In another room beside it shelves held all the canned vegetables and fruit that was put up during the growing season.

One time, when I was going to Harrison School, after lunch we were playing a running game, in the side yard. I watched one of the Pugh twins, a Jones relative of mine, a couple of years younger than I, sink her teeth in a marvelous Grimes Golden apple. I could taste it myself! We didn't have any Grimes Golden at home at that time, but I knew how delicious it was, and my mouth watered.

As I watched her she ate two or three bites only, then raised it in the air to throw it over the fence. I watched that beautiful apple as it soared up, up, high over her head and over, way over, to fall on the other side of the fence.

"Why did you do that?" I asked as I ached for just one bite.

"Because I didn't want it any more!" she said as she ran off to play.

Many is the time I have thought of this incident, as my love for apples has never left me, especially Grimes Golden.

"What is your name, little girl?" A neighbor asked me when I was quite small.

"Catty Buddy," I said shyly.

Buddy for Busby and Catty was my nickname until Mother told me not to answer when called that.

"Why not?" I asked not having a clue as to why.

"It just isn't a very nice nickname," she said. From then on, I was called Catherine by everyone. When I was a Junior in high school, I changed the spelling to Kathryn.

When I was five years old, I had double pneumonia. I was at Grandma's house, upstairs in Gram's bed, with the windows open for the cold, crisp, clean air. Mother came and took care of me. I lay without food and with an extremely high fever. At that time nothing, much could be done for pneumonia.

Mother sat beside me for three days and nights not sleeping. Several times a day she took me into another room, where it was warmer, to put me in cool water. It was to get my temperature down. She had to carry me straight so my chest would be flat.

When my fever broke, she went to bed and slept for twenty-four hours a day for three days and nights. No one could wake her. Mother had lost one baby, she didn't want to lose another. There are still scars on my lungs, which are a grim reminder of that ordeal. When I was well enough, Dad carried me downstairs and stood me up in front of the fireplace. My legs would not hold me and I crumpled to the floor. I had to learn to walk again.

When Dad was a young man, he and his brother, Frank, made a large two seated sleigh with leather seats. It was really great. One year, when we had a very bad snow storm, with many feet of snow, Dad let the boys get it out of the hayloft from the barn, and hitch one of the strong young horses to it.

We bundled up in our heavy clothes against the cold wind and we glided over the thick crusted snow as if it were glass.

Later, after Mother died in 1981, Allen Mills in Vermilion Grove, one of my classmates from high school, asked if he could have it to restore as he collects antiques.

The refurbished sleigh now rests at the side of his house.

That same winter, when it snowed so much and piled up in drifts, we had it deep enough to make an igloo in which to play. It was so much fun digging the igloo, but, much more fun when we actually got inside and played. The drift was right in front of our house and was so high we could not see the road. For days there was no traffic as everyone was snowed in.

We grew up on the farm with horses, cows, hogs, dogs, cats, chickens and goats.

The twins had riding horses, but they were too wild and frisky for us girls. Mary and I would tease Dad to ride the old work horses. Old Pomp was our favorite.

Mary would jump up on Old Pomp at the front grabbing his mane. I had to get close to the fence and jump on from there holding to Mary. She would maneuver Old Pomp out of the barnyard onto the gravel road. Since the gravel was hard on his feet, we would get out on the side of the road and start trotting. I hated the trotting. It shook us so hard we had a difficult time staying on the horse.

"Hurry up!" I would say, "Make him go faster!"

Then the fun began. The most exhilarating ride was produced by Old Pomp loping down the road. It was as if we were in a slow rocking chair. We loved it!

The only other riding experience that equaled our times on Old Pomp was when George and I rode on a swaying camel, in Egypt, when we rode up to the pyramids in Giza, Egypt.

The elephant ride I took at an amusement fair wasn't quite so comfortable, perhaps because I was behind my grand-children Joshua and Devon, and had to sit on the elephants rump. We had expected Larry and Judy to ride with them, but we three had gone up the stairs to the platform.

As I turned to see Larry, our son, and Judy, his wife, they were still at the end of the long steep stairs talking, not paying any attention to us. The elephant was moving out with only Joshua and Devon on it so I slung my leg over and went along! It was an unexpected ride. I enjoyed it but it was not Old Pomp! Nor was the camel ride later.

When I was in the second grade, I did something the teacher didn't like. She asked me to come to the front of the room. She whacked me on the palm of my hand with a ruler. It smarted! I cried.

My grandmother was visiting her oldest sister, my Aunt Pauline, in Baltimore, Maryland, in the summer of 1928 when I was eight years old.

After harvesting the wheat, we tied our cots and large tent to the running boards of our open touring car. All five of us kids, Anna Rose, Charley, Milt, Mary Ellen and I piled into the back seat and off we went to visit them. The car had a hard time going over the Appalachian Mountains as the grades were very steep. There were pullovers going up each peak, and we huffed and puffed, going slower and slower, until we arrived at each one. We would pull over with the car spurting steam, and let the radiator and motor cool down.

At one pullover there was a small wagon on wheels with a man selling hot tamales.

"What's a hot tamale?" I asked, as I had never heard of them.

"It's sort of like a hotdog," my dad told me. "Come here and get one."

He handed me a hot tamale, and mother helped me pull back the corn husk, filled with ground meat rolled in cornmeal dough. I bit a bite off and was very surprised.

"Oh! That's hot! I'm not sure I like it," I said.

"Keep on eating it. You'll like it," Dad said. I ate the whole thing but I wasn't sure I liked it. I'm still not sure I do.

When we arrived at Aunt Pauline's home in a fashionable area of Baltimore, it was raining.

"Here we are," Dad said, as he pulled the car over against the curbing. We kids hurriedly un-snapped the side curtains of leather and isinglass, and slid over and down the tent and cots on the running board, pushing at each other.

I fell on my hands and knees into a puddle which the other kids had jumped over. Everyone was running towards the house when I started crying. Anna Rose came running back to help me.

"Where's Grandma? Where's Grandma?" We children all chimed in, after greeting Aunt Pauline and her companion Evelyn and her maids, cooks and Clarence Pettengill, her chauffeur and handyman.

"She's upstairs. Run along. I know thee want to see her," Aunt Pauline said, but we were already running towards the staircase.

Mary Ellen and I ran as fast as we could, holding onto the railing, as we slipped and slid on the rugs on the landings. As we arrived on the upstairs floor running in every room we were calling "Grandma, Grandma!"

"I'm up here," Grandma called, from another upstairs.

With surprise, Mary Ellen and I raced up those stairs and ran into Grandma who was trying to get down to us.

"I thought I heard Catherine crying!" Grandma said as she folded her arms around us.

Before we went downstairs to see the others, Grandma gave each of us a wicker type ten inch square sewing basket filled with all kinds of needles, thread, pins, ribbons and other sewing needs, which we kept for many years.

Aunt Pauline always sat at the head of the table, with plates piled in front of her, on which she served the food, and passed it to her left. It was to go around the table to the person on her right. We at home put all the food on the table and passed it to each person on our right. Worked both ways I thought.

Will thee have some meat, Catherine?" I was asked by Aunt Pauline, after I had eaten what I had been served.

"I don't care," I said. Such an idiot! I wanted more of that delicious food, but I didn't say the "If I may," or "Please" or something. She took it as "I don't care for any," but I meant "I don't care if I do" which in the west meant, Yes! So I went without the second helping!

We kids could not understand how the maid always came bursting through the swinging doors and stand at Aunt Pauline's elbow when she needed her. One day Charley and Milt crawled under the table and found a button on the floor, which was used to call the maid. While they were playing around with it and pushed it the maid came in, "Did you want something?" So we knew.

Clarence, in his chauffeurs uniform, drove us in Aunt Pauline's big Hudson to the Country Club. We all felt so elegant having a chauffeur drive us. The club was a big wooden structure, sprawling in a large wooded area, with wrap around porches, with rocking chairs and tables. Aunt Florence and Aunt Jenny had come up from Salem, New Jersey, and we all had a wonderful time.

"Would thee like a nickel to spend, Catherine? You could buy a candy bar at the concession stand," my favorite Aunt Florence asked me. I nodded my head yes, remembering the nickel I had in my pocket. I wondered if I should tell her about it.

When I went to the counter and bought a ten cent bar, instead of a five cent bar of candy, Aunt Florence met me as I turned around.

"Thee didn't tell me thee had a nickel, Catherine. That is dishonest." I hung my head with shame.

The conversations amongst my elders were about women's rights, Women's Christian Temperance Union, (WCTU), and Herbert Hoover, who was running for President that year. Everyone agreed that Herbert Hoover would make a good President. Probably, because he was a Quaker, as we all were, and he was our cousin.

We all had an absolutely fabulous time at Aunt Pauline's, but I'll bet they heaved a sigh of relief when we left for home.

School had started, when we arrived home in late September. I loved school so was very happy to get back.

"I know you," the new teacher said to me.

"You know me?" I said with surprise.

"Yes, Jean told me all about you. A lot of the children told me about you," she said, " Your name is Catherine and you've been to visit your aunt in the east."

I loved my new teacher, and was able to catch up with the other students in the fourth grade. There was only one problem. I didn't remember how to spell my name. When I received a letter from Aunt Pauline, shortly after our return home, she wrote my name Catharine and I thought she must know how to spell my name correctly. I spelled it with an a until we learned later that it was Catherine spelled with an "e."

Aunt Pauline had been to Europe several times after Uncle Henry died. One summer, she had Grandma come east, and they bought a lot of new silk dresses, shoes, and beautiful clothes. They were going to Europe that summer.

Then Aunt Pauline came down with lumbago, so they didn't get to go. When Gram returned home from Aunt Pauline's that summer, she brought a large trunk full of clothes. We girls had lots of fun trying those clothes on. It was a great disappointment to all of us, except I was glad to get my gram back home that summer.

One hot, summer day on the farm, I must have been nine or ten years old, when I heard our car start up. That was a clue to run outside so I could go with whomever was going anywhere. To my surprise, it was Mary Ellen, who was eleven or twelve. In the open touring car sat Mary Ellen behind the steering wheel. My cousin Rosella, who was visiting us, was in the front seat beside her.

As I watched, Mary started the motor and began backing up. There was no reason to believe she would do anything, so I watched to see just what she would do.

She jerked the car backward, and pulled out onto the road. As she jerked the car forward I realized she was going down the road. I started running after them.

"Wait for me! Wait for me! I want to go!" I screamed.

Mary Ellen and Rosella kept their eyes on the road, and Mary shifted gears again. She held her back erect, and sat close to the wheel. Rosella kept wanting to get out of the car, but Mary wouldn't stop.

They went faster and faster as I ran after them. They disappeared out of sight as I finally stopped and stared after them.

"I wanted to go!" I cried with tears running down my cheeks.

It was about an hour before they came home. By then Mary thought she knew how to drive the car very well.

"How did you know what to do?" I asked her.

"I have been watching Dad, and just did what he did!" she answered.

"Why didn't you stop and let me go?" I asked. "I wanted to go with you!"

"I didn't know how to stop," Mary said.

Mary drove the car past Uncle Rosie's, turned left, and turned left again, etc., until they came back here.

"Why did you go so far?" I asked.

"I didn't know how to turn around," she said.

I thought she was so smart! I had never thought to watch Dad to see how he drove the car.

The ice wagon was brought to the country two or three times a week. The ice man used steel tongs to pick up the fifty pound block, and carry it to the kitchen, where our wooden ice box would hold it.

We chipped ice from this block for lemonade, which Mother made a lot. She never made much tea as some folks did. The lemonade was made in a large silver pitcher, which would be so cold the condensation would run down the sides. It tasted so good on hot summer days.

Below the ice in the icebox, in a separate compartment, were shelves which held the dishes of food. We didn't have nice refrigerator dishes, waxed paper, aluminum foil, or Tupperware, as we have now.

The food in dishes from the table was pushed and shoved in anywhere it would go.

Before we had the ice box, Mother let food stay on the table, if not finished during the meal. She made lots of slaw that was delicious. It was always on the table, as well as a glass holder full of spoons. The dishes of food were covered with a small white tablecloth.

Many a time I reached in for a spoon and took a bite of slaw. We always had a big bunch of bananas and a big round of yellow, delicious, longhorn cheese, which were my father's favorite foods, I think. Dad kept us well supplied with those two items. I loved eating chunks of that cheese and a banana at the same time. I still do. Mother never went shopping for food. Dad did all the grocery shopping. He went to Johnny Kerns' General store in Ridgefarm, where he bought all our food, except what we bought from the huckster wagon.

A man, possibly from Johnny Kerns' store, I'm not sure, would come to the farm twice a week. I loved to get up inside the huckster wagon and look around finding delicious foods I wanted.

"Can I have this?" I would ask Mother. She usually let me.

One time we unwrapped the package quickly as usual to find the cookies tasted like soap. We tried to eat them but it wasn't easy. Evidently the man had carried the cookies in the wagon next to soap.

Dad bought a fat, round, squat, steel cream separator which was used every time the cows were milked. It was a boon to the separation of cream from milk, as before the milk from the cows was poured in a large blue crock, and let stand until the cream came to the top. Then the cream was skimmed off and saved.

The blue white milk or skimmed milk left, which had no butterfat remaining in it, was drunk or used in various ways.

The heavy rich cream was used for baking and over fresh strawberries, but I didn't want it poured back into a glass of milk as Mother and Dad did. I was a great drinker of blue white, no fat, milk which I am still drinking today.

When Dad sold our cows, there was no more use for our beautiful cream separator, where the cream came out of one pipe and the skimmed milk came out of the other pipe. Dad bought milk, cream, and butter from the new, smelly, creamery in Ridgefarm. I had to go past it when I went downtown, when I stayed at Grandma's home, and gave it a wide birth as I hurried on down the street. It smelled awful!

Mother used to make the most delicious ice cream I ever tasted. The cream mixture was cooked on the stove, then poured in the two gallon steel ice cream freezer, packed with ice and covered with coarse salt. Dad would start turning the handle the minute everything was ready.

Then the man's work begins. Turning and turning and turning. When the cream begins thickening, off comes the lid, and in goes the fruit. Mother tried different fruits sometimes two or three at a time. No ice cream was as good as Mother's!

When it was soft set, Dad would open the lid and remove the paddles, which he let us lick. Then we were given a small bowl of soft ice cream, if we wanted it. I always did! Then he would put the lid back on without the paddles.

The outer part of the freezer would be packed with more ice and salt, and covered with a gunny sack, in order for the soft ice cream to become hard. Then we had to wait. That was the hard part.

When Dad thought it was hardened enough, he would push the ice and salt on top out of the way and open the lid.

Voila! It was fit for the kings!

There were the sparkling, huge, exciting, fireworks on the Fourth of July at Hoopeston, Illinois.

Then there were the fabulous plays, under large tents, and also there were the religious circuit riders in tents, every summer and early fall, where they spread their gospel in Ridgefarm.

When Dad bought the Atwater Kent radio we had a fabulous change of lifestyle. No longer did we sit in the yard or on the porch and fan ourselves.

We listened to music, programs like Fibber McGee and Molly, Amos and Andy, and political news. When we went to Maryland and New Jersey, to visit Grandma's sisters, I knew all about wonderful Herbert Hoover.

My Dad talked a lot about Calvin Coolidge and Franklin D. Roosevelt. They were a boon to farmers, and other people, in need of help from the government.

Our Atwater Kent radio was about two feet tall, and sat on a table, in front of a window, that looked out towards Hute Besore's farm, a quarter of a mile south of us. On Sundays, Dad always wanted us to turn our radio up high, and turn it around to face Hute's home, so he could hear it. "He likes to sit outside and listen to the music," Dad said.

The Besores were big, earthy Germans who didn't talk much. Their only child was Nellie, who was Anna Rose's best friend. She was a beautiful big buxom girl with an hourglass figure. Her waist was so small the fingers of two hands could touch, when placed around her. She had a lovely personality and was very intelligent. We all loved her. Besores moved to a home a half mile down the road from us, when Ira Jones and his family, moved into the house just south of us. He was the grandson of Ira Grover Jones who owned so much land.

Iry, as we called him, and his wife, Washburn, had two children, Sara Frances, and Elizabeth. Sara was a marvelous pianist and violinist like her mother. Later Sara Frances played the piano in Danville, Illinois over WDAN radio.

Aunt Chloe James, was Washburn's mother, and my father's, father's sister, who lived with Washburn after her husband died. She was a wonderful pianist, who loved to come to our house, and would play Mother's piano by the hour, without music. Aunt Chloe was a wonderful, happy person, whom we all loved. When Aunt Chloe remarried, and moved to Danville, her sister Aunt Jenny, came to live with Washburn and Iry.

Aunt Jenny was a little bitty, feisty woman who was a delight. She was in her sixties, when she was wooed by Albert Newlin and soon was married for the first time. The wedding was held at Washburn's home; and after the dinner, they prepared to leave.

Jenny and Albert came outside to go on their honeymoon. After helping her in the car, he started around to the back of the car, to get in the front seat.

We kids had put lots of tin cans on the back bumper, with a big sign, "Just Married," on it.

We younger kids had been told not to let him come that way, so we pelted him harder and harder with the rice. He finally backed off and went around the front, to get in the car.

Later Aunt Jenny told us he had a suspicion about the reason we kids would not let him go around to the back. He stopped the car a few miles from home and got out to check. He found the tin cans and sign. They had a big laugh about it. He then took them off, so all our work went for naught!

On October 29, 1929, the stock market crash came that changed everyone's lives. There were lots of people who lost great and near great fortunes. People jumped out of their windows to their deaths. There was nothing in my lifetime that changed peoples lives more than The Great Depression.

There is a book written on that era that is explanatory as well as anything I've ever read. Everyone should read this book. It is called, "The Invisible Scar," and was written by Caroline Bird and published in 1966. It can be found in most libraries.

Dad almost lost our farm as did a lot of farmers. For years after the crash everyone struggled to live.

I was too young to understand. But now I see the terrible struggle which my mother and father, and grandmother, made. They must have talked about their problems that everyone of their relatives and friends were going through, but I never heard anything.

My life was delightfully pleasant. I didn't have material things, but there was plenty of love and friendship.

As I grew older I was always wanting to do more and have more things. This probably came from having to go through this depression, as well as, never seeming to be able to buy all I wanted. It takes years for people to recover from bad times and struggles. It permeates one's whole soul. One's whole life is changed because of the way one had to live. I was one of the fortunate ones, who has always maintained a happiness and acceptance of my circumstances, which is probably partially at least due to my Quaker upbringing.

One time when Mother had a large shower for Milt, my brother, and Laura who were to be married, the pencils that were used to play games were left in a heavy silver sculptured tray on top of the radio, in front of the window.

The next day we awoke to find pencils strewn all over the front room and blackened curtains. In the night we had had a terrible electrical storm. The lightning had struck our window.

Later, Dad bought a large floor model radio which had a great resonant volume and could be heard all over the house. It was turned on in the morning and turned off at night when we went upstairs to bed.

On Sundays all afternoon there was this fabulous, heart pounding, classical music. They never said what pieces they were playing but I still remember the music and love classical music. I would lie down in front of the radio and let my chest pound and reverberate to the music.

Mother's best friend was a music teacher in Danville. She came down to our farm each week one summer to give Mary and me lessons on the piano, the same piano on which Mother had learned and played, when she was a young girl. Mary Ellen was quite good, but I goofed-off and failed to practice enough.

Years later, Mother gave the upright piano to me after we were married, and my family played on it until we reluctantly traded it for a Story and Clark, as it needed major overhaul. We wanted a beautiful grand piano, which being second handed was almost affordable, but was too large to put in our home at the time.

My bedroom was the coldest room in the house in the winter. I would try to sleep with my sisters, but they never really wanted me to crawl in beside them with my cold icy body. Many times I went to my Mother, lying in her warm bed, and said, "I'm cold, Mommy!"

"Move over, Milt," she would whisper.

"Aw, there's no room for her," Dad would say. He would move, groaning and complaining.

"Oh, Milt, she's so little she won't take up much room," Mother would say, as she would move over against Dad, which was no more than a few inches. Mother would move over slightly, as she raised her covers, and I felt the warmth of her body reaching out to my cold and icy one. She would turn towards me as I would crawl next to her curved warm body. It was like an oven, always so very warm, and I was so very cold. I would lie in the curve of her body with enormous pleasure and fall asleep.

When I would awaken I was always alone, with wonderful smells of perking coffee and frying bacon, wafting up to me from the kitchen. I would jump up and run downstairs to the open fireplace which would be burning furiously, as a new fire does. The warmth and smells of the house will never be forgotten.

I'll give you a dime if you'll find my wart," my Dad would say.

That was fun! I liked to do that. It brought Dad and me together. I would play around with his head, pretending to find his big wart, which was on the right side just above his hairline.

It's not there!" I would playfully say, so I felt around and massaged his head a little.

"There it is!" I would finally say, as I put my fingers on it.

Dad would get a dime from his pocket and hand it to me. We would be all smiles and happiness.

Dad loved to twiddle his thumbs. I teased him so much about it that it became apparent he did it just to get my attention.

I would see him with clasped hands and his thumbs going fast around one another. I would look up at his twinkling blue eyes, to find them staring into my dark brown ones.

I would laugh and we would have our little secret. I had caught him twiddling his thumbs! It became a game we would play many times.

We had no alarm clocks in the house when I was growing up. If Dad had to get up early to go in the fields, he would wake up without an alarm clock about four in the morning.

Usually Dad wanted to get outside by daybreak, so he could shuck two wagon loads of corn before nightfall. When he came in from the field with his full load of corn, everyone started working fast to help him get out in the field again.

He would weigh it on our large flat scales, then empty the load into the corn cribs. He would feed the horses then run into the house, where Mother would have a hot meal for him. He would eat very fast, then run outside and down the sidewalk to the barnyard. The horses were through eating and drinking and were ready to go. Dad would jump up on the wooden wagon seat, on top of the empty wagon, and away they would go to get another load of corn before it got too dark.

During the depression Dad had to give up his hired help, so it was hard to get the crops in. When I was a little pre-school girl my Mother would help Dad shuck corn. She would sit me on the wagon seat while she shucked the corn. She told me several times about this and said she was always so afraid she would hit me, when she threw the corn towards the batter board, which was an extra wide board attached on one side of the wagon, to throw corn against to get it into the wagon.

Harrison School was a beautiful red brick building where we all went to school for our first eight years. Grades one through four were in the room to the right off the hall at the top of the stairs, and grades five through eight were in the room to the left.

It had a large kitchen and a library. We went up twelve steps to the classroom level. We went downstairs to our play area in the basements, the boys on the right and the girls on the left. We had parties in the basement on special occasions.

At a Halloween party my Mother won first prize dressed as an Indian Princess with a rust colored beaded Indian dress, tan moccasins and hair band with a feather in it. Her hair was tied the way the Indians tied it and hung to her waist in the back. With dusky skin, dark brown eyes and black hair everyone said she looked just like an Indian.

Mother wore her long hair longer than anyone else in our neighborhood. She would take it down and brush and brush. I loved to watch her. When she was finished she would twist it around and make an attractive bun in the back. Then she would clean all the long wisps of her hair, that had collected in the brush, and tuck them in a fine china container with a round hole in the center. When this container was so full she could not push anymore hair through the hole, she would take the top half of the container off and take her hair out of the bottom half. This hair was her hair, to make a fetching hairdo. She did this only when she wanted to dress up.

Mother finally succumbed to the scissors, many years later, after most of her contemporaries, and had a permanent. She looked less elegant, but more like everyone else, and much younger.

In Mother's Mendenhall lineage, her grandmother, five generations back, was an Indian Princess of the Cherokee tribe of North Carolina, named Anna Weh Hah, born 11 Oct 1743. Mother was always very proud of her Indian heritage.

There was a huge bear rug in our little room off the end of the parlour. It looked great on the floor in the middle of the room. The piano was on the far side, with the window to the right of it.

Bare feet felt so good in the long black fur of the bear rug. The huge head and front feet were on the left side and in front of the piano, and the rest of the bear was on the window side.

Many a time I laid on that big bear rug and cried with a toothache. That was where I went each time my teeth hurt so badly.

The only doll I remember was inseparable from me. I took it to school, and one day its head was broken on the cement floor in the basement during recess. I cried as if my heart were broken. Anna Rose came over and helped me pick up the pieces and loved me, telling me it was alright. I was about eight years old.

"Come in the parlour Catherine and see what's in there my Mother said one day, after we had come home from school. There I found my doll in a little girls chair that was given to Ann when she was a baby. I stood in front of the doll in the chair and could not move.

"What is it?" I said.

"It's your doll," Mother said. "I had a new head put on the body."

I did not want it. I did not like it. It was not my dolly. It had a new face and head but it had something else.

Something Mother said she thought I would love. It had real hair. I picked it up gingerly and looked at Mother.

"I wish I had my old doll" I said.

It was never the same. I was weaned of all dolls from that moment on.

Once when playing in the school basement on a cold winter day someone shouted, "It's snowing!" Everyone became excited and ran to jump up on the bench to look out the ground level window to get a better view.

I jumped up in a good spot, but girls jumped up on each side of me. The girl on my right pushed her elbow hard against me, to get a better look, knocking me backwards. I tried putting my right leg back down on the cement floor, but she was standing on my untied shoelace. I fell on my back with my arm underneath.

I have been a wild advocate of tightly tied shoelaces the rest of my life, showing the little ones my wicked three inch scar I am still carrying on my arm at the top of my wrist.

"Help! Help!" I heard someone screaming, over and over, not knowing it was me. One of my friends ran up stairs and brought the teacher running. They had backed off and were just staring at me when the teacher ran over to me and helped me up. It was pandemonium as I watched in a dazed condition.

The teacher told someone to get the bus driver. He came running and helped me upstairs and got me in the bus. He took me home, which was just a mile or so down the road. He told me to sit still while he ran into the house and told my folks.

As I watched the house, I saw Charley, run out of the house, and looking over at me in the bus, ran to the garage and quickly backed out the car.

Mother and Dad came running out the door and to the bus. They took me gently out of the bus and into the car. This was the most attention I had ever had in my life.

The doctor in Chrisman, Illinois, set my arm by jerking it into place, and said to take me to the hospital in Danville the next morning to have an x-ray taken, to see if my bones were straight together for good knitting.

The next day in the hospital my arm was x-rayed which showed the bones were not together, necessitating an operation.

"Catherine," my Mother asked "Do you want to have an operation to make your arm straight, or do you want to have an arm the rest of your life like this?" she said as she held her wrist up high in the air as if it were broken.

"I want it like this," I said because I was so scared of an operation, holding my arm up the way she had done.

A large ugly red scar three inches long on the top of my wrist has been the bane of my life.

During this time with my arm, Mother fixed a cot near her bed along side of the wall for me to sleep in case I might need some help in the night.

Another time the hired man came up the sidewalk from the barn, carrying Charley's limp bloody body to the house. Mother was beside herself with apprehension. The hired man had been teasing Charley running toward him with a pitchfork up in the hay loft. Charley had been pestering him and the hired man was playing with him. They both had failed to see Charley had come too close to the loft opening. He fell through onto the cement about fourteen feet below. It was a severe fall and one never forgotten. The hired man had tears in his eyes he was so sorry.

When Charley was about ten or eleven, he had severe pains in his lower right abdomen. Dr. Hinshaw came up from Chrisman to see to him. After examining Charley, the Doctor came downstairs to tell his findings to all of us kids who were waiting in the living room with long, sad faces. What was the matter with Charley?

The doctor stood by the mantle in the front room, and told us Charley had acute appendicitis and would have to be taken to the hospital in Danville for an operation. Mother was getting him ready upstairs.

The doctor saw how upset and worried we all were, as none of us had ever been sick of anything except colds and flus. He put his hand over to the back of my ear pulling his hand forward quickly showing a quarter between his thumb and forefinger.

"Look what I found back of your ear!" he said.

He kept us happy, playing around with us with his tricks, until Mother and Dad came downstairs, helping Charley to get ready to go to the hospital. The coin tricks were a great relaxer and although we felt terrible about Charley, we were told he would be all right. The next day, he was fine but I've always thought the doctor was great for helping all of us kids in our sadness.

Charley and Milt were mechanically minded, following in the footsteps of our father. Dad kept all his threshing machines, and tractors, and combines, and cars all in tiptop shape himself. Dad had a special building in which he kept tools and equipment and parts to keep the farm operating.

The boys learned to be as mechanically skilled as Dad.

When they were in their early teens, they built a little tractor with pieces of equipment and parts they found on the farm. We used to ride it around the farm, as it was just about half the size of a regular tractor, so it was not feasible to work it in the fields.

After Milt married, and had his own farm, Charley was the only help Dad had. He was a great help to Dad until he left the farm in order to get a construction job at Newport, Indiana, during World War II.

Dad sold off his cows and horses and became a grain farmer, as most everyone did. Now we bought milk and butter from the creamery in Ridgefarm, and chickens and eggs at Johnny Kerns' General Store. It was not the same as when we were younger. Dad became a grain farmer altogether with better machinery.

Dad had the first threshing machine, and then the first combine, ahead of anyone in the area.

He never replaced them as he knew how to keep them going.

When the threshing machine, or then later the combine, would break down in the wheat or oat fields, everything stopped until Dad could fix it. Many a time he let all the threshers go home, while we went to Peoria, Illinois, about one hundred thirty five miles northwest, to get a new part for the machine. When I saw Dad come running towards the house, and hearing no machines running, I knew we were going to Peoria. Men would be leaving the barnyard to go home, and wait until we arrived back home and the machine was fixed, and they could get back to work.

The house became a flurry of activity with dad running upstairs to take a bath, yelling at Mother in the kitchen or wherever she was to hurry if she wanted to go along. That meant me, too!

Mother and I would hurry to take baths, and change in order to be ready to go with Dad. We had only five or ten minutes before Dad came rushing downstairs again and we all ran out to the car, with Mother always carrying her silk hose to be put on in the car. Those were wonderful, happy times for me, but hectic and troublesome for Dad. We would, however, get to Peoria and back the same day, and the farmers would be back in the wheat fields threshing the next day.

There came the time when there were no more threshing dinners with lots of people around. I missed all that. It had been fun but hard work.

Mother and some of the working men's wives would cook for days getting food prepared for threshing dinners. Each family wherever the threshing was done would serve the dinner meal. It would be one to three days at one house.

Our dining room table was opened up as far as it would go, with three leaves put in the center. Over a white tablecloth, places were set for as many men as could get around the table. At our large table we would set about fifteen. When the men stopped for lunch, they would rush towards the house, wash up and come in like hungry bears. They lived for this time of eating. The table groaned with large bowls of potatoes, slaw, meats, vegetables, etc., etc. Everything imaginable to eat! The men started eating immediately. They ate and ate, there was little talking.

The women would grab each empty dish and replenish it. Desserts were then brought in and eaten with gusto.

When that group finished they would leave the table and go outside to lie on the grass in the shade under the huge maple trees in the yard.

The ladies would run the empty dishes and dirty plates and silverware to the kitchen, and bring out all clean service and more food to be eaten by the second group.

Dad always sat down for a very short while with the second group. He had been busy checking his equipment and getting it ready for the afternoon's work. Dad ate little before he would jump up to go past all the lounging, gorged men to his tractor and threshing machine. When he was ready, he would yell for the men to get started working again.

Now was the time for the women to relax and eat along with the kids.

It was a lot of work, but I loved it. I think everyone did.

The boys always seemed to get the best of everything, more attention. They were so cute and likeable, and being two of them, they were twice the attention getters as the rest of us.

We all loved sports. The boys were great in baseball and basketball in grade school. They would let me run for them in baseball when they made a hit which was almost each time they batted. They would get tired so I would start teasing to run for them. In high school that running for the boys helped my wind in track, and later when I played basketball.

Charley and Milt would start football practice in August at Ridgefarm High School, then go to school until they had to drop out for harvesting. They did this for a couple of years. It was a shame they could not continue and graduate but the depression changed everything. Dad had always had hired men at the farm but now it was the lean years. The boys were needed on the farm.

One time on Charley and Milt's birthday, Mother made two birthday cakes, one for each of the boys. They were good, as they were not made of left over pancake mix. I can't remember her ever making me a birthday cake. We never received birthday presents and very little for Christmas. There was so little money, it had to go for food.

Charley and Milt were identical twins, which gave them an edge. Family and close friends could tell them apart, but other people often were confused about their identity.

When either boy was chastised at school, and made to stay during recess, or after school, they would take turns staying. In retrospect, I suspect the wonderful teacher, Mrs. Ellis, knew but allowed this to happen. How could she not know? Mrs. Ellis taught all of us at Harrison Grade School. She was an excellent but firm teacher, the best kind.

The twins had beautiful red horses and bicycles, but we girls only had dolls. Then they got cars which eliminated the use of the horses and bikes, so we girls did learn to ride their bikes, but we never had our own. Mary always said Ann and I were close so she had to pal around with the boys. I think in retrospect this was true. I was the baby, and Ann being the oldest, she did take extra care of me.

The year when Ann was to become a Junior in high school, Aunt Pauline took her to an eastern girls finishing school at Westown, where she had an interesting year learning how other people lived other than farmers.

For Christmas, Aunt Pauline sent her chauffeur, Clarence Pettingill to pick her up and take her back to her house for the Holidays. He wrapped a lap robe around her legs in the back seat so she wouldn't be cold. I found a letter from Ann to Mother begging Mother to come and see her. If she couldn't, she asked that they send the boys for a visit. She must have been very lonely for her family.

She came home in the spring with her ice skates, tennis racket, and a pink pillow with ruffles on it, and the name of the school, which was Westown. She never went back.

That summer, when Aunt Pauline was driven over, Grandma and Aunt Pauline thought Ann and the chauffeur were too friendly. So the following year when Aunt Pauline came, she had a new chauffeur, a woman named Evelyn. We liked her and didn't like her. She was sharp tongued with us, wouldn't let us get away with anything, but was so helpful to Aunt Pauline and any of her relatives. She was a marvelous violinist. We kids would beg her to play. We would sit immobile and listen to her. She had played in a well known orchestra.

Mary Ellen was a strong individual who always knew what she wanted and didn't want. I was more laid-back and stood around watching the others.

In the fall of my eighth grade, when all my siblings had gone on to high school at Ridgefarm, Mother became ill and I had to do the cooking of which I knew nothing until this time. I remember the day Mother taught me how to make biscuits, a favorite of Pop. He liked them tall and thick. I didn't, so I would open them and pull out an inch or two of moist center and eat the crusty tops and bottoms. I still do that.

"You put in a batch of flour, and a teaspoon of baking powder, with a pinch of salt." Mother said.

"How much is a batch? How much is a pinch?" I asked.

I would take everything to her where she lay on the sofa, and she would show me how much to put in. I was real proud of those biscuits I made. Pop liked them!

We never received birthday presents, as times were so hard. We were lucky to have food on the table during the Great Depression years, and for some time afterwards. Mother would make cakes out of the left over pancake mix. They were awful. None of us liked cakes very well the rest of our lives. Mother did make good pies which we all loved.

We had picnics at the end of school each year when everyone would take the best food they could make out of what they had. One year someone brought a pumpkin pie which was green. It tasted awful! No one knew what was in it to make it green and taste so terrible.

THEN AND NOW

I was visiting Uncle Ed and Aunt Nora in their farm near Metcalf, Illinois and their beautiful little girl, Martha, and I slept on the floor in the front room. Martha had the prettiest dimples I ever saw.

As we lay sleeping, there was a horrible racket going on. I got myself awake with great effort, and got up off the floor. "What's going on?" I asked Aunt Nora.

"A weasel got in the hen house," answered Aunt Nora "and is causing a terrible ruckus! Ed is down there now, trying do get him out."

In a little bit, the noise was gone, and Uncle Ed came back in the house.

The next morning Martha and I got up and went into the kitchen for breakfast, where Uncle Ed was served his two shredded wheat biscuits soaked in rich cream from the cows. I had never seen anyone eat two biscuits, and never in all that rich cream. It did look good.

"He always has the same breakfast every morning," Aunt Nora said, when I said something about it. "Do you want some like that?"

I didn't! Too much for me!

When they started talking about the night before, I did not remember it all. I didn't understand what they were talking about!

"Why, you were up, talking and seemed as alert as anyone!" Aunt Nora said.

"I don't remember it at all," I said in amazement.

In the summertime every year we went to the Busby reunion. Mother would take two huge baskets full of food to reunions and picnics. In later years I marvelled at how little food people would take to picnics. One woman brought a small dish of cottage cheese, for her husband and herself.

At that church picnic for our four I had taken three or four things that I worked many hours to make. In many years later, like now when this is being written, most people bring one dish to a picnic. Sometimes there is not one crumb of anything left to take home.

I look at the empty dishes and wonder what people would think of the loaded baskets the people used to take to a picnic. Alas, those days are gone! Everyone made her best dishes to take. A lot of it is bought already made, and what is made at home is done quickly, or made from a box and without a thought of pleasing palates.

"I know who brought this!" was said about one of my favorite dishes many a time.

One day when I was in the eighth grade I was outside at recess playing ball when my brother Milt came by in our truck and stopped, and called me over to talk to him. I ran over with a big smile on my face, happy and excited that he wanted to see me.

He berated me. "How could you leave Mother like that? You never washed the dishes, you didn't do anything before you went to school!"

"I gave her a cup of coffee," I said meekly. "That's all she wanted," I said, devastated.

"I'm going up for Grandma," Milt said, "and bring her back. If Mom dies it's all your fault."

I watched the truck pull away fast and go tearing down the road. I walked very slowly back to the ball game.

That afternoon when I arrived home on the bus I hurried inside the house to find my gram sitting down exhausted, with all the dishes washed, but not yet put away. The house was cleaned and sparkling, with Mother feeling so much better. My guilty conscience was eased as I put away the dishes. I was so glad my Grandma was there.

I won first prize of a pen and pencil set when I was a 4-H Club reporter to the Danville Commercial News. There was an award ceremony where I was to give a speech.

"What kind of a speech should I give?" I asked.

"Oh, anything you want to say," I was told.

My main thought in those days was poetry. I read poetry at the Award Ceremony. They were kind to applaud.

My friends were always asking me to write poetry for them. I would ask them questions about their boy friends or something then would write a poem about it. Everyone wanted a poem written about themselves.

All my brothers and sisters were 4-H Club members, Head, Heart, Hands, and Health, started to keep farm boys and girls busy producing and learning how to grow crops, sew, cook, etc.

One year I took up sewing in 4-H and wanted to enter a patched hole in the county fair. My teacher said my made up article of a patched hole was crooked on one side. My teacher told me not to enter it because it was too crooked. I had done a fine job with the sewing but it was shorter on one end compared to the other end. I was devastated, as it looked great to me, so I showed it to the assistant teacher, who was the mother of my best friend Jean Mills, after the main teacher left. She conspiratively told me to enter it as she thought I had done a beautiful job. It won second award. It proved to me never to give up and know what is good. There were a lot of entries but mine was so much better than all the others.

For years Charley and Milt won first and second on their entries of their corn and best of show in the judged competition. We girls wanted to enter corn one year. We pestered Dad to help us choose the corn. He informed us we had to make our own choices. But he did reluctantly help a little.

"That one's all right," he would say.

"Are you sure?" We want to win like the boys.

"Yes, that one will be all right, he said, this one is good, too.

When we ran inside the building expectantly to see all five displays, with the first five winners belonging to the Busby family, we were the most disappointed girls in the world. I'm sure Dad had told the judges to not consider our entries. The First and Second awards were given to Charley and Milt, as usual. Then third, etc. were other kids corn. Way down the line were the Busby girls exhibits, with no one a winner. I looked at each winner to see why we did not win.

It was obvious. Dad had had us put in corn that was not perfect. The boys ears of corn were beautiful, long eared, top choices, while we girls ears of corn were sometimes good and other times nubby ears. Too short and no way near perfect. I suspect my father planned it that way.

"We can't get all the prizes. We have to let others have a chance," Dad told us when we complained.

Chapter 3

Teenage Years

When I was graduated from Harrison School, the graduation exercises were held at Pilot Grove Quaker Friends Church, where Jean Mills and her family attended church. The only gift I received was a pair of white lacy under panties from my Aunt Lois Busby. Ann was graduated from Ridgefarm High School that same year.

Mother wanted to cook a chicken, and asked Mary Ellen and me to get it prepared for cooking. I wanted no part of this.

"I can't do it!" I said.

"Oh, you can, too!" Mary Ellen said emphatically. "Just take it by the neck and wring it."

I got my hands on the chicken's neck and tried desperately, but it kept getting away from me.

"I can't do it!" I was crying by now.

"Oh, you silly! Let me do it!" Mary Ellen yelled at me. She grabbed the Rhode Island Red chicken from me, and pulled its head up above her wrist, placing her hand on its long neck, and swung it around. She swung and swung! Nothing happened. She just continued wringing its neck! I stood watching.

"I can't do it either!" she finally acknowledged.

"I'll put it down here on the cement, and you step on its neck!" she coaxed.

I tried cautiously and gingerly to step on its stretched out neck. "I can't!" I said, almost sick at my stomach.

"You have to!" Mary Ellen yelled at me. "Step on it! Hold it down and I'll pull it loose!"

I tried but the furious movement underneath my foot made me almost throw up!

She pulled and pulled on its legs, while that poor chicken tried its best to stay alive. When it finally pulled apart, I jerked my foot off its neck, and went running away. I looked back to see that poor chicken flouncing around, getting blood everywhere. I never helped, or by myself, killed another chicken, in my life.

So after the first year I was alone in high school. It was lonely and quiet after having so many around. We had been such a happy family with so many cousins and neighbors and friends all around. It was a shift in lifestyle.

Milt had married a girl from Georgetown then Mary Ellen married her brother. Their families were always very close and still are.

Milt and Laura Pearson Busby had five children. The first beautiful, blue eyed, bald headed, boy was named Charles Milton. I called him Charley Milt and still do. He was my first nephew and I doted on him. Then came Lester Lee, then Kay Ellen, named after Mary Ellen and me, then later Bonnie Sue. They had one little boy, Ronald Wayne, stillborn, who is buried in the Busby Mendenhall plot at Crown Hill Cemetery in Ridgefarm, Illinois.

Mary Ellen and Clifford Pearson, Laura's brother, met in the hospital after he was in a horrible car accident that almost took his life. Their love flourished, and they married and had three sons Philip, David, and Stephen.

Milt and Laura were going to a dance one time and asked me if I wanted to go with them. I did. We arrived at the throbbing, pulsating, nightclub, where we were seated in a booth. It was noisy and the dancing was furious and fast.

It was the first time I had ever been to such a place. Laura hadn't wanted me to go, but Milt said I needed to know sometime about things like this.

A young friend of the family had come to the dance by himself and was talking to Milt. They walked to the booth where Laura and I sat.

"He's here alone," Milt said. "I asked him to come sit with us." We moved over, and he squeezed in opposite me.

Laura and Milt got up to dance and left us alone in the booth. He just looked at me. He never did talk much.

"Will you marry me?" he said.

I sat up straight looking him in the eye, aghast.

"What?" I managed to say quietly.

"Will you marry me?" He repeated.

Then I burst out laughing, and acting demur, as I usually did in situations I didn't fathom. I giggled and that broke the seriousness of our situation.

"You don't mean that," I managed to say.

"Yes, I do. I want you to marry me," he said.

Well, it wasn't the kind of proposal I expected to get from a man I loved. What would my life have been like if I had said yes? I know, and I'm so glad I said no.

He married a cousin of mine later, and they lived on a farm the rest of their lives. I had always wanted and expected to marry a farmer, but I had to love a man with deep abiding love first, and anything that came after was icing on the cake.

When I met and fell in love with George, I knew whatever we did and wherever our lives took us it would be great, because we were together with our deep love between us.

One time after Milt and Laura were married, Charley tried to kid Laura, but it didn't work.

"Come here, Hon, and give me a kiss," he said, as he lay on the couch, in the parlor. It was dusk, and Laura had come in from the lighted outside, to a darkened room.

She started towards him. Then, I don't know why, she stopped. "You can't kid me, Charley! I know you are not Milt!" She said.

He laughed and jumped up. "It was worth a try," he said.

One year Dad planted too much sweet corn for us to sell locally. He and Charley took a load of sweet corn in our truck to Danville to see if they could sell it to the grocery stores. I went along as I always wanted to do things rather than stay at the farm.

It was a disappointing trip as most of the grocery stores had their own sources. We were left with a lot of wonderful delicious corn. It was early in the morning, and the corn had been picked that morning, so it was very fresh.

"Maybe we could go door to door and sell it," Dad said.

I was elated. That would be fun! "I know how to sell!" I said, "Let me help!" I was jumping up and down.

"No, you just go along with me. I'll do the selling. Don't say anything," Dad said.

I loved it. I listened and watched. I saw how the women were so receptive to the fresh corn and wanted to buy it. It was a seller's market.

"Pop, let me sell some by myself! I can do it!" I begged.

He fixed me some nice ears of corn and let me go off on my own. It was loads of fun. I think the women were so astonished at a little girl selling fresh corn at their front door that it was a pushover! Pop was amazed, telling everyone I was a better salesman than he and Charley were.

The corn field kept producing so much sweet corn that summer, that Dad decided to take a load to Chicago. He and Charley loaded up our old truck full of corn and off we went.

He and Mother took turns being with me. Charley was driving and Mother was sitting in the front. We planned to drive all night and get to the fresh produce market in the early morning hours.

Just outside Watseka, Illinois, which was about half way to Chicago, we had a wreck.

Dad and I were sleeping in the back on top the corn, where he had fixed a place for us. I heard someone screaming, "Help, help!" sounding as if way off in the distance. Then I realized they were my screams.

A good Samaritan came along and stopped to help us. We were sitting amongst all the corn strewn everywhere.

Charley had gone to sleep and hit an abutment. The truck was on its side, with all the corn thrown out on the ground. We were taken to an upstairs doctor's office in Watseka. The doctor had been called and met us there. Charley was still in a daze but Mother seemed to be hurt quite badly.

"I'll take you in first," he said to Mother, after asking each of us how we were hurt. "The rest of you sit out on the balcony and I'll get to you as soon as I can," the doctor said.

We were very worried at Mother's condition and did as we were told. As I was standing on the open balcony I reeled and almost fell off. Pop caught me and helped me lie down. The doctor came out and said he had done all he could for Mother, and wanted to look at me. He found a very large egg, at the right side of my head, which was causing my dizziness. After looking at Charley and Dad the doctor sent us to an interesting, old hotel downtown.

Charley and Dad went on to Chicago and sold the corn. Dad thought I should stay with Mother and help her. I wanted so badly to go with them, but I wanted to help Mother, too.

So I stayed with Mother. She could not be moved, when they came back from selling the corn, so they went back home without us. We stayed three weeks until Mother was well enough to travel.

As she grew a little better each day, I began to go outside her room a lot, finding interesting things to do. I had the run of the hotel and also the town, I think. There were some young girls and boys my age, with whom I became great friends, and wrote to after we went home. It was really fun after I knew Mother was mending. When the doctor said Mother could travel, Dad came up in our car and took us home. I had had a wonderful vacation, but it had to be at the expense of my Mother and the pocketbook of my Father.

In the fall of 1936, Dad learned from the radio and newspaper that President Elect, Franklin Delano Roosevelt, was going to give a speech at a park in Terre Haute, Indiana, "Terry Hut," as Dad called it. Dad was very politically minded so he thought this was a great opportunity to see him. He liked Roosevelt very much.

"I'll fix a picnic and we can stay there in the park after his speech," Mother said.

Mother was great with picnics, always taking delicious food. She fried chicken and made potato salad and a peach pie, plus other things.

"Are you about ready?" Dad asked.

"It won't be long," Mother said as she turned the chicken once more.

Dad got antsy. It was getting late! Mr. Roosevelt was to be there at twelve o'clock. Mother had been in the kitchen from early morning.

"We have to go!" Dad said sharply. "If we don't, we'll miss him!"

We finally piled into the car, and Dad raced down the road. It was about thirty-five or forty miles to Terre Haute from our house.

The Packard held the road well, but the road was not a good one. When we left the country road onto Route 1 Dad drove faster. I moved from the side back of Dad to the middle and leaned forward. I bounced from side to side holding on to the back of Mother and Dad's seats. Charley had stayed home with Grandma, so I was the only one in the back seat.

"You shouldn't have taken so long to get the picnic ready!" Dad said crossly. They never argued, so I knew he was really mad. I prayed we would make it in time as I could see how much it meant to my Dad.

"Hurry, Pop!" I cried above the motor noise.

"I can't go any faster! I'm going way faster than I should now."

He was definitely right. He was normally a slow driver as he liked to look at the crops. We used to go all around the countryside looking at other people's crops. He would go about 15 miles or less an hour, stopping for him to go over to the fields and pick a head of wheat, to check out how full it was.

This time going to Terre Haute was a wild ride I had never taken, even with my brothers who liked to drive fast.

We arrived in the city and went straight to the park.

"We'll never make it!" Pop said.

"Hurry, Pop, maybe he'll be late!" I said with Mom echoing me.

As we pulled into the entrance of the park I could feel Dad's energy flow away.

"There he goes!" he said.

"Maybe he's coming in," I suggested quietly. But the airplane had just taken off and we watched it gradually fade in the distance.

"I'm sorry," Mother said. "I shouldn't have taken so long with the food."

We parked our car and ate our delicious meal, but it really didn't taste so good now.

When I was a Junior in high school, I teased my dad for a permanent. I had never had one. My Grandma would put my very straight, blonde hair up on pieces of paper. It sometimes curled but parts of the hair would be straight. It really wasn't very good and it didn't last long, just a day or so.

The permanent was three dollars, smelled awful, but was good and kinky. It lasted a year! After I had it a week, I asked Pop if I could get it washed and set.

"You said you wanted a permanent so you wouldn't have to set it," Pop said.

"I know, but the girl said she needed the practice and she would do it for 50 cents," I told him.

So each week on Tuesday I stayed after school and had my hair set for 50 cents.

I would walk two blocks to the main part of town and hunt up my Dad for him to take me back home to the farm. In order to find out just where my dad was I needed only to stand and listen a few minutes. I would hear him clear his throat loudly and I knew exactly where he was. The town was so small and quiet I could hear him anywhere. He was more often than not downstairs in the town's only barbershop.

"I'm through Pop, let's go!" I usually had some studying to do so had to get home to do that. I was the only one at home now, except for Charley, so I got a lot of perks.

"Can I buy lunch today?" I would often ask Pop before the bus came to take me to school.

"How much do you want?" He would invariably ask me, knowing full well.

"Fifteen cents will do," I often said. "Well, fifteen cents for a sandwich and a drink, but could I have another nickel for a candy bar?" I would ask about once a week. Sometimes he had it, and sometimes he didn't.

One time Mother went to Danville on dollar day which happened once a year. She brought me back five dresses, each costing one dollar. I could not believe it. I screamed at each one. When I came to the long sleeved tailored red dress I grabbed it and screamed, "This is the best! I love it! I Love it!" It was, however, really too old for me. My friends were not that sophisticated so I did not wear it too often.

My favorite became the blue dress with a light cream colored top and a blue vest. This later became my wedding dress.

My favorite pastime was reading. Gram and I would read ten books at a time. She and I would discuss them, reading constantly. When we read the ten, from Ridgefarm Carnegie Library, (the smallest library he ever endowed), I would haul them all back, and exchange them for another ten. My favorite author was Gene Stratton Porter. I read every book the library had by this author. My favorite book of all books, in the whole library, was her "Girl of the Limberlost."

Gene Stratton Porter's real name was Geneva, which she changed to Gennevieve, when she was sixteen, then later her husband had her change it to Gene.

Gram and I were moved from her home to the farm, when I was in the Junior class, then I found it more difficult to get enough books to read. I had to delve deeper into our home library. Now, Gram's library was at the farm, so I selected books from both Gram's and my Mother's libraries.

My favorite books there were "Pollyanna," by Eleanor H. Porter, and "Anne of Green Gables," by L. M. Montgomery, (Lucy Maude) "Little Women," was my very favorite story of all books I have ever read.

After Gram and I were moved to the farm, I used to read nonstop hours at a time, curled up in the wide armed rocking chair, as I didn't have so much work to do. Many a time I would get up out of my chair, only to black out, and fall back into the chair. This was too much reading, too little activity, but what else was there to do? I knew I was reading too much, but I never wanted to put down a book I was reading until I finished.

These were the kind of books I grew up reading and loving. Pure, simple, wonderful books. Later they were all made into movies and videos. They can be found at most libraries and video stores.

When I was a Junior in High School, our class play was "Tom Sawyer." I played Becky which was lots of fun. Tom kissed Becky in the play. She was startled and threw her apron over her face. The next day my chemistry teacher, on whom I had a crush, told me my face was red when I pulled the apron down.

Halloween was always a fun time of year. Boys would upset outside toilets, and even put a cow on top of a roof. I was always glad to get invited to a Halloween party.

My Senior year, I dressed in my Grandmother's dressiest dress put away in her attic. It was heavy black satin with beautiful cutouts in the design of the dress, very elegant and gorgeous. I carried her beautiful black parasol, and wore her black pointed, high button shoes. No one knew me. I had told none of my friends how I was dressing.

Charley drove me there. I sat in a chair, while others were walking about, seeing who should win first prize for their costume. No one could guess who I was!

"Let me see your legs," one of my friends finally said.

As I lifted the skirt, and showed my black hosed legs, my friend, Mary Lou Duncan yelled, "It's Kathryn Busby!" All because of my legs! Most of the kids at our age had very thin legs. Mine were a little curved and had some shape to them. I won first prize!

When I was a Senior in high school, the class was given an assignment of "What My Philosophy in Life Is." I had to look up the word Philosophy, and even as I wrote the assignment, I was unsure as to just what it meant. But as I reread it, and pondered over it, I could not change one word of my one and a half page paper. It was short and to the point in which I said I wanted to do as God wanted me to do.

Only three students received an A on that assignment and the teacher, who was the principal of the school, Mr Jones, read those three papers in class. Mine was one of them. I was amazed, and sat in astonishment, as he read it aloud to all the students!

I always loved school. I wanted to be in everything and do everything. It broke my heart to graduate, I cried and cried.

That fall, I attended Utterback Business College, which was upstairs over business stores in Danville, Illinois. Each weekend I would go home on the bus to Ridgefarm and be picked up by Pop, as I had begun to call my Dad. Mom and Pop took me to the college the first day and said they would pick me up for lunch. It was a big surprise to them when I came downstairs at lunchtime with a girlfriend I had just met, by the name of Eloise High. We had hit it off immediately. We were both rather quiet, but had made friends instantly.

For the first time in my life I was on my own. Mother found me a little two room apartment, where I stayed during the week days. I'm sure Mom and Pop felt better about leaving me in Danville after meeting Eloise, who remained a close friend for years.

It was almost Christmas that winter when we got word that Uncle Lon and Aunt Mabel Busby called Mom and Pop to tell them their daughter Irene had been in an accident, and was killed. Six kids were in the car returning from a high school graduation party and their car was hit by a train. We were all so sorry Uncle Lon and Aunt Mabel's daughter was killed. It was such a shock. I went with Mother and Dad to Lapel, Indiana, for the funeral and stayed a couple of weeks after they returned home. We used to visit Uncle Lon and Aunt Mabel in Lapel quite often.

One time we decided to go to a well known department store in Indianapolis. It was the first time any of us had ever seen an escalator.

"Let's go upstairs," someone said.

Aunt Mabel didn't want to get on the escalator and tried to get us to go to the elevator.

"No, this will be fun," I said. "Come on, let's try it."

Mother was standing back of Aunt Mabel who wouldn't try to get on it.

"Just step on. It will move you," I said. We were all laughing and talking so loud we attracted lots of attention. People had stopped where they were to watch us and laugh with us.

Finally, after pushing Aunt Mabel physically and verbally, I decided someone better go forward. Looking down at my feet and trying several times, and getting on it right, I finally started going up and away from Mother, Anne and Aunt Mabel. Looking back at them I said, "Come on!" They finally made it but we had caused a lot of commotion.

After returning from Lapel, I never went back to Utterback Business College, as I felt I had progressed enough to get a job. I had passed all tests except I couldn't quite make that passing grade in shorthand. I was typing seventy words a minute but I was a little short of the eighty words a minute in shorthand required for a secretarial position.

Chapter 4
Meeting the Massings

The following spring I went to the fields and helped Charley and Pop. Milt was farming his own rented farm. He became a successful farmer which left Charley alone to help Pop. Milt sometimes came back home to help farm.

Pop didn't want me to harrow, as he said it was too hard for me, but he did let me disk after the harrowing was done, and before the crops came up. He used to hang around the field (he never really trusted my judgement the way he did the boys), but I loved doing what he did let me do. As a young child he let me ride around with him on the tractors.

One day in March, I had spent all day in the field, and was dirty and hungry, when we went in finished for the day. We had eaten and were relaxing when there was a knock on the farmhouse door.

"Is there a Catherine Busby living here?" a man asked.

That alerted us all!

When I would look in the newspaper at advertisements for a job, I was never able to go on an interview to try to get a job, so I had put my name in the Young Women's Christian Association (YWCA) in Danville for housework, thinking this would position me in the city so I could go on any interview that might come up. It was noted there my reason for work as a housekeeper.

The man at the door was George Clemens Massing, Sr. who had been a 543 acre farmer north of Georgetown. They now lived in Danville and he worked at the Bredehoft Dairy.

My Pop and he talked at great lengths about farming and people they knew, while I decided to go back to Danville with him, and help his wife who needed a small amount of housework to be done. I could go on any interview and could get another job at any time. Perfect, just what I wanted! It certainly set the course of my life in a great direction.

When we went out to get in his beautiful big Nash car, there was a young man in the front seat. Mr. Massing turned to me in the back seat. "This is my son Buddy," Mr. Massing said.

We exchanged glances and hellos then as we started up the road Mr. Massing continued carrying on a conversation. Buddy turned to look at me two or three times to talk. I thought he might be one of the young men from my business college, but I wasn't sure. I couldn't place the name.

When we arrived in Danville at Mrs. Massing's mother's beautiful home on Gilbert Street, I was introduced to all of them, including their other son, little nine year old Joseph, with whom I made a long lasting friendship immediately. He helped ease the situation completely. I had checked Buddy immediately upon arrival and decided I had never seen him before.

They took me to their five room apartment and I stayed forever! In their lives that is.

George knew his people, on his father's side, came from Germany, but he never knew what part. His aunt Mabel said several times they came from Rheiling, in the Saar Valley. He found naturalization papers, which stated that his immigrant Great, Great, Grandfather Nicholas, and his fourteen year old son Peter, came over in the 1840's and that they were born in Sanwintle, Prussia. Not finding Sanwintle on any map he thought perhaps it was a phonetic spelling.

When George and I visited Europe in 1985, we went to Saarbrucken in the Saar, to search for a lead.

A beautiful German girl from Berlin, working at the Rathaus (Town Hall) in Saarbrucken, spoke to us in perfect English. She said George's idea about the phonetic spelling of Sanwintle being

St. Wendel, would not be correct, because that's not the way it's pronounced phonetically. She said it's pronounced, "Sankt Vendel." We left the Rathaus discouraged and downhearted.

We returned to our hotel and George looked at the local telephone directory and found forty four Massing names. We were exuberant and George started calling. "Sprecken sie Englisch?" he asked each one he called. It means, do you speak English? In German. "Nein, nein," each would say with a smile in his or her voice. They wanted desperately to help but could not because of the language barrier.

On Sunday evening all had been called except the last three.

"Shall I forget the last three?" George asked me. "It's almost nine o'clock. People may have gone to bed."

"No," I said, "call the rest of them. We may never be back and we want to know we did everything we could."

The second name called, with only one to go, was Peter Massing who spoke a little English. We all became very excited and he told George we must come to St. Wendel, to get on a train and leave our bags locked up at the rail station and walk two blocks to the police station. He was the Kommissar se Polizei, Commissioner of Police.

When we arrived at his office at the police station, a few hours later, he was very happy to see us, and became very enthused about genealogy and promised to help us. He set us up in a very fine hotel and started searching for records. After considerable searching, by Peter, the trail led us to Namborn, a town near St. Wendel, in St. Wendel District. Peter made an appointment for us all and we were to be allowed fifteen minutes at the Namborn Rathaus (town hall), but we stayed much longer due to Peter's persistence. Peter talked to the two ladies behind the counter very insistently speaking Deutsch with no let up.

"What's he doing, what's he saying?" I asked again.

"Why doesn't he give up?" They finally started pulling record books, both civil and Catholic Church records, and found three more generations of George's family with birth and marriage records, proof of their existence. What a find! We were provided copies of the records found. Peter also found the location of the three hundred year old Massing family home in Namborn and took us there. It is a large two story frame house with no Massings living there now.

Above the lintel is the inscription, Elizabeth Massing 1894, the year she had the house remodeled.

We met the present owner of the house, Mr. Hoffman, who told us Elizabeth had a brother and nephew who went to America. That would have been George's immigrant ancestors, Nicholas and Peter, father and son.

In front were flower beds with beautiful roses in bloom, five or six inches in diameter; and in the rear, built into the house, was a blacksmith shop. So, they were farmers, blacksmiths, and possibly workers in brass, as the meaning of the name Massing/Messing is brass.

In the four days we were there. Peter had us to his beautiful home in Theley two or three times to meet his lovely family, his wife Margret and daughter Iris. We were entertained and fed a fine desert Margret prepared of fresh plums, special candies of chocolate covered carmel, and served an excellent wine made of apples off trees on their land. We were invited, and went with them to see a caravan they wished to buy for their travels.

Our visit there was doubly fruitful. We not only found George's family roots, and three more generations, but met a very fine family, whom we call cousins. They visited us in our home in North Fort Myers in 1987. They plan to visit us again in the near future.

Peter Massing, the fourteen year old immigrant, later married Barbara Speltz, and were the parents of George's grandfather, Joseph C. Massing, born in 1862. He had seven brothers all of whom, including Joseph, when their time came, died of pneumonia. They had four sisters.

Joseph migrated from Ripley County, Indiana, where he was born, to Vermilion County, Illinois, where he owned and operated livery stables and feed stores until he saw the automobile would ruin him, and sold out.

Joseph C. Massing married Flora Ellen Roderick of Vermilion County, Illinois, and they had four daughters and two sons. One of the sons was George Clemens Massing Sr., who married Nellie Leona Parker, (known as Leona), one of six sisters. These were, George, my husband's parents.

Joseph and Flora had a home on North Hazel Street in Danville, Illinois, as well as a farm a few miles north of Georgetown, Illinois, where the family spent much of their time in the summer months.

George Sr. farmed 543 acres just north of Georgetown. They lived on the farm until George Jr. was seven, at which time his Dad took a job with American Railway Express, and later was employed by Bredehoft Meadow Gold Dairy in Danville and Champaign Meadow Gold Dairy for many years.

Two more sons were born, Bobbie Jo, who died at age four of complications from scarlet fever and strept throat.

Joseph P. now resides in Naples, Florida, where he and his wife Virginia, own and operate furniture/home decorating stores, both being licensed Interior Decorators. They have two sons, Kent and Britt and a daughter, Gina.

George's mother, Nellie Leona Parker, was born to Alonzo and Delana Daisy Schooler Parker, well known grocers in the New Village/Georgetown areas. Daisy's father and mother had also been grocers. Daisy's grandfather, Isaac Thornton, who was a Quaker, fired his rifle into the air to avoid killing enemy soldiers during the Civil War.

Alonzo's father, Robert Parker, served in the Civil War, came home with the fever and died. Alonzo's mother, Amanda Jane Baldwin, was a descendent of John Baldwin, George's Baldwin immigrant ancestor, who was one of the founding father's of both Milford, Connecticut and later, Newark, New Jersey, according to historical record.

The morning after my arrival at the Massing family home was washday. Leona, George's mother, jerked off the sheets, causing them to fly up in the air, and changed them for clean ones while I helped a little. I had never seen this done. She made the beds up, then dusted and ran the sweeper. I watched very carefully and helped her as much as I could. I had done very little housework in my life.

The next day I started jerking off the sheets again as she had done the day before. Leona stood and watched me in amazement. "Why are you doing that?" Leona asked. "I'm making the bed, that's what you did yesterday," I said. "I only do that each week when it's time to change the sheets," she said in a small voice. I had a lot to learn. I thank God the Massings were very patient people!

George always helped his Mother with house chores and gardening. Just prior to my arrival, he had been spending all his evenings after school preparing dinner and cleaning up afterwards. It was usually midnight before he got his studies done. His mother had had two nervous breakdowns after Bobbie Jo died. She had not regained her strength.

I liked to work there. I really did get better at doing my chores. I learned to do them the way it was expected of me.

"What do you want us to call you?" Leona asked as we were doing housework.

"I've always wanted a nickname. I never had one. When I was real small people called me Cat or Catty, but Mother told me not to answer them, when they called me that." I explained,

"What would you like for us to call you?" Leona asked again.

"Maybe Kathy or Kay," I said. Leona thought a moment. "We'll call you Kay." So I finally had my nickname I always wanted. For the rest of my life I have been Kay to everyone.

When I was a Junior in Ridgefarm High School I wanted to change the spelling of my name from Catherine to Kathryn. My Mother didn't mind, so I have spelled it that way ever since. It is my legal name because I used it for years before I ever checked on it for legality. My Grandpa Parris had to have his spelling legalized by notary from Paris to Parris, as he was using it.

One day George was fooling around at the dining room table, after the dishes were done, with pen and paper. "What is that?" I asked.

"It is a love knot," he said. He continued making them as I watched.

"Make one on the palm of my hand," I said.

He drew a beautiful love knot, in the center of my left palm, which thrilled me so much. He had to hold my hand in his big one and lean in close towards my face. It was exhilarating and breathtaking to be so close. From that moment on love knots have been a part of our lives.

That was the start of our love for one another, a love that grew and grew, and is still growing.

He still puts love knots on all notes, cards, gifts, and just anywhere. I know he loves me when I see a love knot, and my love for him abounds stronger every time I see one. They bond us together as nothing else does.

One time love for George overwhelmed me. I reached up on tiptoe and kissed him on the cheek. After that, there were many kisses.

After the dinner dishes were finished, George's dad would often take the family for a drive. He would drive us through the nicest sections of town in north Danville. We would cross Lake Vermilion on the causeway and bridge.

George and I would sit close to one another and hold hands in the back seat. Once in a while George's dad would ask if George wanted to drive. I preferred his Dad to drive.

Joe and I became fast friends and I began to become interested in calm quiet George. My boy friends had all been quiet boys, but George was exceedingly quiet. But our friendship flourished and one time I was asleep, actually pretending to be asleep, when he walked into the front room and stood looking out the window.

"Would you like to go to a movie tonight with me?" he asked.

I was immobile. I couldn't move. I pretended I was asleep.

"Would you like to go to a movie tonight?" he repeated louder.

I managed to straighten up and said, "Yes, I would!"

After dinner I dressed up in my only good dress that I had brought with me. He helped put on my light shawl across my shoulders. We walked six blocks to the best movie house in town. He was so polite, I would lose him when he would change from one side of me to the other, so he was always on the outside. I had to turn to see where he was, as he would shift himself to the curb side. No one had ever been so polite to me before. He said later his Aunt Ruth had taught him how to walk right, when on a date.

That was the first of hundreds of movies we have attended. We have made going to the movies our most enjoyable pastime.

The Massing family saw how well George and I were becoming attracted to one another, so Mom Parker, George's wonderful grandmother, gave me her ticket to see him be graduated from Danville High School in June 1938. I was thrilled to go. There were two thousand students in Danville High School with a graduating class of more than two hundred so the seating capacity was limited. It was very impressive, much different than my Ridgefarm High School graduation of thirty-six seniors the year before.

George lost three semesters of school. Once in the second grade as he transferred from Wingard Grade School, Meeks Station, to Washington Grade School, Georgetown, Illinois, because he had been taught no music. He had only been exposed to "America," which was sung every morning as school opened.

The first day George attended Wingard school, which was the same school his Grandmother Parker attended when it was a log cabin, George received a spanking. The teacher knew his folks and knew George knew his ABC's, but he refused to say them. John Milton the teacher, spanked him. George got back at him by puddling on the floor.

George has been stubborn ever since!!

The second time a semester was lost was with an absence of twelve weeks, due to complications of Strep Throat and Scarlet Fever, during which time George's brother, Bobbie Jo, died at age four. George and his other brother, Joseph, were also very seriously ill. The third semester lost was, as a Sophomore in high school, he was again absent for twelve weeks due to complications of Bronchial Pneumonia and Whooping Cough.

After George's graduation, I went back to the farm, as Mother Massing's health was improved.

George would polish his dad's Nash until it shone silvery black and come down to Ridgefarm. We had very little money, so we would mostly drive along the country roads. We found places we never knew were there. We were always trying "to get lost," a thing we continued doing with our children all our lives. We still say, "Let's try and get lost!" It is very difficult to do as all roads lead back home.

When I was quite young we discovered Lodi a hot sulfur springs park in Indiana, not far from Cayuga, where we kids wanted to go every Sunday in the hot torrid summer. It took several miles, then going through a valley of horribly smelling sulfur fumes in the air when the winds were blowing our direction. It was a sigh of relief for all of us when we arrived at the clubhouse and parked.

There was nothing in this world better than running down the hill in our swimming suits and jumping in that glorious pool of sulfur water. Mother always took gallons of water home to drink. George says his grandmother, Mom Parker, at one time used it to heal her delivery horse's leg at her store in Georgetown, when the leg was cut by barbed wire. Lots of people claimed it had medicinal healing properties.

One of the most memorable times there was in the beginning of George's and my courtship. George came down to Ridgefarm to see me, not knowing I had gone to Lodi. After being told by the neighbors where we all were, he drove to Lodi. What a wonderful surprise. I loved it. I left with George early but there was no fresh water in which to wash up and get the Lodi smell off. As the afternoon progressed my Lodi smell stayed with us, especially from my hair.

In August we talked of marriage.

"Gram, George asked me to get married! We're going to get married!" I said.

I had gone in the house late at night with a full bursting heart and ran into Gram's bedroom. I had to tell someone. Mother had made a bedroom out of the parlor in order for Gram to be able to stay downstairs.

"Don't tell anybody," I said after we talked and I told her how happy I was.

Gram and I kept that burning secret for three or four days until George came down again and I could be sure he had really wanted me to marry him. He did! So we told the whole world then!

A few weeks, after George asked me to marry him, he asked me to go downtown in Danville with him. We walked towards town where he took me in Heflin's Jewelry Store on Vermilion Street.

"Will you let me see the rings?" George asked of Mr. Heflin, after introductions.

Mr Heflin said with a big smile, "I would be glad to."

He brought out three beautiful diamond rings to show me.

"George picked these three rings for you to choose one for your engagement," Mr. Heflin said.

They were all so pretty. One had less diamonds and sparkled less than the other two. One had more diamonds than the other two and was considerably more brilliant than the other two. I wanted this one.

It was beautiful. But then my Quaker upbringing got the better of me. When evaluated, the middle diamond ring seemed to be much more beautiful than the less of the three, and when I looked at the largest and more brilliant I thought, "It has to be much more expensive than the middle one, and the middle one is almost as large and bright and sparkly as the bigger one."

"I'll take the middle one." I had talked myself into exactly what they wanted.

"You can get this larger one if you want," George said.

"No, it's too expensive, I'm sure. I love this one. We'll take it. It's so beautiful," I said.

The wedding band had seven small diamonds in it and the large engagement diamond with its two flanking stones was beautiful. The center diamond was one quarter carat.

The summer between my Junior and Senior years I sold Avon Products, by walking around the countryside in about a two mile radius. Finally Charley let me use his Chevlrolet Coupe to increase my territory. When I sent in my order, it was so large the company was elated. At the end of the summer season when I wrote with my order that I would not be selling Avon Products anymore I immediately received a letter begging me to reconsider. I was moving on to better things.

I worked as a clerk in the cosmetic department at Woolworth Dime Store, in Danville before George and I were married. I worked for Doctor Williamson as a receptionist after we were married.

While I was working at the Soil Conservation Office George gave me my diamond ring. I would take it off my finger when I washed my hands, and lay it on the sink. One day after I washed my hands I walked out without it. I forgot it until George and I went on a date, at which time I became hysterical. I insisted on going back to work right then. It was dark.

"No one will be there," George said.

"They might. Sometimes, someone works at night," I said. "Let's go by there and see!"

Imagine our surprise when we saw the light on. I ran up to the door and knocked. Someone saw me.

"Could I please come in and check in the rest room!" I said. "I've lost my diamond ring, and I think I might have left it here." He let me in, and I hurried to the rest room. It wasn't there. I looked all around, but it just wasn't anywhere. Sick at heart, I slowly went back to George.

The next morning, I went in early and stood around, to see if someone had found it. No one said anything, so after awhile, I turned to go.

"Kay," my boss said. "Did you loose something?"

"Oh, did you find it? My ring? I put it down to wash my hands, and forgot it!" I said.

"I picked it up last night and kept it safe for you," she said.

I never quite forgave her, for not telling me in the beginning, and making me wait to know she had found it. That ring was never off my finger again except on my wedding day, and again when I had my babies, the nurse told me my finger might swell, necessitating having the ring cut off.

The ultimate of good looks for a husband for me would have been black curly hair, blue eyes, and definitely dimples. When I met George all that went out the window. I saw what I wanted, kindness, gentleness, softness of a man who put his wife and family ahead of himself always. He nurtured our lives with love and compassion, letting us grow into individuals, hoping to be worthy of his love for us.

George had deep black eyes like his mother's, black curly hair, but no dimples. George says his hair is brown but it always looked black to me. I have to get one thing aestheticaly hoped for don't I?

Aunt Jessie, who married Uncle Fred Townsend after her husband Kenneth (mother's brother) had died, used to come over to Illinois a lot to visit us and especially Grandma whom she still called Mother. Aunt Jessie had been an orphan and said Grandma had been the only mother she had known. After George and I were engaged, I went to Indianapolis to stay a few days with her. The first day I was there was Saturday and Aunt Jessie had invited several adults and their offspring who were my age to meet me. I am sure she was trying to match me up with one of the boys.

"Never marry the first man that asks you to marry him," she told me.

"Why not I asked incredulously. I thought you must be sure before you accept a proposal of marriage. I was! I had never wanted to spend the rest of my days with anyone but George. After I knew him for a few months I knew he was the one I wanted to live with forever. I hadn't even thought of any of my other boyfriends that way.

Aunt Jessie suggested this one young man take me to the movies. I didn't want to go, but felt impolite about refusing after everyone tried to encourage us. It was probably a trumped up deal. Jeff really was a nice young man but I felt I was being unfaithful to George.

"It will be all right," Aunt Jessie said. "He is just a friend."

"I'll have to call George first. I told him I would call him today," I said.

When I went into the dining room to call, the telephone which was on the wall, looked quite different than Grandma's or ours on the farm. I took down the receiver and waited.

No one came on. I hung up the receiver and looked all around to see why it was different from ours at home. When I finally got the operator I couldn't answer her questions properly. As I hung up, Jeffrey came into the dining room from the kitchen where all the kids were.

"Do you need some help?" he asked a frustrated girl! No doubt all the kids in the kitchen had been listening.

"I can't seem to understand the telephone. It isn't like the ones we have at home," I said in desperation.

"Let me try for you. What's the number you are calling?" Jeff asked. He helped me and I was soon talking to George. Jeff had been so suave and I had been so flustered.

I put on my jacket and he and I walked a block to catch the trolley.

When we arrived at the movie Jeff wanted us to sit in the top balcony. I had never sat in the top balcony at a movie house before. As we took our seats, I noticed they were all young couples hugging and kissing one another. I was embarrassed and uneasy. Fortunately the movie started right away. It starred a blonde bombshell, named Marie. It was hilariously funny and I laughed loud and hard.

The couples turned to stare at me and began to watch the movie. Jeff had put his arm across my shoulders fully intending a little loving of his own. I became so involved with the movie he pulled his arm away and enjoyed it with me.

We returned to Aunt Jessie's on the trolley with little conversation. When we arrived at Aunt Jessie's, I went in with the adults, and he went into the kitchen where the kids were. Aunt Jessie gave up trying to arrange any dates for me.

There was an old cliche we kids, especially the boys, would always say when asked to do something.

"Let George do it," was always the reply. When George started coming around there was that inevitable remark to a chore. "Let George do it."

George looked around surprised and got up and did it the first time he heard it. We all laughed and explained. But even after our explanation of the meaning, George insisted on doing things. I cautioned him, "You're always going to have to do things for everybody."

George said "I don't mind."

Many times after that initial episode he continued doing things when one of us said, "Let George do it!" This went on for years long after we were married.

Chapter 5
Early Married Life

George and I were married March 17, 1939, at the Parsonage of the Bowman Ave Methodist Church in Danville, Illinois, where I had attended services with Heloise, my friend from Utterback Business College. The Reverend Otto C Frey conducted the ceremony, and my sister, Mary Ellen and her husband, Kip, stood up with us. I glanced at the clock the exact moment he pronounced us man and wife, and it was 5:15 P.M.

Mary and Kip drove us back to the farm, where all my brothers and sisters and their families were gathered, to celebrate our marriage. We were to sit down at the extended table covered with a damask cloth on which was set Mother's hand painted Havilland dishes, sterling silver, and leaded cut glass tumblers. The Havilland set of dishes, and the salad plates, were hand painted by Mother when she was a young lady while attending Butler University in Indianapolis, Indiana. On the Havilland she painted her monogram in gold and the salad plates she decorated with colorful, paintings of blossoms and buds.

We sat down to a sumptuous meal in the dining room at the old farm house and had a warm and loving time. When we were ready to go, Charley said he would take us back to our furnished apartment in Danville.

As we left the farm house, Mary Ellen gave me a package.

"Did you remember to buy soap and towels and things?" she asked.

I looked at her in surprise. "No I didn't I guess."

I didn't think you would,"she laughed,. "So I fixed you a package of things you might need."

I was so glad to get them. What would I have done without them? I thanked her and hugged her as we said goodbye.

I had asked Charley if we could use his car for a few days before, and he said no.

"It's too late now Charley," I said "we've spent all of our money. We'll just stay up in our new apartment and go to a movie or two."

One nice big room, with a daybed, and a very small kitchen, was where we lived for the next few months. The bathroom was outside our door and down the hall.

The first meal I cooked was the best meal I ever tasted! It was boiled potatoes and green beans and tasted great! They had lots of butter on them, as George worked for Bredehoft Meadow Gold Dairy, so we always bought a lot of dairy products.

He would come home about 2:00 P.M. every day, and I would be at the window watching to see his first entrance into the alley that would bring him home to me. I would yell out the window to him, not caring what the neighbors thought.

When we still lived in this first apartment, one morning George got up early, as usual, to go out on his milk route. It was about 3:00 A.M., the time he had to be at the dairy to pick up his bottles of milk for delivery. As George left the apartment building he heard some noise and looked back to see a naked man running around the house. Someone in the building had a hot party the night before, and it looked as if it were still going on.

One afternoon at the dairy George was upstairs in the annex where all the route men checked up, that is prepared a work sheet on all that days transactions to turn in to the office.

That day Owen West, a curly-headed, blue-eyed guy and one of our "gung ho" salesmen, told George he was wanted to see about a collection at an address down on South Street, which ran parallel to Green Street Danville's notorious "Red Light District." That wasn't too unusual, as George had at one time been a substitute on that route and delivered milk to a few of "those houses."

George drove to the address and found it to be on the second floor of a very large building. Upon arriving on the second floor he walked into a huge waiting room of some sort, as it had gaudy red velvet plush davenports, chairs, tables with gaudy lamps lined up all around the walls. There must have been ten or fifteen of these settees, davenports, etc.

He asked for the lady of the place and was asked to sit down. There was not another person in the room at the time.

George became suspicious after awhile from the appearance of things. However, not having ever frequented such a place, he could not be sure. He finally decided he must have been set up by Owen West, who probably thought George was still wet behind the ears. He sneaked out finally as nothing ever happened.

I was so happy I laughed and giggled at everything. I had always been a giggler, and people had always laughed with me.

"What are you laughing about?" My new neighbor down the hall asked me one day. "You laugh all the time."

One day, I decided to see how far I had to go in order to get stony old George to laugh. I was reading the evening newspaper when I looked over at George and saw him very serious as usual.

I started to giggle slightly, then I giggled a little louder. No response. I began to laugh quietly. No response. I laughed louder and louder. George sat stoically in his chair. I slipped off my chair laughing so hard and loud. It finally caught his attention.

"What's so funny?" He said with a smile finally on his face.

My laughter stopped. I had finally caught his attention! He hasn't changed much.

Our apartment was only six blocks from downtown Danville so we would window shop and go to the movies. George had a heavy duty large bicycle, that his Dad had ridden to work at the dairy in his earlier days, so we bought me a lighter girl's bike. We went everywhere on our bikes for years. We even grocery shopped on them when you could buy two big bags of groceries for a five dollar bill. Everyone around town recognized us because of our bikes.

George made only $16.25 weekly, or $65.00 per month, so we couldn't buy much, but we didn't need much. We lived on love. Of course, we went home to Mother and Dad Massing's a lot in the evenings about dinner time, and every weekend we went to Ridgefarm where Dad picked us up at 6:00 o'clock every Friday night at the bus and took us back Sunday night.

There was the time Charley and Milt pulled a good one on George. George's Dad had quit farming when George was seven, so he did not learn much about farm life and operation of equipment.

They set George up to harrow the field, over by my Uncle Rosie's. They figured he could not get into too much trouble doing that. They got him started, told him where to harrow, then took off for Ridgefarm, to play euchre.

George started out, okay, but before they were barely out of sight, George cramped the front wheels too sharply on a turn, and got them almost squared off. They promptly dug into the ground and killed the engine. That engine had to be started by a twist or two of the flywheel which was pretty stiff and hot.

When Charley and Milt came back, after two hours of card playing, they found George was still trying to start the engine.

I took a job with Doctor Williamson in Danville to help out with our income. He paid me five dollars a week until he saw I had nothing to do in the afternoon, so then I went there for two fifty for half a day. George often stopped by and had some lunch with us.

One of Doctor Williamson's patients taught me how to knit. I had seven nephews and nieces by now, and I knitted a pair of mittens for each one of them that year for Christmas.

Furnished apartments were an easy living for us. We just packed up our few clothes and moved on to another one. We would tire of it and would get a nicer one, or a cheaper one, depending on our situation.

George's Grandmother, Mom Parker, made an apartment for us in her upstairs closed in porch with an entrance room which was our front room. She put the five piece white wicker furniture which Aunt Sudie had made in high school in our front room. The bath room was just down the hall. Our kitchen and bedroom were in the former sleeping porch. I used a three burner coal oil stove for cooking.

My brother Charley was having terrible trouble with his teeth. He came to our apartment at Mom Parker's, to ask us what Doctor to see.

"I have my Dad's old mule forceps," George laughed.

Well, maybe you could do it, I would be willing for you to try," Charley said.

George had the forceps his Dad had used to pull teeth from his mules, on the farm, as well as George's own baby teeth, over the years, when one needed pulling. The forceps were in excellent condition, apparently made of some high quality chrome steel.

First George sterilized the forceps, cleaned his hands with alcohol, and made ready clean cloths. He had Charley swish listerine around in his mouth, to cleanse it. George then went to work, pulling and tugging with the forceps, until he had one tooth out.

"What do you think? How do you feel?" George asked.

"It's okay, try to take the other one out now. You are doing a good job," Charley said.

George pulled and tugged at the other one, twisting it, and working much harder than with the first one. George kept trying and finally, it broke off.

"You should probably go to the dentist and have him look at it and see if he can do anything more for you," George said.

So, George called Doctor Taylor, a well known, and well liked negro dentist, and told him the problem. Doctor Taylor said, "Bring him in."

Upon arrival at the dentist's office, he tried to trip George up, to see if he had done anything wrong.

"You did everything right" said Doctor Taylor, and proceeded to remove the rest of Charley's broken tooth.

My Dad was a very strong man. He could withstand more than most people. When he knew he had to have his teeth pulled, he had half of them pulled, at one time, and went back the next day, and had the other half of them pulled. That takes a mighty strong man. He rinsed his mouth out with whiskey, and I suspect he let a little go down his throat.

When one of my nephews, Dave, was five years old, I wanted Mary and Kip's boys to stay all night with George and me, when we lived at Mom Parker's house. Steve was too small, Phil did not want to stay, so good little Dave stayed with us. He was a delight. I loved having him.

For supper, we had sandwiches and milk shakes. Dave was not a good eater, and was dawdling over his milk shake.

"I bet I can drink mine faster than you! I said.

"I bet you can't!" he said.

We tried to better each other. It was too much for little Dave! He immediately went to the bathroom and threw up.

The next day, we walked to church, about ten blocks. Along the way we saw a dead bird, and stopped to look at it, laying there on the sidewalk. We felt so sorry for the bird.

"He's in Heaven now," I said.

We were late in getting to our Methodist church, so, hurriedly I told the assistant teacher to be sure to keep him in his class, until we came back to get him.

When we went back, after our class was over, Davey was not there!!

I was frantic! We looked everywhere in the halls, in other rooms, outside. Then the teacher suggested, that she take us in her car, to see if he could be found.

"There's no way he could have walked home! He would not know how to get there! We came so far, going down different streets!" I said. I was sure he was lost forever! What would Mary and Kip do? This was awful!

The church was a very large church, and by now it was empty. No Dave could be found anywhere! There was nothing to do but get in the car with the teacher.

She made all the turns, where we had walked, and we were almost home. No Dave! I was positively sick.

"Is that your little boy, sitting up there on the porch, in the swing?" the teacher asked.

"Where? Where?" I craned my neck, from the middle of the back seat, to get a better view. "Yes! That's him! How on earth did he find the place?"

I was crying and laughing at the same time, as we ran up the stairs, and gathered him in my arms.

"How did you ever find your way home?" I asked.

"I saw the bird, and I knew I was okay!" he said.

That is one smart kid! To get out of that huge church and walk all the way back home by himself!

George always wanted a set of "power tools." When we lived at Mom Parker's, on north Gilbert Street in Danville, one day we went to Sears, and bought him the Dunlop line, not their best Craftsman, but adequate. George had had this hankering for a long time. He had taken woodworking in both grade and high schools. We bought a table saw, jig saw, lathe, and other small tools, plus a grind wheel.

My brother Milt found out about these tools, and came with his tractor, and a head full of ideas, for building a tractor cab, to keep out the dust in the fields, as well as, chilling winds and foul weather. They did a lot of figuring, then gathered up the raw materials, and proceeded to build the cab from scratch. They used the frame and windshield from a Model A Ford. They kept several late hours, until the project was finished, with great results. Milt added a radio in the cab, to keep him company. The whole thing was constructed of plywood panels, and straps of metal. The finishing touch was a coat of brilliant farm implement red paint.

After Rosella, my cousin, was married and had a family, she invited Mother and Dad to her house for dinner one Sunday.

"I wonder what she would serve," my Mother said.

"Why?" I asked.

"When we used to go to Maude's house she always served us pork roast," she answered. Rosella's mother, Maude, had died when Rosella, was a little girl.

"Well, did she serve pork roast?" I asked the next time I saw her.

"Yes, she did," Mother said. We had a good laugh. Like Mother, like daughter.

Mother's are very special people, but in a way, we all expect that. Grandmas, on the other hand, are very special people, from whom we expect nothing, and receive everything. My Grandma was super special. I loved her very much.

When Mother told me Gram was not too well, and wondered if I could stay at home and stay beside her overnight, I was glad to do it. George had to go back to Danville to work, but I stayed that weekend to help with Grandma.

THEN AND NOW

Mother, Pop, and Charley all went to bed, while I sat beside my beloved Gram. It was early in the morning, when she became agitated, and began making strange sounds. I tried to talk to her but to no avail. I ran to the foot of the stairs in the front room. I did not want to be gone from Grandma, but I was afraid for her.

"Mother! Mother! Gram's doing something. Please come down," I yelled.

"Milt, Milt, wake up"! I head my Mother say. "Charley, get up! Grandma needs us!"

They were all downstairs in a minute, and we all gathered around Grandma. It was not long until we heard a heavy sigh, and she was gone. She died on her eighty-sixth birthday, nineteen hundred thirty-nine.

Gram was buried at Crown Hill Cemetery beside Grandpa, who had preceded her to heaven by seventeen years. We all missed Gram, but knew she was in heaven where she belonged. She had had a wonderful life on earth.

That fall Mother and Dad bought a beautiful little sixteen foot, well arranged travel trailer and left the cold, snowy Illinois winter for Florida. For a few winters, they traveled to other states finally, settling one year in the Hallandale area of Florida, for the rest of their lives.

After each trip, we lived in the trailer, when they would come back in March to get the farm crops started, and we would live in the trailer until they wanted it to go to Florida the next November after all crops were out of the fields. Then we would move to a furnished apartment, until they returned the next spring.

One spring, we just got the trailer parked, and I was putting everything in order, when I became very dizzy and sick. When George came home from work, I was quite ill. George was beginning to feel bad, too. We rode our bikes to Mother Massing's, who put both of us to bed, in their big bed, as we both were breaking out with the three day measles, by then.

One year Mother and Dad took their sixteen foot trailer to the Springfield, Illinois Fair. Milt and Laura and George and I had gone to the fair arriving at breakfast time. Mother made breakfast for us, and we all started to sit down at the dining room table, which was at the far end of the trailer, when all of a sudden the trailer made a loud noise and moved as if to go down the steep hill on which it was parked. Everyone had sat down except Milt and I.

"Go down to the other end!" Milt yelled. Everyone was so taken by surprise they just sat there.

"Come on, hurry up!" I yelled running to the other end,

When Milt and I ran down to the other end, the movement and noise stopped. We all ran out the door to find the rear bumper jammed in the soft wet muddy earth on the hill. A little more and we would all have been at the bottom of the deep gorge.

Our beloved Aunt Florence passed away in New Jersey, in 1940. Laura and Milt, Anna Rose, Mother and I drove straight through to New Jersey, for the funeral.

Milt and Laura took turns at the wheel, driving all night. When Milt was driving at night, all of a sudden, I realized I was watching the same red tail lights, on the car ahead of us far in the distance, and had been seeing them for a long time.

"Milt, why don't you go around that car? You've been following him for hours," I said.

He turned to me quickly. "No, I don't want to go around him. He is a lead for me. I want him up there. I can keep at a steady fast pace, as long as I see his tail lights. When he turns a curve, or disappears for awhile, I know I will have to do the same, when I get where he is," Milt explained.

That taught me a big lesson I have never forgotten. I thought my brother was very smart to figure that out, and have remembered what he said many times, when we are driving at night.

It was so sad to know I would never see Aunt Florence again. But we enjoyed our visit at the Joshua Waddington home, where Grandma and all her sisters and brother grew up.

We also had a wonderful time visiting cousin Emma Engle, in Clarksboro, New Jersey, before we returned home.

Wendell Wilkie, who was running for president, was coming through Danville, stopping in his train, to give a short speech, from the rear platform. The stop was at the Big Four Railway Station a short block north of where we lived in our trailer.

I decided I'd better get out there and see Mister Wilkie, as he might be our next president. He did not win, of course, but I did like him.

As I stood half way down the block, I heard his short speech, then watched his train leave, with Mister Wilkie waving good bye.

As I turned to go back to our trailer, I caught a familiar face in the crowd. He was hurrying away.

"Hey, Pop! I thought you were a Democrat" I yelled far too loudly, causing lots of stares!

"I wanted to hear what he had to say," he answered me. That taught me to always hear the other side of anything.

When we went to our first voting poll to vote, George and I hardly discussed the issues.

When we came out of the beautiful, palatial Joseph Cannon home where we voted, George was the first to speak.

"Who did you vote for?" he asked as we started down the steps.

"Franklin Delano Roosevelt!" I said, without hesitation.

George stopped in his tracks, and said "How could you! Why did you vote for him?"

I stopped and stared at him in amazement. "Why, what do you mean?" I cried. "It never entered my mind to vote for anyone else!"

I guess I had listened to my dad, and it was ingrained in me to be a Democrat, like him. Since then, I try to see both sides, and when I'm ready, I vote for the man I think is best, and what he will do for our country. But I remain a Democrat, and, more often than not I vote for a Democrat.

In the next presidential election, George, also voted for Franklin Delano Roosevelt.

My brother Charley married Helen Clark in 1940. Their children were: Thomas, Terry, Elizabeth, Richard, twins Michael and Georgia, and Linda. Charley told me if Milt had not named his firstborn Charles Milton, he would have his.

One time Georgia cut a huge gash in the side of her left leg near the knee. She was a little afraid of what her father might say.

"What happened?" Charley asked when he heard her crying so loudly. "What did you do? Let me see it!" He pulled Georgia to him and sat her on his lap. "That looks bad. We better take you to the doctor!" Charley said. As the doctor started to work on her knee, Charley pulled her up on his lap and held her until the doctor finished. Georgia felt so much love for her father then and has always remembered.

Charley and Helen and their family lived near Ridgefarm for a few years then went to Florida, where they lived and most of their children continue to live.

Chapter 6
The War Years

World War II was imminent. It was building up to a huge crescendo. When it came we were all stunned. Everyone knew it was coming sooner or later, the time for the United States to get involved. But when it did come, when President Franklin D. Roosevelt signed the papers to get us in the war, we could hardly believe our ears and eyes, as we saw him signing the Declaration of War, on television.

It meant many of our boys would be killed. Our friends and relatives, perhaps our fathers and husbands, would go away and never come back. We grieved before it happened.

But we must help the world! The United States were in a good position to help Europe, and Japan had blown up our Pearl Harbor, on December 7, 1941.

George was classified 3A because of his eyes, then he waited, expecting he might have to go anytime. After the supply of unmarried men had been depleted, we knew George would be taken as we had no children as yet.

Charley and Milt had children, and had quit farming, to work for the government at defense plants. Ann got a job as an inspector at a laboratory making medications in Indianapolis. Mary and Kip were traveling with their boys from one area to another, building houses for defense plant workers.

George left the dairy, as wages and advancement were very slim and took a job at Wabash River Ordnance Works which was at Newport, Indiana, a few miles from Ridgefarm and southeast of Mother and Dad's. We packed our sparse belongings, and stayed at Mother and Dad's a couple of months. We then decided we were secure enough in George's job and bought new furniture, moving back to Danville, finding a nice apartment two blocks from George's grandmother Mom Parker's home and another block from Mother and Dad Massing's apartment.

When we shopped for a new sofa, there was only one left in the furniture store near our new apartment, and it was called a Victory couch. There was very little furniture made now as the war was taking all raw materials as well as manpower. It was a delicately patterned, pink rose flowered sofa, that made into a very hard bed, but we felt very fortunate to find any sofa at all. We were to keep this sofa, using it for many years. We got used to it being so hard, and, of course, it wore like iron. We later had Rikes in Dayton re-upholster it, because it had become a part of the family. At the end it was relegated to the basement family room. Only after moving to Florida thirty years later, did we give it up.

I wanted a dog, since I wasn't working, so we found a beautiful large white sheep dog, whose eyes were always covered with long hair. He looked at us through that hair of his all the time. I was constantly pushing it back, but it always fell over his eyes soon afterwards. How I did love that "Snorky," as we called him. I used to take him out walking all the time.

One rainy night we were awakened by loud yelling, and banging on our front door.

"Please help me, let me in! I have to call for an ambulance," we heard the man saying.

We looked at one another through sleepy eyes, trying to keep Snorky quiet. George turned on the lights, as he went to the door. We didn't know if we should let him in.

"Please let me use your phone!" The man outside yelled. "I'm a neighbor and friend of your landlady, and she isn't home. I need to call the police!"

George opened the door, with a great deal of consternation. I clutched the covers close to me, as I lay on the open Victory couch, and held onto Snorky, who was trying to get at the man. All I had to do was to release my grip on Snorky, and he would have torn him apart.

"Help me, please!" The man was saying over the phone.

"My brother is lying on the ground. I think he is dead! There seems to be an electric line down over his car!" As he put the receiver down, he yelled, "I think my brother is dead!" He ran out of the house, into the cold wet night.

"Let's get dressed and see if we can help!" I said.

George and I hurriedly dressed, and went outside. We turned the corner and looked upon the scene. A man was sprawled on the ground, between the sidewalk and the parked car. There was a wire hanging from the top of the tall light pole coming down over the top of the car.

"I told my husband to go get our luggage out of the car," a woman was crying and screaming at the same time. "We just arrived for a visit, and we were going to unpack the car. He must have tried to get the door of the car opened, and was electrocuted! I think he is dead!"

Many of the neighbors had gathered, wanting to help in some way.

"Don't touch him!" screamed someone! Everyone stepped back! He was, indeed, dead!

It was horrible to watch the scene played out. We had to wait until someone from the electric company came and removed the live wire. The hot wire dangling from the tall street light, after a strong windy rain storm, had to be cut and removed from the car.

The wife ran to her husband as soon as the workers let her, falling on top of him and crying hysterically, trying to get some response.

After the wire was removed the ambulance crew worked desperately trying to revive him, to no avail. He was gone! Instantly they guessed.

We stood, watching it all, until everyone was gone. We were shook up! It could have happened to any one of us.

We enjoyed a month of heavenly bliss in our new apartment. Then George was let go from his job because they closed the black powder plant at Wabash River Ordnance Works. George was out of a job! He was to remain two months to phase things down.

His old boss, Russell Pollitt from the dairy, came to our apartment and offered George his old job back. George said he'd think about it, as he still wanted another type of work.

George had referral information from his job at Wabash River Ordnance Works. He was told to go to the district office in Terre Haute, Indiana, and see Mr. O'Malley. There were no jobs available in the area, but Mr. O'Malley offered George a job, as a truck driver, at Wright-Patterson Air Force Base, Dayton, Ohio, at the same rate of pay he had at Wabash River Ordnance Works. He asked George if his wife worked, as they desperately needed typists and clerks.

George called home and asked, "Do you want to move to Dayton, Ohio?"

"Why, what happened?" I asked.

"I got a job offer for Dayton, Ohio, as a truck driver at Wright-Patterson Air Force Base," he said.

"Well, sure, I'll go anywhere, as long as you have a good job." I answered.

"Do you want a job too?" George asked.

"Sure," I answered, quickly. "What kind of a job?"

"They said they drastically need clerks, typists, and secretaries," George answered. "He asked specifically if you have shorthand. If you want the job, I have to come and get you today, and bring you back to sign up and we have to be there in three days."

This was Thursday and I had to be there to take tests. George raced back and took me back to sign up for the job.

On the way back home we stopped and talked to Mother and Dad, and asked if we could leave our furniture there. She said she could take part of it, so we drove to Milt and Laura's farm, and asked if they could take the rest, and keep it as long as necessary for us. They said they could, and Milt was to get it after we left. We thanked them all, and hugged them goodbye, and left for Danville.

Our biggest problem was our beloved Snorky. We had become so attached to him!

"I know of an older couple, near Georgetown, who might take him," a friend of ours said. "They live way out in the country. It would be a good place for him."

"That would be great!" we said. We did not want to leave him, but we could not take him with us. This was an ideal situation and solved our problem. When we said goodbye to Snorky, it was very sad indeed!

We told Mother and Dad Massing, and Mom Parker of our plans. They hated to see us go but realized it was for the best.

We left Friday night in a snow storm, which was almost impossible, in order to arrive at the employment office before they closed at twelve noon the next day, Saturday. We stayed the night at my sister Anna Rose's apartment in Indianapolis and got up early the next morning.

When we arrived at the Ohio line, we were pleasantly surprised to find clear roads, as Ohio does more to keep their roads clear, unlike Illinois and Indiana. We arrived at the employment office in Dayton in a cold rain, just in time to take the tests before they closed.

We reported to work at an employment office in Dayton. George signed up immediately, but I had to take a test in shorthand and typing. I hadn't typed in four years, and my fingers were stiff and cold. On my typing test I got forty-eight, which I thought was horrible, when I had been typing seventy four years ago. The woman who gave me the test was elated.

"Look here what this girl did. She hasn't typed for four years and she typed forty-eight words a minute. Isn't that great?" the tester said, running around telling three or four girls, waving my test in the air. Then, she wanted me to take the shorthand test. I was sure I couldn't do it, but she insisted. I took it and failed. So, I was signed on as a clerk typist, instead of a stenographer, or a secretary.

When we asked them if there was a place close by to eat because we were starved, they sent us to the Virginia Cafeteria, about three blocks down the street. It was excellent, and became our favorite eating place for years, until they went out of business.

We were sent to the War Housing Office, about a place to live. They had only one apartment, we took it sight unseen. It was way out on the west side of town, on the far edge of the black section. It had been an old German section of town. The Deshong's were an old

German family and lived in a large two-story home. Our apartment consisted of the upstairs, except one bedroom, which was for their daughter. We shared the bath with her.

Dayton, Ohio, had swelled from a population of 150,000 to 400,000 because of its proximity to Wright-Patterson Air Force Base, which had become a teeming government installation, because of World War II.

Monday morning we drove twenty miles from our apartment to the base, and had to park a mile from where we had to be. The parking lot was a huge field, looking much like a car sales lot. We walked on a cinder based path, to the long length of wooden board walks, which led through the main pedestrian gates.

George reported to the Post Ordnance Garage, to be interviewed by Larry Biddle, for the truck driver job.

"You are too nice of a guy to be a truck driver," Mr. Biddle said. "I think I'd rather place you in another spot I have in mind." He placed him as an assistant clerk in the parts department, which served the mechanics, who maintained about 2500 vehicles on the base.

When I reported, because of my former job with Dr. Williamson, in Danville, I was assigned to the main base dispensary as a clerk typist, where I typed cards on sick or injured people. The head nurse was overbearing, loud, and obnoxious.

It was with a happy heart, when I was sent to Sally Allen's First Aid Station, as an assistant to her. Sally and I became fast friends.

One day Sally was out of her treatment room when a big baby of an enlisted man came to the dispensary with a minor laceration on his first finger.

"I can fix that for you!" I told him. "It just needs a little merthiolate."

"It won't hurt, will it?" he asked suspiciously.

"No not much!" I said, "You really need this on it."

I had a darling new two piece dress on, for the first time. After cleaning the laceration, I opened a bottle of merthiolate, and started to put it on his small open wound.

"Ouch!" he yelled, and flung his arms up in the air, hitting the open bottle. The red medicine flew up out of the bottle, splashing back down onto my beautiful new dress. The enlisted man was very apologetic, but I had a completely ruined dress, which could neither be washed nor dry-cleaned, so was thrown away. It was such a minor wound.

We both loved our jobs. It was a new and fresh experience for us.

During the war years, everyone was rationed certain foods, one of which was sugar. Neither of us really had a sweet tooth, so my coupons were seldom used. Some of my friends complained of not having enough sugar, so we shared our coupons. I always was amazed at anyone using so much sugar. What did they do with it all?

Silk hose became a thing of the past. When we went to work at Wright-Patterson Air Force Base, I had one pair of silk hose, which I wore every day. For years, I wore these silk hose long past the other girls I knew, who were wearing the new nylons, which I hated, as they buckled or wrinkled so much. Silk hose stayed up, and were much more attractive than the new nylon hose.

"How can you keep from getting runners or snags in your hose?" I was asked many times. I never knew how they could get a runner, or snag every other day, as they said they did. I guess I kept my legs tucked under better than my friends. Those silk hose lasted for years.

I guess it was partly because I found leg makeup. I loved that. I was very adept at putting it on. I didn't know that I was, as I thought everyone did the same as I did.

The makeup was put into the cup of the right hand, then quickly transferred to the left hand, and moved around the whole hand quickly, going up and down the leg, and around every part of the skin in order to apply it evenly.

I think the success must have been, that the makeup was equally and loosely held in the hands, then quickly applied to all areas. My legs always looked as if I had real hose on. People were surprised that I had makeup on instead of hose. To me it was very easy to put on, and a very normal thing to do, but for many it was impossible to use makeup on their legs, as they smeared it, or had long streaks or splotches. I couldn't understand why, and told many people how I did it, when they asked me. Of course, it helped to have tan legs in the beginning. Maybe that was the reason for success.

A few months after moving to Dayton, we returned to Illinois, which we did often, and while visiting Mary and Kip, I suddenly realized their place wasn't too far from where Snorky was.

"Hey," I said, "How about you taking George and me riding over to see Snorky on your new motorcycle?" I asked Kip.

Kip had been taking us on the back of the motorcycle. It was great fun. George and I were wearing our horse riding outfits, our jodhpurs and boots.

Kip said okay and away we went. As we pulled up to the house, I saw Snorky and, jumping off the motorcycle, I raced towards the fenced in yard, yelling, "Snorky, Snorky!"

The lady of the house came running outside, flailing her arms! "Stay back, stay back! He'll hurt you!" she screamed.

I had opened the gate, and was running as fast as I could towards Snorky who came bounding towards me, with his long white hair flying everywhere. He did look wild, I thought! I began to slow down, still thinking my Snorky remembered me, but being wary now. Did he? Or was he coming at me to eat me up?

As I slowed down, I said, "Snorky! Snorky, hello! Do you remember me?"

He came to me with a bound. He remembered. He just about ate me up! I was laughing so hard, the lady was still screaming, as she thought he was hurting me. We both fell to the ground, he barking and me laughing and loving him! It was a great reunion! The lady stared in amazement!

"He knows me!" I laughed and cried at the same time. Then he saw George and jumped all over him.

"He's our dog," I explained to the lady, who was non-plussed. We talked with her for some time, and loved Snorky all the while. It was so hard to leave him. But now I knew he was all right. We thanked the lady for taking him, knowing he was in good hands.

In Ohio, George and I bowled a lot. We had fairly good scores, but not nearly as good as George's Aunt Sudie and Uncle Nig, back in Danville. They bowled perfect games which entitled them to belong to the "300 Club."

There was a "cattle trailer," at least forty feet long, that we rode to work sometimes, instead of driving our car. It had benches around the walls, and straps in the center for standees. It was very unpleasant, with no windows or lights. It herded employees from the west side of Dayton to Wright-Patterson Air Force Base. Mostly black people used it, but a few whites did, too. The blacks, during this time, had "bumping days," when they would bump against white people on purpose. Fortunately we were never involved. It was certainly a disagreeable form of transportation to and from work for all.

The Deshong's sold their house on Ingram Street, moving to a nice big home on Dayton Avenue, not far from the Dayton Art Museum, two blocks east of Salem Avenue, just across the Miami River. This was a much better neighborhood; and, when George went to the service a few months later, we put our Oldsmobile in Mrs. Deshong's spare garage.

Chapter 7

Furlough in Florida

George was called up to enter the army, to serve in World War II, in January 1944, a year after going to Ohio. Mother and Dad were living in Naples, Florida, for the winter, so we went down there by bus. It took us three days, so we were tired and anxious by the time we saw the Naples sign for the town. We kept looking and looking for the town but there was none.

"Where in the world is Naples?" I finally asked. Those on the bus around us laughed.

When we finally arrived at the center of town, it seemed like a milk stop. The bus pulled up, at what we were to learn, was Four Corners. It was the section where the Tamiami Trail turned east to go to Miami. On the west side was the downtown area, where Mother and Dad were waiting for us, just as they, or sometimes just Dad, had awaited our bus in Ridgefarm.

Their beautiful three room log cabin at the Gordon's Pass Fish Camp at the southernmost part of Naples was wonderful. They had rented it for the winter instead of pulling their trailer to Florida this year. We had a marvelous time walking on the beach, picking up shells, gathering Fiddler Crabs for bait, fishing, swimming when warm enough, and just lounging around.

We walked three miles north to the nearest store which was called the Corner Store. It was on the corner of Third Street South, and Broad Avenue, with the wide open doors facing that corner.

Sitting on stools, we munched on free hard boiled eggs from a bowl on the counter, and drank soda pop. This gave us the energy to walk the long trek back.

A private plane and a plane from the flexible gunnery school nearby collided in mid-air and had crashed at the southern tip of Keewaydin Island, to the south across Gordon Pass.

While we were there a retired lady doctor from the camp rowed George and Dad across Gordon Pass in her boat to Keewaydin Island and they walked the eight miles down the beach to the crash site. The sun was very intense, and by the time George went to be inducted into the army, he still had blisters on his face and couldn't shave.

"Do you want to make coconut candy?" Mother asked me, the day they walked down the beach.

"What is coconut candy?" I asked.

"Coconut candy!" she said. "You know what that is. Coconut candy!"

"I never heard of it," I said.

"You just make candy and put coconut in it," Mother explained.

We whipped up a batch and Mother grated some fresh coconut from the trees outside our front door. After it cooled, she put the coconut in and we beat it. And beat it and beat it some more.

Finally, we poured it into a dish and ate it with spoons. Evidently the fresh coconut was too moist to let the candy get hard. It was delicious!

The next day, we all went to lovely Marco Island and visited our cousin Merle Jones, whose wife Magdalene was a teacher in the Marco Island school system.

George and I had fallen in love with the sleepy little town of Naples and the surrounding areas, and continued going back there at every opportunity.

George was sent to Camp Lee in Virginia to the Quartermaster Corps where he remained for ten months, attending basic training and various schools. When he was to finish his Non Commissioned Officer School, NCO, he and his buddies were all begged to transfer on to Officer's Candidate School, OCS. Since their time in the service had to be extended to four years not one would sign up to become an officer. They wanted to get out of the service as soon as possible and get back to their civilian lives.

A friend of George's wanted to buy our Oldsmobile. When I asked George if he wanted to sell it, he wrote in his letter to sell the car but try to hang onto the jack, because it was a good one.

"Everybody sells their car with the jack!" his friend said to me. "I never heard tell of such a thing! I need the jack with the car!"

"George told me not to sell the jack. I can't sell it." I was adamant.

Three days later, George's friend called me and said he'd take the Oldsmobile without the jack. I don't think we ever used it for anything.

When I knew George was to be sent overseas, my heart broke. I told Mrs. Deshong I wanted to spend the remaining time he had in the United States with him.

"Will you be back?" Mrs. Deshong asked me.

"I don't know! I have no idea. I'm going to Camp Lee, and stay with him as long as I can," I said.

"Do you want me to save your room?" she asked me.

It had been some time since I had the whole upstairs, as I never used all the rooms anyway. So, Mrs. Deshong had rented out the other rooms, leaving me with only the bedroom. She had me eat with the family. This had been fine with me, but now I had to give up my one room.

"I have no idea what I will be doing. Just rent out this room, if you can." She had been so wonderful to both George and me. I really had no idea what was to happen to me.

George was shipped out on a train from Virginia, after I was with him for only a few days. I was crestfallen, but I went back to Mrs. Deshong's in Dayton.

"Oh, Kay, I'm so sorry! I rented your room right away after you left," she said. "There isn't anything I could do about it now. I'm so sorry. I wish I had a room for you!"

There was a place in the paper that had a room for rent. I caught a bus and went there. I liked it all right. "I'll be back tonight with my luggage," I said.

I called Sally Allen, and told her I was back in town, and asked if she and her Bill would help me move in. That evening, Sally and Bill and I drove down the street, looking for the house where I had rented the room. I couldn't find it!

"Oh, there it is!" I laughed. "They even have their name in the window. Isn't that nice of them? There name is White, and there's the card in the window!"

It was getting close to dark. The shadows were long, so we gathered up my luggage and went up the walk to the front door.

As we knocked, I looked through the screen and saw down the long hallway at the end of which was the woman of the house.

"Hello," I called to her, as I opened the front door. We all came in. "I brought my friends to help me move. Isn't that nice of them?"

We three were loaded down, and, as we came to the upstairs steps, I turned and started up them, with Sally and Bill falling in behind me. The lady of the house came forward with a dish towel in her hands, and we all turned to look at her as she spoke.

"I'm afraid you have the wrong house," she said quietly.

We couldn't believe it! We all had a hilarious time with her before we managed to find out the White card in the window was for the White Baking Company, meaning for him to stop today.

"I forgot to take it out of the window," she laughed!

"I'm so sorry!" I said. "Do you know where the Whites live? I'm sure the house is on this street!"

"There's a White family who live next door," the lady said.

We thanked her and laughingly carried all my luggage back down the steps and down to the neighbor's house. We told the real Mrs. White all about our fiasco, and she got a big kick out of it.

A few days later, I was told by George's friend, Lou Lucius, that George had been shipped to Camp Beale, Marysville, California. I told them at work I was leaving to be with George, and I didn't know when I would be back.

During the war years, a lot of things were done that would not be tolerated afterwards. I left and went to California, not to go back to WPAFB, to work, for many years.

When George went into the Army, I wanted him to have a good picture so he wouldn't forget me. Sally knew of an excellent photographer, Alex Bronson, one who was very particular. One of Sally's friends was sent home without having her picture taken, because when she arrived her hair was not right.

Sally worked on my hair, and we walked into the building, where the photographer had his studio upstairs, to find him waiting at the elevator for us. We had pleasantries and as we walked into the elevator I said, "I brought my hairdresser with me." He nodded, as we rode up in complete silence. We felt awkward, as we walked into his studio, and he told us we could freshen up in a small room.

Sally and I looked around. It was a very small room with a mirror, and chair, and table.

"Well, we better do something," I said giggling. "What shall I do? I already fixed it!" We laughed and she worked on it a little.

When we went out, the photographer had me sit looking at him, and he talked to me asking why I wanted the picture.

"For my soldier husband," I said.

He kept asking questions, getting me to relax, and then started taking pictures. When I went back later there were twenty-five or more proofs from which I was to choose the one that he would enlarge. They were all so great, I had a terrible time choosing.

I also had an inexpensive picture taken, at the Mills Studio where I sat down and was snapped immediately.

The first picture was elegant and perfect but we never could make up our minds, as to the picture we liked best, as the other was so fresh and unassuming, seeming to capture my personality.

George took both of the 8 x 10 portraits to Camp Lee, where he hung them on the inner side of his locker door. An officer, inspecting the barracks, came by and opened the door. He stared at them, wanting to know who they were.

"That's my wife," George said.

"Both pictures?" he said with interest. "I thought they were movie stars."

After seventeen weeks basic training, and an eight week Depot Supply Course, George was sent to the Quartermaster School for eight more weeks training to become a Non-Commissioned Officer (NCO).

Upon completion of training at Camp Lee George was sent to the Philippines for fifteen months, then on to Japan for five more. He was to be in California for a few weeks, en route to the Philippines, so I took the train out to be with him the short time he would be there at Camp Beale California. Johnny Briggs, George's buddy, took us to dinner at a Chinese restaurant in Marysville one of the nights. We had a great time.

We were only together three days when he was shipped out. I was devastated. We just lay in one another's arms all evening the last night in our bunk beds on the base.

The next morning I wanted to watch him leave, so I hurriedly packed my suitcase, and ran outside with it to watch for him marching in formation. I stood in the deluge of rain, staring at every soldier dressed in full combat uniform. I couldn't see him. He had told me exactly where to stand on a certain street corner. I watched every soldier go by, grim in face, and sick at heart.

At the end of their formation, I stared at their backs and cried for George, and all the soldiers. I was so heavy hearted I could not stand it. I saw the bus coming and knew I had to be on it, in order to make my train to Portland, Oregon, where my brother Charley and his family were living. I stood at the spot where George said to get the bus.

The bus came by slowly, then passed me by. I stared at the end of the bus, as it went away from me.

I began to cry uncontrollably. The rain was pouring, so I yelled and screamed, as the unhappy moments overwhelmed me. No one heard me because of the noise of the rain.

As I stopped sobbing, I realized the bus had gone about one half mile, and had stopped there. I started walking towards it, then went a little faster, and as I started to hurry, thinking I might be able to catch it, the bus pulled away.

I had to get a worn out jalopy, their answer to a taxi, which hurtled me vicariously through the rain, to finally get me to the train barely on time.

Charley and Helen were both working at a defense plant in Portland, Oregon. Charley did construction work, and Helen was "Rosie the Riveter." Helen took me around and showed me what she did. She wore wide heavy chaps on her legs, that flopped when she walked, and goggles pushed up over her eyes. Their two little boys, Tommy and Terry were adorable. I enjoyed my short three days there before I got a letter from one of George's friends, who said if I hurried I could see George at Pittsburgh, California, as he was being shipped out, he didn't know where.

When I got to Pittsburgh, George had just left for the Philippines. I was so crushed I sobbed and sobbed. The lady who had told me came outside of her office and held me knowing of my frustration and sense of loss.

Chapter 8
California

My sister Mary Ellen, and her husband Kip, were in the southern part of California, so I rode the bus to their home in El Monte.

There was a change in buses at a place for me to make. I had sat directly behind the driver and had asked him several things about the countryside, one of which was the beautiful landscape around the grape wineries, a landscape I had never seen before. We talked quite a bit.

When we got to the change area, the driver told me I had missed the bus I was to have caught, to continue on to El Monte. He picked up my bag and said, "I'll take care of you, and get you a hotel room."

He explained he would put my bag over in the building there, while he turned in his report, and got his car. I was to wait outside the building until he came back.

After waiting and watching another bus that had come in, I decided I better find out a little more.

" This is the bus to El Monte," the new bus driver told me. "Wait here I'll check this out for you," he said quite angrily.

He came back carrying my bag. I got on the bus, and was on time to see my sis waiting for me.

Kip's best friend was leaving for the Navy. He had a couple of days pass, and came to visit his good friend, before shipping out. He was very negative about the whole situation, very frightened. He had always been a homebody, loving his wife and children very much.

When Mary and Kip were to take him the several mile trip over the mountains, back to his ship, I went along, but the boys stayed home.

The friend and I sat in the back seat, and the four of us carried on a lively conversation that finally lapsed into an uneasy silence.

"May I kiss you?" the friend asked me, to my surprise. He had been talking about his wife and leaving her to go to war, from which he had no idea whether he would ever be back.

"No," I said quietly, shaking my head.

"Please!" he said, "please let me kiss you."

He was feeling so low and did not want to go on that ship, I knew, but I just could not allow him to kiss me when I knew he really wanted to kiss his wife. He needed her to hold him in her arms and tell him everything would be alright!

"May I lay my head in your lap?" he then surprised me by asking. He needed the touch of a woman! I understood.

"Yes," I said, almost whispering. He had always been such a gentle man, and I knew how he was feeling.

Without another word, he dropped down on the seat cushion and put his head gently in my lap. He closed his eyes as I stroked his hair. He was so lonely for his wife and family. I looked out the window as I cried silently for him and all the boys who were going to they knew not where, nor what would happen.

He lay immobile, with thoughts of home, I'm sure, until Kip said, "We're almost there."

He raised up, and with the saddest look I've ever seen, whispered, "Thank you!"

He went overseas and was a good sailor for his country. He came back and was reunited with his family he loved so much.

Mary wanted me to stay with her, and since I felt so forlorn, and lost in not getting to see George, I did. When they left for Inyokern, California, to get construction work there, I went along. I enjoyed being with Mary and Kip and their family so much. They really helped me through a very trying time. Philip, Dave, and Stephen were all such nice boys, and we all got along fine in their thirty foot trailer.

Inyokern, which was in the Mojave Desert, had a normal population of fifty, but during the war years, it became a sea of mobile homes, owned by construction workers and employees of the Defense Department at Inyokern Naval Ordnance Test Station ten miles east of Inyokern. The town itself had a coffee shop at a crossroad, and a few other stores in the same block. The largest building was the telephone company, where I worked for a short time.

There was no grass, just sand. There were very few houses, and I had to go out of my way to see gorgeous, green, green, grass at one of the homes. I would walk very slowly past it, keeping my eyes focused on that beautiful, well manicured lawn.

There were terrible wind storms, when the sand would be blown by the fierce winds up in the air, where it swirled all around. Sometimes, the wind would blow so strongly, that all the sand that was normally on the hard, rocky ground, would be in the air. At these times, even small rocks would be blowing and swirling in the air. They hurt, with a thud, when they hit! The sand would sting terribly, and watch out for the eyes!

Sometimes, the winds were so bad, I had to try to keep the sand and rocks from hitting me, by running from mobile home to mobile home, in order that I could be shielded a little. My eyes had to be shielded, and I could not see a foot in front of me, because of the heavy sand in the air. Sometimes, the rocks would hit my legs so hard, they would crack a hole in my hose. It wasn't pleasant!

The word sandstorm was coined in 1774, according to Webster's Ninth New Collegiate Dictionary, defining it as a windstorm, driving clouds of sand before it. I was always glad when I arrived at our mobile home! We never, ever went out, after we got home on those nights.

One such night I had to go to the bathroom in the middle of the night. Kip had stayed at work that night, so Mary said for me to use a bottle under the sink. It was so bad outside I decided to do that.

"The hole is awfully small, Mary, I'm not sure I can hit it. I might get it all over the trailer!" I said.

Mary, lying in her warm bed, told me, "Sure you can. I've done it. Just stand squarely over it, and go! It's too bad out to go to the toilet!"

"Hey," I said, "I did it! I don't think I dropped any at all outside."

"I told you you could do it," Mary said.

Next morning, she and I had a great laugh! I had used a bottle, with an opening one inch in diameter.

"I use this one," Mary laughed. It was three inches in diameter!

I slept with the three boys which made it pretty tight. Sometimes, Stevie, the baby would sleep with Mary and Kip. One night the kids did not want to go to sleep.

"Do you want me to tell you a story?" I asked.

"What kind of story?" Phil asked.

"Well, lets see. What kind of a story do you want to hear? How about a love story?" Before anyone could answer, I said, "No, you are too young for a love story. How about a Western story?"

"Yes, yes," they all wanted cowboys and Indians. I started, and thought up my story as I went along. Sometimes I would go slow, as that would be the time I was trying to organize the story, but when it came to me I would get right along with it.

They all quieted down and listened attentively. When I was where I thought I could finish, they were very quiet.

"Now go to sleep," I said, "and I'll tell you another one tomorrow night maybe."

The next morning, to my surprise, Kip was the one who brought up the story.

"That was some story you told last night," he said.

"Oh, did you listen to it? Did I keep you from sleeping?" I asked.

"No, I found it interesting and couldn't go to sleep until you finished," he said.

After that night I told them a lot of stories just before they went to sleep.

The school where the boys attended in Inyokern, which was in Kern County, California, had burgeoned from twenty- nine students to two thousand, in one years time, because of the construction of the Navy Test Station, as well as a Marine Base. It was a boom town.

I got a position as a payroll clerk for a private contractor on the base. I had to work twelve hours every day straight through then was off two days. I worked in a large building with no windows, but had bright neon lights throughout. These lights have since been found to cause depression, and other ailments, and known to be very bad for you. After four months I became ill with fatigue and terrible loss of energy. I needed the sunshine and less stress. I left this position. When I was feeling better, I obtained a position at Indian Wells Valley Union Schools, in Inyokern.

Mary and Kip and I picked up the boys from school, all packed and ready to go on a vacation to Dirty Sock. The Superintendent, Mr. Luttrell, came over to the car as they were piling in, and talked to us.

"Would you have a job here at school for me?" I asked him, as he had been talking about the enormous growth the area was going through.

He looked very interested and said, "Come in and see me when you get back from your trip."

He was a very large, good looking man, with piercing brown eyes and curly black hair, through which he kept running his fingers. He must have had a lot of oil on his beautiful hair, as his hands were often greasy.

We drove north to Lone Pine and turned right to hunt for Dirty Sock. We had gone miles when we saw a dirty sock hanging on a stick at a crossroads. We turned left laughingly wondering if it meant Dirty Sock was down that road. It was!

After traveling a few miles down a dusty, narrow road we came to what had to be Dirty Sock. There was a large round body of warm water with a spring bubbling in the center, surrounded by sun burnt brown grass as far as the eye could see. We were in Death Valley which is 282 feet below sea level.

Off in the far distance beyond miles of the brown grasses, could be seen high in the air, the ethereal beauty of Mount Whittier with its glistening white snow capped peaks rising 14,494 feet above sea level, the highest point in California. We couldn't wait to get in the inviting water. Kip parked the car and trailer at the water's edge.

The water caressed our bodies with its warm, bubbling movement as we swam through its glistening ripples, or merely treaded water with only our head exposed.

We had planned on going to Dirty Sock for just a few hours, but it was so wonderful swimming in that magnificent water, we stayed for three days. When we left, we were as brown as berries from the searing sun.

When I went to school to see Mr. Luttrell for a job, my face was bronze, my hair was bleached a very pale yellow, from the sun and hot mineral spring water, and I could not wear a brassiere for days. We had not felt the power of the sun then, but I felt it now. With grease on my face and body, with no brassiere, I got my job.

No other place in the world would have hired me like that! Mr. Luttrell hired me to sort out and clear up the correspondence and records in the office of the principal.

The principal and district superintendent had never had time to work on papers, and they had had no help. Their offices were a complete mess. Stacks of unanswered correspondence, paperwork of all sorts, all kinds of school related reports and filing were piled everywhere. Nothing had ever been filed. I started a filing system.

I started on the principal's office, which was in a Quonset hut, weeding, and throwing out, and filing. My decisions were the only ones made. The principal accepted anything I said. It was a great job! I enjoyed it!

After a few weeks, when it was mostly finished, the principal praised my work so highly, the superintendent, Mr. Luttrell, wanted me to come and work for him and do the same for his office.

The move to the old Spanish stucco schoolhouse was a great advancement for me. The rest of the school was in Quonset huts all in rows.

Mr. Luttrell's office was even worse than the principal's office. I jumped right in, and also became the secretary to the Board of Education, where I took shorthand and wrote the minutes.

The kids were so good and I loved staying with Mary and Kip. But, it made the trailer too full. The teachers were a great group, and I made lots of friends. So after a few teachers tried to get me to eat lunch with them, and then to stay at the Marine Barracks, at the Inyokern Naval Test Station, several miles east of Inyokern, I decided to do that.

I moved to the newly constructed Marine barracks, which was being used for temporary housing for civilian working women on the base, until the Marines would arrive. It really was a great place to live.

The head administrator gave me a bed in a little alcove, right outside her private room. We became fast friends. The rest of the girls lived in the dormitory, so I didn't really get to know the other girls very well.

The weather was so dry in California that when I would do my washing and hang it on the inside line in the barracks washroom, the first clothes I put up would be dry enough to iron by the time I had hung the last piece of washing. That was fabulous. I loved the weather. No matter how hot it got, we seldom sweat because there was such low humidity. I loved California and always wanted to live there afterwards. It was not to be.

Mary and Kip moved on to another construction site elsewhere, but I stayed at the new barracks until George came back from overseas. I enjoyed the barracks life, and realized I would have gotten along fine, if I had joined the Wacs, as I had wanted to do.

I started a Brownie Scout Troop, when I was secretary to the District Superintendent of schools in Inyokern. Some of the girls had been in Brownies before, so had their uniforms. There was no shop in Inyokern, so the others had to wear their school clothes. That didn't faze us. Everyone had a great time.

We gathered after school, in the school yard on Tuesday, and walked together about a mile, to the Methodist Church. All the little girls tried to walk beside me, and hold my hands, always chattering loudly, to tell me things.

One time, they all clamored to be near me, hanging on to every part of my body.

"Why don't you just pick me up and carry me?" I laughed at them.

"Let's do! Let's do carry her," they all screamed.

Before I could stop them, each little girl got hold of me somewhere, and amongst the fifteen or so girls, they hoisted me up in the air, flat on my back, while I was yelling for them to put me down.

"You'll hurt yourselves!" I yelled. "Put me down!"

We were making so much noise the policemen came running outside the police station to see what was the matter.

There were so few places to take my Brownie Scouts on a trip. One day, we all met in the school yard, after school, and walked the two miles to the Inyokern Naval Test Station west of town. When we arrived, we were all hot and sweaty. Two men met us, as we came towards the entrance, as I had called and made the appointment for us to see the place in operation.

We soon gathered around the men who seemed overwhelmed turning this way and that looking us over.

"Where is the leader? Is she here?" One of the men asked as he looked all around us.

"I'm the leader," I said. "I'm the one that called you on the phone."

"Oh," he laughed. I thought you were one of the girls. As he looked the little girls over he added, " Why did you bring them? What is it you want to see? We thought it would be older students, that might be interested in getting into this kind of an operation."

I apologized, telling him there were so few outings we could go on, so I thought this would be interesting to the girls.

The whole group there got into the act then and treated us royally. We had a great time with everyone telling us, and showing us, their whole operation. We all thanked them profusely, for a great time, then we sauntered back towards town and our homes.

Another trip we took was past the Naval Test Station, on up into the mountains, where a School Board member and his wife lived.

The Chairman of the School Board asked me, if I would want to bring my Brownies to his home, to see his rock collection. I thought it was a splendid idea. We were to go on the bus.

At the end of the school day, all my Brownies and I, and one of the teachers, Alice Woolf, a good friend of mine, hurried out to the school bus. The door was open and the motor was running. We all climbed in, and took our seats, with Alice and me sitting on the seat behind the driver. We sat and waited. And waited. The school yard became empty, and we still waited.

"I guess I'm supposed to drive the bus!" I finally said. I got behind the wheel, and Alice Woolf stayed in her seat behind me. I looked back at the school, then shifted gears, and away we went. I did not see the bus driver come running out of the school house door, wildly trying to flag me down. We nonchalantly turned out of the school yard onto the highway, and we were on our way.

I had never driven a bus, and I had never driven in the mountains. The road got steeper, and steeper, and smaller, and smaller. There was no traffic which was good. We were finally in a deserted area, with nothing but one little winding road. I kept looking at the side of the road, which became steeper, and making remarks about it to Alice.

"Do you want me to drive?" Alice asked.

"I'd be glad if you would, I haven't driven much in my life, and never on any road like this!" I said.

Alice took over, and I found she was an excellent driver. She manipulated the bus, over those bad spots, like a pro. When we arrived at the man's house, I was extremely happy I was not driving. I believe I could not have manipulated that big bus, in the rocky uneven area, that was called their barnyard. I was very thankful Alice had come along.

In the front room, they had a huge collection of all kinds of rocks they had collected in the area. A lot of them glowed in the dark, so they had fixed up a dark, light weight blanket, over gorgeous rocks, and put a lamp in there to make them glow brighter. We crawled in, a few at a time to view this area, where we Oh'd and Ah'd, over the gorgeous colors, glowing in the dark.

Other rocks were assembled all through his house. He had been collecting rocks all of his life. The rocks were beautiful and made the trip a great success.

His wife served us cookies and drinks after which we headed for home in a down pour of rain. Again, I was very happy to be sitting behind Alice, as she drove through the cold rain in the dark. I don't believe I could have made it. Perhaps the man and his wife would have let us stay all night with them.

It was a wonderful, happy, trip but we got heck when we got back. The bus driver was worried sick!

I received a letter from George, saying he was being sent home through the Red Cross, because his father was very ill, and not expected to live.

Knowing I would be leaving soon to go back home, I thought this would be a good time to have my hair changed from my blonde hair back to its original color which was a darker shade. I went to a beauty parlor, and asked if they could change it to a little darker shade than I had, but not too dark.

"Sure, I can. I can make it whatever color you want." We looked at charts, and I picked out the proper color.

It was almost supper time when she finished. My hair was black! I was sick!

"I'll wash it out!" she stammered. "That will help." It didn't!

I ran to my barracks room, past a lot of people going to chow. A distance of about a mile. I was panting when I ran upstairs to my bunk. I grabbed my head scarf and put it around my head. When I arrived at the mess hall there was only a teeny bit of black hair showing above my forehead.

When I had my tray of food, and was sitting down, some smart aleck Navy man who I knew slightly yelled across three tables of men.

"Hey, Kay, weren't you a blonde this morning?" he yelled.

I was mortified as everyone turned to look at me. He must have seen me running down the street.

Chapter 9
Army Life by George-
Camp Lee to Southeast Asia

The following is George's recollection of events which happened during his twenty-seven months in the army. He was classified for "limited service," due to legal blindness in his right eye.

Tales from Army Life
by
George C. Massing

During World War II, I received one of those letters from my draft Board. So, I was inducted into the Army February 8, 1944, at Fort Thomas, Kentucky, along with a large contingent of mountain men from Hazard County, Kentucky. The only thing missing was their squirrel rifles. Here we were issued our too large uniforms, and my size 10 1/2 Charley combat boots that wore blisters on my feet.

I was mustered out twenty seven months later on May 4, 1946, at Jefferson Barracks, Missouri. During the time in between, a few amusing things happened. I was first shipped to Camp Lee, at Petersburg, Virginia, for seventeen weeks basic training, in the Quartermaster Corps. Heretofore, they never had to take basic training, because it was considered they operated behind the lines, to keep supplies rolling. Not so anymore.

This kind of war, the enemy took the combat right behind our lines, to interrupt the supply lines, so the Quartermaster's had to learn to defend themselves. This had happened at Wake and Guadalcanal. So, we took basic infantry training, hand to hand combat, forced marches, obstacle courses, rifle range, explosives, gas mask drill, and lots more, the works.

The things that stood out here were if one screwed up in any way, the whole platoon was punished, so everyone would have a hand in seeing it didn't happen again. They took it out one night on a young Italian boy. When taps sounded he found he had been "short sheeted," with crackers in his bed. When short sheeted, the bunk was made up special with the bottom sheet turned up half way, so when you shoved your feet into bed everything stopped half way in, this time with crackers in the bed, too.

Then there was the time I froze up on the obstacle course. I had to walk several feet across a board that was two inches thick on the edge, ten feet in the air, between two posts. I started across and got part way and froze, just couldn't move. A young assistant platoon leader, a smart aleck Corporal was all for pulling me down, but the buck sergeant platoon leader, with a little more experience, was for talking me down with a little kindness.

I finally crossed and came down with his coaxing. "Come on Massing," he said, "you can do it."

Then there was the time when I went on to NCO school (Noncommissioned Officer), at the same camp. We all had to take turns commanding the platoon in close order drill. Well, I got them started off marching alright, right towards the reviewing stands. Then I forgot my next command, which should have been, "To the rear march!" Naturally, without a change from my original command, they all started piling into the reviewing stand. So, that didn't go over so hot. I did get a lot of hoots and razzing from them.

They begged us to transfer into OCS, (Officers Candidate School). They were crazy for asking, because it was next to our school, and we saw what training the candidates had to go through. My wife said, that I should have done it as I would have become an Officer and a

THEN AND NOW

Gentleman, instead of being a noncom, and she would get to travel with me. But you also had to re-up for at least four more years, which I didn't want to do. Out of my platoon of about thirty men there were only two who accepted and went to OCS.

After being graduated from QM School I was shipped on a troop train to the west coast for overseas duty. My wife joined me at Camp Beale, Marysville, California, and we were together every possible moment before I was moved to the overseas staging area at Pittsburg, California, for departure for an unknown destination overseas.

Our Army Transport Ship The USAT Sea Barb which had been converted from a cargo vessel, left the United States underneath the Golden Gate Bridge at San Francisco, California. We took a zigzag course after passing two hundred miles off Hawaii to make a harder target for Japanese submarines. We were traveling only eight knots per hour. When the alarm sounded at dusk each evening, all troops moved quickly from all corners of the ship to stand on deck in life vests until an all clear was sounded.

Dusk is the time a ship is an easier target. All smoking was forbidden as even the tip of a lighted cigarette could be picked up by an enemy submarine periscope.

One thing that happened on board was a drawing held to receive a hunting type knife with a broad blade and a sheath. The drawing was held as there were not enough for everyone to have one. I was one of the lucky ones as my name was drawn. My buddy Johnny Briggs, who was crossing with me, didn't get one. As we spent a lot of time together he carved my initials, in gothic letters, G C M, vertically on the front of the sheath. I've always been proud of this knife, and still have it. A Filipino Ranger used the back of the blade one night, after we arrived on Leyte, to show all of us how to open a coconut husk to get at the shell and pierce the nut to get the milk, then open further to get at the flesh.

Christmas day 1944 we anchored in the harbor at Finchhafen, New Guinea. The Captain and his party were the only men who went ashore. I was not included. On board, we all enjoyed a traditional full course American Christmas Dinner with turkey and all the trimmings, including pumpkin pie.

The twenty-one days on the ship we were bombarded with the Captain's favorite music, "Walter, Walter, Lead Me To The Alter." A few days before our arrival at our destination the Captain announced he would be playing a tune which would give us a hint of our final destination. But, few of us got it until we arrived at Leyte. We were nonplused as to why he was playing "Lady be Good" so many times among the other tunes also interspersed with Walter.

I was assigned to a replacement depot on Leyte, Philippine Islands. I pulled duty at the ration dump one night, and at the ammo dump the next, alternating night after night, part of the twenty one days I was there.

The camp commander lit up our life one day calling us together to announce, " Men, when we requisitioned you we needed clerks, now because of a few reverses like Wake and Guadalcanal, we need basic infantrymen." You could have heard a pin drop. Some of my buddies did go that route, with First Cavalry Division.

One night in the ration dump, we were given a box of concentrated chocolate bars, to pass out among only five or six of us. Everyone of us made a mistake of eating several of these concentrated rations like candy bars. Sick? You said it! I guess we were supposed to know better.

One day I wanted to wash my hair. We had to use our steel helmets for a wash pan, taking out the light weight helmet liner with a sweat band. I knew I'd been told salt water soap and fresh water don't mix. I did it anyway and my hair became as stiff as a board and stood on end. My buddy Johnny Briggs, from Sebring, Ohio, and a few others got a good laugh out of it. One of life's little lessons.

One good thing to make me smile I found in our camp. One day at the ships store that had been set up, I spotted a small package of Chuckles, orange slice gum drops, from my old home town of Danville, Illinois, which boasted of a Chuckles factory. It made me homesick.

When we left Leyte, we went to Luzon by way of Lingayen Gulf, where we landed at Dagupan, Pangasinan Province. When we first arrived all showers were not ready or were overcrowded, so where did we take our baths? Well, why not in the river which flowed past our campsite? Did we have spectators? Yes, men and women alike, lined up on the opposite bank and watched as we bathed in our all together. What do you suppose they thought?

When we reached San Fernando, Pampanaga Province, we set up camp on the capitol grounds. This was to be our permanent camp, and was about thirty-five miles north of Manila.

Here they put all ten of us new men in an eight man squad tent. With the flaps up, it would hold ten. The same night we erected our tent it rained, it poured. Do you know what happened in the middle of the night? About half our tent stakes pulled out of the ground. No one had told us not to tighten our tent stake ropes too tight. There was bedlam in that tent, that night. We had even selected a site low in the center, so we had a lake there.

All of us were issued cigarettes and were able to get candy bars from the PX. These were things the Filipinos did not have, but had a hankering for to satisfy their cravings. They had bananas, a fruit called duat, (like a small sour cherry,) small watermelons, and a root looking like a cross between a turnip and a radish- pretty good. I traded some of my items for the fruit. One girl brought bananas I liked best, and as I recall, were called Lantania or some such name. I would say, "Be sako sagin." (I like bananas.)

We were attached to Sixth Army Headquarters, with General Walter Kreuger as our commander. We all admired him. One day in the Post Exchange (PX) line, where we took our canteen cups to get our ration of Coca Cola, a "brown noser" met his match. He approached the General, and complained he couldn't get shoe polish at the PX. General Kreuger told him he was under field conditions, not stateside, so he really didn't need shoe polish. He told the soldier, where we all could hear, to go get a banana leaf and try that for a shine.

I then spent five months in the land of the Rising Sun. Several of us visited with a Japanese family, most of whom spoke very good English, since the father, Shinwo Inouye, had studied in America at Princeton, and had been an official of the Southern Manchurian Railway. One night I took one of my buddies with us to visit, a rebel from Bay St. Louis Mississippi, named Woodrow Wilson Webre. You wonder why we called him "Woody"?

The Inouye's sometimes served one of their only available snacks, hot roasted soy beans, and I do mean hot, hot! We all knew this except Woody. When I passed them to him I used a teaspoon and just dumped them in the palm of his hand. He didn't hold them long. He flipped his hand and they were scattered over the whole room.

I left Yokohama for the United States on a huge Army transport, the USS General Polk, with 5000 troops returning home. On the way home, I was wearing a pair of new fatigues without my staff sergeant stripes sewn on. Another soldier and I were picked out of the departing mess line by a soldier in fatigues. He wanted us to pull fantail duty, and dump garbage over the ship's rail. We followed him from the ship's galley, up the gangway to the open deck.

We looked at one another in the dusk, and as the mess guy who had pulled us out went toward the fantail of the ship, we turned the other way and melted among the soldiers on deck, in the darkness. We heard him yelling, "Where did those guys go?" No one answered him. We were a little apprehensive for a day or two that he might recognize us in the chow line. But didn't we all look alike? I could have lost my stripes.

We arrived without incident in the harbor at Seattle, but we had to wait there three days to disembark because a man who went to sickbay tested positive for typhus, and we were all quarantined.

In the meantime, while the brass was trying to work out that problem, the local USO turned up with Hula girls on an open deck boat, in that cold March air to entertain us. Their small craft went back and forth before us while they put on a lengthy show. I'm sure those poor girls were frozen. It all turned out all right. The man in sickbay had been inoculated three times for typhus in a short period of time, so he really was super immunized. They then, let us go ashore and head for our next destination. In my case, was home on a 30 day furlough to visit my Dad, who was seriously ill. He recovered from three major operations he had in ten days time.

My overseas time would be up when I would have been part way back to Japan. So, they extended my furlough thirty days after which I was mustered out, at Jefferson Barracks, Missouri, which was near St. Louis.

Chapter Ten
George Returns

George's father, George, Sr., had cancer and was to be operated on. The Red Cross was able to get him home for the operation, which turned out to be very serious, with three major operations in ten days time.

George told me to go home and meet him there. I had waited all this time in California in order to be able to meet him at the entry point, wherever it would be on the West Coast. I had been as close as I could be to him.

I went home to Mother Massing's and waited. And waited. Finally, I tired of waiting, and decided Joe and I could take a couple of hours and go to a movie about ten blocks away. We walked there.

The movie was getting really good, when my name was called over a loud speaker.

"Your husband is calling from Seattle, Washington," the manager told me. I was so excited.

I ran back to Joe. "Joe, you stay and see how the movie turns out," I told him and started home. I ran all the way, arriving panting and out of breath. But, then I had to wait as George had talked to his Mother for awhile and then hung up, expecting me to stay at the movie. That was a long hard wait.

"Hi, Sweetheart," he said, when he finally called, "they've kept us quarantined for three days in the Seattle Harbor, but now we're released to go home! I'll be home Tuesday. Meet me at the railroad station at three o'clock, in the afternoon."

"I'm going with you," Mother said, as I was getting ready to meet the train. I stared at her.

"No, you're not! I said, We'll hurry home!" I said gently. She let me go by myself.

My heart was beating so fast as the train chugged down the tracks. I could hardly breathe, as I watched four or five feet from the lowered steps, and watched as many soldiers and civilians got off and on the train, people pushing me on each side with me not paying any attention to them.

There he was! So handsome. My George! I watched in a trance as he took those few steps to me. We fell into one another's arms and all my pent up emotions erupted into sobbing, and laughing, and hugging, and kissing.

We finally pulled away from one another, only to realize the area was void of any people. We had not noticed the stares or commotion of anyone. We had been alone with all our happiness and hopefulness of our future life to come.

"We'll have to hurry," your Mother wants to see you!" We clasped hands and started to run. We were so crazed with happiness, we ran into an area where we couldn't go through, and laughingly turned and went around.

After Dad's three operations, and getting on the road to recovery, George was mustered out in St. Louis, Missouri, May 4, 1946.

After Dad Massing was out of danger, George and I went to the Second National Bank of Danville, to get my money I had deposited by mail, while working at the Inyokern schools.

"You are the one!" the bank clerk said to me when I explained I wanted to take my money out. "You cannot imagine what we all went through when you sent the first four checks to an account we didn't have."

I had thought it so simple. Where else would I have sent my money to save. I had lived on the allowance from George's being in the army and it sufficed, as my lunches, food, and housing had been minimal.

"And the checks kept on coming!" said the clerk. She called several other clerks and told them who I was. We had a great time.

"I didn't have any place to spend it," I explained, "Not many places in the Mojave Desert!"

The money I had saved, paid for a lemon of a car, but one we truly loved, and the down payment on our first house, Pinecrest.

We went back to Ohio and lived for thirty years.

Part Two
Married Life in Ohio

Chapter 11
Pinecrest, Crystal Lakes, Ohio

Not really. It was thirty years, from the time we first went to Dayton in 1943, to the time we left Ohio in 1973. But who's counting? That's inclusive of our time spent in the army, and California, and getting back to Ohio.

Mother and Dad took us to Ohio with their trailer after they came home from Florida that March of 1946. They helped us get set up in their trailer at Osborne Trailer Park, on a hill just outside of Fairborn, Ohio.

We mentioned to the people who were helping us move in that we needed a car. They said there was a sergeant, who lived on the other side of the park, who had a nice looking car for sale. When we went over there, we liked it very much. It was a big, beautiful, black, four door sedan, a Lincoln Zephyr. We bought it with part of my savings from my work in California, the biggest lemon of a car we could have found. I guess it was worth the nine hundred ten dollars we paid for it, as we kept it for several years.

The trailer park was located just three miles from where George went back to work at Wright-Patterson Air Force Base, WPAFB. He returned to the same Ordnance Office from which he had left to enter the army.

That fall, Mother and Dad were ready to use the trailer to go back to Florida, but we hadn't found a home yet. Wanting a house instead of an apartment, we had looked all summer. However, there were no houses we could afford, on our little pittance of George's salary.

"Why don't you try to find a home near where we live?" George's good friend, Boggsy, at work said in early November. "Come to Crystal Lakes, and see if you can't find something there."

"Where is Crystal Lakes?" George asked.

"It's two miles from Medway, about half way between Dayton and Springfield. It's about nine miles from work," he said.

They were not home, when we drove to their house, so we drove around on our own.

We liked the area where they lived very much. It was a small group of nice homes around four lakes, one lake being much larger than the other three, it being the swimming area. There was a clubhouse on an island across the lake from the swimming area.

When we drove up Pine Road, at the crest of the small hill, Mary Cohagen was stooping down holding a For Sale sign, while her husband Dick was pounding it in the ground with a sledge hammer.

"That's a cute house, George!" I said. "I like it, let's stop." We stopped, we looked, we bought! It was perfect for us!

Walking down a colorful brick sidewalk, we walked up steps onto a small peaked porch, at the sides of which we later planted wisteria. The lavender scented blossoms of the wisteria grew to ten inches long and permeated our whole existence. It was fabulous!

Inside, we entered a large wide living room, with built in low cabinets at the far end, under a large window, and three large connecting windows facing the street. Through a large opening on the right side was the dining room. The kitchen was in the same room at the other end.

The hallway went from the side of the kitchen to the living room. At each end of the hallway was a bedroom, with the bathroom in the middle. It was a small house, but perfect for us, having lived in apartments, and a little, although well organized trailer. We were delighted with the home and area. We were to live there for twelve years, at Pinecrest.

Mother and Dad came over from Illinois, and moved the trailer to our driveway. They and I stayed in the trailer and empty house, while George went home to Illinois to get our furniture. He rented a truck, and went from home to home, where we had left our furniture when we came to Ohio, almost four years before.

He started back to Ohio late in the evening, only to run into a severe snow storm. The windshield defroster stopped working, which made it impossible for him to see, by the time he drove into Indianapolis. He stopped at a service station, where they were able to rig up a simple contrivance, that enabled him to drive on through the soft, moist snow, which was rapidly accumulating. They squeezed an oil filler spout underneath the hood, which caused engine heat to be directed at the windshield. This kept the snow and ice melted.

He arrived at our new home about two o'clock in the morning, where we were all gathered on the floor, waiting for him. He was frozen and exhausted, but had managed to get there, thank God! We all pitched in and helped him unload the furniture, after we heard of his escapades.

In the morning, after breakfast, Mother and Dad started for the Sunny South with their trailer.

That winter, we quickly settled in, waiting for the birth of our first long awaited baby. I kept busy knitting and crocheting gorgeous pink baby Afghans and clothes.

About a month before our baby was due, we had a wonderful house warming, with all our friends arriving for fun and eats. We played games, ate heartily and unwrapped gifts. Some stayed for a late buffet dinner.

Pinecrest, our first home! It was perfect for us. Our family grew healthy and happy, we made many friends, life was good.

Lawrence Busby Massing arrived May 28, 1947. I quickly added white, blue, and green to his layette.

When Larry was to be born, I was doing all right, until I heard moaning and screaming in the six, bed room for expectant mothers. George was beside me and going through it all with me. When my water broke I didn't know what had happened and sent George for the nurse.

"The doctor is on the way," she said. "Just hold your legs together," and she tightly squeezed them together. I wanted to have the baby then, but ever so often she would come back in the room and squeeze my legs together again. After Doctor Schauer had come and had examined me, he stood at the foot of my bed.

"You are going to have your baby," he said.

I stared at him. "Of course, I'm going to have my baby. Why did you say that?" I said in a loud voice.

He tried to quiet me down. "Well, I mean you weren't sure as of two weeks ago, you had false labor. You are definitely having your baby now." he said.

I quieted down, and sure enough, they were soon wheeling me on a Gurney to the delivery room.

Above the birthing table on which they transferred me, I could see a mirror right on me. "Oh, wonderful," I thought, "I'm going to get to see my baby born." That thought was short lived. A mask came down on my face with the anesthesia. I fought hard, trying to get it across to them, that I wanted to see my baby born.

I had asked Doctor Schauer, in my early pregnancy, if I could have the new technique of childbearing, which allowed a mother to see and participate in her baby's birth. He had said he could not do that. Since I had had Doctor Schauer ever since we had come back to Ohio, and liked him very much, I had to give up my idea of seeing the birth of my baby.

So, here I was seeing it, I thought, when down came the mask on my face, and I struggled wildly, to no avail. I gradually succumbed to the ether and knew no more.

"You want to see your baby?" Doctor Schauer was bending over me. "It's a boy. You had a perfect little boy! He weighs eight pounds, four ounces."

"Yes," I whispered, as he called the nurse to show me my baby.

He looked about the recovery room. He walked over to a crib and looked in it. He came back to me. "Oh, I'm sorry! They've taken him out." I had a great feeling of disappointment, then I promptly went back to sleep.

Later when he was brought in, that beautiful little bundle of joy looked like an angel cuddled in the arms of a nurse. I had raised up to see him better, but fell back, exhausted, as the nurse walked away with him.

The next day, a nurse brought Larry to my bedside where George was standing. We stared at our beautiful baby boy. His gob of dark brown hair was standing straight up, his wrinkled face made him look like a little old man much like George would look, fifty years later.

The nurse pulled open his blanket and showed us his long beautiful slender hands, and lifted up his darling little feet with their long slender toes. Ten of each. Ten little fingers, ten little toes. He had beautiful hands, which have remained beautiful and long and sinewy. I have never seen more beautiful hands on anyone. I always thought George's hands were so beautiful, when he made my love knots in the center of my palms, but here were the most beautiful hands in the world, and still are today.

Two days later, I was anxiously awaiting his arrival, for nursing. The nurse walked in with the darling, little pink faced, baby girl, looking down at her cooing, as she carried her to her mother in the bed next to me. The nurse went out of the room and I watched intently for her to bring my baby to me. She came in the room, slinging my baby back and forth, on one arm. "I wonder what the other guy looked like!" she said, looking down at him. I didn't think that was very nice of her.

As she threw him down on my arms, I stared at him. He did look as if he had been in a fight. His red wrinkled skin was beginning to peel, especially around his mouth where the milk from nursing, would build up.

When I was allowed to get up and walk the next day, George and I walked to the nursery. I stood looking from my baby to my husband, and thought if anyone walked up to the nursery window and looked at George and the babies in the nursery, that person would definitely know which baby was his. He looked exactly like a miniature George. He changed later and took on the appearance of a Busby, but when he was born he looked like a George.

Larry's black hair came out, and was replaced with beautiful blonde hair, almost white, like both his grandfathers had been when very young. It didn't turn darker for years, but now is dark brown with streaks of grey through his beard and hair. He is still a handsome man, very likeable, and much of which to be proud, as his father and mother were, when looking down at him when he was a baby.

It seemed as if I had wanted a baby all my life. I loved all my nieces and nephews and wanted a baby of my own for so long. George hadn't wanted me to have a baby until he completed his time in the service to his country, so we waited. When he did come back we couldn't get pregnant. Now May 28, 1947, here was my firstborn! He was everything I had hoped for!

The day George brought the baby and me home, a young girl, Margaret Brosey, from Medway, came to help us.

"Do you want butter, or jelly, on your toast?" Margaret asked me the first morning, after I finished nursing the baby. She placed him in his little crib standing beside my bed. I thought a moment. I had never made a choice of butter or jelly! I used both!

"Jelly," I managed to say, surprised at the question.

That's the last time I ever had just plain, jelly and no butter, on a piece of toast. It's awful. To this day, I always butter my toast first.

It reminded me of the time I was living in Danville, when I went to the Deluxe Cafe every morning for breakfast, before going on to business college. I always ordered hot buttered toast and hot chocolate which I enjoyed immensely. One day, the nice waitress asked me if I would like her to bring me the toast un-buttered, and let me butter it myself.

"You will save a lot of money that way," she said. I wasn't sure but I acquiesced.

"Butter it yourself right away, and it will be the same," she told me. She was wrong! I did, but it was never the same as it was when the butter was slapped on while the toast was still hot. I never enjoyed it after that. But, I never had the nerve to change the order back, as she had been so nice to me.

My instructions from the doctor were to bathe the baby with only baby oil for his first few days. When it came time for his first water bath, Margaret came to me.

"Do you want me to bring the bassinet in by your bed, and you watch me bathe the baby?" she asked.

"Yes!" I said quickly. "That would be great!"

"I could show you how to do it," she said.

"I need that! Yes, I've never seen a baby have a bath before," I said.

She brought the bassinet just inside the door, filled it with warm water, then proceeded to bathe the baby, while I watched very carefully from my bed. As she held my beautiful baby with one hand and washed him with the other, she put him gently down in the water. He let out a shrill scream. Evidently, he was shocked at the feeling of the water.

"Do you think he shouldn't be put down in the water?" I asked anxiously.

"No, he's all right. He just was shocked at the change. He'll be all right. She was younger than I, but had had a child of her own, so I felt she knew what she was talking about.

As I watched her gently handle Larry he became used to it, and then gradually seemed to enjoy it. She was so good with him. I relaxed and watched, as she talked to me about what to do.

Larry was a few weeks old when we found a used handsome, decorative, expensive baby carriage for him. It was large, bluish gray, and made of heavy vinyl, with high sides to keep Larry from falling out. There was a back rest for him to sit up when older, which could be lowered for him to stretch out. It was trimmed in chrome, with wire wheels and a chrome push bar. It had a folding top which could be used raised or lowered.

Doctor Schauer told me to take Larry outside to sunbathe naked, one minute on his tummy side, then turn him over and leave him in the sun one minute on his back. Then the next day, leave him two minutes on each side, then the following day three minutes, building up to twenty minutes on each side. One day, when lying on his back in the baby carriage, we saw a fountain going straight up. I had to jump up and wipe him off. As he got older, a large quilted, comforter with cotton backing, that Mother Massing had made for us, was perfect for sunbathing. By the end of summer, he was as brown as a berry.

I loved the sun. If I couldn't go swimming, I loved to sunbathe on the two empty lots, which we purchased, next to our house. There was a wide grassy area, where there was all sun and no trees.

One day, as I was lying on Mother Massing's comforter in the open area, in a skimpy two piece bathing suit, an airplane roared above me flying rather low to the ground. "I wonder where he is going? I wish I were up there flying somewhere," I thought.

I waved my hand sideways, as I was lying in a prone position, to catch the sun. Much to my surprise, the pilot blinked his airplane lights, as he flew over. After that, when I was out sunbathing, I would wave, and the pilot would blink his lights on and off.

I became uneasy, and stopped sunning myself in the afternoon right after lunch. In a few days I never heard the plane again.

My neighbor began going outside about the time I would sunbathe, and would call over to talk to me. He was so obtrusive, since all I wanted was to be alone, that I finally gave up my sunbathing at home, and only did it at our beach.

We filled Larry with vitamins and he was a very healthy, beautiful boy. Everyone loved him. He was such a delightful young fellow as he grew, very happy and contented.

I could hardly wait to take Larry home to see his Grandparents. On the way to Illinois, we went through Richmond, and stopped at Miller's Cafeteria, to get my favorite food, an ice cream cone. I couldn't wait to give Larry his first bite of ice cream. "Do you think it would be alright?" I asked George.

"Well, I don't know," he said, "I suppose so."

"Look here, Sweetie," I said, "look what I have, you're going to like this." I held the cone so the ice cream would touch his lips. He went into shock, opening his eyes wide, and stiffening his body. He started screaming.

"Oh, what have I done!" I cried. "George, take the cone quick!" I pulled Larry up against my chest, patting him on his back, saying, "I'm sorry, Sweetie. It was just too cold for you."

Mother and Dad thought we had a fine boy, to add to their other eleven grandchildren, at that time.

That summer, the neighbors behind our house on the next street moved, and an artist, named Eleanor Von Schildnecht, and her husband moved there.

She was fat and jolly, and became a wonderful and delightful friend. I always had the urge to paint. My Mother, my Grandmother and her sisters had all been artists. Their paintings hung in their homes.

Eleanor encouraged me. After I put Larry down for his afternoon naps, I would haul out my paints and canvas, and work on this first painting. I counted the hours I spent on it. All told, it was thirty hours, sometimes only fifteen minutes at a time. Eleanor gave me information and instructions over the back fence.

This first picture of mine was taken from a Christmas card. It was a beautiful snow scene of a red grist mill and water wheel amongst fir trees. I had to hurry to get it done for Christmas.

When George unwrapped the gift of my painting for Christmas, I watched in anticipation. He looked at it, without much interest, and put it aside, to pick up another present.

"Did you see what that was?" I asked, with pounding heart. He reached for it and looked closer.

"What is it?" he asked, holding it close and looking at it.

"It's a painting I did!" I said.

"You did that!" He was astonished! "When did you learn to do that? How did you do it? When did you do it?" he kept asking, and I kept telling him all about my newly developed talent, which I had kept secret from him.

We bought an old second hand wringer washing machine, which was a far cry from Gram's wash tub and board. I was so happy with the hand wringer, as it saved me a lot of hard work. There was no place to put it except outside on the small back porch.

In the winter months I would run the clothes quickly through the wringer, and run in the house with them, to hang them on lines run back and forth throughout the kitchen-dining room area. The heat from the coal furnace, in the basement, would cause a steam bath all through the house. But they got dry! Diapers and little baby things dried fast, but sheets and heavy clothing took more than a day sometimes.

The Bridesmaids, by Judith Balaban Quwe, tells of how Grace Kelly hung her washings all throughout the hallways and into her back workroom in her first living quarters, after marrying her Prince Ranier. The apartment had been the former bachelor digs and had no facilities for drying clothes. I was in good company!

In the summer months, my clothes were hung outside, on lines in the back yard. They all smelled so good, after hanging in the hot sun all day. They were always so white and pretty!

When Larry was six months old, I bundled him up warmly against the cold wintry day, and we got in our lemon of a car, the beautiful Lincoln Zephyr, to go to Springfield, Ohio, one Saturday morning.

The night before, there had been a deep snow, which was causing the car to slip and slide. George had to leave the main road, Lower Valley Pike, as the river was out of its banks and the bridge impossible to cross, and turned north on Tecumseh Road. As he drove towards the steep hill, near George Rogers Clark Park, he gave the car a little more gas and started up the hill.

A small truck had been parked in the center of the road, at the base of the hill. After passing the truck the car moved up the hill slower and slower. A man from the park, who had parked the truck, was spreading sand or cinders, starting at the top, to give traffic better traction. As we approached the top, the car finally stopped, with the rear wheels spinning. The brakes didn't hold! George slammed on the brakes again and again, but we started moving backwards, and down the hill, towards that parked truck.

"Get out! Take the baby, and get out!" George yelled.

"I can't!" I screamed.

"You have to! I'll slam on my brakes real hard, maybe they'll hold long enough! Hurry up!" George was yelling.

We were going backwards too fast! The car was slipping and sliding! I held my baby close to me, my darling precious, little bundle. As I yanked the door open, George slammed on the brakes, and I was able to jump out, in my heavy coat and goulashes, into the ditch, with my baby, and slipping and sliding, I managed to get behind the open door, and slam it shut.

The car went backwards, faster and faster. George turned the steering wheel, and slammed the rear of the car into the ditch, against a two foot high abutment on the other side of the ditch. I watched with great consternation. Holding Larry tightly in my arms, I slipped and slid down the steep hill, until I was near the car.

"Are you Okay?" I screamed. "Why did you do that? What happened?"

George, trying to explain to me said, "I could not go backwards down the hill. I was afraid I would hit the truck parked in the middle of the road, so I turned the car into the ditch hoping that would stop it. It did!" He was terribly shaken.

The caretaker of the park, who was the man at the top of the hill, came running and sliding down to help us. He took us in his truck to the park headquarters, in the beautiful old stone farm house. His wife made hot chocolate for Larry and me, while George called Mr. Watterly, at his home at Crystal Lakes. This was the first call of many, for such help, for this car

The Watterly's lived in the southern part of Crystal Lakes, and Irvin had a soft heart where we were concerned. He drove to wherever we broke down, whether it be south Dayton or any other place we broke down, and hauled us back, and fixed the car, at a price we could afford.

Upon examining the car, this time he found the brake line had rubbed against some part of the car, making a small hole which caused all the brake fluid to pump out on the ground, when George jammed on the brakes. He was our angel in disguise. Until we got rid of that Lincoln, we had lots of problems. Mr Watterly was up to every predicament in which we found ourselves. He kept all of our cars in good running order for all the years we lived at Crystal Lakes. We didn't attempt to go to Springfield anymore that winter season.

Chapter 12

Friendships

There were lots of wonderful people living in Crystal Lakes, people with whom we were friends all the years we lived there, many of whom have remained our friends still.

Our next door neighbors were the Atkins family. They were the mother, with her two married sons, and a younger son. One of the sons Clyde, and his wife Bert, became very good friends of ours, playing cards and spending a lot of time together. We missed seeing Larry take his first steps, as he was over at their house, as he was so often, when he took three steps for the first time. This broke my heart.

The Amil Roe's, with their two girls, and two boys lived next to Atkins.

Thelma and Ced Wolter, with their four beautiful blonde Swedish children, lived at the foot of our hill. Their daughter Sandy was a special friend of Larry's as she was his age and they grew up together. One day, when the kids were about eleven, Sandy tackled me in a football game. The boys had never tackled me before, but Sandy had no such compunction. I slowly got up, with my aching body, vowing never to play a scrimmage again.

Rita and Bill Kelly who lived about a block north of Ced and Thelma, were special friends, who had three boys, with Billy being Larry's best friend growing up. Bruce, their second son, was a very good friend of our second son Monte, with their third son, Mark, being younger than the other four.

Rita told funny stories of her sons at our bridge parties. She kept us laughing all the time about the funny things they said or did.

Up near the fourth lake were our good friends, Jean and Russ Miller who had a girl and a boy. She and Thelma were home economists and belonged to a professional group, to which I was invited as a guest many times.

On the other side of this lake lived Bill and Jackie Neill, who had five boys. One Christmas the baby, Rondie gave me a pair of delicately knitted footies, saying "For my favorite baby sitter."

On the southern most street in Crystal Lakes lived our good friends, Lorraine and Danny Collins. They had three girls, Jeannie, Sally, and Kathy, and one boy, Danny. At one time, years later, Danny, Senior was George's Division Chief at the base in Data Automation.

We had many more friends, too numerous to mention, and such a wonderful life living in Crystal Lakes.

God is the most important thing in my life. God, Jesus, and the Holy Spirit, The Trinity. Without these my life would be barren. I accepted Jesus Christ as my savior, when I was an eleven year old girl, at the Friends Church in Ridgefarm, Illinois. Grandma and I walked the five blocks there every Sunday morning, with me beside her, carrying her little square pillow, as our benches were hard and without cushions.

I take everything to God in prayer, my problems, and my happiness, my asking for help, and my thankfulness for his help. He has never let me down. Sometimes, He has rearranged my thoughts or my life, but He has always been there for me. In every walk of my life, He goes with me.

When we went to Ohio to live, the only Friends Church we could find in the area was six miles away in Fairborn. It met only once a month.

So, we attended Medway Methodist Church, which was two miles away from our home, and liked it very much. The congregation was wonderful, and we were to remain there, for the rest of our thirty years of life in Ohio. I am so glad we did. It was where I grew in my religion, and my strong love for God and man.

It was not hard for me to go from a Quaker Church to a Methodist. They held similar beliefs; the fatherhood of God, Jesus Christ as Lord and Savior, The Holy Spirit. There was more ritual in the Methodist Church but the deep down beliefs were similar. The Quaker Church, founded by George Fox, broke away from the Puritan Church in England, during the reign of Oliver Cromwell, 1653-1658.

There was never a better friend, nor long lasting, than Martha Fitzgerald, who, after her husband's death, became the wife of Arthur Yowler. She lived in a home across and down the street from Medway United Methodist Church, which allowed her to walk to church, a practice I never was able to do after leaving Illinois. It is my thought that this is the ultimate, to get outside and walk in the refreshing morning air, going to the best place in the world, God's house, to be closer to Him, and to see my friends.

When I was raising my little boys, painting, having a great time doing things with our friends, Martha was being an excellent librarian at the Technical Library at WPAFB. She became the head librarian there, then spent the next two years commuting to the Library at Headquarters in Washington, D. C.

Martha was leader of the Junior Department of Sunday School at Medway United Methodist Church, a job I later held, when she retired from her librarian position in Washington, and became an artist. She took the Famous Artist's Course, and has sold many paintings.

Martha is the loveliest of all women, with a smile as big as the whole outdoors, with her enormous dimples flashing in and out, even as she talks. She is the ultimate Christian, in my life. So kind, so dear, so sweet! To everyone! She is what Christianity is all about. She is a very knowledgeable person, well read, and personable.

Our very close friends, Paul and Betty Styer, had three children, Vickie, Stephen, and Paula, all of whom were very thin and wiry, like their parents, and always ready for a good time. They lived in a large roomy house in the center of Medway. There were lots of parties at their house, as we had a lot of mutual friends.

When the boys missed their school bus, and I had to run them over there, or had to talk to their teachers at Medway Elementary School, next to our church, I oftentimes stopped at Betty's, and had breakfast with her. When they moved to Florida for a few years, we stopped off and visited with them when coming home from visiting Mother. Then, they moved back to Ohio, to Park Layne just west of us, and we renewed our great friendship.

Ann and Charles Glancy, with their four little girls, lived across and down the street from Styers in Medway. Charles was an engineer, and Ann a graduate of Ball State University, Indiana, where she studied Home Economics. Charles was our Sunday School teacher, and worked as a B-57 Project Manager, at the Base. We had lots of good things to eat at their house, and played a lot of cards with them.

After many years at The Base Charles was sent to Houston, Texas, where he and Ann went to live and raise their four little girls.

Ann was a member of the Professional Home Economists, along with Thelma Wolter and Jean Miller. It was a great pleasure, to me, to be asked to be a guest at one of their meetings.

One time, when I was teaching a Junior High Class in Bible School, with the young minister's wife as an assistant, her son kept breaking up my concentration on my teaching trying to get attention, from the other kids, as was his wont to do. I had my back to him, when I heard more activity and giggles. I turned quickly, and stared at him.

"Eddie, will you stop doing that!" I yelled. There was instant and complete silence. No one had ever called him down! This was the problem. He was always allowed to do anything he wanted to do!

"How do you expect these other kids to learn anything when you are always acting up!" I finally got my breath back. What was I doing, yelling at the preacher's son?

"No one can learn," I said softer and quieter. I didn't need to yell now! Everyone was petrified! "If you aren't quiet, no one is going to learn anything!" I said more gently.

There was never anymore trouble with Eddie after that. We had a smooth running class from then on. A few times he would get hyper, but I would see his Mother give him the eye and he would quiet down.

I taught Junior High students at Summer Vacation Bible School held each year. When Vacation Bible school time was near, I told all my friends I could not see them until the school was over, that I had to give it all I had.

I loved Vacation Bible School. My first time to help was when Monte was less than a year old, and would not stay with the baby sitter for the Vacation Bible School, Betty Styer. He screamed and cried the first day I left him, every moment, for his Mommy. So the next day and from then on, until the end of the two week session, he was glued to my hip, while I tried to be a good assistant to the teacher.

My favorite group to teach were the fourth, fifth, and sixth graders, called the Junior Department. They were so alert, and aggressive in their search for knowledge. It was hard to get teachers for that group, but I found the classes to be enlightening and rewarding. I learned right along with them.

When a question was asked by one of the students, that I didn't know the answer, I would say, "That's a good question! Why don't we look it up tonight and talk about it in the morning?" Then both they and I would come to class the next day and have a leisurely discussion of the subject in question. It was wonderful!

The older ones had different attitudes, and seemed to be unwilling to work the problems out.

The smaller children were adorable, and I loved them, but they didn't challenge me. Most of the mothers wanted to work with the little ones, so I always got to handle the inquisitive ones, the ones who were the easiest to mold, and help in their religious education. Of all my work with children, I loved my summer church school best. The children were so ready, and willing to develop their religious thoughts and activities. I think they got a good start at Medway Methodist Church.

I progressed to teacher status the next year, then to Director of the whole program, and finally for the last three years, I held both the position of head teacher for the Junior Department, as well as Director of the whole Bible School, which had an enrollment of one hundred and fifty children each year.

These were busy, sometimes difficult, times, getting teachers and materials organized before time, then correlating the whole two weeks of the Vacation Bible School, and presenting a program, at the end of the school, showing what we had learned to the children's parents. I finally had to give it up. It was too big of a job for me. No one wanted to be the director, and no one wanted to teach the Junior High students. So, I told them I couldn't do it anymore. No one would take over my demanding jobs. The next year they didn't have Vacation Bible School which made me feel terribly guilty. But, fortunately the following year, a young lady offered to be the director. They chose to have bible school one week only instead of the two we had always had. I could not begin to understand how the Vacation Bible School could be held only one week, and teach the children any good, but they are continuing to hold it only one week today.

We had Tupperware lawn parties, went picnicking at all the parks, went to dances and activities at the American Veterans of World War II (AMVETS), and lots of parties and activities at our Crystal Lakes Clubhouse. We helped operate the clubhouse parties and activities. It was a fun time of living, always something to do. Never a dull moment.

Swimming was so marvelous at our swimming area, that I wanted to go all day. Morning, afternoon, and at night, if I were able to get George to go when he came home from work. There was no problem getting the boys to go any part of, or all the day, as their friends were there, too. We spent most of our summers at the beach, or visiting friends, or going to the clubhouse on the circle. There were afternoon parties, or card games, or just visiting all summer, and until the snow and cold weather kept us mostly indoors.

When summers were over, and the children went back to school, we women had get-togethers in the afternoons and sometimes at night. We played all day bridge from ten to school-out time. Tupperware parties were fun and frequent. Church women's clubs were usually held in the evenings.

Since I wanted to be with George and the boys in the evenings, I attended things in the daytime, but usually curtailed my activities to those in which George and I or the boys could participate in the evenings.

Pinochle and euchre parties were great throughout the years. Always fun! Then it was the bridge parties. They were even more fun. More concentration and effort were required for bridge, the more we played the better we got. I have belonged to bridge clubs all my life, after first learning to play.

One day, Jackie Neill asked Rita Kelly and me if we wanted to learn to play bridge. Of course, we did! A friend of Jackie's, who was an officer's wife, was going to take lessons at The Base (WPAFB). She thought if she could teach us after each class what she had learned, she would learn how to play bridge much better and faster. We were so pleased to be asked!

After four or six lessons, this friend of Jackie's decided it would be good for us to play with a group of her friends, who were all officer's wives. We certainly didn't think we were ready to play with bonafide excellent players, but we were told they were a great bunch of gals, and it would be good for us. We succumbed, with much trepidation.

On the way to Jackie's friend's home in Medway, we were all so nervous, especially when we talked about this one Colonel's wife, who was known to be the best player of all. We wondered who would get her as a partner. None of us wanted to have to play with her, as she was such an excellent player. Guess who got her!

When I sat opposite her, I looked at each of my friends at other tables, who were sitting opposite their partners, and received looks of pity for me and thankfulness for themselves that they didn't get her as a partner.

The first round of bidding was started by my partner, the Colonel's wife. She opened the bid at two hearts. I almost fainted! I hardly knew what that meant. It was the highest bid she could have given.

I looked at my skimpy hand, of a count of six, with four hearts, which was a bust hand. My answer to her should have been a bid of two No Trump, meaning I had nothing!

"Six hearts," I said shaking all over. That meant a great hand and let's go to slam! I realized from the shocked looks of every one from the other tables, what I had done.

"Oh, I didn't mean that. I mean two No Trump," I finished lamely.

"No you said six hearts. That stands," my partner said.

I felt smaller than small. I wanted to slip underneath the table. I knew my face was flushed, red as can be, when I laid my cards on the table. Everyone craned their necks to see what I had!

My partner was a real gem. She never flinched but started to play her hand. She was such a fantastic player that she went down only two tricks. I remained sick the whole game, and was the happiest person in the world, when the game broke up and I could go home.

We all became proficient at bridge, starting a new bridge club of two tables.

Jackie Neill's husband, Bill, already knew how to play bridge, but Rita and I taught our husbands. George and I have enjoyed playing bridge ever since.

We became fast and true friends with Danny and Lorraine Collins. Their beautiful blonde daughter, Jeannie, babysat for us when we went out in the evenings to parties and dances.

One day Lorraine was going to help me with some sewing, so she asked me to come to her house for lunch.

While she was working on my dress, I asked her, "What were you going to do today, before you decided to help me with my sewing?"

"I have to iron Daniel's shirts," she said. She always called him Daniel. Everyone else called him Danny.

"I'll do them for you!" I said quickly. "That's the thing I know how to do best, as when I married George, he came with five solid blue long sleeved shirts, some with French cuffs. I had become adept at ironing these shirts."

"Oh, no! You can't!" she exclaimed.

"Yes, I can. Why not?" I said.

"Daniel is so particular about his shirts! I have to do them! He won't wear them if there is a wrinkle in them!" she said.

"You're looking at a person who never leaves a crease. I've ironed George's shirts every week," I said.

Lorraine was still arguing with me, but this was one thing I really knew how to do perfectly!

"Where's the ironing board?" I demanded! "If you don't like them, you can always dampen them down and redo them."

She helped me set up the ironing board, and I proceeded to iron out in the kitchen, while she stayed safely in the front room, working on my dress.

"How is this?" I asked her, holding the perfectly pressed white shirt, hanging with buttons all fastened on a hanger. She stared in disbelief.

"Well, I guess that will do!" she said quietly. I laughed, and went back to the kitchen, where I finished ironing all of his dampened down shirts.

George and some of his friends started American Veterans of World War II (AMVETS) Post 78 at Crystal Lakes. This was a very active post, with a very active auxiliary, which consisted of the wives of the AMVETS. The associations and activities of this group of American Veterans of World War II were a great part of our lives. George is a past Post Commander of this Post, as well as having held other offices, and still holds the original charter of the Post.

Quite a few officers stationed at Wright-Patterson Air Force Base (WPAFB) chose to live at Crystal Lakes instead of base quarters. We made a lot of close friends amongst them. Colonel Bob and Hilma Curlee lived a block south from us on Oak Road. Bob and Hilma were starting a soon to be large family. Hilma and I were very close, being pregnant at the same time, each of us with our first born, soaking up the sun together, and swapping recipes. We four didn't get to play a foursome in bridge too often, as Bob was studying so much at that time. Hilma and I belonged to the same bridge club.

We met Col. John and Bea Honaker, at the Crystal Lakes Clubhouse, during a big party, where I was having lots of fun, serving as a waitress. We knew almost everybody there, but John and Bea were newcomers to the community.

"Can I do that?" Bea asked, "you look like you're having so much fun!"

"Sure. Come on! I'll show you what to do," I said. She did a bang up job and we became fast friends. They lived a short distance from us, on Queen road.

John and Bea had three boys. Their son, Bobbie, was given a BB gun for his birthday. He loved that gun but one day he killed a bird with it. The authorities were called by a neighbor, and he was chastised. He never shot another bird.

Chapter 13
Birth, Death, and Polio

Our families in Illinois came over a lot. We were always glad to have them. We went home a lot too, which was always fun.

Mother and Dad came over from Ridgefarm to help, when our second child was to be born. They brought two of my nephews, Charley Milt and Phillip, to play with our three year old son Larry.

A week before the baby was due, I was sitting on the sofa, when an ambulance pulled up in front of the house.

"Mother, Mother! Come quick! There's an ambulance here," I yelled from the front door. I heard a lot of commotion and went outside to see what was going on. As I watched, two men were trying to slide George on a litter from their ambulance door.

"What is it? What happened?" I waddled down the porch steps and on the brick path, I fell to the ground, quickly jerking myself upright.

"Help my wife, please! I'm all right." George was raising his head up, trying to see what had happened to me. The men dropped him, and ran towards me, helping me up.

"What is wrong, George? What happened?" I was so alarmed.

"I'm alright, I've just had a nervous breakdown," he said. "The nurse was supposed to call you and let you know I was being brought home. Didn't she call you?" She hadn't.

He was brought into the house and put to bed. I lay down beside him and stayed there most of the time for a week. I was so thankful Mother and Dad were there to help us.

We talked some about his condition, but a lot of time we just lay together. We poured through books of baby names, trying to decide a boys or girls name, whichever we got.

A week later, on a Sunday morning, my pains I had had all week became stronger. When George awakened, about seven my pains were five minutes apart. I called the doctor, and he said he would meet me at the hospital.

Mother and Dad drove me twenty miles to Good Samaritan Hospital, in Dayton, Ohio. Dad was going so slow I thought we would never get there.

"Pop," I said, "Go faster!"

He looked at me in surprise. "I thought I shouldn't shake you up!" he said.

"No, go faster! I might have it in the car if you don't!" He sped up.

The baby was born August 13, 1950 at Good Samaritan Hospital in Dayton. Mother was always so pleased she was the one to identify the birth of the baby, when the nurse brought him out.

The next morning, he was brought to me. He looked just like Larry had looked, but not red and tough skinned. Their baby pictures are so similar, we had to put their names on the backs of them, to be able to tell who was who.

"What do you want to name him?" The nurse asked.

"Monte Kevin," I said without hesitation. George and I had studied names all week, so I was sure of the name we chose.

When Mother and Dad came in the next day, they brought a note for me from George. "How's Timothy today?" he had written at the top of the note.

I was flabbergasted. I thought, for sure, we had decided on Monte Kevin. I wondered if I could change it, but decided I better not try. So Monte Kevin was our second son's name. My pregnant friend, Florence Warlin, who had stayed with George and the children when I went to the hospital, had a boy three months later and named him Timothy.

I was brought home in an ambulance. Larry was running around in the yard with Charley Milt and Phillip. The ambulance drivers pulled the litter, on which I was lying with the baby on my chest, out of the ambulance and started carrying us up the sidewalk to the house.

"Come here, sweetie," I called, raising my head up off the litter. "Come and see your new brother." He stopped playing and stared, standing stiffly in the grass. The drivers had stopped for Larry to come over to see me.

"I guess he'll have to see him later," I said. I watched Larry the rest of the walk to the house. He just stared. We had talked about it, but now was the big moment, when his new brother had arrived.

After I went to bed, and the sleeping baby was ensconced in Larry's baby bassinet, I tried again. Larry came slowly, and looked at his brother for the first time.

"His name is Monte Kevin," I said, "Do you like that name? We'll call him Monte. Isn't he beautiful?" He looked from Monte to me, then back at the baby. "Won't you have fun playing with him?" He wasn't too sure but they became fast friends, although their likes and dislikes were so different. Larry wanted to do everything, to get involved in lots of things, whereas Monte was slow and easy going like his father, and slow to become involved in new things.

When George had his nervous breakdown, we curtailed all activity, except what we had to do. He wouldn't let me out of his sight. So, where one went the other had to go. The babies went along with us. We made a tight little foursome, everywhere we went. It was hard, but it made us a stronger family. Bill and Rita helped us, getting groceries for us sometimes, and coming over to play pinochle. Bill would do anything we asked him to do. They were great friends.

After three months, George was able to go back to work. He had a lot of problems for years, but tried to control his feelings in order to function. It was a terrible thing for us to go through, but we did the best we could. In retrospect, I think we did quite well. With our love for one another, and our help from our God, we got through it all.

When we took Monte back to Ridgefarm for the first time, we stopped at Ann's in Indianapolis as usual. Ann had always made so much over Larry, so when she came to the door, I just held Monte out to her. She took him over to the sofa, sat down with him and held him. Larry followed them, pressing against her knees, never moving away, as she tried to play with the baby. Was he trying to protect his baby, or was he afraid, his baby was usurping his presence with his Aunt Ann, who had so clearly loved him? Probably both.

"Larry, is this your new brother?" Ann asked, drawing him closer. "How do you like him? Isn't he a nice little baby?"

I could see Larry relaxing. I breathed a sigh of relief.

We went on to Illinois visiting both sets of Grandparents where he was received with lots of love and admiration.

The snow came early that year, 1950, causing a very bad storm. We awakened one morning to a beautiful white snow drifted against our windows, and piled high in huge drifts. It was gorgeous!

George had been building a large wooden sled for Larry, with large initials LBM on top in a rounded circle like a monogram, cut out on his jigsaw. The snow had come too early so, the sled was unpainted, finished but for the paint.

"That doesn't matter," I said, "Go on and take Larry for a ride in this gorgeous snow. I'll hold Monte up to the window, and we'll watch you, he's too young to go out." He was only three months old.

Monte and I watched and yelled at them, well, I guess I did the yelling, while Monte gurgled and watched and kicked his little feet. I wanted to be out there in the snow with them so much! But I was holding my little baby. I wanted him to enjoy it, too.

Larry was all bundled up in a new light brown snow suit and hat. He fit into the darling little sleigh very nicely. They were laughing, as Daddy pulled him around. They made snowballs and threw at us, so we got in the action, too. Later, George did get the sleigh painted, but never was a better time had by all as that first day of the heavy snow of nineteen fifty.

One of our friends had a baby that night of the heavy snow. They couldn't get her to the hospital, so she had it at home.

The following summer, Rita and I were walking home on a beautiful, moonlit night, from a Tupperware party, laughing and talking. As we came towards our well lighted house, we saw George come out on the porch and clutching the side post, he called to us, "Come in the house Kay. Rita, you come in, too!"

"What's the matter?" I asked.

"What's wrong?" Rita asked, "Is something wrong with Bill?"

"No, just come in the house, both of you!" George demanded!

"What is it?" I planted my two feet firmly on the walkway, and dropped my two clenched fists towards the ground. "I'm not going anywhere until you tell me what's wrong!"

"We received a telephone call," George finally said. "Your Mom called. Your Dad just died. He had a heart attack."

My legs became rubbery, and my body began to go limp.

"Oh, Rita, grab her. Don't let her fall." George cried.

He ran towards us and, with Rita on one side, and George on the other, they caught me. My legs had completely given way and I was falling. They dragged me up the steps, and into the front room, where I fell on the sofa.

"What? What happened? When did she call?" I couldn't believe it. We had just been home the weekend before and he was fine.

"He had coronary thrombosis, and died in fifteen minutes," George said.

I sobbed and sobbed. I had one arm across the back of the sofa, and just laid on it, and sobs tore from me for fifteen or more minutes. George nor Rita could console me. What could be said to a young woman, who just found out her beloved father had died, almost instantly.

"We'll go home in the morning," George said.

"No," I cried. "Tonight! I couldn't sleep a wink. No use to wait. We'll get ready right now!"

"I'll go home and send Bill back to see if he can help," Rita said, and left.

When Bill came, I was packing. We got the kids up, and all helped to get us into the car, and on the way. I drove the whole two hundred and thirty miles, as George had had his nervous breakdown less than a year before and was still doing very little driving.

We arrived home at seven in the morning, to find Uncle Ed on the front porch beside himself. He was so close to Dad.

"Where's Mother?" I said in a tremulous voice.

"Upstairs, I think," he said, "I don't know if she's up yet."

I ran upstairs and burst into her room. She had just got up and dressed and was standing in the middle of the room. Anna Rose was standing in the doorway to the bedroom next to Mother and Dad's bedroom. She had come over from Indianapolis to the farm, and they were all planning on leaving this morning to go West and visit Milt's in California, and Mary's family in Oregon.

Mother and I threw our arms around one another, sobbing.

"What are we going to do without him?" I cried.

After I said it for the third time, Mother jerked away from me, and looked me in the eyes.

"Well, we're just going to have to get along without him!" she said sharply.

It was such a shock, which I needed. I backed off, turned, and ran out of the room into the hallway and collided with Uncle Ed. He had come upstairs and was standing outside the door, listening to us with a broken heart. We stared at one another, then I hurried on past him. No one felt the death more than my Uncle Ed and Uncle Rosy. They were very close to him. He was their big brother, who always looked after them.

The funeral was held at the Friends Church in Ridgefarm, after the huge gathering of friends and relatives at the farm. They were gathered in the house, all over the yard, the farmyard, and out on the road. All drove to the church in a convoy of cars.

When we went into the church, we found it full of people, who had not gathered at the farm, but were waiting at the church to pay their last respects. As I walked in, I saw, through my tears, a whole pew of the poor, what people call in the cities, Street People. Dad had been a good friend to all of them, as well as the most influential people who lived in and around Ridgefarm.

Tears rolled down my face all during the service, during which were said many wonderful things about my father.

He was buried in the Crown Hill Cemetery, in the Busby Mendenhall plot, where he was laid beside Grandma and Grandpa Mendenhall, leaving a space for Mother.

That fall, George and I drove Mother to Florida in her Cadillac. Larry was three and Monte one, it was their first trip to Florida, and they loved it. The hammock, on the patio in front of the trailer, was a favorite place of theirs. Larry would crawl in there by himself sometimes and swing in his cowboy outfit, with wide brim hat and fancy boots.

Henry and Millie Miller, who lived close by, in the same Royal Palm Trailer Park, in Hallandale, had been good friends of Mother and Dad. They became even closer friends, helping Mother with all the extra things, now that Dad was gone. They would take Mother back to Illinois, and stay a month or so with her on the farm, putting out the spring garden. They were the best of friends. When Millie died several years later, Henry remained her best friend, helping her in many ways.

Ruby and Dorothy, Uncle Frank's two daughters, helped Mother a lot, too, as they lived near Miami now, in Hialeah.

Henry and Mother took us to the train station in Hollywood for us to return home to Ohio. We had to wait quite awhile for the train to arrive, so we sat outside on the station platform seats. Monte was fidgety, so I pushed my pocket book to the side of me, next to the armrest, in order to care for him better. When the train came, we jumped up and ran to get on, saying our good-byes to Mother and Henry.

It wasn't until about a half hour later, that I reached for my purse, and it wasn't there. I was frantic! Where was it? The only place I could think it could be was back on that settee. The conductor was very solicitous to our dilemma. He said he would contact the train station at our next stop, and ask them to look for it. I thought I would never see it again. But, voila, it was found where I had left it on the settee. It arrived in our mail the next day about the same time we arrived home.

There were two lovely teenagers on the train, and they became enamored of our sweet little Larry. They took him to their seats and held, and talked, and laughed with him all the way home. Our "baby sitters" hated to see us get off the train, with Larry, when we arrived in Dayton, hours later. They wanted to keep him!

The summer the boys were two and five we planned to go on a vacation. Joe, George's brother, drove over from Illnois, in his new car, and we were all going camping together Larry became ill, lying around listlessly, not getting any better. His legs would jerk uncontrollably.

We called a local doctor, at Crystal Lakes, who came over to the house to examine him.

"Now, Mother, he's going to be all right. Don't worry!" he said, after his examination. After the doctor came the second time, with the same results, we took Larry to the Miami Valley Hospital in Dayton, to be checked, as he was getting no better. He just lay with no strength or appetite, with his legs jerking.

The doctors wanted to do a spinal tap, and asked us to wait in the waiting room.

"Mother! Mother!" I heard Larry's little voice screaming for me. I jumped up and ran to the door. George caught me and held me tightly. "You can't go in there! They said to wait here!" he said.

"I don't care! If I can just be with him and hold him, just to let him know I'm here, and that I love him!" I cried through my tears.

"He knows that! It won't take long. They'll do a better job if you stay here," George said to me.

When they wheeled him into the hallway, in a hospital baby crib, and he lay so still in it, I knew the verdict. He had polio. We helped the nurse place him in the room, still in his crib amongst eight or so children.

"You musn't be here," the nurse said, "you'll have to go."

"Where will we go? I can't leave him like this," I cried.

"You could go outside and stand in front of the window. I could push his crib over there near to it," she said.

For nine days, we stood outside the window, morning until night, while Larry lay in his crib, not taking his eyes off us. When my legs swelled twice their size, and I could not stand the pain any longer, I would drop away and go over to a nearby tree to sit under the shade.

"Don't go!" Larry would say.

"Sweetheart, Mother has to get off her legs for a little while. I'll just be over there in the shade and I'll be back soon," I said.

Joe was handling Monte, who at the age of two wanted his mommy.

It certainly wasn't easy for any of us. When Joe came up with Monte, pushing him in his stroller, I asked Joe how he was doing. Joe had come to spend his long awaited vacation with us, which turned out to be a baby sitting job.

"You should see what he did to my new car!" he said.

"Oh, Joe, what happened?" I asked.

"He wet the whole front seat," he said, through clenched teeth.

The panic of polio was substantial at Crystal Lakes, as twenty-two children got it that summer. It was called an epidemic. Several children died with it.

Danny and Lorraine Collins' two younger children, Kathy and Danny, had serious side effects, after having Polio, which necessitated a long period of rehabilitation.

Jackie and Bill Neill lost Murray, their first born, and their next two boys had bad side effects of polio. They and Larry had to be taken to a children's hospital for therapy for months.

When I looked at that beautiful, blonde haired, five year old boy, Murray, in his little casket, I was heartbroken. I sobbed as I realized and said, "That could be our Larry, but for the grace of God." He had been one of Larry's best friends.

I sobbed and sobbed. He had been a big favorite of mine and it was as if I had lost a son. Jackie and Bill later lost another son in a car accident.

When we wanted to trade our 1950 Chrysler Windsor Highlander in for a new car, I gave explicit instructions to the two boys.

"You kids picked holes in that beautiful plaid seat!" I said. "You sit on those spots, and don't you dare move. We don't want the salesman to see them!" When I had seen them for the first time, I was livid. There was no reason for them to have picked two or two and a half inch holes in the beautiful plaid covering and the soft rubber underneath.

"Under no conditions are you to move off those holes!" I said. "If the salesman sees them, he won't exchange our car for a new one!"

When we all took a ride to show the salesman what a nice car we had to trade in, he drove and George and I sat in the front seat with him. The boys were in the back sitting on the holes.

I saw the salesman look in the back two or three times, I'm sure he wondered why the boys sat up straight, never moving. They stared him in the eyes each time he looked in the back seat. The plaid looked beautiful. It was a beautiful car. We got top price. I have, however, remained with a guilt complex about it all.

Chapter 14
Matisse and Camping

The summer Larry was born, and our neighbor Eleanor got me started painting. I couldn't stop. My life was full of painting, art work of all kinds, arty friends, art shows, artistic endeavors of all kinds.

George was a very willing and able helpmate, in designing and constructing most of my art equipment. He fashioned a thin limber board into a palette shape, with the thumb hole and a protrusion for the fingers. He made it of the plywood panel in which our new refrigerator was shipped. The palette was given a smooth polished finish for mixing of paints and medium, which facilitated my efforts to the greatest degree. It is a fabulous palette, which is better than any I have ever seen.

Using his power tools which we brought from Danville, George made me an adjustable table easel which I used for many years. When I wanted to go out on field trips to paint, I had to have a free standing easel. He used my old ironing board legs and formed a not-too-steady standing easel. It could be folded into a compact carrying easel for going on painting forays.

An old wooden suitcase of ours was cut down to a six inch thick case and compartments were installed to separate and store my turpentine, paints, brushes and tools. A hinged rack was included to hold my palette. The outside he covered with treated masonite, making it a very sturdy carrying case for my art supplies.

In the beginning, I painted on canvas boards, which most beginners use, then George started stretching my canvases which enabled me to do better and larger work. Some he framed, but oftentimes I painted the edges using no frames, as was often done in those days.

I loved and breathed art! It was the main compelling force in my life. I read art books, studied art, and made friends in the art world of all surrounding areas.

Throughout the following years, I took classes from many art teachers, exhibiting in many art shows, and belonged to several art associations.

Fairborn Art Association gave me an outlet that helped me grow tremendously in my art work. There were classes where I learned my art, there were art shows where I showed my paintings, and won prizes with many.

My first art exhibit was after classes by Madge Harrah, who was a wonderful, exciting teacher, instilling a great desire in me to do better and better. During her first class she asked us to do a collage. I hardly knew the word, and barely understood what was expected of me. I thought about it all week, not knowing what to do.

"I better get at it," I thought, "Class is tonight. I have to take in something."

It was quiet at our house, so I could think. I set up an arrangement on the table with two tall glasses and a tall pitcher. I sketched, then cut out, of different colored paper the forms I saw, using our flowered curtains in the back of my setup. Then, I pasted my completed pieces on a large canvas board. I had to hurry to get dinner ready for the family, then rushed to my classes in Fairborn.

"Look what Kay brought!" Madge said excitedly. She came to me quickly, and took my large picture from my hands.

"It's a Matisse!" she said excitedly. She held it up high, and went all around the room, holding it up for everyone to see. It's a Matisse! It is wonderful! I love it!

Needless to say, she was crazy about it. And here I had wondered if I had done what I was supposed to do.

"It's perfect," she said.

For the next class, I was to paint a picture, from the collage, with my oil paints. When I took the oil painting of it into class, Madge was delighted.

"You've lost a little, but not much! It's very good! I'm proud of you."

When we had an art show after the classes were over, I won second prize with it from about three hundred entries. First prize went to a professional international artist, and third prize went to my teacher, Madge Harrah.

"Your painting won a ribbon, Kay! Come down and get your picture taken for the newspaper," I was told over the phone, a few months later, after the next show was opened. I had worked so hard setting up the show and helping get it ready, and had gone home to rest and get a bite to eat.

"Which one of my pictures got the ribbon?" I asked excitedly.

"I don't know! It had your name on it," she said.

"Which one was it?" I queried. I couldn't believe I had won.

"It is called "Fall," the girl on the phone answered, as she read from a card. I was stunned.

"That can't be mine! I don't have any with that title." I was nonplussed.

"Well, your name is on the card. Come on down, and get your picture taken, so we can put it in the paper, with the other first and second place winners!" she insisted.

"Well," I said slowly, "I'll come down, but I'm sure that isn't mine. I can't think of anything I entered named that."

When I went into the big hall, all laid out beautifully, with hundreds of pictures, I hurried over to my painting that had won, and then I laughed.

"It is mine!" I couldn't remember by the way it was described to me! At the last minute, a friend of mine told me I hadn't named my painting. It had to have a name. I had taken a quick moment to name it, then promptly forgot the name, as I was so busy. It was definitely a fall scene! I had won a second ribbon in that large exhibit.

All media fascinated me, but my true love was oil painting. There were fabulous teachers from whom I gleaned my (or their) best, but also those teachers who found it hard to pass on their great ability.

Madge Harrah was a great teacher, pushing us towards greater accomplishments, from ability that we didn't know we had. John Nartker was fabulous. He came up from Cincinnati, where he taught all phases of art to young ladies in a Catholic girls school, College of St. Joseph on the Mount. He was a huge success as a teacher and an accomplished artist as well.

Often, a teacher can teach well, but cannot always themselves produce excellent pictures. Often they can do the work better than they can teach it. John Nartker was excellent both in teaching and producing his own work.

He and I were on the same wave length. One time, as he was going around the class of artists, giving instructions to each one of us, he finally arrived behind me. He stood looking at my work.

"Don't do too much more to that, Kay," he said.

"I'm not! This is my last stroke!" I exclaimed as I hit the canvas in the right place, and threw my arm with the brush in my hand up in the air. I was so happy he and I agreed on when to stop. A lot of people do not understand when to stop. They overwork their pictures, and it shows.

They do not retain their spontaneity and freshness.

For the first picture I sold, I received seven dollars. Now, that doesn't sound like much, but, to me, it was fabulous! It was a windfall! All these pictures I was doing, were gathering all over the house. It was great to start selling some of them.

With that first seven dollars, I rushed to the art supply store, and bought a fantastic sable brush, which I had wanted, but felt I couldn't afford. I had been using my mother's old paints and brushes, but I really needed this new wonderful brush. I had never spent so much on any brush before, but it was well worth it.

Polly and Pete Marras lived across the street from the bank on the main street in Medway. They had a beautiful little baby girl, Pam.

Polly was a beautiful woman, with a very lovely face. She had been a model, wearing broad brim hats, and perfect makeup. They moved to a large apartment in an old 1800's house near Salem Avenue in Dayton, a very exclusive part of town. After a few years, they bought a very nice home in the eastern part of Kettering, south of Dayton, where we visited them often.

She and I painted together once or twice a month, sometimes more often. She didn't drive, nor ever wanted to learn, so I always went the twenty miles to her house, when we would get together. She was an excellent cook, always having a special meal for me. George and Pete, and our children, were together a lot. We had great cookouts and parties, as well as our painting classes and forays. Polly and I took art classes together, worked out our artistic endeavors together, and became the best of friends.

One New Year's Eve party, at their house, we were snowed in, while playing our games and eating great food, so Polly insisted we stay all night. The other guests lived closer so they all managed to get home. Since we had the boys with us, there was no reason for us to try to get home, and perhaps have a wreck. So we, all four, stayed the rest of the night with them. The next morning, the party continued as a lot of the night before guests, came back. It was the best New Year's Eve we ever had, as it continued the next day. We finally got in our car, and fought the heavy snowdrifts, laughing all the way.

One time at a New Year's Eve party at our house, I had invited all of our close friends. We played games, and had lots of special fancy food. One of the games we played was to pick up cotton balls, which had been poured on the top of a card table, and picked up with a spoon, by a blindfolded individual. It is not easy! Especially, if the hostess keeps moving the lightweight cotton balls away from the spoon, as I did, when Pete was trying his hand at the game! He persevered, with his ever present patience, amid the howling laughter! The crowd finally turned on the hostess me, and to preserve my integrity, I had to stop teasing him, and let him find his cotton balls. But Pete was always that way, he never showed any malice, he always laughed at a good joke whether it be on himself, or anyone else. He never held a grudge, so we remained friends.

Since George didn't feel like being with people much, after his illness, we went to all the state parks. We went to George Rogers Clark State Park, the one where we had had the wreck when Larry was a baby. It was a wonderful place; we always had a great time. Larry and his Dad would go off together, while Monte and I would hang out together. He never wanted to be far from me. He would hang onto my legs all the time. He barley came above my knees, so he would hang onto one of my legs a lot whether we were at the park, or cooking a meal, or anything. That was fine with me. I always knew where he was.

Larry was always full of noises, no matter where he was, by himself or whoever, I always knew where he was, by his little noises.

When we took them to grocery shop, or anywhere, I would have them hang on my skirt, and by their softest touch, I knew they were with me. If they let go, I knew instantly, and would explain why they should keep touching my skirt. They were both such good little boys and grew into such good big boys!

We always shared everything equally. One time when Monte found the only mushroom on a field trip, I cooked it and cut it in four pieces. It was a delicious Morel and we all wanted more, but we shared, as usual.

As the boys grew older, they had lots of friends to our house, and they were allowed to visit all over Crystal Lakes. It was a marvelous area in which to grow up.

When Monte was barely walking, we bought a pup tent, and went to Fort Ancient, near Lebanon, Ohio, for our first camping trip. It was near a railroad crossing, where trains went by every two or three hours. There were also hounds baying, on a scent most of the night. Monte was awakened by the noises, and his allergies, so many times, we packed up the next morning and left for home.

We didn't give up camping but went many times with that little tent, and enjoyed the out doors, until we found a used umbrella tent. It was opened like an umbrella. George had to get inside the partially opened out tent and pop the roof up into place. The canvas flooring was about ten feet square on which I made pallets of blankets. We traveled a lot with this tent, our gasoline camping stove and paraphernalia, staying in camp grounds and parks.

George cultivated a large plot of ground, one hundred by one hundred feet, on an empty lot opposite the front of our house, on the other side of Pine Road. It was a huge endeavor, but excellent therapy for him. He planted and cultivated lettuce, kale, spinach, brussels sprouts, radishes, beets, turnips, sweet corn, popcorn, beans, cucumbers, tomatoes, cantaloupes and acorn squash. He worked hard all that summer in the garden, and, by August, everything was big and almost ready to eat.

He had always loved to work in the soil. As his Father farmed the fields, he had helped his Mother work in vegetable gardens, and flowers, as he grew up. But all of this huge garden grew to maturity at the same time. All of the vegetables were going to be ready during that three week vacation we had planned. It made us think of all that hard work, and the beautiful, weedless garden, full of almost ready-to-eat vegetables. The thought of the corn and tomatoes especially, going to waste while we were gone, caused us no end of concern.

We debated whether to cancel our vacation plans, but we really wanted to go to Niagara Falls, where we had never been. So, we decided to go.

But first, we told several of our friends to check on George's gorgeous garden, and use the bountiful huge and delectable vegetables, so they would not be wasted.

When we came home from our fantastic trip to Niagara Falls and Canada, the first thing we did was run over to our garden, hoping some of the vegetables were not too mature for us to eat. We were sickened by what we saw! Weeds everywhere! But more importantly, the corn had grown into huge ears of large kernels, hardened by three weeks of maturity, and the tomatoes and most of the other vegetables were overgrown and too mature to eat. I was so mad! Our friends were too lazy to even pick our marvelous vegetables, which were far better than what they could buy at the market. It was the best garden we had ever raised.

"We picked one batch," Thelma, down the road, said. "We thought we should leave the rest for you!" No one else had even checked on the garden!

We started picking and canning what we could, and stuffed ourselves with what couldn't be canned and threw the rest away.

The boys were five and eight when we went to Niagara Falls, the number one U. S. attraction. It was so fabulous it takes your breath away, however, it was so cold we decided to get us a cabin. That was a mistake. The ancient, unheated cabin, was made with unpainted boards, with wide cracks between, through which the cold wind whistled all night.

The next morning, we put on every warm piece of clothing we had, and went out to see the magnificent sight of Niagara Falls. The water rushes down the Niagara River, plummeting off the edge, to the gorge below, crashing upon the huge boulders. It was a breath taking sight and sound.

We crossed over to Canada, and asked a lady who worked there how to get to the view of the Canadian side of Niagara Falls.

"I'm sorry, I don't know," she said, "I've never been there" How could anyone live there and be so disinterested as to never see that gorgeous view.

We ate at an interesting place, which was so hard to find, that when 20 years later, George tried to find it, I just knew he couldn't. He went right to it without any wrong turn! I was amazed.

Crossing the southern part of Canada we camped at Rondeau Provincial Park, in Ontario, where we put up our tent to camp and attempted to stay. The rains that we had been trying to escape started again as I was dishing up our lunch. After eating in the tent with the downpour of hard pummeling rain, we decided to go home.

It was too wet to break camp, so we decided to go downtown and go to a movie. It was dark and dreary, still raining on us, when we entered the only movie in town. It was Prince Valiant, with Robert Wagner. It lifted our spirits, in his wonderful portrayal of Prince Valiant. We were in such high spirits when we came out of the movie to find a bright sunny, perfect day. We decided to stay another night at our campsite.

As we neared our home at Crystal Lakes we counted our money. It was the lowest we ever got on a vacation. We stopped at a little store on the highway, and bought a loaf of bread and a bottle of milk. George put the pennies it left in his pocket, and we sailed home fat and sassy.

Chapter 15

Florida Again

The first time we drove to Florida, in our car, we stopped at a motel in northern Florida in the dark. The next morning, when I got up and went to the bathroom, I saw a beautiful sight. The window blind was closed, and the sun was beaming strongly against the window. A beautiful shadow of a lovely palm tree was etched on the blind for us to see.

"Come quick, George! See what I see!" I screamed. "Isn't it lovely?"

He agreed, and we stood transformed into the land of beauty!

It was winter and we had traveled two days through burned up trees, shrubs, and grass. It was a gorgeous transformation into lovely green palm trees and luscious foliage, of the Florida we came to know and love as our own.

Now, I awaken every morning to the beauty of the Florida sunlight forming a beautiful picture, of our three Phoenix Roebelenii palm trees George planted for me outside our window, etched on my closed Venetian blinds. It brings to mind that first morning in Florida years ago.

In the winter of 1955, we packed the boys up, and drove to the pure white sandy beaches of Fort Walton Beach, in the panhandle of Florida. While George inquired at Eglin Air Force Base about a job transfer, the boys and I spent our time at the beach. We only had to step outside our cabin to be on the beach, to make castles in the sand, swim in the gorgeous aqua water and gather colorful shells. When George came back, with his sad story, I was as disappointed as I could be. I had such high hopes! I loved Florida, and wanted to live here!

"The highest position they could offer me is a GS-9," George told me. "That means I would have to get less money than we make now, as I am a GS-11. The highest man, in my field, Director of Materiel, which includes Supply and Maintenance Divisions, is only a GS-12. I would never be able to attain that position, as there are so many ahead of us. This is not like WPAFB, where I would have a chance to advance."

How had we ever thought it possible! The jobs weren't plentiful, as they were at WPAFB, which is a Headquarters.

If it had been left up to me, I might have been stupid enough to come down, just to be in Sunny Florida, but fortunately, I listened to George.

"Okay, I can see where it wouldn't be fair to you, but you have to promise me we will come to Florida every chance we get," I said.

He promised. And he kept that promise, bless his heart!

There was an old southern style, wooden house, in Pensacola, Florida, called Ma Hopkins Boarding House, which we heard about.

Going to that boarding house was a terrific experience for all four of us, one which we have enjoyed every time we have traveled anywhere near there.

We entered the foyer from a large porch, and sat in tall straight-backed wooden chairs, waiting to be called. The people waiting on lunch were as interesting a lot as any we had ever seen. We thoroughly enjoyed the conversations about this place and the surrounding areas.

When we were called to eat dinner, we entered a large two room area, which formerly had been a living, dining area. There were several huge tables, each one seating twelve people, in each room, with dishes of food filling the center of the table. As soon as one person was full, he was replaced with another. Fortunately, we got to sit together. Food was passed constantly, but there were times when someone asked for something.

THEN AND NOW

Everyone ate, and ate, and ate. There was no talking. It was strange.

A lovely blonde woman surprised me when I heard her say, "Please pass the collard greens." She ate as if she had the appetite of an elephant, I never saw anyone put away food as she did! I had not known what that was and hadn't taken any. Never having tasted them, I decided to try a little. They were delicious! We ate several dishes we had never eaten before, all Southern cooking.

All four of us waddled out on the porch and down the street to our car with our avowal we would be back!

On that same trip, we also went to New Orleans, and it was fabulous. New Orleans is like no other city in the world.

It was bitter cold, and extremely windy, as we four walked through Pirate's Alley, towards the square, in front of the cathedral, where some brave artists were trying to show their paintings, which were for sale. The wind was so strong and cold, whipping against our faces and keeping us bent into the wind. One brave artist was trying to get a customer to pose for a portrait.

"I'll do this little one for Twenty dollars," he said to us.

"How long will it take?" I asked.

"It's too cold," I said, "We'll freeze." I saw the disappointment in his face.

"It would only take me twenty minutes," he said, much to my amazement. How could anyone paint a portrait in twenty minutes.

"You can go around the corner, to the coffee shop, and keep warm, while I paint the little one. They have great hot chocolate. My wife will show you there," he said.

I hadn't seen her, but she walked forward, and we smiled at one another.

"Okay. It's so cold!" I said.

I hated to leave Monte there by himself, he was only five years old, but we were freezing, and I wanted a picture.

In twenty minutes, we went back out from the lovely warm coffee shop, where we had found the hot chocolate, which had warmed us through and through.

He was almost finished! It was beautiful. I loved it! I was not a portrait painter, but had the greatest admiration for those who were. This man's work was excellent.

"I'll do the other one, if you would like," he said, "but it will take longer."

When he was done with Larry, we came back from the coffee shop, with warmed up Monte to a frozen Larry.

"He's not quite finished! Do you see why I told you it would take longer?" he asked.

I asked him why it did.

"The young are so uninhibited they sit quietly. But when they get older, they try to pose, and it makes them harder to paint." he stated.

Both pictures were beautiful, and always have had a special place in our home. Today, they are hanging on the wall at our house entrance with all the rest of our family portraits.

The artist signed Larry's picture, Fedorsky '55 New Orleans. He had signed Monte's picture, Fedorsky New Orleans "Pirate's Alley."

It was too cold and windy to stay long in New Orleans that year, but we were to go back to New Orleans in the future several times. One of the things we found that year, and enjoyed each subsequent visit, was the fantastic New Orleans coffee, near the Market Place, at Cafe Du Monde, in the French Quarter, where they serve Cafe' Au Lait. It has chicory in it and is very strong, then they fill half the cup with cream. It is delicious! The hot Beignets (French Doughnuts) which are served with it are delicate, crunchy, morsels!

A big beautiful, muscular, black man was walking with purpose, near Bourbon Street, with this little old man running beside him, stumbling over the curbing several times, trying to keep pace. It was obvious where they were going, which was more abundantly clear, when we saw the old man, sometime later, walking down the street, with a contented smile on his face, and oblivious to everyone.

My brother Charley, built a concrete block house with terrazzo floors and plaster walls, a true Florida style home of the time, in West Hollywood, Florida, near U. S. Route 441. It was a well built house with three bedrooms, a very well organized kitchen, that was open to the dining area, and front room. It had a concrete patio area in the back, a covered car port, with a storage room attached for the washer and dryer.

Charley and Helen lived there with their brood of seven, for a few years, with Mother staying with them in the winter months.

After Charley and Helen moved to Ocala, we would drive Mother down on our vacation time, for her to stay the winter, then Henry and Millie Miller would drive her back to the farm for her summer months and stay on for awhile.

While we were staying with her one time, Monte dropped his beautiful ceramic alligator on the terrazzo floor, and it broke into a hundred pieces. To placate Monte George said he would put it back together.

"You can't do that, George! It will take forever!" I objected. And the time it would take! I wanted to go somewhere! Anywhere!

"I can fix it!" George said. "Monte wants it fixed!" So we sat and watched George working on that darned alligator!

Monte and Larry picked up their guns and walked outside to the grassy lawn, where they proceeded to play cowboy and Indians. George stopped working on the alligator long enough to go out and take movies of their gun battle. They had on their cowboy boots and hats and gun belts around their waists. After they tired of whooping and hollering, they came back in to a quiet house,

The kids were still wound up from their gun battle, so I thought it was a good time to take them somewhere. Mother, who never wanted the car to go anywhere without her, was at the sink in the kitchen. I whispered to the boys that they and I would sneak off, and go down a couple of blocks, to an Indian Teepee, where they sold Indian souvenirs.

"Don't look up, just listen!" I whispered to George, as he continued gluing the alligator together. "The boys and I are going to run down to the Indian Teepee. We want to go alone."

"Do you have the keys to the car?" he asked quietly, so as not to alert Mother's instinct.

"They're in my hand," I said, looking up to see Mother turning around from the sink, to see what was going on. "Hurry up, Boys! Let's go!" I said, dragging them outside fast. We quickly got in the car, and I zoomed out of the driveway as fast as I could.

It wasn't that we didn't want Mother to go along, but she seemed to want to be attached at the hip, never wanting anyone to do anything without her. Of course, I felt guilty! But we had fun, just the three of us, looking all over the millions of Indian things for sale. I bought Monte a tomtom and Larry a tomahawk, both decorated with paint and feathers, which they kept on their dressers for many years.

"I guess we better go back," I said, thinking it had been so nice to be with my boys alone.

"Couldn't we get an ice cream cone?" Monte asked. "No, we better not take the time," I said. I was feeling real guilty by then. "We've been gone a long time."

When we went into the house, Mother was right there!

"Where did you go?" she asked.

"We just went down to the Indian Teepee," I said, sheepishly.

"I wanted to go there! I haven't been there for years!" she said.

Talk about feeling guilty! After that, Mother went everywhere we went.

She was never any problem. Always kind and gentle, always ready to do anything we wanted to do, oftentimes suggesting places to go, and things to do! My Mom was a wonderful person, never arguing, always trying to keep people interested. She could be a very quiet person, or do anything anyone else wanted to do. I would guess I got all my habits, good and bad, from my Mother. That's not so bad, is it?

One time when we went to Mother's in West Hollywood, we took a ride on the racetrack at Hialeah, in a horse drawn surrey, with fringe on the top. It had poured down rain so the track was muddy and slippery, but it was a wonderful ride as we could clearly see the most beautiful bird in Florida, the pink colored flamingo. There were twenty-five or thirty tall flamingos on spindly legs, in the center of the track, moving about.

The boys were delighted, as we all were, riding on the track and watching the flamingos strut themselves, showing off.

One time later, when we were visiting Mother in West Hollywood, we drove through beautiful Hollywood Hills, to return home after being downtown.

"This is a nice section of Hollywood, Mother," I said.

"Yes, it is," she replied with a great deal of interest.

"You ought to buy a house here. That is, if you plan on coming down to Florida every winter," I said.

After Dad died she had gone from her mobile home in Royal Palm Park, Hallandale, to the house Charley built in West Hollywood. It was a nice home, but was not in the best area of town. We were afraid of leaving her by herself, even though Ann, my sister, and her husband Connie, would go down for a month or two in the winter and Milt, my brother, sometimes lived with her.

"This is a pretty home," I said.

"Yes, it is," Mother agreed.

"Want to stop and see it?" I said.

"Yes, let's do!" Mother said.

George stopped and we looked at the house. The sign had been outside saying it was open. It was a lovely three bedroom, two bath home, with a circular drive in front and a sunken living room. We all fell in love with it.

Mother bought it and lived there until two and a half years before she died, when we took her to Naples to a care center near us.

George's brother Joe had fallen in love with a petite, black haired, beauty with blue eyes, Virginia Ross, daughter of A. L. and Anne Ross. She was everything we would have wanted for Joe. They had a lovely wedding, on March 28, 1954, with George as best man, and I pouring punch with George and Joe's Aunt Sudie, at the refreshment table at the reception. Ginny, as we called her, was a vision of loveliness, in white satin and lace, with a long sheer lace veil over her face, to be folded up over her beautiful black hair.

After the honeymoon they went back to the large home Joe had bought in the north end of Danville.

They later moved to Peoria, then to Pekin, Illinois, where he went to further his career in his chosen field of retail furniture sales and interior decorating. We visited them quite a lot, and they, in turn, came to Ohio a lot.

Chapter 16

Our Trip East,

and Looking for a New Home

We asked Mother to go camping with us one summer. We were going to the East and knew she would like to go back to visit her mother's ancestral home. We knew it would be crowded in our car but felt we could manage.

Mother had always done wonders with old fur coats, that Aunt Pauline had given her, when she bought new ones. The beautiful soft furs, and the gorgeous twenties dresses, she worked over for herself, were the best in our community. She always looked stylish, except for her long hair. Then when she cut that, and wore it with a flair, I thought she was the best looking mother around.

So, when we decided to make the trip East, I was not surprised when she walked out, with a fur, to our packed overloaded car.

"What is that?" I asked her.

"It's my fur," she said.

"Why did you bring your fur stole, Mother? It will be too hot to wear," I said.

"I thought it might get colder and then I could wear it," she said.

"Where will we put it? There is no room! We are overloaded now, with camping gear, and our clothes and things!" I reasoned.

"I'll hold it on my lap," she said.

This beautiful cape probably was the only fur piece she had ever bought herself, although she, in the past, had had all kinds of beautiful long coats, stoles, and fur pieces to go around her neck. At one time she had a gorgeous fur piece of a full sized red fox, including head, legs, and fluffy fat tail.

Mother held the fur stole on her lap the first day. We tried to find another place to put it, as it was too hot. The next day, after we broke camp, I noticed she didn't have it on her lap.

"Mother, where is your fur piece?" I asked in an alarmed voice, thinking it might have been left at the campsite. I was looking everywhere for it.

"I'm sitting on it," she said.

We laughed but I'm sure it must have been uncomfortable and hot. It must have been better than holding it, as she continued sitting on it. She never got to use it, as the heat stayed with us.

There were lots of places to visit everywhere, and with Mother guiding us, we saw so much we wouldn't have, if we had gone by ourselves without her.

"Your Mother knows more about our family affairs than I do," Cousin Emma Engle said when we stayed with her for a few days, at Clarksboro, New Jersey. She was amazed that Mother knew so much.

Cousin Emma took us to see her/our relatives about a mile or so down the road in the little village of Mickleton.

The large, beautiful main house was nestled in formal shrubbery and huge old trees. We stood at the front door, as Emma knocked, chatting away.

"Hello, Cousin Amos, look who I have brought to see thee. Our cousin from the West, Georgia Mendenhall," Emma said to Amos and his beautiful wife. "They are staying with me for a few days."

We were warmly welcomed, and a lively, interesting time was had. Mother and they talked of the past, which was always interesting to me, to hear stories of our Quaker family heritage.

Cousin Emma showed us all around their home and grounds. Everything was beautiful. I was surprised at their taking all rugs, mostly oriental, up in the summertime to be professionally cleaned and put back down in the fall for winter. We walked around on beautifully polished wooden floors, on which area rugs were thrown.

We were to go back to visit Cousin Emma and her cousins, the year after Mother passed away, and we felt her presence with us everywhere we went.

Emma took us outside and showed us the huge grounds of the estate. We strolled among the gardens and saw the well groomed Boxwood, which seemed to be a favorite of everyone in this little town, and huge old Oak and Maple trees.

We walked down the path to their guest house, outside of which were several well kept tennis courts. We saw Amos' office and den, in a separate building, in which many famous people had visited and been entertained by him, both socially and for business.

Walking across the lawns, we came to their private airplane hanger where Amos' airplane was kept. Right outside was a monument, brought back from Europe by Amos, to commemorate a famous event.

We walked back past the beautiful low barns where sheep were contentedly grazing on the barnyard grass.

We crossed the road to a house where Amos' son lived. He was a famous professional photographer, who had just arrived home that day from a trip to Africa, where he had taken photographs for a car commercial, for television.

We visited their horse barns where they kept beautiful riding horses. Larry and I wanted to ride, but it was too near dinner time. They had us for dinner that evening.

Amos, who was a lawyer, had become a millionaire, on one case for the government, following World War One, which required him to cross the Atlantic twenty-two times. It took years to settle.

That night we slept in Cousin Emma's delightful old huge house, going up the long wide stairway to our high four poster bed.

The next day as we entered the front door of Cousin Amos' house, his wife said, "Well, look who's here!"

"Yes," I said, "We came back to see you."

I was chagrined when she quickly said something nice about that, then continued talking in an excited way, looking past us.

THEN AND NOW

"When did you get back?" she said to her son who had come in behind us. "I didn't know you were home! When did you get back?"

It was obvious he had just arrived home to host our dinner last night, and must have been too tired to call his folks. I felt guilty for keeping his folks in the dark about his return.

Afterwards we all went outside to the lovely backyard, where, of all the incongruous things, there was a large beautiful hammock!

"Oh, you have a beautiful hammock," I said, "May I sit in it?"

"Of course! Amos bring out some chairs, and we'll sit out here and talk," his wife said.

That was the most beautiful, comfortable hammock I have ever swung in. We stayed there for tea in the afternoon, while the kids and I monopolized the hammock.

The next day, we drove down to Salem, where my grandmother, Sallie Waddington Mendenhall, had been born, and lived all of her life, until she went west to visit her Uncle Wil and Aunt Emma Vanneman. We visited the beautiful Quaker Church in downtown Salem, where she and her family attended, then went on down Main Street to the beautiful brick walled Quaker burying grounds, where we found Grandmother's family buried. We stood underneath the huge Salem Oak tree were they were buried. Under this same oak tree, a few feet from our families graves, John Fenwick stood, when the peace treaty was made with the Indians in 1675, and he established a new homeland for the Quakers and named it Salem, meaning Peace. It was also known as Fenwick's Colony.

Then we drove past the large two story Waddington town house, and several miles down the country road, to the farmhouse where Grandma and her siblings had been born and raised. As we turned down the lane, to our left was a huge barn, still in excellent condition. Continuing down the lane, we found the beautiful, tall, and splendid, old fashioned farm house in a setting among huge old trees and neatly kept Boxwood.

Aunt Jennie met us at the door, so happy to see us all. As she and Mother turned to the right to go into the front room, I asked, "Where was Grandma's room?"

"Upstairs, to the right," she said. "She and I slept in the same room." As it looked to her that I wanted to go up there first, she continued, "Yes, do go on up. Just turn to the right of the stairway, and it's the room on the left."

I couldn't wait! I could hardly feel the steps, as I bounded upstairs, with my two little boys right beside me. We almost fell over one another, trying to get there.

As I stood at the door, I felt I was on sacred ground! My beloved Grandmother lived and slept and studied in this room! She told her sisters her secret thoughts. Oh, how I wished I could turn back the clock, and listen, and watch! It was still an old fashioned room, holding all those memories. I was much more subdued as we went downstairs, to join the rest of the family.

We drove south out of Salem, along the scenic route, to Hancock Bridge, site of the 20 March 1778 massacre, of a group of about thirty local patriots, by the British, at Hancock House. This home was built in 1734 by William Hancock, son of John Hancock, who emigrated from England in 1679, and Elizabeth Champnes Hancock, my lineal ancestors. The men were stationed there to watch over the nearby bridge.

The house provides an outstanding example of ornamental brickwork peculiar to early manor houses of Salem County. It is famous for the zig-zag striped brick pattern, of laying the bricks, and the initials of the owners, WHS, William and Sarah Hancock. The area is steeped in history of resistance to the British.

We drove to New York City to see the sights. We saw the fabulous skyline as we approached, and could see the Empire State Building, which we planned as a stop. We had traveled the New Jersey turnpike and passed through Newark and entered New York through the Holland Tunnel. We walked around Battery Park at the tip of Manhattan Island looking out on the bay.

Then we drove to Times Square and the shopping district, seeing the sights along the way. We were fortunate in finding a parking space one block from the Empire State Building. It was right near the corner of a busy street. We all traipsed up the street and went as high as we could in the elevator to the very top. What a wonderful sight. It was like being on top of the world. It was fabulous. Every one of us was impressed.

We came down out of the elevator, and to the street, happy but tired. It was getting late in the afternoon, and time for us to hit the road out of New York City.

"Look!" I said. "That looks like our car out there in the middle of the street!" Disbelieving my eyes, all shook up, I looked over at George.

"It does look like it!" he said.

"It can't be!" I said. "What would it be doing out there!" I cried, almost hysterically.

We all ran down the street, to the intersection. A policeman was directing traffic around our car. George ran over to the policeman and started talking to him.

"I believe that's our car!" he said. "What's it doing out there?" he asked!

"This is your car?" the policeman yelled above the traffic. "Well, move it out! I've sent for a wrecker to pick it up. I found it out there where it had rolled."

George got us all in the car, then noticed a note under the windshield wiper, to come to a precinct Police Station to find out what had happened, it said, because as the car rolled away it scraped a passing car.

Evidently, George had left the brake off, and the car out of gear, as it had crawled down the street, going a little into the line of traffic.

We were mortified! How in the world could this ever have happened.

At the precinct Police Station, they told George our car had grazed a car in traffic as it rolled away from the curb. The owner of the car it grazed said it did little damage, as his car was old, and he would not prefer charges.

So, other than a little scolding, so it wouldn't happen again, they sent George on his way. They had been very kind actually for the trouble it caused them. They did not issue a ticket or fine. George thought it was because we were travelers. We were so late in leaving we had to search immediately for a motel.

We took the Pennsylvania Turnpike to return home so, we took a side trip to Lancaster, Pennsylvania, where we stopped at Seven Sweets and Seven Sours to eat dinner. It was a fabulous, fantastic layout of food. It was smorgasbord, and all of us filled our plates more than once.

For desert there were many selections, but behind my seat was a refrigerator full of small cups of ice cream. Monte and I leaned over the refrigerator contemplating which flavor to eat. The first bite told us it was the smoothest, most delicious ice cream we had ever eaten. The rest of the family ate pies, cakes, other things, but Monte and I kept eating this ice cream.

I can't believe I ate eight little (they were little!) ice creams but Monte continued. He really was not a big eater of regular food, so I let him fill up on the ice cream.

"Want another one, Monte?" I asked, and as he sheepishly nodded his head yes, I reached back of me and took another one for him. I didn't even have to get up. They made it too easy! He ate his fifteenth ice cream. We all waddled out.

Years later George and I couldn't wait until we came to Lancaster, and arrived at our fantastic dining room, only to find it moved and changed. It was more elegant and much larger but still a good place to eat. It is called Miller's now. We ate so much we were not sure of desert. Our waitress came over and tried to talk us into desert.

"How about a piece of Pekin Pie?" she asked.

"Pekin Pie," I said. "What is that? I never heard of Pekin Pie." Joe and Ginny, George's brother and wife lived in Pekin, Illinois, at this time, so I thought it must be named because of Pekin, Illinois.

"I'll warm it for you. It's better that way," the waitress said. When she brought it heated to us, it was the best pie we had ever tasted.

"It must be pecan pie," I mused. "It is so different than I ever tasted, though!" We loved it, but have often laughed at our not catching her accent and knowing that pecan can, and is, pronounced several ways. This pecan pie had chocolate bits in it which, when heated, melted over and into the more or less regular pecan pie, George's favorite pie.

Dad had wanted a Cadillac for years, finally getting one a year or so before he died. He had had big touring cars, heavy Hudsons and Packards, but he always wanted a Cadillac. It was his pride and joy. He finally had his Cadillac! We all envied him.

Mother never drove the cars. Very few times did she get behind the wheel. After Dad died, Ann came home from Indianapolis, to live with and take care of her. Ann took lessons to drive, as she had never driven, either. She was very particular about the car, never letting anyone else drive, and always washing the windshield before she got in the car to drive.

One fall, after the car was packed for their trip to Florida, she remembered she had not washed the windshield. She hurried back in the house to get the cleaning materials. When she came rushing out, she twisted her foot on the porch steps, breaking her ankle. That slowed them down on getting to Florida that year! It was a few months before she could drive that long trip.

Charley's and Helen's seven kids were staying on the farm in Illinois with Grandma and Aunt Ann, for awhile in 1956 or 1957. Dick recounted this story as to what happened when they were all sitting around, with nothing else to do.

"All my brothers and sisters and I talked Grandma into driving over to Uncle Rosie's house, and Aunt Ann had gone with friends somewhere, I don't know where she went. Anyway, we got tired of sitting around the house, so we talked Grandma into jumping in the 1951 Cadillac. She couldn't hardly see over the wheel, the steering wheel, well, she couldn't see over the steering wheel. We were sitting in the front seat, Mike and I, telling her to go left or right. We made it over there, and she just did all right," he said with a chuckle, "and then we got over to Uncle Rosie's. We never left there until Aunt Ann got home, and came over there and picked the car up and drove it back to the house."

"Was Ann mad at her?" I asked.

"Yes, Aunt Ann was madder than a wet hen about it all, but anyway, we went for a ride!" Dick said.

Chapter 17

Oakhaven and Art

"We're bursting at the seams!" I said to George, one day. "There isn't enough room anymore for all of us. The boys need a room of their own, and we need more closet space, and just more room!"

We looked on our own for awhile, then worked with real estate people. Nothing was right. For three years we looked, every free moment we had. It came to my knowing when we pulled in front of a house, whether I liked the house or not.

"I'm not even going inside," I would say. "I don't like the outside and I know I wouldn't want it, even if I liked the inside!"

One day in the summer of 1958, working as Bible School Director at our church, I heard two mothers talking. One, who owned and rented a beautiful log house about one block from where we lived, was complaining about not being able to sell the house. She knew we were looking for a house and said, "We have ours for sale. Why don't you come look at it?"

My eyes opened wide in astonishment. "We couldn't afford your house!" I said, "It would be way too much for us!"

"You never can tell. Why don't you come look at it?" She said.

It was a large, three bedroom log cabin, which I had always thought, was the most beautiful home in Crystal Lakes. A few months later, I was praying to God so hard for Him to help us! We needed more space! I prayed every waking moment, I think. It was constantly on my mind.

"Please God, help us find the perfect home, one that will care for all our needs. If it is pretty, that will be wonderful! But just help us find a house we can afford and one that we can love." I prayed.

One day soon thereafter, at five o'clock in the morning, I awoke with a start. My eyes flew open and I stared at the ceiling.

"Go see about the house on Oak Road!" A voice said inside me.

No! It couldn't be. We couldn't afford that beautiful place! I lay there tingling all over! I was wide awake. Why didn't George wake up? I lay there thinking, until I heard his first movement about seven o'clock.

"George!" I said, excitedly. "We must go over to the log house and see about buying it!"

"Oh, Kay, you know we can't afford anything like that! We don't make enough money to buy that place." He was getting into his clothes.

"George! I don't understand it, but it is very clear to me." I told him what happened to me two whole hours ago.

"I haven't been able to sleep. I think the Lord must have given us a message. Let's go see about it, at least!" I said. "Well, okay," he said slowly. "I'll call them."

I had prayed so long for us to find a place that satisfied all our needs. "Also," I would say, "if it's pretty, that's all right, too. But just let me know for sure!" I was so tired of looking and wondering if we could manage the price and arrangement of houses. I prayed I would know for sure!

The door opened and there stood the owners, the McFarlands.

"Come in," Mrs. McFarland said, as she stepped back from the door.

I took one step, looked around at the openness of the rooms, and stared at the beautiful stained shiny log beams. I couldn't move. It was gorgeous!

"This is it!" a small voice within me seemed to scream at me. "This is it!"

I felt a slight pressure on my back, and, realizing George was still hanging in the doorway, I moved into the room. He loved it, too! We were speechless.

The further I went, the more I loved it. It was perfect! Only one street over, but what a difference.

It was a log cabin, with the exterior\interior having the solid logs as the wall structure and the ceiling all open cathedral style. The walls dividing the inner sections were knotty ponderosa pine where the bedrooms and bath were.

We entered the large living room, with its beautiful brick fireplace on the left side of the room from the entrance door, and the hallway to the master bedroom just beyond the side of the fireplace. It was a very large room with high windows on two sides. This room had been added onto the cabin later, and it enhanced the rest of the house with its large area, and closets. There was a large picture window overlooking the lovely back yard.

The two smaller bedrooms were straight ahead from the front entrance, with the bathroom situated between them and the master bedroom. A back door went out the bathroom to the backyard enclosed with a six foot split stockade fence.

At the right of the entrance was the dining room, then the very compact kitchen, through which we went from a landing to the full basement or outdoors where there was a free standing garage of logs. The whole front and side of the yard was surrounded by a split two rail fence of chestnut.

It was perfect! Absolutely the most beautiful home in the world, with everything included that I had wanted. Why hadn't I prayed so strongly for it years ago? Thank you, God! There were private rooms for the boys. Larry chose the smaller bedroom with the two windows, while Monte got the larger bedroom with only one window. George and I were so happy with our huge bedroom. We all loved our "Oakhaven," as we named it.

The price was right, and they bought our smaller Pinecrest, to rent out. The people who were renting Oakhaven, moved to our Pinecrest, the same day we moved to Oakhaven.

It was a bright, sunny, November day when we moved. Many of our friends had offered to help us move, and we gladly accepted. I stayed at

Pinecrest to help engineer our moving out while George commanded the Oakhaven operation. There were times when some would collide with others, but those times were few, and laughingly corrected. It was a big undertaking, moving from Pinecrest to Oakhaven at the same time as the tenants were moving from Oakhaven to Pinecrest.

I told George every place I wanted our things. When I found the time to go over there, I was amazed to see that everything was in its proper niche!

We worked hard, but with planning and cooperation, it was a breeze, thanks to our many friends. Finally, after three years looking, we moved from a far too small home, to the most beautiful home in the world. Thank you God!

After we settled in following our move to Oakhaven, my interests in art accelerated. There were so many things to do.

We went to Yellow Springs where the artistic Antioch College is, and met some interesting people. Yellow Springs itself was a delightful arty town, with its college kids doing great things in all media. Allan MacBeth maintained a consignment outlet for their works in his home, which was right in downtown Yellow Springs. He later expanded his home to include a coffee shop.

When George took a course in sculpture from Allan, using Monte as his model, he made a fantastic bust. The bust of Monte was well done, George having utilized the sculpture methods Allan taught, which included use of wire armature and other procedures.

George, Monte and I would go to his interesting unique home, and absorb his way of living, activities and mind. We talked art for hours while he helped George with Monte's bust. He would pop a big pan of popcorn to perfection in a pressure cooker, and when we ate it, the huge, crisp kernels would melt in our mouths. It took George the whole ten lessons to finish the bust, but it was a learning experience for all three of us.

George later took pottery classes from Cindy Metcalf of Yellow Springs, learning much about pottery, concentrating mostly on throwing both on the electric and kick wheels. She implanted enthusiasm in George with her teaching methods and superb skill with clay. She was graduated from Alfred University and taught at Antioch College. Her father was a famous stained glass window artist. This enthusiasm for pottery has forever remained steadfast in his future artistic endeavors.

As I became more involved in art, my table easel was too restrictive. George bought me a large, strongly constructed standing easel. It was so much easier to paint with it! I could paint so fast and accomplish a lot more. My body would move from area to area, my mind and hand keeping pace.

After I saw the boys off to school, I would redd up the dishes and quickly make up the beds, then stand in our master bedroom, catching the best light, and paint from the moment the boys left for school until they returned home in the afternoon. It was so exhilarating. I could hardly wait to get started.

At noon time, I always had a picture well started to view and study while I ate my lunch. I would eat half a cheese sandwich and drink a glass of milk. By the time I finished eating and studying my picture, which I would prop against a chair in the living room, I was ready to rush back to my easel and finish my picture.

By the time the boys would come home from school, I would have a painting about finished. They would come into the bedroom, sit on the edge of the bed, and watch as I would be nearing completion of a new picture. They seemed to be as interested as I in how my paintings were developing.

"Mother, could I have your left over paints, when you are finished?" Monte asked me one afternoon.

"Sure! Then I won't have to clean them up and save them," I said, happy to have them used.

That first painting Monte did was entered in the Dayton Montgomery County Fair that fall, and won first prize in its children's category.

The next afternoon Larry asked for the leftover paints. So both boys became good artists, using up my daily leftover paints. They both did very well, and I was as pleased as punch.

George didn't want to be the odd man out, so he got into the act. His first painting was made, standing back of me while I was painting a picture of our house. He painted quite a good picture of me standing in front of my easel, with my ever present Herze, our Dachshund at my feet, and our log house for the background.

THEN AND NOW

George never actually finished his only painting he ever made, which might have won an award on the international art scene, as the paintings in exhibits there were painted in this manner. The artist whose painting received the first award, in my first exhibit, was painted in this fashion. George painted all over the canvas, as I taught him, but he just never put on the finishing touches, as we were taught to do.

Larry painted an Indian when I was in my Indian phase, that was excellent. Joe wanted one of my Indians, so I let him choose. Of course he chose the one I liked best. I hated to see it go to Illinois when he and Ginny took it home with them.

I joined the Dayton Art Institute and learned on a higher level. I constantly poured over their exhibits, and went to all their shows. When they had a fall exhibit and show, where they sold art work, I went with all my best paintings and ceramics. All my ceramics sold, but not my paintings. Some people didn't sell anything. Even then, when abstract paintings were taking over the whole world, they didn't go over in Dayton. One never knows what others want. That is why I paint for myself. I will not, nor have I ever, painted for anyone what he wants. He has to buy what I do from my soul. This is why I haven't become famous, I'm sure. I paint for myself! And if anyone wants to buy what they see, I'll sell. I have sold about one hundred paintings or so, altogether.

Now the art world is different. Your whole life is colored by some kind of art. You want to do it all. When you hear of something, new you've never heard or read about, you have to get involved in that, too. Fortunately, my husband was just as interested in the art world as I was. Even the boys painted and made ceramics.

We entered all the art shows, winning many ribbons, entered our art in the fairs, where we won hands down, and even stopped along the highways, and byways, any time we saw a display of art work. We attended anything suggesting art.

One such exhibit was on the west side of Dayton, at the George Washington Carver Center. It was black art, absolutely fabulous. I wanted so desperately to buy one particular picture, of five or six black people, in a swirl of black and gray, and muted colors.

At the time we hesitated because of the price, but it was a magnificent picture of pure art.

My favorite of all the art shows we attended was the fantastic Chrysler Exhibit at the Cincinnati Museum of Art. It gave me the biggest thrill of any show I have ever seen. My artistic bent is abstract art, so not until we moved into the huge room of abstract paintings did I go into a trance. The other rooms were great, but when we entered the room with a collection of abstract work I was thrilled with the whole collection. I was taking a long time looking at all the abstracts.

Then I turned and saw pictures of Jesus, and I became immobilized! I could hardly move. It was so fantastic! I loved every one I saw. But when I stood in front of one portrait of Jesus, I could move no more. It sank into my very soul. The look of Jesus, saying, "Why?" broke me up. Tears began to trickle down my face. I was right there with Him, as he was carrying His cross to Calvary Hill, and I, too, was asking, "Why?" I told George and the boys to go on, but I stayed near Jesus.

I sobbed and sobbed, for what my Jesus had to go through. I saw it all! More vividly through this great picture, than I had ever seen it before. What had we done?

It was not a large picture, but the pain and compassion in Jesus' face was overwhelming. Tears glistened in his eyes but did not flow down his face. He was looking upwards towards His Father in Heaven. He was holding a cross in front of his chest. It was a heartbreaking picture that seared my very soul.

The room was so crowded with people, the heat and humidity was so high, my tears melded with the sweat. The anguish on my face, must have mirrored the agony and torment on Jesus' face and in His eyes, as I stood in front of Him.

When I finally was able to move on, I found George and the boys in the impressionists room of Monet's pictures. This was a perfect place to regain my composure. His Water Lilies were so serene and beautiful! I looked at all his lovely, soft, gentle paintings and thought of Jesus. It was as if I were in a real garden where I could contemplate the past and get ready for the future.

One time when I was going through a red, black, and white period, a good friend of Larry's, John Gunning, had bought several for his home. He and his wife had come again to see what else I had done in those colors. He was attending the University of Michigan at Ann Arbor, and had come home on one of his visits to see his mother, a good friend of ours. He and his wife were sitting on the sofa as I was showing them my paintings. He began to show a great deal of interest in one of them. It was a concentrated red, black, and white painting that was my favorite.

"It's God," I said. He looked surprised. I started explaining what I saw in it. "Now when I make an abstract, I don't think, this will be God, or anything else. It just evolves. This is His head at the top, and He has his arms and hands held at the sides of the picture, to the whole world, saying, "Come unto Me!"

John looked perplexed. I hurried on, as I could see he was not liking what I said.

"This is the world, and down here are all the people, that God has made," I explained.

"Well, you spoiled it now!" John said. "I was going to buy it, but now I don't want it."

"I know John, that's why I told you," I said quietly. They left soon thereafter.

"Mother, can I have that picture?" Larry asked, as he stood entranced, in front of it, after they left.

"Yes!" I exclaimed. "Of course, you can!" I was so pleased that he wanted it. He saw in it what I saw. Larry has loved that picture as much as I have, and he has always given it a prominent place in his home.

Chapter 18
More Art and Fun
and a New Home

"Let's go by Pinecrest and see how it looks," I said, a few weeks after we had moved.

As we drew close to the house, I was very excited. I loved that little house, we had done a lot of living there.

"Look! They've torn down our lovely window boxes you made! Why in the world would they do that!" I exclaimed. When we left, they had been full of huge, lovely, flowering blossoms that trailed down on the outside.

"And look!" I cried, "They have taken down our gorgeous wisteria!" It had taken years to grow, and had been thick with gorgeous foot long blossoms with a fragrant scent that permeated the air. I was sick! I had wanted to take some roots to start my plants at Oakhaven, but George said that wouldn't be the right thing to do.

Then I got a glimpse of the hedge, which had been full and beautiful. It had all been trimmed out, showing the whole root system a couple of feet above the ground. I became very quiet as the car moved slowly past the house.

"It doesn't look a thing like our homey little house," I said as we continued down the road. "I do kind of like the way she trimmed up the hedge. I've never seen anything like that," I begrudgingly said. "It looks kind of like the boxwood back in New Jersey."

"I wonder what she did to the inside," I said.

"I don't want to go down that road again," I said. It was years before I wanted to look at my little house again.

The Cub Scouts needed a new leader. They were about to fold, so I said I would take them. There were only five, but more started coming, until I had a basement full of boys. They were pretty good, but there were three boys, all brothers, who liked to play and fight together, always wrestling with one another. One day I had had enough!

"Hey, you guys! You want to fight?" I had caught their attention.

"Do you want to go outside and work this out?" I asked again.

"Yeah, yeah, yeah!" they looked excited.

"You can go outside and get it out of your system! Hurry!" I said. They were all smiles, getting up and jumping up the steps, pulling at the bannister, and jerking side to side, rushing up towards the door to go outside. They were all elated, happy and excited!

As I turned back towards the rest of the kids, all were staring at me in anticipation. They expected me to say, "Let's go watch them!" I didn't.

"Let's continue with what we were doing. They can come back when they are through," I said. When they came back sheepishly, a few minutes later, we all looked up.

"Are you through now? Come and get started on your work here," I said, trying not to smile. Those kids never gave me much trouble, after that. They turned out to be pretty good kids, after all!

Monte loved Cub Scouts, but after he joined the Boy Scouts, he lost interest after awhile. Larry continued from Cub Scouts into Boy Scouts and found it rewarding and a great pleasure. Their Boy Scout leader was Harry Stuck, from Medway.

Harry had a way with the boys that was excellent. He seemed like one of the boys, but at the same time, he was able to lead them through an education of knowledge and skills of scouting and life. The scouts went on many named, designated, trails and overnight outings and George and I were always among the supporters.

"Why do you always go with us wherever we go?" Larry asked.

"We always go with you because someone has to be with you, and not too many people want to do it," I said. I didn't tell him we always looked forward to it and jumped at the chance to go.

One day in the hot summertime, we drove in a caravan to Kentucky to beautiful rolling hills near Lexington. The boys walked up and down the winding roads for twenty miles, as we drove in our cars past them and down the road to their destination, which was at the top of a hill where a beautiful house had been burned and was in complete destruction. The boys straggled up the hill and fell down in the green, soothing grass and just lay there immobile, with sweat and sometimes tears, I think. We felt our hearts go out to them. We were plenty hot too, but there was the wonderfully cool breeze on the hill where we were.

The boys finally came to life and began to perk up. We gathered them into our cars and took them back to camp. Twenty miles was the longest walk they had ever done. They received a medal and ribbon to wear on their uniforms for each trail completed.

Although Larry did accomplish a lot in scouting, he fell short of the highest honor of being an Eagle Scout, on which we really encouraged him. Only one percent of scouts manage to achieve this coveted award.

When we took our summer vacation one year, we went on a camping trip to Bagnell Dam, on the Lake of The Ozarks, in Missouri. We drove our 1955 Buick, four holer, as we called it, due to the four holes on each side of the hood.

Near Bagnell Dam was a sort of a tourist attraction with all kinds of things to see and do. There was a place called Dogpatch, like Li'l Abner. It had an old outside bar, complete with jugs and bottles of fake booze, an old jail, and an old outside privy. When I opened the door, I let out a scream, as there in plain sight was an overall clad figure, with his pants down, sitting on one of the two holers. The scene was so real!

While there at Bagnell Dam, we visited a dude ranch, complete with a hay ride, and a wiener roast afterwards. From Bagnell Dam we took a side trip to Meramec Caverns, which were pretty nice, but mostly noted for having, at one time, been Jesse James' hideout.

My sister, Anna Rose, told us about this famous eating place, Virginia McDonald's Tea Room in Gallatin, Missouri, recommended by Duncan Hines. So, we drove an extra one hundred miles to eat there, and we bought her cook book which she autographed for us.

This trip we took Herze with us, so not wanting to miss a thing, he sat in the middle of the boys upright, with his back against the back seat, and his front paws hanging in front of him, turning his head side to side to look out the windows, just as the boys did, to see the flowing wheat fields, and other passing vistas.

We were driving back to the main highway, enjoying the countryside, when George said, "I'm hungry! What do we have to eat?"

"All we have are bread and potato chips," I said, after thinking about it for awhile, "Do you want a potato chip sandwich?" I asked, laughing.

George thought a few moments. "Yeah! Make me a potato chip sandwich! I'm starved!" The kids and I laughed and hooted.

"Who ever heard of a potato chip sandwich?" we asked. But he insisted, so I made it.

"How is it?" I asked after he took his first bite.

"It's not bad!" George said, while the rest of us laughed.

"Why don't you have one?" He asked.

The boys and I hooted at him. "No way!"

"All you need to do now is crow like a rooster," I said.

"Cock-a-doodle-do!" he crowed, before his next bite, as we drove down the empty highway. We laughed.

The sunshine was on him, and as he ate the sandwich and I watched him take big bites and imagined what it tasted like.

When he crowed, the sun shone on his face and mouth, as he opened his mouth to crow. It was a picture I'll never forget. It was as though I was watching a movie with an eerie light shining on a man eating a bulky potato chip sandwich, driving down the highway crowing.

We had such fun that year on that camping trip.

We were stuck on Buicks. We traded every two or three years, always second hand cars, until we decided it was time for us to get a brand new car.

"All of us get a say as to what color we want," I said as I looked at a brochure. My pick was a gorgeous soft orangish looking color, with soft delicate leather, tannish, orangish seats. It was a convertible, which we all wanted.

"Where is the one that is like the picture?" I asked, as we had looked for a long time and couldn't find it anywhere, when we went to New Carlisle, where we had bought cars for several years.

Oh, it doesn't come in that color. That's just the lighting by the photographer, the salesman laughed.

I couldn't believe it! It was a trick. Why in the world would anyone put a picture of a car in a brochure that wasn't even for sale!

"Well, that's the one I wanted!" I told the family. "I guess I won't get it. So what's your choices?"

"It only comes in white, black, or red," the salesman interjected into our discussions as to what our choices were. We were all nonplused! Red, white or black! Who wanted any of those colors?

After talking over amongst the four of us, we agreed on a red bottom, black interior and white top which was usually down. It was really snazzy! A sharp car!

On the Fourth of July, in 1967, when Monte was 17, we received an urgent call from a hospital in New Liskeard, Ontario, Canada saying we needed to come for our son Monte as he was stranded there. Monte's friend, an elderly furnace man from Ashland, Ohio, whom Monte was assisting on a job, had a heart attack at the lake where they had gone on a fishing trip for walleyes. White Lake, an H shaped lake, was approximately 200 miles west of New Liskeard, the closest hospital where he was admitted. They told us Monte was fine, but would be better off at home as there were no facilities to take care of him. He was in good hands being entertained by the volunteer candy striper girls working about the hospital. These girls were needed to fulfill their duties helping the nurses.

So, we rushed about and packed to go to New Liskeard, Ontario, Canada on a moments notice. From home at Crystal Lakes, Ohio we drove north to Toledo, Ohio then on to Detroit, Michigan. We entered Canada at Windsor, Ontario and picked up highway 401, the Queen's way, for Toronto, about 250 miles. We drove fast to keep with the bumper to bumper traffic flow, 60 to 70 mph. George became tired and sleepy so went to sleep in the back seat while I kept up that horrible pace toward Toronto. During a lull in the highway traffic one guy even flirted with me since he probably supposed I was driving alone. As we neared Toronto a radio announcer came on appealing for anyone to come into the city as he was lonesome. He said the city had emptied out as everyone was headed somewhere else to celebrate their great holiday, Dominion Day, similar to and on the same day as our 4th of July. Anyway, we didn't take him up on it as we turned north through miles and miles of countryside, with lakes, forests, bridges and highway, past Barrie, Bracebridge, Huntsville, and North Bay and on to New Liskeard, the northern edge of where the watershed reverses and flows north to Hudson Bay, instead of to the great lakes.

We found Monte having a fabulous time and his friend in intensive care. So we visited a local eatery and gathered up Monte after he said his good byes and headed for home after seeing some of the local sights. (A few weeks later his friend was flown home to Ashland, Ohio.) As we left New Liskeard behind, and in areas where there was little traffic, George allowed Monte and me to sit on the folded down top, and dangle our feet in the back seat.

We traveled many miles sitting in this position. It was marvelous, sitting so high and looking around at all the wild flowers and beautiful countryside.

Monte later became a great outdoors man, taking gorgeous pictures of wild flowers, and the outdoors, which he dearly loved.

We drove back to North Bay and headed west for an alternate route for the return trip. We stopped off in Sudbury, Ontario, 78 miles from North Bay. It is a mining town supplying 4/5 ths of the nickel to the world. Also available from the area is copper, gold, silver, platinum and other minerals. We drove to an area where we could get a great picture of a huge nickel coin mounted high in the air on a hillside.

Driving on we reached Sault Ste. Marie where we turned south crossing the upper peninsula of Michigan to The Mackinac bridge which we crossed. We stayed on I75 and stopped in Royal Oaks in north Detroit to look up Wil Adair, an army buddy of George's, having served together with the 34th Machine Records Unit in the

Philippines. We had a nice visit, with them insisting we stay over night with them. We begged off and continued on to our home north of Dayton, Ohio at Crystal Lakes. We had covered a lot of mileage.

There was always suspect in the judging of any art exhibit in which I participated, or was merely a viewer. Why did that picture win when this picture didn't? Study them as I might, sometimes I could not understand the judges choices.

Most teachers will not judge their own students, rightfully so. A teacher knows who is the best overall student, the one that gives his or her best efforts, and who is inconsistently the best and hardest worker. But, I think, the judges are often prejudiced towards, or against, a certain way of painting. I never want to be a judge. It has to be the worst position in which to be.

One summer, I decided to have a class of art students. So many young girls in our area wanted to learn more about art, so we went to the basement, and gathered around the huge long Cub Scout table, which was our pool table covered up with a table tennis top.

This group of students produced so many excellent paintings, that when we had our exhibit at the end of the summer, I asked my friend, Pauline Marras, to be our judge. She was an excellent artist from Dayton, a very good friend, and an excellent judge.

The day of the exhibit, the paintings were all arranged beautifully under the shade trees in our front yard. The sun shined through the trees above the paintings. All the students and their parents came for the exhibit. Polly, as I called her, arrived late for the judging, then she and I walked around looking at the paintings. I agreed with all her choices for winning, except for the coveted first award, the best of show. She wanted the first ribbon to go to a painting that was done by a girl who traced her work.

This one shows so much talent, and is done so well!" I said, about another picture which I thought was better, trying to get her to change her mind.

"Yes," said Polly, "that is very nicely done. I was thinking of that one for first," she said. It was a beautiful picture, so well done with excellent workmanship. It was definitely my choice, from the beginning. The artist had done well all during our classes.

"But look at this one!" Polly said, as we walked over to the beautiful picture of another student. Look at the ripples in the horse's legs and body. It was a picture of a horse very nicely done.

"Yes, they are done well, but the horse itself was traced, not drawn by hand. I would have disqualified her immediately because she had not drawn the horse herself." I said.

Polly looked at it quietly for a few minutes, while we all waited. The judging should have been done before they came! But everyone was standing around, waiting and listening.

"I have to go with the horse picture. It is so well done!" Polly finally said. She was the judge! But the other girl and I were so disappointed I wanted to give both girls a blue ribbon, but I had only one to give. Polly finished judging, then left, as she and Pete had to go somewhere.

"I was hoping you would stay and talk to my girls, and have some refreshments with us!" I said to Polly when she said they had to leave.

"I wish I could," she said, "but we are late now. I didn't realize you had so many paintings in the show."

"I had hoped," I said, "that you would stay and give my girls a critique of their pictures! They need a different perspective than just my ideas." But they had to leave. I had to do the critiquing.

My girls had all done so well, and were so happy that summer, that several of their mothers asked me to have a class for them. I was flattered, but told them perhaps next summer. Teaching isn't easy, when you, yourself, want to paint. It took so much out of me, although I loved the girls and their response to painting, but I didn't get to paint enough myself.

Martha Fitzgerald Yowler's life paralleled mine, although at different times. When I was home painting, she was head librarian at WPAFB, where I would later work, at the Technical Library, after she retired and became an artist, during the time I had started working back at the base. Our lives were intertwined, from the moment of our meeting, as our lives were so full of the same interests.

She was a wonderful person, with a great deal of savvy, and one whom I have loved from the first time I met her, not to mention the gorgeous deep dimples in her cheeks! Why do I have such a fascination with dimples? As she talks they flash in and out, and when she laughs, they become stationary for awhile! She was a lovely person, inside and out.

Her attitude in life is to live and let live, with never a condemnation of anyone. A lovely, lovely lady, whom I dearly loved. (Martha passed away in 1999.)

Our favorite friends of all the WPAFB officers and their wives were Captain Bill and Kay Smith. They had two girls, Anne and Sue, about the same ages as our two boys, and we all got along fine, we were so close. They decided to move back to the base officer's quarters, from their home at Crystal Lakes, but we continued our friendship.

We were invited to dances, parties, and even were allowed to go to their Ceramic Workshop, as guests. We learned how to pour ceramics, and how to glaze. But, the really fun activity was to work on the potter's wheel. George was really good at the wheel, making all kinds of things.

The same winter that we learned to work on the wheel, Mother was taking lessons in Florida, learning how to hand mold gorgeous flowers, and making pitchers and boxes, with the coil method. When she came home, and told us about it, we were so thrilled that we taught one another what we had learned. It was fun! Neither one of us had known the other was embarking on a new extension of life. George and I bought a small kiln, and put in the basement, then we bought a bigger and better kiln later.

One time when visiting Kay and Bill Smith, we met Nancy and Harold Ashenfelter, the later being Larry's band leader when he was in Olive Branch Junior High School. They were lots of fun, and our meeting turned into a strong friendship.

Nancy was a blonde, pert faced German girl, and Harold was a handsome, excellent musician. As a boy growing up, he had practiced his clarinet four hours every day. He became a music teacher at the Junior High School, and also played his clarinet in a dance band combo, on the west side of Springfield, Ohio, where we danced. We attended Springfield Philharmonic Orchestra performances with Nancy, while he played.

Many picnics and barbecues were held in our back yards. They had two sweet little boys. Nancy liked my art work and had several of my pictures on her walls.

"How did Kay Massing get down here?" Harold asked, one time at a friends house where they were visiting in Kentucky.

Nancy had given her one of my pictures which was hanging on their wall. They taught us about music, and we taught them a little about art. Good exchange!

I had never been to a Cocktail party before when George said they were having one at the Civilian Club at the Base after work.

"Would you like to go? You could meet me there," he said.

"Sure! What would I wear?" I asked.

"I don't know. I suppose most of them will go over there from work," George said.

The only thing I could go by then was what I had seen in the movies and read in books. So, I dressed in a nice little sleeveless dress, with a large collar and a full skirt, wore a broad brimmed hat, and white gloves.

The second I entered the room, I knew I was all wrong. Yes, they did all come from work and they didn't wear a hat nor any gloves. I quickly took off my gloves as I saw George coming towards me.

"I'm dressed all wrong!" I said, as he came closer.

"You're okay. You look great!" George said.

Everyone was staring. I felt way overdressed, and wished I did not have that broad brimmed hat on. George took me around and introduced me. As we went to the table, I took off the hat and carried it. I had a good time and made several friendships and often went to later parties.

Bill and Kay Smith wanted George and me and the two boys to go to Maryland with them and their two girls, to say goodbye to Kay's father, as Bill was being transferred to California where they were going to live in Rialto. They wanted to make a trip to see her father, as it would be a few years before they would see him again. We were tickled for the opportunity, gathering things together and packing our supplies, etc., in their four cylinder Volkswagen van. We had a great time going over to Maryland.

On the way, we stopped at Bill's folks at Braddock, a small suburb of Pittsburgh. Their house was on a steep hill. Dinner that night was a heavily laden round table of all kinds of food. With all of them, and all of us, and Bill's brothers and sister, and their family, it looked like a thrashing dinner to me, the farmer's daughter. It turned out to be like some threshing dinners I had seen, too, the way people helped themselves to dishes, picking up a dish in front of them, and not passing it on to any one else. They laughed and talked, and had a wonderful reunion, while I eyed certain delicious looking bowls of food I couldn't reach.

The next day, we drove down their hill and up and around to a park on a high hill, above the confluence of the Ohio, Monongahela, and the Allegheny rivers. At the overlook we saw the whole of Central Pittsburgh, with its haze from nearby smoke, pollution emitting, steel mills, with its seething swirling smog almost obliterating the sunlight. It was a thrilling sight to see all this activity, with belching smoke, and the hustle and bustle of a teeming city.

The next day we drove to Georgetown, Maryland where we had fun and relaxation at her father's hideaway cottage on a river front. We sunbathed, caught fish, played cards and enjoyed each other's company for two weeks. Kay's father was very nice, a joker, and kept things lively. The time went all too fast, but we had to hurry home in order for them to get ready for their move to California.

"Why don't we go through the mountains, going home?" I asked Bill, as we started home. "I never get to go through the mountains because George doesn't like to drive in them. Do you mind driving in the mountains, Bill?"

"No, I don't mind. Let's do it!" He turned off the Pennsylvania Turnpike, driving south, and went on a less traveled highway that would take us to the highest peak of the mountains.

I was thrilled! I enjoyed this with every fiber of my body, until the heavy rains began to pour. The driving became slower and slower. The van could hardly make it up the grades. Bill had to slip into second gear over and over, with a grinding sound coming from the motor or transmission. It was a terrible situation.

"Kay, are you enjoying this?" Bill yelled to me from the driver's seat.

"Yes, keep going! I love it!" I yelled back.

The view from the van was superb, with its mountainous greenery and the wide overall view. I couldn't get enough of it. I looked side to side, then in front, then again to the sides. Each view was better than the last. I was in the mountains! It was glorious.

Then I heard a noise. What was that? Then another and another! and another!

"It's raining harder," I cried!"

"It sure is!" Bill, and Kay who was in the front seat, said at the same time.

But the rains became worse the highway became slippery and very hard to manage, with the van acting up. All of us sat up straight, trying to see what was going on. The world got darker, with less visibility all the time. Drivers turned on their car lights to see better.

We were right up there where the storm originated. The sharp, crackling, snapping was continuous, while huge white balls of fire lashed at us. Bolts of lightning crashed all around us, and, were extremely penetrating, while the thunder roared constantly. It was frightening, becoming worse every minute.

The sky got darker and menacing, the sun was no longer shining, and the noise became louder and stronger. In a matter of minutes, the whole world changed.

The outside of our van became a horrible, hideous mess, with loud, huge drops of rain splattering all over. Then came big balls of hail that clashed against the van, making even louder noises. The sun had completely disappeared, and the whole area that we could see was dark and menacing. Then came the tremendously loud cracks of thunder from the bolts of lightening that lighted up the sky ominously. The van faltered, and slipped around. Bill leaned forward and gripped the steering wheel tightly.

"Have you had enough, Kay?" he asked.

"Yes!" I almost screamed. "Let's get out of here."

He drove to the right amidst all this horrible, hideous storm, and drove down the off ramp of the road. In a few miles we were out of the mountains, past the storm that was still going on up there on high ground.

It had been so eerie. The beautiful day that made me glad to be alive and there so close to God had turned so quickly into the devil's horrendous playground.

We drove a few more miles and we came upon a beautiful, peaceful sight, turning westward onto the main curving highway. It wasn't long before we were all asleep. All but Bill, that is. Of course, he was still driving.

That fall, after a few weeks, they were on their way to California to stay for several years. They wrote to us when they arrived at their new home in Rialto, that they took the van to be serviced, at which time they were told they had been running on only three cylinders, for a long time, quite possibly when we were coming back from Maryland. Wow! No wonder we had problems in the mountains! Our heavy load, plus the roads, grades, and the storm, took their toll on the poor van, which had only four cylinders to begin with.

They kept wanting us to come visit them. We thought it would be great to go west, while they were out there. I loved California, and had wanted to move there after George came back from WWII, but we had settled back in Ohio. It was time to make a visit to my beloved California.

I was tired of the ball games, scout programs, the parties, everything. I wanted something else in my life.

One day in March 1961, when I was in Fairborn, I got the urge to visit my old friend, Sally, with whom I had worked years ago. I headed towards Titus Junior High School in Huber Heights, where she now worked as a nurse, after leaving WPAFB where we had been such good friends. When I walked into the large brick school building and up the stairs to the nurses office, I wasn't really sure what I was doing there.

Sally greeted me with lots of warmth and happiness. We talked and I told her I was thinking of going back to work as life had become so predictable.

"Why don't you go across the road to the office building, and apply for a job here?" she asked.

With both anticipation and trepidation I went to the superintendent's office to see if I could get an interview. They hired me on the spot. I was to work in their office that spring to help with the backlog before the summer season.

It was nothing like my work in the superintendent's office in Inyokern, California. Everyone was tense, talking loudly on the phone, and, in general, it was a very nervous atmosphere.

The head secretary was very demanding and excitable, very pressured in her job. I hurried to do everything she asked me to do, but had time on my hands with no decisions to make.

One day, after an important letter was edited and finalized, she handed it to me to type. It was a rush assignment, which I hurriedly completed, obtaining the signature, from the superintendent. I put it in its envelope and placed it in the outgoing mail basket.

"Where's the letter, where's the letter!" The secretary screamed, looking everywhere for it.

"I finished it," I said quietly. Here it is in the envelope ready to be mailed.

"Why did you do that?" she screamed.

"I was finished with it, and I just assumed you wanted it to be sent," I said.

"You don't assume anything in this office!" she screamed. "I'll tell you what to do and you will do what I say and nothing more!" louder than ever. Everyone was staring at us. I handed her the stamped and addressed envelope with the letter in it. She grabbed it and went into her office, and slammed the door. I sat down in my chair and shook, staring out the window.

After that tirade, I did what she told me to do, and never initiated another movement on my own. I sat quite often looking into space, along with the other girls.

Chapter 19

A Trip to California

That summer of 1961, we took a long vacation, to visit relatives, and our best of friends, Major Bill and Kay Smith, and their two girls, who had wanted us to visit them ever since they moved to Rialto, California. Milt and Laura, my brother and his wife, and their children had gone to California years ago, and their children were all married and had children of their own, except Bonnie who had come along later, and was now, nine years old, at the time of our visit.

Our car was packed to every free inch of space, when we pulled out for California with our camping gear, etc. It was quite a trek going westward, stopping to see the historical sights on the way. For the first time ever we left our beloved Herze in a kennel while we were gone.

We headed for California by way of Odessa, Texas, so we could visit George's favorite Aunt Ruth, youngest and last of his father's family, and her husband Uncle Harold Dysert, where they lived near the oil fields where he worked. It was a long grueling trip in the hot summer heat, to reach Texas, then it took us five days to cross the state. At the Texas state line, at Texarkana, we had a pleasant experience. We bought our first yellow watermelon. We stopped at a roadside table, as we left town and ate it. The meat was very yellow with black seeds. It was very sweet and tasty, so we enjoyed it very much. We now sometimes find them at our local supermarket.

The first day in Odessa, we told George's aunt about my playing bridge, so she wouldn't have it any other way than that she would get together a duplicate bridge group. The next day she spent hours calling and preparing eight or more tables for bridge.

I tried to get out of it, but she would have none of it. I had never played duplicate before, and wondered about the different rules. She said that you played the same as any bridge, but you kept your same partner and went to each table to play.

"I'll put you with a real nice lady. She's a millionaire, but just as common as anyone. You'll like her," she said.

I didn't think so. Play bridge with a millionaire?

When I saw my partner, I couldn't imagine her being a millionaire. She was a little old hausfrau type. But when she started to play, she meant business! I made three grave mistakes in the beginning and thought I did a completely lousy job the whole evening.

I looked over at the kids and George, out in the family room, having such a good time with Uncle Harold, I wanted to be with them. However, when Aunt Ruth counted up who won, she kept saying, "You did all right." I thought I couldn't have.

It was, however, a big surprise to me when she gave me my money, for which I didn't know I was playing. I was right in the middle of the high and low winners. It was my first time to play duplicate bridge, and I was very sure it was going to be my last. It was!

The few days we stayed, Aunt Ruth and Uncle Harold took us out on the town to a Mexican restaurant, where we had our first Tacos. She also tried to introduce us to red hot chili peppers which she ate like so many peanuts. They were too hot for us! We couldn't understand how she could eat them.

Uncle Harold had us drive around Odessa and showed us how the oil wells where he worked were situated right in town among the houses, and explained their operation to us. He showed us the first oil well to "come in" in Odessa. It was right in the front yard of a home.

We were so thankful that we had stopped to see them, as George's Aunt Ruth passed away the next year after we were there.

We crossed the United States-Mexican Border at El Paso, Texas, and walked into Juarez, Mexico, where we spent a day, leaving our car on the United States side. It was hotter than Hades that day.

Aunt Ruth had explained to us how to bargain when shopping in Mexico, so when I saw a special pure white goat skin throw rug, that I was crazy about, I asked the price.

It was extremely soft, long haired and gorgeous. It would have been perfect at my side of the bed to step out on. The young Mexican man said thirty-five dollars.

"I'll give you fifteen dollars," I said, as I thought that was what Aunt Ruth said to do. Then when he would counter offer, I would counter offer his offer, and we would finally get together on a price.

The young man jerked away from my hands that gorgeous white rug, that I was willing to die for, so fast all I could see was his backside, as he walked away from me in a hurry, and went clear across the room so I couldn't even talk to him. I kept watching him, as we gradually went on down the line of shops, looking at other items, thinking he would come back and we could discuss price again.

As we went along, I saw a few things which I bought, but nothing I really wanted the way I wanted that beautiful white rug. Only once did I see him glance our way. He did not come back to us to get a better deal. As we left the large sales room, I looked back at him one more time. He was not looking my way. I thought, but for Aunt Ruth, I could be walking away with a luxurious, gorgeous, long haired goat skin rug, in which to wallow and pamper my feet.

As we left the building, we began to walk in the hot, hot sun to return to the car. It was quite far, and the scorching heat from the sidewalk penetrated my thin leather soles. A darling little Mexican boy had been following us, working up courage to ask for money, I thought.

"Give some money to him. He is so adorable!" I said, "I have to get off this cement walk!" I started running and when I looked back, George and the boys were giving this precious little fellow some money. I ran until I found a little shade, from a cantina, where I stopped and waited for George and the boys to catch up.

THEN AND NOW

"I guess he did want money," George said. "He was very happy when we gave it to him." We thought he was especially interested in us because of Larry and Monte, as they were young boys like him.

I wonder what that little boy is doing today. I often wonder what people are doing later in life. What kind of a life did he have? Where is he now?

We resumed our trip to California the next day, after seeing Texas for five days. As we passed through El Paso, I saw a strange sight.

"Hey, look, kids! Look at that old holey T shirt, hanging on a hanger." We howled with laughter. Can you believe that a young man, in an old dilapidated car had a holey white T shirt, hanging on a hanger in the back window of his car?

I wonder if that was his best shirt, or his extra shirt he didn't want wrinkled, or a joke? It had all kinds of holes in it. I have thought of it often, and laughed as heartily as I did then.

We were headed for the Mohave Desert when we came to Hell. It had a population of twelve. We stopped, and were talked into buying a side window desert cooler for our car, as it was "hotter than hell going through the Mohave Desert!" as the man said. It was put on the outside of my window, and the cold, cold air was blown in above and past my head. My head was always freezing, as the cold blast of air blew constantly. It did keep us cooler, but we did survive the hot, hot heat of the desert.

When we entered California, by way of Indio, we passed groves of date palms, with paper bags covering the dates to protect them.

When we arrived in Cathedral City, we stopped at the home of Milt and Laura's oldest son, Charley Milt. It had been so long since I had seen any of them, and here was my little Charley Milt all grown up. We talked way into the night.

Charley Milt was my first nephew, and we were all so crazy about him. He had a little round face with big blue eyes the color of the sky, and a perfect round head, which remained bald for many, many months. He was the cream of the crop. Everyone loved Charley Milt, as I called him. His parents called him Buddy, then shortened it to Bud, when he grew older. Since the same thing happened to my George, I wasn't too happy with that nickname, so I chose one of my

KATHRYN BUSBY MASSING

own. Charley Milt, he was to me, then and now. I call him Charley Milt and he loves it.

We were so very tired from the trip and sick from the horrible heat, especially me. That night I had to go to the hospital, and when there was treated for heat exhaustion and nerves.

After visiting with Charley Milt, the next evening we left for our good friend's home in Rialto, crossing the San Bernardino Mountains at night. It was great fun seeing our good friends Kay and Bill Smith, and their two girls, Anne and Sue, after such a long time. We cooled off in their swimming pool, and went to bed at a late hour, in their guest house near the pool, having made lots of plans for the next few days. In the wee hours of that night the telephone rang and rang in the big house.

"Kay! Kay! George! You are wanted on the phone," Kay called to us, pounding on our door. We poured out of bed to pick up the phone. Who could be calling us? For what reason?

"Oh, Kay," Laura said. "I'm so sorry to have to tell you this. But Milt couldn't wait to see you, so he decided to drive through the night. He wanted to see you and not wait for morning. He had a wreck! A terrible wreck, when he tried to make a curve in the road!"

"How is he? Is he all right?" I cried into the phone. "Why did he do such a thing? We would have been back there in a few days to see him. He should have come in the daytime."

"I know! But he wanted to see you so badly he couldn't wait!" Laura said. "He's bad! Very bad! That's why I'm calling you. They don't think he'll live!"

We left the boys with the Smith's, and George and I drove back to the Palm Springs Hospital immediately. The boys had a great time with the Smith girls, and were taken lots of places, where we had all planned to go.

Milt was in bad condition. His eyes were crossed and he had bruises and breaks. His car was demolished, completely totaled. He had gone to sleep and ran off the mountain road and splintered a utility pole.

Milt was taken to his son Lester Lee's lovely home in Palm Springs, where he was kept and nurtured until he became well and whole again. Laura loved him so much, and was there most of the time.

Laura hovered over him, doing everything for him that she could.

Laura brought a group of Christians from her church to talk to Milt. He accepted Jesus Christ as his Savior, for which I was so very glad! He was precious to me, and I wanted to see him in Heaven.

"Put your hand on my chest, Sis," Milt said to me one time when he was better.

"Why?" I asked laughing.

"All the girls say I have a chest that feels like velvet. They all want to touch it and run their hands over it," he said.

When I touched his bare chest, as he was lying in bed, with only his boxer shorts on, I felt a quickening of my senses.

"It does!" I said in delightful amazement. "It really does feel like velvet."

"That's what the girls all say," he said.

"Why? Why does it feel like that?" I asked.

"I don't know," he said, "but it always has."

I'm much smarter now than then. The reason is, that good, beautiful, velvety, skin came down through the generations of Waddington families. My wonderful Gram had a lovely skin which awarded her with compliments, to her dying day, when she was eighty six. My dear Mother was also complimented many times, about her lovely skin.

I in turn, have been blessed with great skin most of my life. It was just normal to me. I never thought of it until in later years, so many compliments were given me, that I tried to figure it out. It was a gift from God, one of His many gifts that were given to me. As I look at my children, grandchildren, nephews and nieces, I think they all have lovely skin.

As Milt had improved Les and Charley Milt took us different places. We went by Palm Springs famous homes. Frank Sinatra had a life size chess set outside his home. We saw the store where Walt Disney's wife would order a certain shoe in every color, often ordering forty pairs of shoes at one time. We saw the home of Bob Hope, and many, many more. We saw the cable car that crossed the mountains.

Les took us up on a construction site where we could look over all of Palm Springs.

When we had to go, we hated to leave Milt, but George had to get back to work.

"I'm sorry I messed up your vacation, Sis!" Milt said.

"I'm just sorry you had to have that wreck," I said. "We didn't get to do things together."

George and I sadly drove away, waving good bye to the family as they all stood there waving at us.

We drove back to Rialto, visited a day, then took our boys and left for Ohio. When we came into Oklahoma, we noticed the trees all leaning southward along the highway. The north winds must be strong here. Then the humidity started getting to us! It became more humid and miserable as we passed through Oklahoma. They have a lot of tornadoes spawned there.

"I'll never live in Oklahoma!" I said. "I want to go back to California again. I wanted to go to Inyokern, go see and swim at Dirty Sock, and do so many things!" It was a very unfulfilled trip. But it had been fun, too, seeing our family and friends, although it was in such adverse circumstances.

Chapter 20

Working at the Library

When we arrived home, I anxiously sifted through the mail to see if there was an offer of employment from Titus Junior High School. There wasn't.

The next thing we did was to get Herze from the kennel, where we had left him on Gerlaugh Road with the Greenes. George had ridden to work a few times with Eva Greene in the same car pool. They said after we left Herze had pined away, until the owners, the Greenes, were afraid he would die, so they took him into their home and allowed him to sleep near the kitchen range. They kept him there the rest of the time.

Herze came bounding to us when we stopped to pick him up, looking fine and healthy. The Greenes said that was the most energy he had ever shown. He was so happy to see us. We decided we would never leave him again. From then on he went wherever and whenever we went.

It was late September when we arrived home from California, and after washing and cleaning and doing my housewifely duties, I decided to run over to school to visit Sally at her nursing job.

"Do you know of any positions open? I was hoping to get a full time job this fall," I said to her.

"Yes, I do! It's good to have a friend in the right places!" She laughed..

I got excited. "What is it?" I asked, quickly.

"The librarian left, and, as far as I know, it hasn't been filled yet. Why don't you go over there now and see about it!" she said.

Voila! Could this be what I was looking for?

It was late in the school day, but I went over to the superintendent's office and asked if there was a job available to me.

"Would you be interested in being the librarian? We have an opening there." He offered.

Would I? You could bet your bottom dollar on that. There was no better job in the world for me. It was perfect. This was Friday, I was to start next Monday!

I loved being a librarian more than anything in the world! The kids were great, I had no trouble getting students to help in the library. I took to this job like a fish thrown back in the waters.

"Did you bring any lunch?" Sally asked when she came downstairs to my library the first day.

"Heavens, no! I never thought of that! Don't they serve lunch here?" I asked.

"Yes, but it's with all the kids screaming and talking," she said. "I'll share my lunch with you. I'll come down at lunchtime."

She came downstairs, bringing her little paper bag of lunch, and opened it up to share with me. She had one sliced in half, uncooked hot dog between two un-buttered slices of white bread. That was it! Sally was never one to eat well. She was a tall, ultra thin, attractive blonde with no visible fat on her anywhere. Eating is the least of all her desires.

We walked down to the cafeteria and bought two cartons of milk. I glanced around, my mouth watering. But then I went back to the library and ate my half of her sandwich.

"It's delicious!" I laughed. I guess it's the company, I thought.

The next day I brought my own lunch, and sometimes I would go to the noisy cafeteria and eat at the teacher's table. It wasn't too bad. Good food! I never had an uncooked wiener in two pieces of un-buttered white bread!

All that fall, I kept wanting to paint. There was no time! With my housewifely and motherly duties and activities, there was no time left. I wanted to take a special course in Library Science, so I started

THEN AND NOW

to Wittenberg University in Springfield, Ohio, the subject being dictionaries and encyclopedias.

It was wonderful. When the instructor asked our opinion on anything, I was always ready to give it. I was sure! Even when another student would say Compton's was a better encyclopedia, I was sure it was World Book. Actually, I still think I am right!

It was a great experience for me, but I began to have serious attacks in the night! It was overwork. I had to quit. I cried. But, my family came first, then my job, my secondary family of kids. I just couldn't manage everything I wanted. My life settled down after I quit college.

George bought me a little red Renault, but it seemed to give out fumes inside the car. After a year, we traded it in on a darling little dark blue Renault Caravelle convertible, which I dearly loved.

One time I had to go home in new soft snow so deep it had me making tracks where there had been none before. I went the back roads and loved making the first tracks over beautiful white snow. But this one time, it had come down so fast, and with hard ruts of snow and ice underneath it. I was scared, but I knew I had to get home. No one could help me. I had to do it myself.

When I left the school I was very careful. It was alright on the back roads, but when I got out on route two thirty-five, I noticed it was much harder to drive. I had to stay on the right side of the two lane road. With the snow covering the top of the hardened ruts, it made me hang on for dear life.

My car got over at the side of the road where the curbing was, and no ground near it. My car slid off the curbing throwing the car completely sideways. I kept my hands tightly on the steering wheel, took my foot off the brakes, turned the car around to the front again, and accelerated the car on the smooth snow, just in time to let an oncoming car go by me. Then another car, and another. I was sick! I could have caused a big accident! I drove so very carefully, the two more miles I had to go, and went immediately to bed to relax.

My Junior High School Library was a great job. The pay was very small, but I loved the kids, and got along fine with them.

"This is a library! You are to be quiet and read here. We have lots of books, which I will help you find, if you need my help. You are not to talk, except in a quiet voice, so as not to disturb the other readers," I told them.

The school teacher looked at me in amazement! She had brought her study hall students in, and was walking up and down the aisles, letting the kids talk to any one they wanted to. There was very little studying, and hardly any reading, of my library books. After two days of my keeping the children quiet, and helping them, the teacher was amazed.

"Do you mind if I go to the teacher's lounge? You seem to have them under control. I'll be just across the hall if you need me," she said. I never saw her again.

Every period there would be a change of kids to my library. One study hall time the students used my library for studying, but the rest would come from the cafeteria which was used as a study hall for larger groups of students. If these students wanted to use my library they came with passes.

There were a lot of kids who wanted to have fun during one study hall period. One kid in particular, was as cute as they come, and was so mischievous, always wanting attention. But I noticed after my helping him there would be moments of decency and quiet.

One day, the kids in the library got out of control and caused a lot of commotion. Some kids went back to get the teacher in the study hall and she came in trying to straighten out the problems. She was blaming the cute kid who was always causing trouble.

"Mrs Massing, you know I've been good and I didn't cause you any trouble, did I?" the boy asked.

I turned and looked him in the eye, while I thought, to be sure I would give him the right answer.

"No, you didn't. You were a good boy, all the time you were here! You never caused any of the trouble."

The teacher stared at me, as if she didn't believe me.

"He never said or did anything," I said. He just sat in his seat looking at his book, while all the commotion was going on. The teacher gathered the troublesome kids and took them back to her study hall.

I was so glad to be able to say that. It really helped him tremendously. From then on he was the best student in my library.

By Easter time, I had ached for so long to paint, that I decided, during the break in school, that I would try.

In between house cleaning, regular cleaning and washing, and feeding my family and their friends, I would run downstairs where I had laid out all my art supplies, then up to clean, and feed, and whatever, I painted.

I decided watercolors would be faster than any other medium, not my favorite, but, at least, I would be painting! Out came my large water color paper, and my inks. I decided this would be better than paints, faster at least, and I would have a finished project.

I worked awhile, putting ink on my wet paper, holding it and moving it about. The inks I used needed to be rolled around and changed ever so often but they also needed time to soak into the paper at times and not allowed to go further. It became alive! I thought it needed drying a little, so, I ran upstairs, with glee and great happiness, did some cleaning, and ran back downstairs to check my watercolor, put more and different colors on the wet paper, and ran back upstairs to work. I kept this going for a few hours.

When I finally calmed down, and looked at that picture, I thought it was gorgeous! I was so thrilled, I decided to do another one. I did the same thing, but this time, I used smaller amounts of ink and in a more all over pattern.

When I completed the second one, I couldn't decide which one I liked best. I had worked at such a frantic pace, I was completely frazzled out! So exhausted, I could hardly crawl back upstairs, but delighted with the results.

The first watercolor I did that Easter Holiday won a first ribbon, the first time I exhibited it. The second one, which was never entered in an exhibit, an agent wanted to sell for me, saying she could get four hundred dollars for it. I never sold either one, as by now, I knew there would be no more paintings from this old girl, and I had to have some for myself. To this day, they continue to occupy a special place on my walls.

One day, when Larry was five yeas old, George and the boys and I were shopping in Fairborn. We heard the Fairborn High School Band coming down the street, so we gathered at the curb with other spectators. Larry became so excited we had to caution him to come back and sit on the curbing as they proceeded and passed in front of us. As we looked at the receding band members Larry jumped up and down, saying, "I want to be a bad boy! I want to be a bad boy!"

"You want to be a bad boy?" I asked Larry.

"What do you mean you want to be a bad boy?" I asked.

And as I leaned over him and he repeated what he was saying, I realized I had misunderstood him.

"I want to be a band boy!" he repeated.

He started his lessons with Harold Ashenfelter in the eighth and ninth grades. He started playing the saxophone, eventually playing all four saxes. He later turned to the clarinet, which he played the rest his time in the band. Our family became close friends with the Ashenfelters, spending considerable leisure time with them.

In the tenth grade he became the Drum Major of The Tecumseh High School Marching Band under Bandmaster Mr. Allen. His first performance as drum major was in front of the grandstand at Clark County, Ohio Fair. At that time they marched in black trousers and white shirts. Larry wore a beautiful white uniform, with the traditional tall white bushy hat, when he led the band onto the football field. He made a very impressive young leader, as he stepped out in front, of the band. The tall white drum major's hat, was similar to the hat, which has been worn by the British Guard since the 1850's, and is called a busby. The bandmaster Mr. Allen had him direct the band at a football game half time in Springfield.

At the Tecumseh High Homecoming game, one Halloween, the band performed in costumes and danced the Twist at half time. Larry, as drum major, used a toilet plunger for his baton.

Larry was drum major only in the tenth grade. In grades eleven and twelve he rejoined the ranks with his clarinet.

Monte took piano lessons for three years and played the drums very well. He and three of his friends formed a band and went to places like anniversary parties to play. One time George and I went to our good friend Martha's house and sat on her porch with her in order to hear their band play down the street at an anniversary party. It was quite good as well as very loud! The whole town heard them, I'm sure.

Monte always wanted to practice his drums upstairs, as had Larry with his wind instruments, and of course the piano was located in the front room, where he practiced. The drums were so loud we had to vacate the living room when he practiced. One day, his playing vibrated a couple of good glasses in my antique cabinet, that used to be Gram's, and they fell to the floor breaking to pieces.

"You get that drum set downstairs!" I yelled at Monte. "It makes too much noise up here, and now it's broken part of my good set of glasses." He sheepishly took all the seven pieces of his drum set down to the basement, which was set up as a family room. He never played too much after that, although I told him he could bring his set back upstairs, but he never did. It was a sad day when he sold his drum set.

On November 23, 1963, Mr. Zimmerly the principal of Titus Junior High, made an announcement on the speaker.

"We have heard, on the radio, that, as of a few minutes ago, President Kennedy has been shot in a motorcade in Dallas, Texas!" he announced.

Those of us in the library were paralyzed, wondering how this could be possible. Not long afterwards, he made another announcement. "We have heard the President of the United States has died."

All students in the library lifted up their heads, as one, looked around in stunned silence, then each one got up from his or her desk, and started out the door.

"You don't have to leave!" I said. No one said anything, but I realized everyone was in complete shock. I signed their passes to go back to their classes quickly, and in a moment, they were all gone. I sat alone, wondering and mourning. What a horrible thing to happen to the most influential person in our world at this time. What is going to happen now? What will happen to his family? What will happen to the United States?

There were no answers. We had to wait and see. In the days ahead, we stayed glued to the television, and mourned for our young president and his family.

Over thirty years later, all questions have not been answered and probably never will be. It was a horrible shame that anything like this could happen.

KATHRYN BUSBY MASSING

In the fall of 1966, there was to be a raise for secretaries and librarians. When I received my notification of my raise, I almost died! $.05 on the hour! The secretaries had received $.15 on the hour. Since I worked only six and a half hours each day instead of eight, I was not paid for my lunch time, so my raise in pay was nothing. I quit. I had been there five years without a raise.

Chapter 21
Our Boys

Larry had several great friends, one of my favorites being Bruce Osborne, who lived a very short distance from us, so would spend lots of time at our home. He seemed to be at our house a lot at lunch time, so, I would invariably ask him to stay to lunch with us.

At night when I cooked dinner, I always tried to have leftovers for a hot meal the next day. Our favorite was a dish made of macaroni, beef and onions. The next day I would beef up the leftovers with a lot of cheese which I melted over the top. It was better the next day!

One time we took Bruce and his girlfriend, who later became his wife, to our weekend retreat at Eagle Creek, Kentucky.

"Are you the one who makes such great leftovers?" the girl asked.

I couldn't believe it! This was years later, and he was still remembering it.

"He often talks of your great leftovers!" she continued. "How did you do it?"

I told her it was much easier than making sandwiches or most things people had for lunch. And it was far better! It just took a little planning.

I often thought of Bruce as my third son, as he was a fine young man, never arguing or causing a moment of disruption. He blended in and fused into our family as one of our own.

After Larry was graduated from Tecumseh High School, he attended Wright State University for a few weeks. He was discontented with college, and decided to go into the Coast Guard. George was in San Antonio, Texas, for several weeks, working on a computer system, with a large contingent of people from WPAFB.

I was to take Larry down to Cincinnati for his lantern test for color perception, to get into the Coast Guard. It was below zero, snowing, windy and raw. I bundled up in my big winter coat, and away we went. No parking spaces anywhere near the Coast Guard building! We had to walk several blocks in that raw, cold, damp, snowy air. It was almost impossible to get to our destination.

After sitting with all my heavy clothes on for awhile in the extra hot room, waiting for Larry to be called, I was finally warm enough to take off my heavy coat, gloves, scarf, and stocking hat, when Larry jumped up and ran out of the room. I thought he was running to the bathroom, and after waiting for awhile, thinking he must be sick, I saw him coming back to me.

Let's go," he said.

"Go where?" I looked around. "Where do we go?" I asked, stupidly.

"Home!" he said.

"What do you mean?" I asked. We had waited so long for his testing, I certainly didn't want to make another trip in a snowstorm to Cincinnati!"

"It's all over," he exclaimed.

I still didn't understand! My brain had become numbed from the weather, I thought.

"I took the test, and it's time to go home!" He was getting a little testy with me.

"You've already taken the test?" I almost screamed at him.

"Sh-h!" he tried to hush me. "Yes, I've taken the test!"

"Well, that didn't take long!" I said. "I thought you went to the bathroom! Did you pass?" I asked, excitedly.

"Yes, come on, I'll tell you about it." We gathered all our heavy clothes and put them on, and rushed out the door and down the street. It was impossible to talk, in the harsh, brutal wind, so we waited until we got in the car.

"Well, tell me about it!" I said excitedly. I really didn't want him to go to the Coast Guard, but if he were dead set for it, I had to go along with it. "Did you have any trouble?"

"Well, once I did, I guess. I called out white when the lantern turned green," he said. "The fellow who was giving me the test made a suggestion that maybe the color was white, and I said, yes. I passed."

In the next few years, when Larry was in the Coast Guard, I worried a little about that. But no harm was done, so I guess he was able to check out lantern guidelines alright.

The first time Larry had a furlough, I could hardly wait to see him. He called us one evening after work and said he would be coming home on the eleven o'clock plane. I was thrilled! I had missed him so much! It had been a very quiet home since he had left, as Monte and George were very quiet people. I had just taken a bath and washed my hair.

I enlisted George's help, and we rushed around our house, sparking it up until it shone! By the time we had to leave for the airport, our house was cleaner and more beautiful than it had ever been. The logs were sparkling and the fragrance of cleaning solutions permeated the air.

My hair wasn't dry yet so I draped a scarf around my head, and off we went to get our boy.

When I saw Larry coming through the door at the far end of the room, filing along with other service men in uniform, and other passengers, I jumped up in the air and screamed, "There he is! Larry! Larry!" George, with his usual quiet aplomb, told me to be quiet.

Larry ran toward us, grinning from ear to ear. He was as happy to see us as we were to see him. I threw my arms around him! We hugged and kissed. It had been so long. I had missed him so much! We gathered his luggage, and hurried home.

When we entered our Oakhaven, he walked into a perfect house, cleaned and sparkling just for him. He walked through the kitchen into the dining room and stood stock still. Then, he took a few steps, looking down all through the house from side to side in the living room and through the hallway into the master bedroom. He just stared at HOME! I was as thrilled as he was, I say it as if I were he, having been away from home the first time in his life for so long! I was so thankful we had spent the whole evening cleaning and making his home the most beautiful home he had ever been in. I knew how he felt, as I felt the same way. Oakhaven was a perfect home for us. He went back to the Coast Guard a very happy boy.

While Larry was home on his first furlough from the Coast Guard, he told us they had looked at his teeth and filled five, saying he had bad cavities. I saw red! No way did he have one cavity! We had taken our Larry and Monte both from the time they were six months old to our dentist, who was an excellent dentist from New Carlisle.

"The fellows who did it were going to school in dentistry," Larry said, "They might have wanted to practice on the new recruits."

I was fighting mad, but Larry calmed me down, saying it was all right. There wasn't anything to do about it. To think he had to have his beautiful teeth filled when there was absolutely nothing wrong with them! I still seethe when I think about it. We were so cautious about our children's teeth because I had had a bad time with mine. When I was in high school, Dad took me to our Ridgefarm dentist, who was my favorite teacher's husband, Dr. Rice. My teeth had so many cavities, he had to fill several and pull two or three, because they were so bad he could not fill them. This caused my teeth to be pushed to the side instead of being straight.

"You have beautiful teeth," I have been told several times in my life. I can't believe I hear correctly. They don't look closely.

On the other hand, George's teeth are strong and healthy. George's are hard and without many fillings. He eats nuts and hard things men eat all the time.

"Eat nuts! They are good for you," he has told me many times. Baloney. Don't believe it! That's when my teeth will chip, or crack, or just plain get another cavity.

Larry and Monte fortunately have had excellent teeth like their father, except for those five filled teeth Larry got in the service.

Bruce Osborne came over one day, and the boys were wondering what to do.

"Why don't you go bowling?" I asked, "I used to be pretty good. Aunt Sudie and Uncle Nig used to bowl several times weekly, and he used to bowl in tournaments. He was in the 300 Club having bowled a perfect game. I'm certainly not that good, but I love to bowl!" We drove out to the west side of Dayton where George and I used to bowl.

The first time I was up, I made a gutter ball. I was mortified. For the second try, I made another gutter ball. As I went back to my seat, the boys tried not to notice my chagrin at making such a goof!

"You haven't played for a long time," they tried to soothe my ego. "You'll do better."

When I was up again, I surprised myself making another gutter ball, then another! What was the matter! I couldn't understand it.

The next time I was up, I thought I had it all figured out, what I was doing wrong. I tried again. I got two gutter balls again, doing the same identical way!

I wanted to quit! But I don't believe in quitting at anything! Try, try again, and you will succeed was my motto.

With a great deal of trepidation, I got up for the fourth time, and threw two more gutter balls!

Getting sicker and sicker, trying to understand what I was doing wrong, I managed two more times. Two more gutter balls.

"I won't give in! What is wrong?" I was trying desperately to keep those balls out of the gutters! "If I throw two more balls in the gutter, I'm going to quit!" I said to myself.

I put myself in a perfect position, eyed the situation, and threw with gusto and expectation of success. We all watched with great hope, but the ball caught at the side and wrapped into the gutter! I died!

I'll try my next ball, I said to myself. "If it goes down the gutter, I've had it." It did! I was mortified six times up, and twelve gutter balls.

The boys were sympathetic, but what could they say? It put a damper on the rest of the day. I've never tried my hand at bowling since!

It was a beautiful, crisp fall weekend when we decided to visit Anne and Connie in Chester, Illinois. Monte, George and I drove to Ridgefarm, Illinois, to pick up mother and Florida friends, Henry and Millie Miller, who often came to the farm for a month or two in the summertime.

We all piled in mother's Cadillac, as it would be much roomier than our car, with Monte driving. He was just of driving age and did not have his first car yet, so he was pleased as punch to drive mother's big Cadillac.

We had a great time at Ann's as usual, and since George and I had to be back at work Monday, we left Ann's at six o'clock Sunday morning. We passed through the beautiful, wide open space of Illinois farmlands. Traveling smoothly down Illinois' wide highway, we glided with only two or three cars passing us in a one hundred mile stretch. Monte was behind the wheel, with George and me in the front seat, and Mother, Henry, and Millie in the back.

The constant steady drone of the motor, and the smooth highway, lulled us all to sleep.

"Sure drives nice, doesn't it, Monte?" were the last words I said to Monte, before falling off to sleep.

We were awakened by a state police coming up behind us, with his siren blaring, charging down on us as if we were criminals.

"What happened?" George and I were saying. "What did you do, Monte?"

"Don't say anything! Let me do the talking!" Monte blurted out, as the patrolman walked up to his window and leaned over.

"What's going on?" he asked, looking us all over. "Do you realize you were going ninety miles an hour?"

"Ninety miles an hour!" I whispered to George. "I never knew anyone who went ninety miles an hour!"

"Will you get out, please?" the patrolman said to Monte.

"Let me see your driver's license," I heard the patrolman say, as they walked to the back of the car.

When Monte came back to the car, after fifteen or twenty minutes, he crawled back in the driver's seat, and started the motor. It was nip and tuck to get anything out of him. I think the patrolman must have done a good job chastising him, but all he would say was that he gave him his choice of paying now or coming back next week to court. Of course, he knew he would not be able to come back from Ohio, to pay a thirty dollar fine. They know how to get you!

"Did you pay it?" I asked.

"Yeah!" he said quietly. That's the last we ever spoke about it. I thought he had had a good lesson! He was always such an excellent driver all his life.

I told Monte, when he first started driving, that if he ever got a ticket for speeding, he had to pay it, as I didn't believe in speeding. So nothing more was said.

Chapter 22
A New Job

After leaving school, I tried to get a job in Dayton, going on interviews wherever the employment office sent me. Nothing appealed to me.

Finally, I was sent to a Readymix Concrete Company which hired several men. As I was going inside to meet the interviewer, there was a long loud whistle. I turned and looked into the blue eyes of a young truck driver. I smiled, unsure of what to do. I hurried inside the building. I liked the atmosphere and the many late model business machines. I loved good equipment. I toyed with the idea of accepting the position. I would be boss and with all these machines, I would be in seventh heaven.

"I could get more if I went to the Base," I said to the young good looking interviewer.

"Sure you could. But wouldn't you like to work here?" he said. He thought a minute, then added, "I could go up another ten dollars on the week."

"I'll think about it. I do like it here, and I believe I would like to work here, but if I could make so much more at the Base, I guess I should go there. I wouldn't have to drive as I could go to work with my husband." I told him.

As I left I noticed two or three sets of eyes watching my every movement.

"You'll get used to the men. They won't hurt you," he said. I wasn't so sure.

The next week I applied for a job at WPAFB. I took tests, all the tests I could think of that I could do. I stayed up studying all night, the night before, as it had been so long since I had had a job.

George and I had gone downtown on Ludlow Street in Dayton to Wilkies, the best book store in town and bought helpful books on Civil Service Tests. We found ARCO Study Books for Civil Service Tests the day before I was scheduled to take the first test. That evening after supper, I studied all night. After breakfast, I drove to Dayton to the testing station for the Clerk-Typist Test. It would qualify me for a General Schedule (GS-2), the lowest rating for beginners.

"Could I have some paper to practice my typing? I haven't typed for twenty-one years," I asked the girl who was to give us the test.

"I have no paper. There is no paper, for practice. If you wanted to practice, you should have brought your own paper," she said in a nasty way. Years ago when a person took a test, practice paper was always given to use ahead of the test.

When the typing part of the test came, I started typing quite fast, but I became panic stricken when I heard the girl next to me run away with her typing. She was going twice as fast as I was. My fingers froze. I stopped and I said to myself, "Just relax! Go slowly, and do not make mistakes."

I put my fingers back in position on the keyboard, and slowly started to type. I gradually typed a little faster, and in rhythm, while the girl beside me was going faster than ever.

"You were going great! You must have made a really high score!" I told the girl, when the test was over, and we were leaving.

"I didn't pass!" she said.

"What do you mean? You were going six times faster than I!" I said. "I made too many mistakes," she said.

"I've taken this test three times and I get so nervous I always make too many mistakes." We were allowed only three mistakes, and had only to type forty words a minute.

When I received my score the next week, I had passed both the typing and the written tests, with a score of 86.5 which wasn't too bad. I went all through the house, after opening the envelope with the information in it, with my hands raised to the Lord saying, "Thank you, God! thank you, thank you, thank you!"

I wanted to take all the tests I could. The next one was for a GS-3, a Clerk test. I received 100 on this test. The next test was a library assistant position, for which I was really going. I passed the GS-4 on this test. There was no numerical number. Now I was ready to accept anything!

When I talked to Personnel at the Base, I was told there were no jobs available then, but it would behoove me to accept a temporary 2, (there were no 1's, so this was the lowest grade there was), in order to get on the Base, then I would be placed quicker than if I would wait for a 2, or 3, or 4 that might turn up.

I did this and was given a temporary 2 in the Personnel Office, where I worked for three long months, waiting to be placed.

The person who was to place me had every question I asked covered with an answer with which I could not deal. I felt she did not place me because she didn't like me for some reason. I got along fine with everyone, man and woman, except the placement woman.

One of my questions, after two and a half months working there, was why I wasn't placed yet? The head librarian at the base technical library had had me to visit her several times, and I was very anxious to work there.

"They keep trying to give me someone else. I don't want anyone else. I want you!" she said to me.

That made me feel good! I liked her very much and thought we would get along fine.

So, why wasn't I placed with her? "There are others ahead of you!" This placement lady told me.

"I passed my test with one hundred. How could there be more than one hundred?" I asked, perhaps too heatedly.

"There could be a service woman or a service man's widow," she replied rather unconvincingly.

"What does that mean?" I asked.

"A service woman who just got out of the service could pass the test at one hundred, and get ten extra points, as a former service woman. A service man's widow would get an extra five points on top of the one hundred she might have on the test." she said.

She didn't say she had anyone in either of these categories, but implied they could exist. I thanked her and went back to my desk to work on temporary two work, which was quite basic. I realized the men and women in the office were staring at us, or hanging their heads so they wouldn't look at me as we were talking pretty loud.

The next day the placement woman sent me out on another job I didn't want.

George did some checking and found an opening for me. He was a GS-13, so had quite a bit of clout. He told me about a major who wanted someone in his department. I went to his office and was interviewed by him. I liked him very much. He was the first black man I had ever seen in such a position, but I could understand how he got there. He was very intelligent, very kind, and thoughtful. He took me out to meet a supervisor over payroll personnel.

Until I met that supervisor, under whom I would work, I was ready to take the position. He was apparently overworked and harried, a nasty, hateful, one armed man with a grudge at the whole world. I wouldn't have worked for him if I had to stay a temporary two forever. Anyway, numbers were not my forte.

When I walked into my office, my placement lady came at my heels and jumped all over me. The major had already called and said he wanted me to work for him. She was beside herself, asking over and over where I got the information that he had a job available, and why did I go there without her sending me! I couldn't tell her that. Then George would be in jeopardy, perhaps. Perhaps not though, as she was only a GS-6. I decided not to tell her, so she kept after me for a day or two, then dropped it.

She spoke so badly to me, and I didn't really want to work under that one armed supervisor, so I refused the job. The major wanted to talk to me and I refused to talk to him. After he called a few times he gave up. I always wanted to tell him my reasons, but, of course I couldn't.

One day not long after that, my immediate supervisor, Charlotte Blair, who was a fantastic supervisor, and with whom I got along well, and did everything she wanted immediately, was looking over some of my work, when she started talking real loud. She purposely, I know, sat at an empty desk, three desks from me, so she had to yell in order for me to hear. All heads between us and at the sides of us jerked up staring at her, and then at me, continuing to listen and stare as no one could get out of the hearing range of her voice.

"Kay Massing. Kay Massing! This is a beautiful piece of work," she said. "You do a beautiful job of typing these reports with proper spacing. You rework them so they make more sense and the finished product is well done!"

I was amazed! Didn't everyone do that? I looked over at the placement woman who was staring and listening intently as I realized she was my supervisor's reason for doing this. I felt like blowing a kiss to my supervisor.

Later I looked at the reports of a couple of black girls who were cute and likeable and temporary 2's as I was. I was amazed! It was the sloppiest work I had ever seen. No real sentences, all jammed up against other printed work, and a lot of misspelled words and grammatical errors. I couldn't understand why they kept their jobs.

Two days later, I was placed at the head library in Area B at WPAFB, where I had wanted to go all along. I tip my hat to you dear sweet Charlotte at personnel.

The placement woman got even with me, she placed me where I wanted to be, but she made me accept a GS-3 for the GS-4 Librarian Assistant position on which I had to work several months before I received my GS-4.

It was not all fun and games. It was the hardest job I had ever had in my entire life. Going from Junior High School Library to the highest Technical Library, was too big of a jump. I had lots to learn. There were ten or fifteen book cards on almost every book in the library as there were so many subjects in each book.

"You are going to burn that typewriter up!" one of the librarians said to me one day. I tried to slow down but it's hard to do when you have so much work to do. I was finally where I wanted to be.

Then I was sent to work as an assistant secretary to the Division Chief, Russell Donahue, at the main office of our Base Headquarters. I found the people friendly and fun to work with.

I think Russ was trying me out for working for him later. He was sent to the 2750th Air Base Wing, as the civilian director, and asked me to go as his personal secretary. I really wanted to go back to the library at area B, but I did as he asked. It shouldn't be too long, then I could go back to my library. I went, and hoopla! It was lots of fun!

Base Special Services was composed of happy people, lots of fun along with the work. If everyone had a job like that, no one would be unhappy with their jobs! We were the organization which assisted base non-commissioned officers with their personal lives.

I was still a stickler for protocol and things done right the first time. One time I changed the wording of Russ's letter to read better. He questioned me on it. "You changed my wording," he said. I really hadn't expected him to notice.

"It is better to put the word, however, in the middle of a sentence." I had changed his word, however, from the beginning of a sentence to: It is, however, such and such. He studied it for awhile.

"That's a matter of opinion," he said.

"Yes, it is," I said. Then after a pause, I added, "Do you want me to change it?"

"No, it will be all right," he said.

I never changed his work after that. I think he liked it that way, but what difference did it really make? We had a great rapport and I wanted to keep it that way.

There were lots of parties, with our party loving gang who worked hard during the day, but kept in mind always that we all worked to help people have a good time. That was our job. We had lots of reports to make and correlate lots of red tape, but we were able to attend luncheons, dinners, dances, etc., where we always had a great time.

George was always with me after hours, as when his day ended he was free, so he would come to whatever was going on with my group. We would party. Fun! We had gone to lots of dances but this was different. I was involved more, and yet freer with everyone out for a good time.

We did live it up in those days, going to the Officer's Club for special occasions and hobnobbing with officers, some of whom were our best friends. We had special occasions when we went off base to great lunches, but mostly our work and fun were on the base. Everyone was happy compared to the heaviness of some of my friends on other jobs. It wasn't that we were a wild bunch, it was just clean fun.

There were great house parties some of which George and I hosted. Oakhaven was a great place for partying. Larry and Monte would stay in their rooms a lot during these parties, but would come out and have fun themselves, and to get good punch and food. This was a happy time for us all.

I learned how to read palms, and became a big hit at parties, reading the palms. It really seemed to hit the fantasy of my friends. Different friends and I went to seances, worked the Oiejie Board, and I read a lot of books on the subject.

At one reading, I was told I would never have children, "You're barren, like me!" she said! I didn't believe that! Thank God I was right!

Fortune telling, astrology, palm reading, and handwriting analysis became very interesting to me.

But there was one reader who impressed me as knowing a lot about my past and future.

Along with a friend, I went to a house on the southwest side of Dayton, where we had an appointment for ten or fifteen minutes. She became so excited, and we hit it off so well, she kept me between half an hour and an hour. Everything seemed to work.

She talked about my grandma and my past. Then after a thoughtful pause, she surprised me.

"I see a beautiful blue eyed baby, sitting in your lap," she said.

I could think of no blue eyed baby that could be. "Well, I see him there!" she said.

"I don't see how it could be anyone I know. It wouldn't be any in our family. Both George and I have brown eyes, and both of our sons have brown eyes," I said.

"It is as clear as a bell. He has beautiful blue eyes!" she said.

"Even our daughters in law don't have blue eyes. One has deep brown and the other hazel," I said.

After she continued I finally thought of a friend. A friend of mine, Sudie, from work, has a beautiful little boy, and he has beautiful big blue eyes. He was adorable! And I did have him in my lap!

She went on to something else, but I thought about that when less than a year later, I had my first grandchild on my lap, and he had great, big, beautiful blue eyes and blond hair!

THEN AND NOW

My seance continued until there was a terrible racket, banging against the wall, and voices from afar off.

"Oh, there are the angels!" my reader said. It made me sit up and take notice!

"It is time for me to let you go," she said. "The angels are getting nervous and agitated."

Of course I had no doubt but that some one in the next room made the noises, but it was plausible that it was angels! Not probable!

One of my friends Gloria Dye, made gorgeous gold and silver jewelry. I bought several pieces from her, and had her make me a ring. In the center, she formed a gorgeous, artistic little Virgo on a huge, gold ring, and placed birth stones of my children and that "little blue eyed, blond baby grandchild on my lap," in strategic areas. As I had more grandchildren, she added other birth stones.

When we went to Naples to live, we became very good friends of our minister and wife, Reverend Alfred Jodie and Nancy. He said all this was of the Devil, so I had my friend to take off the beautiful darling Virgo and place a cross there. That made my children and grandchildren hang onto the cross!

I burned my books! It had been fun, but I wanted nothing to do with the Devil! To hell with him! That's where he came from, that's where he'll stay, as far as I am concerned!

Often, the Oiejie Board wouldn't work with people, but the minute I sat down, it would start working furiously. When others would ask questions and the Oiejie Board was sluggish, it wouldn't move at all until I put my fingers on it and started asking questions. Then, it would work so fast and furious, we could hardly keep our fingers on it. What did I have that other's didn't? I will never know.

One time, the Oiejie Board said Martha was going to marry a man from BAHA. "Where's BAHA?" We laughed so hard. We had to discuss where that was. We were astounded.

"Have you ever been to BAHA, Martha?" I asked laughing.

"No!" she exclaimed.

"Do you ever plan going there?" I asked

"No!" she said.

So, I asked the Oiejie Board, "Where did you say?" It spelled it out again.

"Are you sure? It said, "Yes!"
" We can't imagine that! Have you made a mistake?" I asked.

And for about the eighth time, we asked again, and the Oiejie Board was positive Martha would marry someone from BAHA.

Martha married a widower from next door who had been a long time friend. He was not from BAHA!

At a party at the Noncom's Club, George and I were dancing when the orchestra started a slow polka. Now there is no dance I love more than a polka, but after about three whirls George is too dizzy to continue so, as we were walking back to our seats, a friend grabbed me and we started whirling faster and faster.

The band kept going faster and finally, after asking me two or three times if I wanted to stop and receiving a no answer, he stopped as he had reached his limit, and we started back to our tables. Another man grabbed me and whirled me so fast, I hardly knew what was going on. The band kept going faster and faster. We were the only ones left on the floor. The band had almost stopped when the big blond man grabbed me, so the band now was hitting an all time fast pace. I had to stomp so hard on my heel, the right one popped off and flew up and out landing underneath an empty chair. Everyone was watching as we went faster and faster and faster, swinging and turning and twisting. It was fabulous, but I finally couldn't take it anymore.

My heart was beating so fast and furious I could hardly make it back to my chair. But, Oh, what a wonderful dance that was! It was the fastest and longest polka I had ever danced.

At one party, I danced so well with one of the men. This was the first time George and I had met him and his wife. We just glided beautifully together. It was fantastic

"You two dance well together," his wife said, as we passed her and her dancing partner. You really look great!"

Later, she told me he taught dancing at Arthur Murray Dance Studios!

"That's why he's such a great dancer and so easy to follow!" I said.

George had a friend, a young lieutenant from the base, who liked to go with us to dances. He and his former wife were professional dancers on the Hollywood scene. He was so light on his feet and danced with an easy grace.

He would do some fancy footwork, which I was surprisingly able to follow, then he would throw me up in the air above him and gently ease me back to the floor, at which time we would do more fancy stepping. It was exhilarating and exciting, twirling and gliding with him.

Then, there were the Kidds, Orran and Helen. They were such beautiful dancers, just gliding along, and around and around, with great sense of beauty and poise. Helen worked for George at Area C, WPAFB, in Base Supply, and we've stayed good friends, and continued to see them at every dance we attended.

They made such a beautiful splash, twirling all over the floor, and they would come early, and get people up to dance. They sometimes would have to go around the floor a few times, before the rest of us would venture out there. We wasted so much time! Not really. It was a great deal of pleasure to watch them do their magnificent ballroom dancing!

But with all the fun and new friends, I wanted library work. Books have always meant so much to me, and I still wanted to do that kind of work.

"You are not leaving until I leave," Russ said. I would argue with him about going back to my true love, books. So I stayed until he left and Colonel Battista came to take his place. He was very low key and hesitant, being new. I was given carte blanche to run the office with very little instruction. In fact, he asked me and I taught him what I knew. Russ had known how to do everything, but now I was teaching our new colonel. He was nice, caused no waves, but the office changed without Russ.

I started talking of going back to my library. Finally he released me after hiring a new girl. He made me interview the girl to take my place. Here I was interviewing a GS-6 for the job I had handled as a GS-4. I thought they should know more than I, but they were either too nervous, as one beautiful girl was, so much so she couldn't take shorthand at all, or so well worn they couldn't answer questions. I finally settled on one, and chose her to take my place. She was vibrant, attractive, and I thought she was great compared to the others.

The next time I talked to my friend Nancy Earley, who was secretary to the chief, she said she was terrible, even to the point of taking off her shoes and going barefoot, as she never wore hose. I couldn't believe it!

"Well, I got rid of her!" Colonel Battista told me about three months later when I saw him.

"What did you do?" I asked.

"I got her a better job and passed her on," he said.

I was livid. I bet he had never been talked to as I did that day. "How could you do that? You gave her a raise to a GS-7, and I worked here as a GS-4, and no one ever said how great a job I did."

But this is the way it's done in the government service a lot of times. If you don't want a person you get rid of them with a better job. I worked as hard as I could and fought every inch of the way to ever get advancement. I got fun, love, and happiness, but wouldn't it have been terrific to get advancement in my pocketbook? Oh, well, I have good memories, I know I did a great job and everyone liked me.

The Technical Librarians were glad to have me back and it wasn't long before I felt settled in.

Chapter 23
My J A G Library

Then an opening came from the Judge Advocate General's (JAG) Office for a position. My head librarian offered it to me. I was so grateful. My own library.

I had to move over as a GS-4. I wasn't too happy about that, as I had worked hard, and most people would have had a raise to go anywhere. Except me! I was always held to my former grade.

My own library! With ten thousand books, and more arriving every day. Fabulous! There were hundreds of regulations, stacks of which had been left un-posted and unfiled on the desk. I worked so hard getting that library up to par, as it had been let run down. I replaced a GS-7. I was a GS-4 and had to wait a year and a half before I got a GS-5. Does that make sense? George said, "You were screwed by the fickle finger of fate." The library had two large rooms, and I had two large desks, one facing the entrance door, and one facing the room. It was spacious and wonderful. I reorganized the library and arranged all the regulations left undone on one of the desks. I was given a helper to sort out and clean up the mess left by an unwilling worker who knitted all day. She probably was unhappy because her salary was only a GS-6 instead of a GS-7, which was held by the prior librarian, who was a man. Here I was a little GS-4 cleaning up their messes. The story of my life!!

When my good worker helper and I had put the library back into the Dewey Decimal System, where all good libraries should be, she was taken away from me. I had to go it alone then.

The Generals, Colonels, Majors, Captains, Lieutenants and civilian lawyers couldn't find anything after I had put the library in the Dewey Decimal System, so I had the huge job of putting the books back where they were, so they could find them. Law books are in series, and they had been put where the men could get to them easier. They were always in an absolute, no time situation, and needed the books they wanted immediately.

There was no time for them to relearn the correct position of the books they needed. I saw this and changed them back to where they were when I first came. When they came in for a book I would ask them the "Dewey Decimal Number," which, of course no one knew, so how was I to find it for them. I admitted defeat and went back to their system.

Colonel Solamine was over one section of men. I used to go into his office and talk to him. He always appreciated my company, asking me to sit down and talk. He needed a rest, he would say. He was a great friend to all his secretaries. They all became wonderful friends to me, coming to my library to rest and talk.

When they had a pressing military case, they had to type constantly until they were finished, but sometimes they had free time to kill, waiting for another case. We were all great friends and went to luncheons and parties together. They were a great bunch of people, both the men and women, in the Office of the Judge Advocate General (JAG).

The Technical Library staff had been staid and uncommunicative. They were mostly older women who were of the old school of nose to the grindstone and no joviality.

Colonel Solamine did an interim stint in Thailand for about a year. When he came home, he brought me a set of gorgeous, hand carved, wooden elephant candlestick holders, which now rest beautifully among Larry's large elephant collection.

There was a young, handsome, black Captain attorney, who would frequent my library, at which time we often had quiet conversations, about a lot of different topics. He grew up with Malcolm X. He said

THEN AND NOW

he had a long talk with him when he went home to visit one time, and although he had changed a lot, he was still a lot like he used to be. The two of them had a really good time the evening he spent with him, talking over old times, and all about the new era in which they found themselves that day.

When he came back from his summer vacation, he came rushing into my library, smiling and beaming.

"I brought you something!" He said. "It's not much, but I thought of you when I saw it."

It was a darling pin made of a flat rock, about two by two and a half inches. On the outer side was painted a gray cat in a graceful reclining position. It was beautiful and I thanked him very much for it.

"Why do you suppose the Captain gave me that cat?" I asked my George that evening? "Do you think he thought of me as catty? I never talk about people!"

"He probably thought you were the cat's meow!" George said.

I still have my pussy cat. It is favored amongst my jewelry collection.

Larry came back from Alaska, where he had been assigned at a Coast Guard Station in Seward, and on a Buoy Tender for about a year, to attend Electronics School at Groton, Connecticut. Upon being graduated, he was sent to Bermuda to a LORAN Station (Long Range Aid To Navigation) as an Electronics Technician, his duties being to operate and keep in repair the LORAN equipment. He was quartered at barracks on the Naval Station toward the east end of the Island.

A few months after he was stationed there, we visited him for seventeen days. We took a taxi to our nice little, one hundred year old cottage in Padget, about midway of the island, which he had rented for us. It wasn't far from his base, so he lived with us while we were there. We quickly discovered Bermuda is one of the most beautiful places in the world, if not the most beautiful.

George rented a Moped, but he wouldn't let me rent one, as he said I get my right and left mixed up too easily! We had to drive on the wrong (left) side of the road, and he was afraid I would have problems! The newspaper was full of accidents by tourists. So, I rode on the back of Larry's Yamaha Motorcycle. It was loads of fun! The second or third curve we went around, Larry looked back at me.

"Mother," he yelled, "What are you doing? Are you leaning the wrong way?"

"I was just trying to keep us from falling!" I screamed back at him.

"Well don't do that! You will make us fall!" he said. "Lean with me."

So I had to learn to lean with the motorcycle and Larry. I did it gradually, but I did learn, and it really made us have a super smooth ride. By the time we left, we were riding at a forty-five degree angle, going around the many curves, and, there I was, leaning over there with him!

The profusely blooming yellow Frangipani, red and yellow Hibiscus, and white, pink, and fuchsia Oleander, lined the winding roads, with green foliage everywhere as we moved up and down the hills. The rocks and scenery made this island so beautiful, and just great to ride through! We rode 625 miles while there.

Bermuda is twenty-five miles long, with the airport near one end and the naval base near the other.

In the middle is the beautiful town of Hamilton, where in the center, stands a uniformed Bermuda policeman, in an open cage, at the main intersection on Front Street. He directs both pedestrian and vehicle traffic.

The huge tour ships line the waterfront along Front Street. There were fabulous shops and eateries everywhere downtown, which we frequented.

On our last night there, we invited several of Larry's friends whom we had met to a big steak dinner, at our cottage. They all came on their motorcycles, and we had a wonderful time. We hated to leave, but we had a fantastic time.

Monte met a fine young girl, Cindy Bleigh, a few miles from us, and they had a good relationship going. Monte had gone to a vocational school in Springfield, Ohio, where he had done very well, even teaching his fellow students, on closed circuit television, how to laminate formica topped kitchen cabinets. That summer, during school vacation, he had worked at a cabinet shop on Lower Valley

Pike, near home, where he learned how to laminate formica, as part of the cabinet making process.

The summer before, he had stayed at Mother's farm, and had been taught a lot about carpentry by his Uncle Milt, who was staying with Mother at the time, remodeling the house, including installation of a second bathroom.

Larry was stationed in Bermuda for two years. He seemed preoccupied, and sort of jumpy, when he came home. I questioned him about it, and he finally told me why.

"I've met a girl!" he said.

"Hey, so that's what it's all about!" I said. "Tell us about it!"

"Well, I like her a lot. I promised to go back and see her graduate from her high school," he said.

"Oh, she's still in high school?" I asked.

"Yes, but she seems a lot older than she really is," he said. "I don't know whether to take her a ring or not." We were amazed at his statement.

"Oh, you mean you might ask her to marry you?" I asked.

"Well, I don't know!" he said. He finally decided to get a ring and take just in case!

When we received his call from Bermuda, George and I, and Monte, were all listening. Larry introduced Judy over the phone to us and we chatted a little, and then there was a pause.

"Well," I said, "What's cooking?"

"I asked Judy to marry me!" Larry got out before we jumped on him.

"You did? We wondered!" We were all talking at once, laughing and carrying on.

Judy came home with him and stayed with us a month, for us to get to know her. It was a great time. We all thoroughly took her to our hearts, and we have kept her there.

She is a fine young girl, always up to every situation. She and Larry make a perfect couple.

Judy left us after a month to go back to Bermuda to get ready for their wedding.

While preparations were being made in Bermuda for Larry and Judy's wedding, Monte and Cindy had a quiet wedding, with their best friends standing up for them, August 29, 1970, at the Park Layne Methodist Church, which Cindy attended, and was a Sunday School teacher. Cindy was very lovely and Monte was handsome.

Bruce Osborne was in the process of completing The Famous Photographers Course and was thrilled to take their wedding pictures.

After the reception at Cindy's parents, they left for their Honeymoon, laughing and dodging the rice thrown at them. After their Honeymoon they went to housekeeping in a mobile home near their work in Dayton, later moving to Crystal Lakes, a few blocks from our home, Oakhaven.

Larry left for Bermuda two weeks before his wedding. George and I left one week before the wedding. We arrived in Bermuda amidst the hustle and bustle of getting ready for a large wedding. It was so much fun. Bridesmaids running in and out of the house activities. Reggie, Judy's father working so hard, trying to get everything ready at the house, and her mother, Delores, running things from her work as a clerk with the Royal British Navy, made it all hectic but delightful.

Bruce Osborne arrived to be Larry's best man, and entered into the activities, having a great time in all the preparations.

It was busy, busy, busy! Presents were put on long tables pushed to the side of the dining room, the men fixing up lights, etc., so much to do! They also saw to it that the buttery was well stocked with soda and all kinds of refreshments for the reception to be held on the large patio.

The night before the wedding, we all stayed up to prepare food for the reception. We spent hours making sandwiches that night. The Bermuda fruitcakes, both plain and fancy, had been made by a baker. Sandwiches, cakes, drinks, everything was ready!

In Bermuda, everyone was invited, by way of living on the island! If someone were going down the road, and saw a wedding reception, he or she would stop by.

The next morning, Beverly, Judy's sister, was putting the yellow Frangipani through greenery piled on the mantle. These flowers, like Hibiscus, remained in full bloom a full day without water.

When George and I got up, two of the bridesmaids were fighting over who was to run the sweeper for the last time. It was hectic! Judy and her brother, Michael, had a face to face screaming combat, their Mother tried to stop it!

We all got to the wedding on time; and it was the most beautiful wedding I had ever seen! Four beautiful bridesmaids followed the darling flower girl and ring bearer down the aisle, with George as an escort, as Judy's oldest brother, David, had come down with Hepatitis. He lay on the sofa in his Tuxedo, sick as could be, so at the last moment George had to step in.

The wedding party was carried from the church a half mile down the road to Rushy Hill, Judy's beautiful home, in a caravan of small convertibles. Judy had wanted horses and carriages, but settled for the convertibles.

There was much partying, toasting, eating, laughing, a great reception! The Chief of Police of Hamilton, serving as bartender from the buttery.

Larry and Judy were taken to a beautiful hotel on the beach, for a few days honeymoon, before they had to leave for the States. They boarded the plane before we did as they had first class seats, taking our beautiful new daughter-in-law with us to our home and hearts.

Larry and Judy stopped at our house for a short while as Larry was going back to college. He had made the choice of Southern Illinois University (SIU), at Carbondale, Illinois, which was a short distance from my sister, Ann, at Chester, Illinois. She became their surrogate Mother for the following years.

Larry took a Photo Journalism course and was graduated with a four point average in two years and eight months. He came out looking gaunt and sick. He had to take and develop numerous thirty-six exposure rolls each week. How he ever did it, I will never understand. Judy had a job on campus and helped him with his school programs.

He was graduated in 1973. Ann was as proud of him as I was, as they had become the children she never had. It was good for her to have them close, and it was good for them to have her close. The first time she held Larry, when he was three months old, she just held him and looked at him with so much love. I thought she would never hand him back to me.

One day, when things had settled down from the wedding, my boss Mr. Brown called me from the JAG Office, Area A.

"We have word from Headquarters in Washington," he said to me, "we have to give them a report on your library."

"What kind of a report?" I asked. I had never had to make a report before.

"How many books you have, how many people read them, things like that going on in your library," he told me.

"How soon do I have to have the report done?" I asked.

"Next Tuesday," he answered.

"Next Tuesday!" I exclaimed. "It's impossible! That will take a long time."

"Well, do the best you can," he said. "It is due at the Washington library Tuesday."

"It has to be done! The head librarian wants to have a report on every library under her," he told me.

As soon as I hung up, I stopped doing the work on which I was working, and started in on the report. When the report format came through the interoffice mail, and I saw what I had to do, I was flabbergasted.

That will take two weeks! I thought. There were many more questions on the letter than my boss had intimated.

This was Friday. I was frantic. In all my life I had been doing reports, but never given such a short amount of time. I couldn't possibly have it ready by Tuesday. I had to work over the weekend! There was no other choice.

"George, would you come down to the library with me, and help me get my report out?" I asked him?

"No! Why should I do that!" he exploded.

"Please, Honey. You know I can't do it by myself!" I said, "Tomorrow is Saturday and we could work in the library without interruption, and maybe we could get it done. We work so well together! I know the two of us could get it done."

I begged and begged George to help me. I did not want to go to the office by myself when no one else would be anywhere in the library building.

So, bless his loving heart, he went with me and the two of us did the whole report Saturday and Sunday, working until we were exhausted. Neither one of us had ever worked so hard and so fast on anything. Here he was a big shot and helping little old me, a nothing in the pecking order of government service.

When I took that report, it would take too long to send it by mail to Area A, early Monday morning to Mr. Brown, there was never a more surprised man in the world before or after.

"When I said Tuesday, I didn't mean you had to get it done Tuesday," he mumbled, astonished. "It could have been later. It was just due on Tuesday," he ended quite lamely.

"But you said it had to be in Washington on Tuesday. It has to have time to get there," I said.

Well, I guess he didn't see things the way I do. In my book, if someone says something is due Tuesday, that's when it is due! Get to it, and get it done by Tuesday! He never called me again and gave me an ultimatum. I guess he was a little thrown by my attitude. In fact, after that, I hardly ever heard from him. I guess he thought I could handle my library without his help.

There were sixty lawyers who used my library. From Generals to Lieutenants, as well as very intelligent civilian attorneys, all were easy to help. They didn't demand things, but just told me what they needed, and I did every thing I could for them. They were a fine bunch of library patrons!

Also some law students would be sent to work on cases they were studying. We kept all our volumes current and bound, except the ones that came in paperback to update each bound book. We had regulations and current case histories. I loved my law library.

There was a bevy of girls who were secretaries to the lawyers, civilian and military. In the same building there was a cafeteria and credit union office. The head secretary was a wonderful black girl, Bernie Milliken, who was married to a minister. Karen Kirves, (later Karen Grogan) was an excellent secretary, who later became the head secretary in the Judge Advocate's, Colonel King Simmon's office, then later went into the lucrative computer field where she attained the grade of GS-12 before retiring in 1993.

One time at one of our parties my George was introduced to Colonel King Simmon.

"I've never met a king before," George said.

Everyone laughed as Colonel Simmon shook hands with George. It eased the situation as everyone was a little uptight in having our boss at our party.

As part of his work, once each month, George was required to brief one to three Generals, heads of Directorates, on the condition of the Air Force Logistics Command support of the overall aircraft and missile fleet.

In the four years I was at the Base, this time, I went from a temporary GS-2 to a GS-6. When I tried to get a seven, the counselor asked me how much time I spent on Regs (regulations). I could not lie. I never have been able to lie! I wasn't about to start.

But because I spent approximately twenty minutes a day on keeping regulations posted, the counselor could not give me a seven although I kept all the other books in excellent condition. (I was told by everyone I kept the "regs" more up to date than anyone on the base).

People from many other offices would check my regulations because they knew they were current. He apologized for it gave me ample opportunity to say I spent less time on the regs. I could not compromise my Quaker beliefs and lie. I did not get the raise to Grade Seven.

I left the base in 1972 as a GS-6. Counting the almost two years I worked there in 1943 and 1944, and my sick leave which I hardly ever used, my time working for the government was about eight years, a very important part of my life.

Chapter 24

Trips to Florida

That fall of 1972, George was still working, but he took time off to drive Mother and me to Florida for her winter stay at the home in Hollywood.

We opened up the house, and I prepared to stay with her for a visit. We all loved Hollywood, and her home was very liveable. It had a sunken living room with her Victorian furniture from Grandma's house on a higher level, along with the dining room furniture to the right of the living room. There was a long walkway through the front of the house with an ivory iron railing that led to the kitchen. At the other end of the kitchen was a cozy breakfast area with a door into the garage. Through sliding glass doors along the living and dining areas was a long spacious lanai.

On the other side of the house to the left of the front door were the large master bedroom and bath and two smaller bedrooms and bath opening off a long hallway.

A picturesque curved driveway with shrubs and Adonidias enhanced the front of the house. An immense Schefflera stood close in front of the kitchen window. It was a lovely home in the beautiful Hollywood Hills section of Hollywood.

A short time after our arrival in Hollywood, and George had returned to Ohio by train, I said, "Mother I think you need a new car, don't you?" She did, of course! The car was the most important part of her life, other than her homes.

Early the next morning, we drove to Fort Lauderdale to the Conner Brown Cadillac sales lot. Walking around the lot, and looking at the few cars that were there, Mother fell for a 1969 Cadillac Calais. We whispered together, I trying to get her to be quiet.

"Sh - don't let him know you are interested!" I said.

The salesman took us into his office, and had us sit in front of him.

"Is there one particular car you are interested in?" he asked.

"The gold one, with two doors. I want that one!" she blurted out, loudly.

The salesman's eyes and mine met in astonishment. How could I dicker? No way. He and I stared at one another, without saying anything. Then he dropped his eyes, and began talking again. He told us about it while Mother could only say, "That's the one I want!" Finally, he got up. "I'll see what I can do with the boss," he said. "Maybe he could do better, for you."

"Mother, you shouldn't have insisted that was the one you wanted!" I said to her, as soon as he was out of the room. "I thought I would get him to come down on the price."

"But that's the one I want!" she said again.

"I know that, but you don't say that to him!" I said.

When he came back into the room, I looked at him, exasperatedly, hoping he would give us a good deal. He dropped his eyes, when he spoke. "My boss said he could give it to you for fifty dollars less," he said meekly.

That was a slap in the face. He knew he had a deal! We had to go for it. With my Mom so sure what she wanted, and didn't want, an attitude she had lived with all her life, and even passed on to her children, there was nothing anyone could do now. She was to pay for what she wanted, a fact that was of little concern to her.

We drove away in that beautiful, gorgeous car which was the delight and pleasure of Mother's and ours for the rest of her life and long afterwards in our family, with almost no trouble with the engine or anything. It was the best buy we ever made.

When Mother died, she still had that Cadillac. By now it was pretty old, and worth very little, so I let Larry and Judy have it to keep it in the family. They used it much longer than they should have, because the air conditioning kept going out on it. That was about the only thing we had as a problem, and in Florida that is a big problem.

Judy drove the Cadillac, while Larry drove their other car, as he drove about seventy miles daily, to and from work. The heat poured out on them so terribly on hot days, I finally told Judy they should get rid of the car. It was too hot for those little babies, even though the windows would all be down. It was a great car and served us all well. I was very proud to tell Mother, "This is your car," up to the time she could not go in it. We took her for drives up to the last of her life and we always went in "her" car so she would feel good. She always seemed to know it was hers.

Now I wanted Florida license to drive this beautiful car that just seemed to glide down the streets. I had a license since I was in my teens in Illinois, so I stood in a long line for applicants, listening to them talking of the test we were to take to get my Florida license. I picked up some information I didn't know about Florida rules. I had no idea what questions they ask, but about four young people before me were talking about questions and answers to those questions. They started talking about Pi.

"What's Pi?" I questioned them. "Why do we have to know anything about that, anyway?" I said.

When they told me, I remembered studying about Pi in school, but who would ever think of it again?

When I started taking my test, I was shaking all over. But I did okay! When the questions were asked I was able to answer all of them, even the Pi! The only question I missed was how many can legally sit in the front seat? My age gave me away.

Two, was my written answer.

Of course, when I was a teenager, we could never let that third person in the front seat. I thought all those years when we had a third person in the front, ever widening seat, was illegal. In Florida a third person may legally sit there.

I stayed with Mother for a month. She and her wonderful Florida friends did not want me to leave. I didn't want to leave either. Every time I mentioned going home, she would beg me to stay. We went everywhere, in her new car, all around Hollywood, Hallandale, Miami, Fort Lauderdale, etc., everywhere we could think of going, and having a great time. We were both gadabouts, not wanting to stay home, when we could think of somewhere to go. It was a wonderful month that November with Mother.

I began to insist I had to leave, but both Mother and Henry, who was often with us on our gadabouts, kept telling me George didn't mind, he could take care of himself. I felt so guilty, having all this fun while he was still going to work. He should be here with me!

A few days later I did go back to Ohio on the train, to George, getting a promise from Henry to look in on Mother, even though we had Marie, a housekeeper to see to her needs. George was beginning to wonder if I was ever coming back.

The following spring George and I flew to Hollywood to drive Mother back to Ridgefarm. Mary and Kip had lived there for the winter and promised to be out when Mother came back the next spring. But it was a cold spring and they had not moved out.

They were bundled up in the dining room which they had fixed up as a living room against the cold that winter. It was so cold, and thinking of her warmth and comfort, we decided to take her home with us until the spring weather would arrive.

The next morning after arriving home at Oakhaven George went to work. Mother slept in Monte's bed, which was made from her grandfather's walnut tree, from his farm in New Jersey, and Gram had slept in all the time when I visited her. This was the same bed I helped make up, as a girl, and watch the fluffy featherbed settle which was such a delight to sink into.

Mother didn't get up, so about 11:00 I went in to see. She wasn't feeling well and was dizzy. After we talked a while, I knew something was wrong. She sat up laboriously and threw her legs over the side of the bed. She tried to talk,

"Something's wrong," she managed to say. "I feel strange."

After trying to get her to talk more to me, I had her lie back in bed, then raced for the telephone.

"George, can you come home?" I cried. "I think there's something wrong with Mother!" I told him how she seemed to be. "I think we ought to take her to the doctor," I said.

"Let me see if I can get off. I had a meeting to attend in a few minutes, but I'll see if someone else can take it." He called back, saying he was coming home.

"Hurry," I said. "I don't like the way she looks and acts."

After the doctor examined her, he talked with us. "Your Mother has had a stroke. She doesn't seem to be too serious, but it's hard to tell. Take her home and watch her. She knows what we are saying, even though she cant talk. She understands but cannot put thoughts into words. You'll have to help her and take care of her, but she will probably be able to talk and do things after awhile."

She could walk but never used her speech facilities too much, after that. After therapy she talked a little, but one day I said, "Mother you never talk anymore!"

"Everything I say is wrong," she answered.

"No, it isn't" I answered. "You need to talk!" But she gradually talked less and less, until she said very little.

Mother didn't get much better. From that time until her death in 1981, she was unable to take care of her business and personal affairs. Since I was the only one left near her home, I was the one who took care of her for the rest of her life.

Charley's and Helen's youngest daughter, Linda, had married a young handsome, dark haired and black eyed Italian, Mario "Mike" Lanza and they had come to Dayton, Ohio, for a stint in the military. They had their first baby, a boy, August 14, 1972, while living in Dayton. It was so nice to have family near us. and I couldn't wait to see her newborn baby.

"Do you want to see him?" she asked us when we went into the hospital room at WPAFB to see her.

"Yes," I said "I can't wait. I love babies."

"I'll go down to the nursery with you," she said. "They let me go inside to be with him. There are only three babies in there right now. They put a sterile robe and mask on me, and I can go into the nursery, and hold my baby." She was so proud.

George and I were told to stand outside the large nursery window and watch. Linda would pick him up and bring him over to the window for us to view him.

As we stood there, looking the babies over, one of them caught our eye.

"Look, George! Look at that little baby on the end!" I spoke excitedly. "Isn't he beautiful!"

He had coal black hair, and beautiful features. We continued looking and talking about this handsome little baby.

"Hey, maybe we shouldn't let Linda see how excited we are about that baby. Maybe that one isn't hers," I said.

So we continued smiling, but tried to calm down, as we saw Linda getting her robe, hat and mask on. She looked over at us where we stood outside the large window, and we watched anxiously to see just which baby she would pick up.

We sighed with relief as she walked towards this gorgeous little creature we had fallen in love with, and picked him up, bringing him over to the window.

He awakened gradually out of his sleep, as Linda held him and talked to him. His black hair, black eyes, and tan skin, made him a gorgeous little creature. I loved him! I wanted to hold him!

We continued to watch and wish we had another baby, or a grandson, for this little one took our breath away.

Mike was stationed in Dayton for a few months, but they soon left to go to the Philippines, and we didn't get to see this little baby grow up. He was to have a brother and a sister later.

In 1973 Larry was to be graduated from Southern Illinois University at Carbondale, Illinois. Mother had had her stroke that spring, and I had retired in June 1972, so I encouraged George to retire in June 1973.

George did retire that June, taking early retirement. They gave him and two other fellows, who retired at that time, a retirement party. One was Martin Connolly, George's division chief. The party was a festive affair, and everyone had a great time. One of the Fett twins, Karen, made a beautiful flowered long dress with low rounded neckline and sleeveless, for me. She made a darling little bag to go with it. I was the best dressed gal there. She and her family were good friends, members of our Medway United Methodist Church.

George was given a fishing rod and reel and several flower and plant books for Florida. He has used the books ever since, they are the Bible of gardening, but the fishing, he has yet to get a good mess of fish with that pole! Fish in Florida are bigger, and more feisty, than those generally caught in the north, so a larger and sturdier pole has to be used.

That June In 1973, we all went to Carbondale, Illinois, where Larry was graduated from Southern Illinois University (SIU) and watched our little six foot boy receive his diploma. He was handsome in his cap and gown, so happy to have his diploma, after study and constant concentration on his class work for two years and eight months, full time.

Mother, Ann and Connie, George and I, and, most important of all, Judy, who had slaved at a position at SIU, were all there to watch him get his diploma.

This was a turning point in our lives. Larry and Judy came home to Oakhaven, and we sold our beautiful Oakhaven to them, where they stayed for five years, until they Came to Florida to help us with our business.

After three years in commercial photography, Schwartz Studio, Inc, Larry became co-owner, for two years of Massing-Patterson Photography Studio, which was engaged in commercial photography. Judy had a very good job at Twyman Films, a firm which distributed film productions all over the country. This is what they left behind when George became ill and we needed their help with the business.

Monte and Cindy both had good jobs, Monte, a Surveyor Crew Chief, with Lockwood Surveying and Engineering Co., and Cindy an accountant with ALCO Manufacturing Company.

We went to the farm in Illinois with Mother and stayed the summer and early fall with her. It was a great time for all of us. We needed a rest. Being at the wonderfully quiet old farm homestead, was the best medicine we could have, when we took Mother to Ridgefarrn to stay with her, until time for all of us to go to Florida.

George set up our kiln and he worked on pottery, throwing on his wheel and creating slab pieces, such as a bird feeder, a candle lamp, several wind chimes, creating several noteworthy pieces of his own design.

We settled down and lived a quiet beautiful life of relaxation, getting back our equilibrium and stamina. We had been going at such a fast pace that it was pure pleasure to just relax and rest.

Part Three
Flourishing in Florida

Chapter 25
Going to Florida for Good!

That fall, October 12, 1973, George drove our car with our twenty-one foot Utopia Travel Trailer, all packed up for the trip, with essentials we needed on the way, and when we would arrive in Florida. I took Mother with me and drove her 1969 Cadillac, following behind George.

We planned to stay with Mother for awhile until we decided to build or to buy an existing home.

It was fun, driving together in our convoy, I behind George, so I wouldn't get ahead of him. George took our Dachshunds, Harry and Katie with him. They slept with their heads on his right knee almost all the way. They whooped and hollered, when we stopped and they saw me. They were as happy as we were.

None of us realized it, but this was the last time Mother was to see her beloved farm, except for one short trip when Cousin Ruby took her back. They just sat in the front room mostly, and talked. I think Mother felt her home was in Florida now and she was happy to get back down there.

It is sad to leave a home, but when you go back to visit that home, it is never the same. It is full of memories, but is not home anymore. Home is where your hat is, where you are living at the moment.

When we arrived in Alabama, near Mobile, we called Kay and Bill Smith, our long ago great friends. They asked us to come and spend the night with them. We did, but stayed the night in our travel trailer rather than in their home.

They lived high on a hill, in a large beautiful home, with a large building housing several Great Danes as they raised and sold them.

She still had their horse sized Great Danes and they still backed up to the sofa and sat down on it like a person. Kay said she had never taught them how to do that, they just started doing it. They had done it several years before when we visited them at Merritt Island, Florida.

Their house was warm and relaxing, as it had always been, wherever they lived. It was so good to visit them. It had been quite a few years, since we had all been such good friends, together constantly. Now Kay was sick in bed with cancer, but she was still lively and thrilled to see us. She died sometime later. It was a great loss.

Kay had always been a vivacious person, full of ideas and activities. Ann, their oldest daughter, had cooked supper of delicious pot roast, which we devoured.

Their younger daughter, Sue, was married to the Grandson of the Nestle chocolate clan.

They wanted us to stay longer, but we were anxious to get settled in Florida.

"Mother, that hat would go perfectly with your dress we like so well," I said excitedly. It was a cloche that pulled down over the eyes. It looked great on me, and felt so good on my head.

I put it on Mother's head and she looked fantastic. It looked like hats I had seen her wear when I was growing up. It was a darkish flowered, tight fitting hat with burgundy leather trim.

"It's almost the same flower pattern as your dress," I said. "It will be beautiful with it!"

The dress was made of extremely soft fabric, covered with darkened gold, rust and burgundy flowers.

After we arrived home and put them together, they were almost identical, the pattern and shade of the flowers went perfectly with her dress that she and I loved so much. From, then on, she was the best dressed woman in any group.

When we stayed with Mother in Hollywood George and I, and sometimes Mother, attended the beautiful Hollywood Hills United Methodist Church. I loved it, as they had a tremendous bell choir that played the bells better than any other choir I ever heard. The resounding bells, reverberated all through our bodies and held us spellbound.

The bell ringers choir were all large men and women, who would file in from both sides of the sanctuary at the same time, strong and elegant in their red robes, and standing erect, would pick up their bells, which were on the bannister in front of them. The choir loft was high above the sanctuary, and we had to only raise our eyes to watch them. They were bigger than life, and they played music that was terrific!

At the snap of the first note to the end of the last strong note it was riveting to watch and hear. Those large men and women would snap the individual bells with strong aplomb and beauty. It was the outstanding part of the beautiful service. They were so superb that they were invited to Europe to perform.

The area from Fort Lauderdale, to Miami, with Hollywood in the middle, was full of interesting places to go.

Mother, George and I, and often Henry Miller, would go out every day and do something. The beaches were fabulous along the ocean front, affording us constant fun and relaxation.

Wolfie's in Miami Beach and Creighton's in Fort Lauderdale were our favorite eateries. Wolfie's was a thriving, bustling beehive of activity noisily serving up mostly traditional Jewish dishes on Collins Avenue. Our favorite dinner there was Bavarian cabbage rolls, the best we have ever eaten. They served a mean Reuben too, which often satisfied George.

Creighton's in Fort Lauderdale was a lovely southern colonial restaurant on the Intercoastal Waterway. A gorgeous white grand piano was in the entrance room, where someone played beautiful melodies on it most of the time, to entertain the dinner guests. The dining area was elegant, light and airy, decorated with foliage plants, as in a garden. We dressed up to go there, where the decorum was of the best. The food was French cuisine, elegantly prepared and served. Creighton's always served dainty sticky buns as the bread, and we found them to be excellent. When we went back to Creighton's sometime after we had moved to the west coast, it had closed, never to be opened again. Imagine our enormous disappointment as we had gone over there just to eat in that lovely restaurant and enjoy it's ambiance.

Wolfie's had moved away from downtown Miami Beach, and was now down the street from where Creighton's had been in Fort Lauderdale.

Going into Wolfie's we compared the new one to the old bustling Wolfie's in Miami Beach, but it was not the same atmosphere. In Miami Beach, the Jews who frequented Wolfie's lived down the streets in motels and apartments, and everyone knew one another. They were so friendly, and always accepted us as their own. However, we did get our delicious Bavarian cabbage rolls, which were just as good as ever, at Fort Lauderdale.

Many, many times, we found ourselves on Collins Avenue in Miami Beach at midnight, ending up going home from an all day outing of fun. After awhile it became a joke. There we would be, going down Collins Ave, heading back home from Miami to our home in Hollywood. We loved Collins Avenue, especially at night with all the lights on, going the full length in Miami Beach to Hollywood Boulevard the road we turned on, to Hollywood and home.

Going to the beaches was great fun. We always managed to shop in the area and to buy a lot. At the Hollywood Beach, George and I found jackets alike, made of orange nylon, which we still have over twenty years later. We bought them to wear on our new Schwinn bikes which we bought when we first came to live in Florida, as we left our old bikes with Larry and Judy. We bought new Schwinn, three speed, bicycles in Hollywood for the two of us, George's being green and mine being yellow. It was fun riding around Hollywood Hills on our new bikes.

We hated to give up George's Dad's old heavy bike, a Liberty Autocycle, which he used to ride to the dairy to work. George used it when we were first married and continued to do so as it was far better than any bicycle we could afford to buy. It had become an antique, however, now about fifty years old. So we opted not to bring it to Florida.

After we bought our orange jackets, we went to another store nearby. There was a large bamboo hassock there that looked to me as if it were made for Mother. It was perfect for her home, for her to put her feet up. She didn't have any kind of a stool, so this was something she needed.

It is now in my home in Fort Myers, perfect for our home. I'm so glad I talked my Mother into getting it that day!

There was a wonderful Fish market Mother and Dad used to frequent, on the road to the beaches, at Sunny Isles, where we could buy excellent fresh or smoked fish. There was a wonderful park at the Sunny Isles Beach. It had a train that ran through the park, which was fun, and the beach itself was one of the best. Nearby, Mother treated us to our first taste of "Pizza Pie." We are still eating it every chance we get, we try them all.

We also loved to go to Breeding's Drug Store in Hallandale, where they kept jars of guava jelly and orange preserves on the tables in the eating area. We sometimes had breakfast or lunch there.

We decided to build our future home in Naples where we had the land Mother bought for us and we took over and paid for. We drove to Naples, looked at homes, and decided we liked the Sunbrella home the best. Our builder said he could make one very similar to the one we had chosen.

Our new home was put in the middle of slash pine and cypress trees. The builder took out all our trees but three in the area where the house was to be built. We had asked him to leave all trees they could, just take away the trees that needed to be taken away to get our house among them.

We were torn asunder the first time we viewed the beginning of the building, as they had cleared all trees on our land for one hundred twenty feet deep. We were sick! Mad! Upset! The first time we saw him, we laid into him as never did anyone before in our lives! We loved our trees! The area was full of trees, an area we could have kept as a beautiful jungle, as did most of the future home builders and home owners who came after us.

But no, our builder had to cut all the beautiful pine trees down. We had a house like the ones in the city! We lived in the country, wanted a country home, but here we were, with only three trees and a wide expanse of sand.

We were the first ones to build on this street, and the first ones in a square mile area. We had to arrange for the electrical power and telephone to be brought to this area, and had to manage without them for a month, as the house had been finished before they could be brought in the seven miles from Golden Gate Subdivision.

"Do you want your street to be named Massing?" the County Clerk said when we went to the court house to apply for a street number and find out the name of the street.

"Yes!" we said in amazement. "That would be fantastic!" we laughed.

But before we left the office, another clerk came in and said it had to be 6th Avenue SW, because it was in the southwest corner of a huge plat. Our happiness was short lived.

George and I pulled our little Utopia travel trailer from Hollywood to Estero, Florida, thirteen miles north of Naples, and left it at the Imperial Mobile Home Park, to be used to stay the nights we would go over there, from Hollywood, to check on the progress of the house. We later parked it at the Covered Wagon Park just south of Estero on Highway 41.

The wife of the builder was an interior decorator, and let us use her card to look at furniture in a Decorator Showroom in Miami. She couldn't come to meet us from Naples, at the time we wanted to look at new furniture, so we went by ourselves.

We had picked out living room furniture on our last trip to Dayton, Ohio, at the Mudd Furniture Store recommended by my good friend, Sally Allen, and it was to be drop shipped as soon as the house was ready.

The Mudd store in Dayton, Ohio was going to drop ship some new front room and dining room furniture, but we were to get two bedrooms of furniture in Florida.

All that new furniture was so beautiful! It was so great to be buying new furniture, as I had lived with antiques all of my life. We were amazed at all the beautiful furniture from which to choose. It was a fairy tale for me. I didn't even ask the price of anything until I settled on what I wanted!

There were two choices for our large master bedroom. I knew I should take the light Country French Provincial set, which was lovely, more feminine than the other, but I fell for the heavy, gorgeous eight piece Thomasville Mediterranean set, which boasted of a huge king sized bed, with a large nine drawer triple dresser, over which were two tall narrow mirrors, two large night stands, and a large armoire consisting of four drawers and two shelves, the shelves and one drawer concealed by triple paneled doors, perfect for sweaters, linens, etc., etc.

The set included a free standing moveable, swiveling mirror. We took them all, and added another tall narrow chest for small things. This outfit I'm going to keep until I die! I have never been sorry. It is so gorgeous and heavy and luxuriant.

It was much more than George expected to pay, but I reasoned we would have it for the rest of our lives, so why not! I still love it as much as I did when I first saw it on the showroom floor.

For one of the guest bedrooms, we chose a Thomasville, regular size bedroom set. It is a creamy, light yellow color with a bamboo motif.

We bought the guest bedroom furniture later, when we moved over to Naples, but the larger master bedroom set we had to take out of the store now as they had a sale on it. So, where did we put it? In our bedroom at Mother's.

"You can't get that furniture in here!" Mother said. "Put it out here in the hall and throughout the house, anywhere it will go."

"I think we can get it amongst the furniture in our bedroom," I said. "We won't be moving for months. You don't want it to be all thru the house."

When the furniture arrived at Mother's house, we had the delivery men put all the pieces in our bedroom. We didn't let them put it in the hall even, as Mother suggested. We didn't want to clutter up Mother's beautiful home.

So we arranged and rearranged our bedroom until every piece was ensconced in our bedroom. As there were only little trails to get out of our bed and get to our bath room and out into the hall. But Mother and her friends were not inconvenienced in any way.

It wasn't bad. I don't know how they got all that bedroom furniture in the room but it was the master bedroom of the house and it kept reaching out towards those movers, saying, "Come on, I can hold some more!" So it all went in there, and we were still able to get around, enough. Not easily, but okay.

When we were able to move into our new home, made specifically for us, and to our specifications, our new furniture fit absolutely perfectly!

It reminded me of the time Larry had a piano for Judy put in his bedroom until Christmas. We were their guests at Oakhaven that Christmas and had to sleep in a bed pushed against the wall and with only one and a half feet from the piano. It can be done.

Soon after we moved in we quickly sowed grass, which never became a beautiful stand of grass in that sand, and went looking for plants, etc., to landscape.

Fortunately, George began to sell plants and shrubs after a few months of living there, so we were able to get first choice of beautiful plants. When we left our new home eleven years later, our real estate lady estimated five thousand dollars worth of plants, two being huge coconut palms for which we traded George's boss, Russ Stahlman, our Utopia travel trailer.

I always wanted an olive tree. They are so gorgeous with their heavy, thick branches, causing a beautiful, full shade, of which we have little here in Florida. So we planted a little beauty right out in front where it could grow and cast a heavy shadow. It never grew in that sandy soil! It just got to a shrub like appearance. One day, when I was busy helping George prune the shrubbery around the house, I looked over at this pathetic tree, and momentarily forgot it was a tree!

"Gosh, that looks awful, all scraggly, going every which way," I thought. I ran over and started trimming and pruning it way down. "There, that looks better!" I said, as I went back to prune around the house.

"What on earth have you done to that olive tree?" George asked, when he came around to the front of the house.

I stared in amazement. I stood looking at it for a longtime!

"I forgot it was our olive tree!" I said in tears.

"Well, it will grow back!" George said. Bless his heart!

But it never did! It stayed a small bush until we left. I never had my gorgeous olive tree I wanted!

That Christmas, Monte and Cindy were expecting their first baby. Shane Lucas, was born January 16, 1974 at Good Samaritan Hospital, in Dayton where Larry and Monte were born.

The first morning after Cindy and Shane were brought home from the hospital, I went over to see them.

"Do you want to bathe Shane?" Cindy asked me.

"Yes, I would love to!" I exclaimed.

"Will you bring the bathinette, where I can watch you?" she asked me. So, I gave Shane his first bath in front of his mother, just as his father was given in front of me in his bathinette. As I bathed my beautiful little grand baby, I talked to Cindy, as my hired girl had talked to me, explaining how to proceed. Cindy reacted as I had done, being very alert and interested.

Two years later Seth Matthew was born December 10, 1975, at the same hospital.

Chapter 26
Casa Masbu - Return to Naples

We moved from Mother's home in Hollywood to our new home in Naples, June 30, 1974, bringing with us the two, beautiful, new bedroom suites we had bought in Miami. They fit our two bedrooms perfectly.

Our third bedroom was to become a hide all for excess stuff we couldn't get rid of, and a room for Katie and Harry, our dear little Dachshunds. I ached all the years we lived there to clean that room up. We really never needed it, so it never got done.

We named our new home Casa, which is Spanish for House, Masbu from Massing and Busby, thus, House of Massing and Busby. Our home had a Spanish flavor which went well in Naples, as many buildings in Naples are of Spanish architecture, or are of old Florida style.

When we moved there, to get to Casa Masbu, we went north on the Tamiami Trail, turned east on Pine Ridge Road, and continued on to a gravel and soft sand road.

Trees almost came together in a thicket through this area forcing the car into the middle of the road through an area of soft sand, then onto, would you believe, onto Ridgefarm Road? I told George I had come full circle.

"It's just like going into a cocoon!" I said one day, as we turned into our area.

When new neighbors down the road one-forth mile, Jim and Joyce Walston, came to see their house being built, she saw our house almost finished.

"How dare they!" Joyce said. "I thought we were going to be the first house built in this area!"

"George!" I said about the same time. "Do you know, there's someone building a new house right down the road? We're going to have new neighbors." I thought we were going to be living out here all by ourselves, darn it! We soon became fast friends.

We had gone to Mudd's Furniture Store in Dayton and picked out a sofa made by Pullman, two avocado lounge chairs, a love seat, and a few other things. They were drop shipped to our new home in Naples. We later bought a southern cotton rattan sofa for the family room with rattan rocker and rattan dining room set. At the open breakfast bar we placed four high backed rattan stools bought in Naples.

When the furniture was brought by Wheaton Van Lines from Ohio, the two young movers worked hard placing the furniture in the right places.

Our Mediterranean sofa from Oakhaven was put in the front room, along with the new love seat from Mudd's which rested in its own alcove. The new wing back green corduroy chairs flanked the sofa.

"You have worked awfully hard," I said. "You've done a great job. Would you like a bite to eat before you hit the Alligator Alley?" They had told us they were going to Miami to pick up another load to take up north.

"Well, yes, if it's not too much work," the driver said. The other young man who was a bit shy just smiled.

"I want you to taste the best fruit you've ever eaten," I said, as I put their sandwiches on the breakfast bar, with a plate of sliced mangos.

"Mangos? Is that what you call that?" The driver asked as he looked at the plate, interested. "I thought Mangos are green. They are up north."

"The vegetable we eat up north is green." I laughed. "This is a southern fruit, peachy yellow in color. We think it's the best of all fruit."

He took a piece and tasted it. "Hmm," he said. He took another bite. He reached for another piece. "That is pretty good!" He continued eating pieces of the mango along with his sandwich. His helper had not attempted to eat any at all.

"Don't you want a piece, too?" I asked him," You'll like it. It's delicious!" He just shook his head and continued eating his sandwich.

"I can't wait until I cross the Alligator Alley," the driver said. "I can't wait to see all those alligators!"

"What alligators?" I asked.

"Well all the alligators on Alligator Alley," he said, in surprise.

I laughed.

"Well, aren't there a lot of alligators on Alligator Alley?" he continued. "Why else is it called Alligator Alley?"

All this time, I had noticed out of the corner of my eye, his helper, that had been so quiet, had reached over gingerly with his hand and had sneaked a piece of mango off the plate to try. I looked at him full in the face.

"How do you like it?" I asked.

He grinned for the first time, surprised to be caught.

"Pretty good," he said, not over enthusiastically. I noticed he continued eating them.

"Back to the Alligators," I said, "we have crossed Alligator Alley many times, and we have never seen but one alligator. Every time we used Alligator Alley, I looked for them. George saw one once. Some people say they see them. Maybe we just look ahead too far."

"I suppose years ago there might have been a lot of alligators on that land." I mused. "One time, there were hundreds of darling little swamp rabbits, all over and along side of the road nestling against the heat of the cement road, as it was such a cold day, and high water had pushed them from their lairs. George had to slow down, real slow, to avoid hitting them. Some cars had hit them as there were dead ones all over the pavement."

While we were getting settled in Naples, my two twin brothers' boys, Charley's two oldest boys Tommy and Terry, and Milt's two boys, Charley Milt and Les, all worked on the Alaskan Pipeline. They helped build it from beginning to end, completed in 1977. It stretches from Prudhoe Bay, Alaska to Valdez, Alaska, sometimes in the ground, sometimes above the ground. It brings crude oil from Alaska to U. S. Refineries. It was a fabulous idea, which brought work to a lot of men who were game enough to endure the hardships and go up there in weather many degrees below zero, and work hard to bring the crude oil to the refineries.

One time, our neighbor's son of fourteen, Jimmie, was walking past our house, as the lightning crackled horrendously. He crouched to the gravel road and held himself in a ball. The lightning started a fire in the woods across from our house. I ran out of our door alarmed.

"Are you all right? Are you hurt?" I called to him.

He looked up and started moving on.

"I'm okay," he said.

I was so frightened for him. The lightning can be so bad in Florida. It kills a lot of people.

One day, we walked down to their house to visit them. As we came up to the front door, I smelled a distinctive, pleasurable aroma wafting from the house. When the door was opened, there was a freshly baked pan of warm Nestle Toll House Cookies, just waiting to be eaten! Their little ten year old girl, Liz, had just removed them from the oven, they were the best Toll House Cookies we had ever eaten. Possibly because we ate them while they were very warm.

George became stuck in the soft sand with his Toyota several times. The first time, a Florida Power and Light bulldozer, working nearby, pulled him out. Another time, a neighbor, in a Volkswagen, who lived several streets from us, pulled our Toyota out of the sand. The neighbor told George to drive fast over the soft sand area, "because when one slows down, the car will sink in the sand."

Before we knew it, another neighbor came, and then another. The streets were straightened out and seven or eight years later Pine Ridge Road became a four lane highway, connecting to I-75. We no longer lived in our little cocoon, but we continued to love it.

When Sally and Bill Allen came to visit us in Naples, from their home in Cape Coral, where they moved after their retirement, Sally was amazed that I had settled into the Floridian lifestyle so easily, from my background of the more formal living with antiques.

"I'm really surprised at you!" she said laughing. I guess she didn't know me as well as she thought she did. I'm always ready for change, if it is better, or suits me better, at the time of change. Some things I will never change.

George and I could hardly wait to get our flowers, trees and shrubs put around our place in Naples. We had two and a half acres of land in a beautiful area. There could be two horses and twenty-five chickens, although not many people had the livestock.

We loved our freedom, we loved doing nothing but just what we felt like doing. We were beach bums, all hours of the day, ferreting out the different haunts along the Western coast of Florida, as we had done on the Eastern Atlantic coast. It was much more quiet here, and the sand was whiter. The gentle waves from the Gulf were always pulling us towards them.

The beaches were the best. We fished off the pier at Naples, took enumerable pictures, swam in the beautiful peaceful Gulf. This was relaxing, getting our worn out bodies back to nature and slowing down to a comfortable, enjoyable retirement.

We found all the delightful, little eating places, but we also went to McDonalds once in awhile. There were many delicious fish and sea foods available. We became knowledgeable about everything in Naples, as it was relatively small and quiet. It was our town!

Later, it grew so fast, it seemed to have a mind of its own. We felt overwhelmed. Too many people found Naples-on-the-Gulf! It had been named Naples-on-the-Gulf, originally as it reminded the founders of Naples, Italy, so the story goes.

I joined the Naples Art Association but it was not very active then, so I dropped out. I continued my Daughters of the American Revolution, in the Big Cypress Chapter which was quite active. We had card parties and shows at the Trinity-by-the-Cove Episcopalian Church in Port Royal, a very exclusive area of Naples.

I originally joined the Governor Bradford Chapter, in 1973 with Mother, and we attended meetings in Hollywood, then transferred membership to Naples when we moved there. I also became a member of the Daughters of the American Colonists (DAC), Naples-on-the-Gulf Chapter, and the Henry of Navarre Chapter of the Huguenot Society. George became active in the Naples Chapter of the Sons of the

American Revolution (SAR) and The Exchange Club International, which is a service club.

"Isn't that a Bravo Croton?" I asked the salesman at a special advertised Saturday sale at Stahlman's Nursery, when we were looking for plants for our home. "How did you know that," he exclaimed. "Yes, it is! Most people just come in and buy what they like. They never know what anything is." As we talked, he could tell that George and I knew a lot about plants.

George knew all the trees, plants, and flowers in the north, so when we moved to Florida we became interested in all growing things in Florida, too.

This man, Joe Jackson, was part owner of the Stahlman Landscaping and Nursery. He offered George a job.

"We are thinking of starting a retail sales outlet," Joe said. "We've just done commercial landscaping for years. Now, we want to go into the retail business."

Both George and I enrolled in a ten week crash course at Edison Community College in Fort Myers, of Joe Vance, who was a teacher from whom we learned an enormous amount of information on Florida planting. His vitality and enthusiasm helped us for years to come. He also had a very informative, and helpful radio program, with call in questions and answers about gardening and landscaping.

George became manager of Stahlman's Retail Nursery Outlet on Airport Road. Our Twenty-one foot Utopia Travel Trailer we had brought from Ohio was used as an office. We had traded it to Russ Stahlman for some large coconut palms.

This was a happy time. George was in his element. It was only a mile from our home and we had the advantage of getting first choice of the gorgeous plants brought in from Homestead on the east coast, and other growing areas at Apopka, just north of Orlando.

George was happy as a lark. We were tired of being retired and wanted something to do. This was perfect. With George's background of growing things, and my appreciation of them, this was the best of all worlds.

But, it was short lived! George had to go to a dermatologist who told him to get out of the sun. There was no way of doing that without quitting his job. He had managed the garden center for only a year and a half, and hated to leave but we knew the doctor was right. He continued to work, only on our own plants utilizing the knowledge garnered at Stahlman's.

Joe and Ginny and children, George's brother and family, had wanted to come to Florida for so long. When we had come down, they wanted to come to Florida too.

Joe came ahead of Ginny, and found them a beautiful four bedroom home with pool, that had belonged to the Baron Collier family. Mr. Collier was the founder of Collier County in which Naples is situated.

Joe and family moved to Naples, bought a furniture store in Bonita Springs north of Naples and settled in. It was so nice to have family here.

George and I went north and picked up Mother Massing who had the first airplane ride in her life, from Indianapolis, Indiana. I had visited Larry and Monte and their families in Ohio, and met George with Mother in Atlanta, for us all to continue to Naples.

"How did you like your trip, Mother?" I asked as George pushed her in the wheelchair towards me. My plane had arrived earlier and I had had a long wait in Atlanta.

"All right," she said quietly. She wasn't sure. We were all amazed that she let George bring her.

"How in the world did you get her here?" I whispered. I was amazed, as she was afraid of everything.

"I didn't have any trouble with her at all!" George said.

It had to be because if she didn't come she would have been bereft of both her beloved sons and this she couldn't handle. No way did she want to be left in her apartment in Danville, Illinois, by herself for the rest of her life.

Mom Parker, Mother's mother and George's grandmother had passed away several years before. Mother had been living with her and they were watching the Red Skelton show on TV. Mother looked over at Mom Parker and saw that she was leaning back laughing, at least she thought she was. Mom Parker had died. Such a happy way to go. Mom Parker was a wonderful person whom everyone loved.

So here was Mother, calmly using her last chance to come to Naples.

THEN AND NOW

The airplane hit an air pocket, then another. I looked over at Mother who was sitting between us. She had hardly said anything from the time I first saw her in the airport.

"That's just an air pocket. It isn't anything," I said to her, and tried to believe it myself. It was the worst air pocket I had ever experienced. As we bumped around more, I really became alarmed but she remained quiet, as if she had believed me. We finally flew through it and everything was calm again. Joe had found her a nice, little one bedroom apartment, half way between their home and ours, so we could both help her.

George and I usually took her grocery shopping. She was so slow! She looked at every jar and bottle, to see what the contents were, she walked as if she were asleep. I used to push the shopping cart but, everything went so slowly that I would sometimes wait out front for them. She took an enormous amount of time with finding out what she was to pay, getting out her checkbook and getting the check written, and finally getting the change or coupons, and getting her purse put back together.

"We are holding everyone up. Everyone is looking at us," I said. George was so patient with her, he couldn't get her to hurry at all.

"I am doing my shopping and I'm going as fast as I can. I am not going to hurry any more," she said.

"Why don't you help her?" I asked George. "At least, you could write her check for her!" He never would, as he thought she needed to do it herself.

After that sometimes, I would let George take her by himself. We thought she needed help. Bless her heart!

When Joe took her, when George couldn't, he let her out at the front door. He let her do all of her shopping by herself. She enjoyed grocery shopping, and it gave her something to do.

One time, we took her to Beall's Department Store, where we looked for a dress for her.

"Look at that little old lady, isn't she adorable?" I heard the lady say to a friend. I looked around, and saw that she was talking about Mother, "Who's she with?" The lady said, looking all around. I was hid from her sight, behind some dresses, and she couldn't see me.

251

"She can't be by herself, where's the person taking care of her? She's all by herself!"

"I am!" I laughed. "She's alright. She loves to shop. We're looking for a dress for her."

"Oh, I didn't know," she said. "I didn't see you over there and I thought she was all alone. She's so adorable."

When we first went to Naples, we transferred our membership from Medway First United Methodist Church to Golden Gate First United Methodist Church, where Alfred Jodie, the pastor, and his wife Nancy, became good friends of ours. He was an excellent minister, having become a minister later in life.

Not everyone has a mystical experience in religion. When I was 12 and Mary Ellen 14 we went to the alter and accepted Jesus Christ as our Savior. I know that shaped my life. With Christ with me my life has been wonderful.

"That's just a crutch," someone dear to me said.

"If it is a crutch, then I want it," I answered. It has made a big difference in the way my life has been lived and other peoples unhappy lives. I have had God's gift of grace with me throughout my life. I have sinned like everyone else because I am not perfect as Jesus was, but I know I am forgiven as everyone is who asks for forgiveness and tries to live better.

The Methodist Church, which we joined when we moved to Crystal Lakes, Ohio (in 1946), believe in the Holy Trinity which is Father, Son and Holy Spirit. It was not hard for me to accept the teaching of the Methodist Church after being raised a Quaker. A mystical experience I had when we moved to Naples was in Miami at a Catherine Kuhlman church rally when I prayed that the Holy Spirit would enter my body. I was holding my hands in the air and there was a tingling that started in my fingertips and continued down my arms to my head. I remember wondering what would happen when it got to my head. I felt the same sensation move onto the top of my head going down through my head to my shoulders. Always moving down the sensation continued through my body to my heels. There the Spirit, which it was I know, moved out to my toes and left me. I was really excited knowing it was the Holy Spirit. I went to the stage where the woman prayed over me as she was doing with many others.

She barely touched a fingertip to my shoulders and I found myself going backwards. I was slain in the Spirit. A man caught me so I wasn't hurt.

I was not so lucky the next time. In a meeting I was slain again and no one was there to catch me. My head hit the sharp top of a chair and I fell backwards in pain.

Another time I was slain at the alter in our Methodist church where our good friend Rev. Jodie officiated. "What happened?" he said excitedly to a friend. "Was she slain?" I was, he was so glad.

He wanted to be slain in the Holy Spirit. He had never been slain. He wanted me to talk to God so he could be slain. When they came to our house the next day I prayed for my vessel to be emptied so the Holy Spirit could go through me and into Rev. Jodie. He really didn't believe it could happen, but he wanted it so badly. After a few minutes of praying, Rev. Jodie was slain. He was the happiest person I've ever seen, crying and laughing at the same time. It was an exhilarating experience for all of us.

I know the Lord loves me and I love the Lord. I pray to be a better person and I try to be but I know I fall short.

When the Jodies were transferred to a new church in Cleveland, Florida, east of Punta Gorda, we decided to change our membership to North Naples United Methodist Church, as it was closer to our home. We enjoyed this church and had a lot of friends there. Joe and Ginny and their family, and Mother Massing, all joined the North Naples United Methodist Church. We took Mother Massing with us and she and I attended functions at the church.

Joe and Ginny took over the selling of Ted's Sheds, which belonged to the son of the woman who sold Joe and Ginny their furniture store in Bonita Springs. When George left the nursery because of the sun damage he was getting, he thought he might try another kind of work. Joe suggested he take over Ted's Sheds in Fort Myers. Joe wanted to keep the lot in Naples which would have been better for us. We arranged to open a shed lot in the Fort Myers area, locating on a small lot next to the post office in North Fort Myers.

The influx of people coming to Florida caused a need for sheds, as everyone wanted a basement or storage attic but had neither. Most people had more furniture or things to save than they could house in their homes they bought. Some wanted to store their lawn mowers and others their yard tools and fertilizers. A Ted's Shed was the perfect answer.

George and I took out a ten thousand dollar loan from the Small Business Administration. We bought an inventory of sheds in 1977 and rented a lot with a run down building on it from a nice old man, Mr. Price, who owned most of downtown North Fort Myers, including the post office building next to us. He was a kindly old man and we enjoyed his acquaintance. His son Jack Price administered our lease from his dad.

Monte came down from Ohio and helped us clean up and repair the building, and get the lot ready. The toilet and entire bathroom was jammed with hundreds of pieces of undelivered mail, left there by the mail carriers who didn't want to, or couldn't for some reason deliver them. We all worked awfully hard getting ready to open, but it was fun. We had our own business!

It was with great happiness that we watched those Ted's Sheds brought in on our cleaned up lot, filling up the empty space. They were beautiful.

We thought small in those days, being fresh and unknowledgeable. We started out with hope! And lots of guts!

We sat and waited for customers. For three weeks we went every day to North Fort Myers, and sat and waited. We enjoyed it, but it was no place for a person with no retirement to live on while getting started. We would go back to Naples to our little cocoon every night.

When the first shed was sold, a 6x8, we were the happiest people on earth! George called Joe and arranged to borrow his delivery van and small trailer. George and I headed for Page Mobile Home Park, across from Page Field to deliver that shed.

"George, how are we going to deliver this by ourselves?" I asked. "We need someone else to help us!"

George saw a young man walking in the ditch beside the road, just before we got there. He stopped and called to him. "How would you like to have a job?" he asked him. "We have this shed to deliver and could use some extra help." He agreed and crawled in the van with us. The three of us managed quite well installing the shed, and the new owners were very happy. We paid off the young man, and dropped him where he wanted to go.

Later, when we made another sale, it was suggested to us to go across the street to find a delivery helper at the neighborhood bar. George found Tom Brower, who worked for us for several years as a delivery man and sometimes salesman. His girlfriend Roselyn, and his grandmother, also helped with the sales and management.

After using Joe's delivery equipment for a few months, we bought a 1976 Ford 250, and soon after, Tom found a trailer that could be used for deliveries after he rebuilt it. Tom was a good worker and handy to have around. He stayed with us until George became seriously ill and Larry and Judy came from Ohio to take over management of the business.

I was so ready for grandchildren, but was beginning to think I was never going to have any. Maybe if I let my hair go gray, and looked like a grandmother, I would become one, I thought. So, I did just that. My bleached blonde hair gradually grew to be lightly salt and peppered.

Monte and Cindy finally had a gorgeous, big blue eyed baby they called Shane Lucas.

A year or two before his birth I had gone with Sally Allen, my good friend, to a fortune teller, who told me she saw a big blue eyed boy on my lap. I told her I knew of no one like that.

"A friend of mine just had a big blue eyed baby boy," I said.

"Maybe that's it," she said to me, and then went to something else.

When Shane came several months later, I thought, "did she really see our Shane?" I never really put much stock in these readings, but to this day, I wonder.

Cindy was a little afraid, so as she lay in bed and watched me, I gave the beautiful little boy his first bath, and explained how to do it. She watched with great interest then wanted to do it the next day.

Shane grew to be a beautiful, gentle, quiet little boy. His brother Seth Matthew came along two years later. Seth was more rambunctious, but doted on his older brother. They were a great pair. I hope they will always be close as they were as children.

When Seth was just a few days old the family came down to Florida for Christmas. We were really anxious to see our new grand baby, and as we arrived at the airport to pick them up, we met them coming up the escalator. As we hurried forward towards them with great excitement and expectation, Cindy, who was carrying the baby, held him way out in front of her. I grabbed that precious bundle and laughed and cried and hugged him. Now I had two wonderful grandchildren.

Then Larry and Judy had their first son, Joshua Paris, October 20, 1977, who was named for his two ancestors, Joshua Waddington and Parris Mendenhall. Larry said he wondered when I told him there should be two r's in Parris, but he didn't want to change it, as it was already on his birth certificate with one r.

That Christmas they came to Florida to let us see him. They arrived Christmas Eve. We had a great time with the beautiful, healthy, fat cheeked baby of one and a half months, until they all went to bed. Then out came Mr. and Mrs. Santa Claus and put presents under the tree. We worked until everything was perfect. The next morning, I ran out to double check our tree with all its presents.

"To Everyone, from God," was a placard across our beautiful little baby with wide open eyes, lying in the middle of all the colorful presents. I laughed and cried yelling for George and the others to come see our best Christmas present ever.

About two years later, George was sent to the hospital with pneumonia in both lungs, heart failure, and other ailments, remaining thirty-two days, at which time he was sent home still carrying a low grade fever. The next year he was in the hospital for nine days with a blood clot in his leg.

Each time we would go up north we would ask Monte and Cindy to come to Florida to help us with the business. Monte demurred as he didn't think he could stand the heat. As a surveyor he always was happier in the cooler weather. We always stayed at Oakhaven with Larry and Judy, when we visited up north. One evening, after we had said goodbye to Monte and his family, we were sitting in front of the fireplace, at Oakhaven with Larry and Judy, preparing to go home the next day.

"You always ask Monte if he wants to go to Florida to help you," Larry said, " You never ask me."

My head jerked up in surprise. "Would you come to Florida to live?" I exclaimed. "It never entered our minds that you would come. You have your thriving photography business here. Would you leave that?"

George was excited and saying all the things I didn't, about being glad that they might be interested in coming to Florida.

"Well, we might," he said looking over at Judy, who was smiling.

"We'd love to have you. Of course we want you to come!" I screamed. We never dreamed you would want to come.

Larry, Judy and Joshua moved to Florida, staying in our house with us, using that third storage bedroom, until their Mobile Home, they bought from Joe was manufactured, and delivered and set up in San Souci Mobile Home Park, in North Fort Myers, at the junction of Business 41 and new U. S. 41.

It was a spacious, three bedroom, double-wide home. They traveled back and forth to work in North Fort Myers, every day, taking the baby with them.

George recuperated while they were managing the business.

When Devon was born 10 May 1980, Judy's mother came from Bermuda to be with her. We had driven up from Naples and stayed the night in their large double wide Mobile Home. Early in the morning Judy came into the living room in labor. Larry hurried her off to Lee Memorial Hospital with her telling us he could get her there without our help.

"Let's follow them anyway, just to be sure she doesn't have it on the way," I said.

We arrived at the hospital without seeing them, and when we saw the empty car there, we knew she had arrived there on time. We started pulling away, when we saw Larry come popping out of the door, with a blanket, running towards the trunk of his car.

"What are you doing here?" he asked, when he saw us.

"We just wanted to make sure she made it alright!" I said.

"How is she doing?" I asked.

"O. K.," he said, grinning.

We left, and later learned everything was fine with a new baby boy in our family. He had the most gorgeous, blue eyes like all the father's of Judy, George, and mine, with jet black hair stiff as a poker. The nurses loved to fix his hair by plastering it down, but it was starting to spring back up by the time they brought him to Judy. The nurses threatened to charge twenty-five dollars for the hairdo.

Larry and Judy called him "electric shock." Both grandmothers thought that was a terrible explanation for their new, beautiful, little grandson. Larry said don't take him out without a bonnet on his head.

But he grew to be an adorable little boy, whose hair had become flaxen by five months old, never to change from the light golden color. At this time his hair was so long he had to have his first haircut, as it was hanging down in his eyes.

Chapter 27

Fun with the Kids

One time after Larry and Judy moved into their new home, Larry was complaining about Judy calling her mother Delores all the time.

She calls her mother and talks to her an hour or more!" he said.

I thought a moment. "How much does it cost" I asked, "to talk to Bermuda for an hour?"

"Twenty dollars or so," Larry said.

"How often does she call?" I asked.

"Probably once a month!" he said.

"When we were young, and moved away from home to Dayton, I wanted to go home every payday," I said. "That was twice a month, then payday changed to every other weekend."

"That cost a lot more than those telephone calls. You are getting off pretty easy, I'd say! What if Judy wanted to go home ever so often, like I did? Judy needs to talk to her Mother and sister."

Larry never mentioned that again. Judy has a wonderful rapport with her Mother. She has always talked things out with her, and when her mother comes to America for a visit, they sit up all night talking.

And they still have those long telephone conversations.

Judy has three brothers, David, Michael and Colin, all of whom live in Bermuda, and one sister Beverley, who married an American Navy flyer, and lives in Maryland with her husband and two sons, so there are lots of family things to talk about. Her brothers and families love to come to visit Florida. We enjoy them when they come. They all have beautiful Bermudian English accents, and are very nice people.

Judy's father, Reggie, came to Oakhaven, when we lived in Ohio, then we took him to Illinois, to see Larry and Judy who were at Southern Illinois University (SIU), in Carbondale. That fall he went with George and me when we took Mother to Florida. We enjoyed Reggie, he was a very likeable man. But he had heart problems, and passed away when Joshua was a year old. Judy and Larry had taken Joshua home to Bermuda to visit his ailing Grandfather. After visiting a week, they went home to Ohio. The next week Reggie died of a heart attack. "I'm so glad we went home, so Joshua and his Grandfather could get to know one another," Judy said.

Larry and Judy needed another set of wheels, so we had them use Mother's old Cadillac, a 1957 Cadillac Calais, built to withstand the years, George would say, "Built like a Sherman tank."

That was the best car. We hardly ever had any problems with it except later on we had to get the air conditioner fixed. When Mother was in the care center we would take her rides in it.

"Mother, this is your car!" I would say. "Remember?"

She would look around and pat it, and seemed to understand.

We let Larry and Judy use it after Mother passed away. I hated to get rid of it. It had meant so much to us.

One day, I was standing besides the car when Judy was at the wheel. She had just picked up the three little ones and they were all looking at me. As I leaned forward to talk to them, I felt a horrible amount of heat pouring past the children and into my face.

"Judy, this air is hot. What is all that heat!"

"Oh, it's the air conditioner!" she said, "We've had it fixed several times, but we've given up on it ever being right," she said.

"But it's so hot for the children!" I complained!

"Yes, I know. We're going to have to get rid of it," she said.

It was about 100 degree weather, then having that heat come out of the air conditioner. It wasn't long before they sold it. It had been a great car! Well worth the money we had paid years ago in Fort Lauderdale when Mother fell for it!

Larry and Judy, and George and I bought a very nice seventeen foot boat, which Larry named Kestrel, for the hawk of that name. We went out in the Caloosahatchee and other waterways. There was one time only, when we talked Larry into going beyond the waterway into Gulf waters. We were coming down the Caloosahatchee towards the Gulf, when the waters became so fierce and choppy, that Larry, did not want to go out into the Gulf.

"Aw, come on Larry," I wheedled. "Let's go on out into the Gulf. We have never been out in the Gulf waters, and I have always wanted to go!" So, like the good son he is, he piloted us in our own little boat out into the Gulf, and close to the coastline of Sanibel, he took us just past our timeshare Condo, Shell Island Beach Club, and back. It was terribly rough, but lots of fun!!

The family would haul the boat, on its trailer, to a boat ramp, and put it in the water by backing the trailer into the water to let the boat float free.

One time, at the boat ramp on Route 80, at the Orange River, when we were trying to get into the boat, the young ones made it very well, as usual, but I had trouble.

"Come here, Larry, and give me a push, I yelled at him where he stood at the controls

"How can I do that?"

"Just push me up. I have no push to my body anymore! I just can't do it," I exclaimed.

He huffed and puffed, with Dad, and they hoisted me up into the boat, and at one time they had my body parallel with the boat and water, and there I was looking up at the sky.

"Keep pushing! I'm getting there," I yelled at them. My arms and legs were all I seemed to be able to move, but I finally hooked my legs over the bow of the boat. They pushed some more and I was in! That was the last time we entered the river at the side of the water. After that, we put the boat in at a dock!

The little boat was fine for the children to run around in, as it was a center console fisherman.

After the children grew older and bigger and more active, we traded the little seventeen foot boat for a twenty-one foot, center console Aquasport fisherman, called Stargazer II.

Judy and the children often sat up front in the bow of the boat like a figurehead. Larry went very fast. It was great and so much fun! We all loved it!

George and I sat back of the pilot and oftentimes watched the beautiful, sparkling wake. There is nothing so wonderful as owning a boat and using it every weekend.

When the fun gets thin and people have too many other interests, that intervene, it is very sad. The best time for an owner of a boat is in the beginning, when he first buys his boat, and the worst time, or some say the happiest time, is when he sells it.

Actually the worst time is watching it deteriorate right outside your window for years before you try to find a buyer for it.

Watching the beautiful churning wake behind the boat and being in the sun so much, did a great deal of damage to my eyes.

Now, our beautiful Stargazer II languishes on its trailer in front of the barn, awaiting the next trip out.

Chapter 28

An Unfortunate Happening

When we first came to Florida we asked around in order to find the best eye doctor, as George has always been legally blind in his right eye ever since he was a small boy.

That doctor became my doctor, too. Now, he told me I had one hemorrhage, possibly two, in one eye. He sent me to Bascom-Palmer in Miami for the examination.

We drove over the Tamiami Trail to my appointment, to have my eyes checked by a specialist, at which time the technician took seventy-five pictures of my eyes. I counted them! After the third one, the light from the camera was so intense that I could not hold my eyes open.

I held the eye of which she was taking the picture as long as I could with my fingers, then she held them open with her fingers. It was horrible!

After having my eyes tested, I felt pretty low. I waited at Mother's home for the telephone call that would tell me my prognosis.

When he called me, "There is nothing that we can do for you. Your Macular Degeneration is too far advanced. If you had come in before there were so many hemorrhages, we could have used laser on those hemorrhages, and controlled the bleeding. But, you have too many now, and there is nothing that can be done for you."

"What can I do?" Isn't there something I can do so it won't get any worse?" I asked, sick at heart.

"No, there is nothing we know that you can do," the doctor said over the phone.

"How long will it be before I go completely blind?" I asked, hesitantly.

"You will never go completely blind with what you have, macular degeneration." he said.

"Well, how long before I get so I can't see much at all?" I insisted. "I wanted an answer!"

"It's hard to say," the doctor didn't want to commit himself. "Maybe two years," he finally said.

"Two years!" I screamed.

"How will I ever live? How can I get along? Why didn't my doctor help me sooner!" I was almost hysterical!

"I don't know. But, now there is nothing more we can do for you!" he stated.

I hung up the receiver, and cried. My life was over!

How could this have happened! Why did my doctor in Naples have let me go so long without help! My eyes could have been helped with the laser surgery. It could have stopped my hemorrhaging! Now I would be blind! My heart was heavy when we headed back to Naples. Judy, my wonderful empathetic daughter-in-law called me several days later from Fort Myers.

"There is a place called the Florida State Office of Blind Services, where you can get a player, and tapes of books to read," she said, over the phone. "I just heard about it. Do you want me to find out more about it?"

"I reckon," I said, a little up, but not much. "What could it be?" I asked.

"I don't know, but I'll check into it," she said.

I didn't have my hopes up. I felt my life was over. I was in the depths of despair. How could I get along without my books to read! I saw my grandmother sitting all alone, doing nothing, for years. Now my mother was doing the same. They had both been very active, but in their older years, they sat, doing nothing, for hours on end. I had been so active in my lifetime! I could not fathom having to live with no eyesight.

"You have to have two doctors to sign a paper, saying you have macular degeneration, and that your eyesight is such that you can't read anymore," Judy told me on the phone, after she found out about the Talking Book Program.

I sent the doctor's letters to Blind Services Headquarters in Daytona Beach, Florida. In a few days, voila! My life was changed completely!

I was sent a disk player and a portable tape player, the latter of which enables the reader to go anywhere. I devoured my Talking Books, I read every second of my life that wasn't filled with something I had to do. George fixed a stand on the center console of the car, to hold my tape player.

"Dear God, help me not to loose my eyesight before I finish reading my bible one more time," I used to pray when I knew my eyesight was getting dimmer. But, I procrastinated, and had to finish it the fourth time through my Talking Books.

I thought my life was over, when I could not read my wonderful books and magazines, etc., that I had read and enjoyed all my life so diligently.

Then I found out about the Talking Books through the State Office of Blind Services.

The first year I devoured them, I had a book or magazine going every second of my life. It gave me back my life! I could think again, live again, through my new Talking Books!

The Library for the Blind and Handicapped in Daytona Beach sends out yearly catalogues, with monthly supplements, which lists new readings by wonderful people who take their precious time to read, with their good beautiful eyes, (or eyesight), for us men and women, who, for one reason or another, have lost their vision, or have some other handicap or ailment. I thank God often for my readers and other persons who have set me back to living. I thought my life was over, but I felt differently when I found out about Talking Books. It put me back in life again.

And television is wonderful for me. One day we were picking up some new glasses for Mother Massing at her optometrists when George found a fancy looking pair of small binoculars on the counter.

"Look at these Kay," he said, showing them to me.

When I looked through the two lenses that stuck out in front of my eyes two inches, I could see a lot better!

"Hey, these are great!" I exclaimed. "I can see a lot clearer with them!"

" We arranged to take them home to try out. They were fabulous to watch television, which I was doing more and more lately.

We don't take the newspaper, although I used to devour it immediately upon its arrival, to find out what was going on in the world, so now I try not to miss the news programs on the air.

I love the afternoon soaps on the CBS channel.

"Those are my friends," one older lady said when someone asked her how she lived. The consensus was, it was a terrible thing for a person, or anyone, to think of the soaps' characters as friends.

Let me tell you, it's like visiting them and loving or hating them, that keeps me going. I love people, so I still like to go to the movies, where we always sit way down front, have real live friends when they have the time. I always have the time, and I still love my television soap friends. Don't knock it, unless you've been there! It is a lot better than sitting in a chair growing old and stiff and unable to function. Give me my Talking Books, my television, and throw in a possible group of friends, and I am relatively happy with my life.

The ever present growing flowers and our travels to faraway places and nearby points keep George and me happy and well.

For my seventy-fifth birthday, September 18, 1994 (today as I write) George gave me what I asked for, a white Rubbermaid rocking chair for the lanai. I love it! As I sat in it at Builders Square, in the shopping mall several miles from us, I thought of nothing but pure pleasure. George laughed at me when he came back to where I was. He knew how I had always loved to swing or rock.

"It's what I want for my birthday!" I said.

Last night, at almost closing time, we drove over there and bought me one of those great rockers.

George banged around in our garage, trying to surprise me with the newly bought rocker, until I went out to the garage.

"Come inside," I said. "There isn't enough room to put it together out here. I know what you are doing!"

I helped him carry the pieces to the front room, where he had it together in a matter of minutes.

I couldn't wait to settle in my newest rocker! It was fantastic! It is fantastic! I thank you my precious George, for always getting me what I want!

It is still in the front room, but I will move it out tomorrow, after my birthday!

We traveled so much, even around town, that this was a boon to my existence. The only thing is, in deference to George, who is my wonderful guy, I have to listen to an awful lot of cowboy stories. Of course, I like them a lot too! Especially our favorite Western writer, Louis L'Amour.

My whole life was changed, I lived again! After devouring books for months, I became a normal person again.

I talked about what I read, and lived through my books. I had a new lease on life. Judy, bless her heart, came through for me again, when she found out more about the Disabled and Blind Services benefits.

Any blind person could have a visiting technician, who would help train blind people to function in their homes. Ellen, who was going blind herself, was my visiting technician. She was excellent. She visited me in my home monthly, for months, until I thought I could get along by myself. I had a severe blow to my life, but now I could function again!

"You are so busy, with all the people you have to visit. I think I can get along now by myself," I told her one day.

"I think you can, too," she said. "If there is anything I can do for you, anytime, you get in touch with me!"

"I just have to practice the things you've taught me to do," I said.

"There is a place where you can go, and live, where you will be shown and helped to learn how to function as a nearly blind person," Ellen said. "Would you be interested in going there?"

"Yes! That sounds great!" I answered quickly. "How do I go about it?"

She sent in my application, and I was accepted without too much delay.

The class was to run for twelve weeks, during which time I would learn how to function as a blind person in a sighted world.

"George, will you promise to visit Mother just as we have been doing," I asked him. "I can't go, unless I know you will be looking out for her, the same way I would have been doing, if I were here."

"Of course, I will," he answered. "You go and do the best you can. I will take care of things here, don't worry about us."

George drove me to Daytona Beach School for the Blind and Handicapped. George helped me unpack, then he left me to embark on a scary but rewarding endeavor.

The first week I was there, our head teacher had a Spelling Bee for the whole class to see in what category we belonged. It was fun. All of us would yell out the spelling until he said, "This won't work. I'll call you by name." So from then on he called out the word and immediately afterwards would call someone by name.

He eliminated one after another who would misspell a word or two. There were only two or three persons left. Finally I was the only one left spelling the words. He went faster and I spelled faster. The others sat erect with a great deal of interest and alertness.

The words became harder and harder. Finally he said a word that I had never heard, I tried to figure it out.

"I never heard of that word," I said.

"You didn't?" he seemed surprised.

"Are you sure it is a word," I laughed.

"Yes, it is a word!" he said.

I tried and missed. It was a very long word with two or three a's in it. What did it mean? It started with para, but I had never heard of it before.

The teacher got up and opened the door to our classroom.

He walked down the corridor to the next classroom where he stood talking to the typing/shorthand teacher who came back to our classroom and stood by our door. "Kay, will you come here, please?" the teacher said. "You will be taking more tests with this teacher to see where you stand."

I walked back to her room where she sat me down and went through more tests. She gave me a spelling test and a reading test verbally as I could not see to read.

The next day she said I had passed one of the tests at the doctorate level and one at the masters level. Imagine my surprise! It all came from my love of books and reading constantly when I had the time! Anyone could do it.

If I ever ran across a word I did not know or heard a person use a word which I questioned, or had been said wrongly, I looked it up in the dictionary or Roget's Thesaurus.

I didn't fare so well with the Arithmetic tests. I was never good in arithmetic, although I loved basic algebra. My tests with arithmetic came out as seventh grade level. It was that high because just outside the door as we were waiting to go in to take the tests, I listened to some of the students.

"What is Pi? I asked one of them who was talking about it.

I never heard of it! I said wrongly. I had it in school along with my fellow classmates but had completely forgotten it. Who in the world ever used Pi in their living? But I got the answer right as I had asked and listened to the answer very carefully.

The second week I was there a class was started for healthful activity to teach us we should be active and healthy. The teacher was so ineffective in accomplishing her ideas to the blind students that I felt sorry for her and also the students, who were just standing there.

"Hold your hand up high like this!" I surprised everyone by saying loudly. "Kick high like this." As one girl tried it I said, "That's it! Higher!"

The teacher was as surprised as anyone and after the girls started doing better I didn't have to say much more.

They were now acclimated and did the exercises well.

"What do you teach here?" the teacher said afterwards when the class had been dismissed. I laughed.

"I don't teach. I'm a student here too. I just saw how they were not paying attention and I just tried to help," I explained to her.

She was very glad I had done that and said for me to be sure and come back to the classes and keep helping.

At the school we learned how to feel to count money, how to handle and identify, how to type from written dictation.

The school gave me the opportunity to learn better how to care for myself when I left and how to make some good friends. It was a good experience for me.

The class in art was most fun of all. In the few weeks I was there I molded a sugar and creamer, and other things in clay and also learned how to make beautiful complicated macrame wall hangings and flower pot holders.

In a special after school knitting class, I crocheted and/or knitted some lovely things, including starting an afghan and a vest. There was a woman who came in twice a week to help us to crochet or knit.

I took a class in flower arranging with foliage, greenery and gorgeous blossoms in decorating projects.

That was rewarding for me as I loved being able to have the pieces to make anything I wanted to make. I was told it was great being here at school in the fall just before the holidays as there were so many lovely flowers, etc. to use.

The school funds were winding down when I was there, so there were lots of things they didn't have and couldn't get until their next allotment of money. But there were lots of things we could use and with imagination a lot of things could be made.

The teacher took me over to the greenhouse and let me pick out my plants I wanted for my project.

When I left school I had seven things I had made from this class. I gave some to friends and relatives and kept some for myself.

After learning to tap with my white cane around the school's hallways and our sleeping quarters I was taken outside to walk down the streets. Crossing the street was a little tricky. We had to come to the curb and run our canes around on the street at the curb to determine if it were clear enough to step down off the curb into the street.

We had to stop and listen to the traffic carefully to be sure when to cross. If there were a stop light we waited until we heard traffic going forward the same direction we wanted to go and heard the cars pull up in front of us and stop. Then we knew it was time for us to tap our cane and cross. It was pretty tricky for those who were totally blind and a little tricky for me who could see a little. It wasn't long before my mobility teacher gave me my card saying I could walk alone.

One sports activity at the school was bicycle riding.

That interested me as I've ridden all my life. When I went out for a ride with one of my teachers, who was to be my guide, there stood a beautiful tandem bike. I'd never been on one except in Danville, Illinois, when George and I were young and rented a tandem bike once in awhile. The teacher got on first and I got on behind him. As we pulled away we wiggled and wobbled until we got a good start. Finally straightening out we went sailing down the road. It was exhilarating and thrilling.

A busload of students were taken to a festival not far from Daytona Beach. Most of us were totaly blind. The driver took us, along with the young man helper who attended college but used his free time to help guide us places. We all liked him very much and wanted him to be with us. On the way there we tried to commandeer his services, but the bus driver/teacher had other plans. He would have been a great help to us, but we went on our own through the high grass to see and hear the activities.

I took Ginger on one side and two more girls on my other side, two of them being totaly blind. We fell and stumbled through the tall uneven grass to the open tent where I tried to guide them under, and get them seated in chairs. We all ran into the ropes holding up the tent, as well as the uneven ground, laughing and making lots of noise. Some kind people sitting there helped us get inside to seats, after which I and the other partially blind girl left for food to take back to the others.

It really was a rather trying trip, which I never wanted to make again. When we left to go home we ran into the kind guide who told us he had just been wandering around most of the time by himself. How we could have used him. The man who was supposed to help had sat most of the time inside a building.

There were trips to the wonderful Daytona Beach. The first time I went it was all young men in our van and although I tried to get in on the conversations I couldn't get a word in edgewise, as everyone was in a happy mood all talking together. So I sat back and listened. Sometimes the sentences were pretty raw, but not too bad really.

As we came to a corner of A1A, just prior to getting to the beach, there was a big animal on the corner.

"What is that?" I said loudly. This put everyone in a state of shock.

"Who's that? I didn't know there was a woman in here!"

I wouldn't have said anything if I'd known. "Why didn't you speak up and let us know you were here! Who are you!" Each one had something to say. I laughed inside, but considered, and rejected answering any of the questions.

"What was on that corner?" I said again to the driver.

"It was a man dressed up like a big bear," the driver said.

"What is he doing there?" I asked.

There was not one sound out of the boys in the car.

Soon we had gone over the hill and down the slope to the sandy drive on the beach.

"We're here!" the driver said to the ever quiet boys. Not one sound was heard. We all jumped out of the van.

"Stay on this side of the driveway, and we'll walk down the beach," the driver said.

"Could I walk over on the other side, please, so I can take off my shoes and walk through the water? I can see quite a bit and I"ll keep my eyes on you and walk along with you only on the other side of the driveway," I begged, as he thought about it finally gave in to me.

As I crossed over the drive to get on the water side, six or seven young men started to talk all at once.

"I'd never have said a word if I had known she was in the car. Who is she?" I heard them all talking at once about me and the situation. I was giggling and found it was fun to be quiet and listen to others sometimes!

One time the same young man guide we all liked took us to a mall. We had lots of fun and several of the girls did some simple flirting with the young fellow. On the way back his car stopped along the highway and he couldn't get it started again.

"Do you want us to get out and walk?" one of the girls I will call Betty asked. I was sitting next to the young man in the front seat where Betty had planned to sit. Then Betty was on my other side.

"No, heavens no," the young man said. "You can't walk along this busy highway." He kept trying to get the car started but to no avail.

"Let's get out and walk. You are never going to get this car started," Betty said. "Kay, don't you want to walk?"

"Sure, I'll walk if everyone else will," I said. The battery was completely dead. What else was there to do?

Betty jumped out of the car and stood there holding the door open.

"Come on, Kay! You said you wanted to walk!" she said.

I turned and said to the young man, "What do you think? Will it be all alright for us to walk? It isn't too far."

"Well, maybe" he said, really unsure. "It's just down to the turn, and then up the hill, and you'll be at the north end of the school."

"Come on, girls. We can make it okay. I'll help you," I said.

I jumped out of the seat, and Betty jumped back in the seat to the middle, and sat close to the young man immediately. I couldn't believe it. She had tricked me! She had wanted to sit next to this young man worse than I thought.

"Come on, Betty, you're the one who wanted to walk!" I said.

"Oh, no, I never said I wanted to walk. You said you wanted to walk. Go ahead, Kay and walk. We'll see you when we get the car going."

I lined the other four girls up, one on each side of me, and the other two back of us, but holdilng onto us three in front. I don't know how we did it. It wasn't easy! But we all laughed and talked and did fine until we started walking up the hill. The girls on the side kept getting over too far and trying to fall on the uneven ground. More cars turned down this road than we had on the main highway but they saw our dilemma and went slow, with some people asking if they could help us.

"No, thanks," we said, "We're just going to the blind school up the road."

We made it! But when we arrived hot and sweaty a very nervous young administrator was terribly upset.

"Where are you coming from?" she asked us collectively.

No one spoke.

"What happened? Where is your driver!" she kept asking questions.

Before we could get our tongues working to answer so she could understand, in walked Betty and took over. She was so sweet, and told untruths, while the rest of us just stood around, looking scared. Betty was so plausible and convincing, that the administrator had no choice but to let us all go. Betty and I never spoke together again. She had put us in a terrible predicament which we should never have been in. We other girls, one by one, left the room while the administrator tried to get us to come back and tell our side of the story.

After five weeks of school I had my first evaluation meeting with the school psychologist. He asked me questions about my family and how well I was getting along in school. He seemed so terribly tired and worn out. He held my meeting with him for only ten or fifteen minutes after which I was to meet with the school's counselor who was very friendly with me and everyone else. She was tops.

"I don't think I should be here," I said as I sat down in front of her desk.

"I don't think so either!" she surprised me by saying.

I stared at her. I had come for a twelve week period and here it was only five weeks.

This was Friday before Memorial Day weekend and George was coming to visit me. We were going to stay in a motel for the weekend, and go to the marvelous Daytona Beach I had really fallen in love with, and a lot of things. I stared at the counselor.

"I've done about everything there is to do here," I said.

"Yes, you have," she said.

I continued to stare at her.

"Maybe I should just go on home with George when he comes up to be with me this weekend," I said slowly.

"I think that would be a good idea," she said.

I couldn't believe my ears! I was going home! I had learned a lot here and I was so thankful I had had the opportunity to come to this wonderful school, but I really was ready to go home!

When George came I was elated to tell him the good news.

He was wary, as he thought I was rushing it to leave so early, but when I said the counselor had said she thought I was ready to go home, he was delighted, too. No more trips up there to visit me.

THEN AND NOW

It was a four hour drive during which he always had to fight sleep. I wasn't beside him to keep him awake!

We picked up all my flower arrangements and put in the car. I took George down the hall in the main building to the art department to pick up my things I had made only to find the art teacher had left for the weekend. I left word for my good friend Ginger be given my hand molded sugar and creamer which had not been glazed, as yet. Then I picked up my other pottery pieces and macrame projects I had made.

Then we headed towards the manual arts room where I picked up my wooden pieces I had made. We went back to my bedroom to pick up my knitting and crocheting and my suitcases.

We told everyone goodby as we left. I felt a little weapy, but I was glad to be going home.

Going to the school helped me function to a fuller more manageable future. I am glad I went there and I thank God for that wonderful school. I call it my Alma Mater.

I continue to go back and see Lillian, my personal representative at the talking book library, who sends me books I want. George and I visited her recently and I told her I was writing this book. She told me when I had it completed they would read it for me and put it on talking books in their library for all totally blind and handicapped people who use the library to read. I want all of you blind and handicapped people to know I have a very strong attachment to you and I love and pray for all of you and many thanks to all you wonderful teachers and management who made it possible! God bess you everyone! And God bless my Alma Mater! Lillian retired and was replaced by Shirley Rucker who continues to offer great service.

I would be remiss if I didn't recognize our branch Talking Book Library here in North Fort Myers so aptly managed by Barbara Ferris. She is totally dedicated to her work and a joy to have as my librarian. We go in to see her often and take her one of George's gorgeous hybrid hibiscus blossoms, when we have one in bloom. She keeps me well supplied with books I would like to read. Although these books are on talking tapes or disks I still say I read them rather than listen to them. Most readers are great, with their intonations and accents which make the books come alive. I get so involved in my books that it seems as if I am living these stories.

Barbara Ferris later retired. Everyone who has ever worked there has been extremely pleasant and helpful.

Chapter 29
Our Loss - Death of a Matriarch

We made trips back and forth, from Naples, Florida, to Hollywood, Florida, to visit Mother and see that she was well cared for. She loved to eat at London Ben's Fish house, and we would always take her there.

Marie took care of Mother until she herself became ill and couldn't do it anymore.

George and I drove over and brought Mother to Naples, where we entered her in the Greater Naples Care Center, the best in the area. It was only seven miles from our home.

She was happy there, as she knew she had a longer life at her home than most, and all the attendants and nurses were very kind and friendly with her. She was ninety-two when we brought her back to Naples, and just past her ninety-fourth birthday ten days, before she passed away.

We attended all the parties with her, visited her once or twice a week, and took relatives and friends to see her. Once Dick, her grandson, his wife Judy, from Orlando, came down with their three small, beautiful children, and we had a real nice visit with her. We all took her in her wheelchair to the lake they had on the premises and watched and fed the ducks and other birds on the lake. Often picnics were held there under the shelter, equipped with tables and seats. On our visits we usually took her to this peaceful area, which she seemed to enjoy.

There finally came a time when we realized Mother didn't have much time left. She had had a good life, a wonderful life full of much happiness. She had lived on this earth ninety-four years.

We received a telephone call from Mother's nurse at the care center.

"Your Mother hasn't long to live" she said. "I expect her to go any minute."

"We'll be right there!" I said quietly.

We rushed to the care center to Mother's bedside.

I leaned over Mother, and spoke quietly to her. I knew she was going. She became agitated, squirming and jerking around.

"The Lord is my shepherd, I shall not want," I said, knowing this was her favorite passage of the whole bible. "He maketh me to lie down in green pastures." She became very still, listening quietly, as she always did when I quoted the bible to her.

As I continued with the 23rd Psalm, she relaxed and became perfectly still. When I had finished, I kept leaning over her. There was no response.

I continued holding her hand, as I sat down in a chair beside her.

As I sat there watching her face, I realized she had opened her eyes, and was staring at me intently. Her eyes penetrated mine. It was as if she said, "You've done a good job. Thank you, Catherine. I must go now. I love you!"

As I watched her, I got up and leaned over her. But her eyes had closed, and she gave a shiver, and was gone. Gone from me, but had entered the Kingdom of Heaven.

We buried her in Crown Hill Cemetery, in Ridgefarm, Illinois, beside Dad, and her Mother and Father, and my brother, Charley, and two little babies.

She had on a lovely light green, voile dress with pearls. "She looks like the elegant matriarch of the family from which she came," George had said as he and I stood together looking at her.

"Yes, she surely does," I said. She had been a wonderful Mother, and had grown old gracefully, fully tending her sheep, and now it was time to go home to rest.

All the clan gathered, coming from far and wide, to give their last respects to the matriarch of our family. It was a huge funeral with many relatives and friends who remembered her.

The family and close friends were invited for a lovely meal, prepared and served by Ridgefarm Friends Church women. After the sumptuous meal, the family went out to the farm, and visited and reminisced.

We drove back, a few weeks later, to the farm, to dispense with all the furniture and belongings, as the farm was to be sold to our good neighbor and friend Spud Spesard.

As I came out of the kitchen and through the dining room in a hurry I felt a huge wave of something. I turned around real fast and started back into the kitchen, at which time I was enveloped with a huge smell and shield, which smelled like the odor that Mother had sometimes. It was not a bad odor but, unmistakenly hers. It was so overpowering I felt Mother's presence.

"Mother is that you?" I said before I realized it. I told George about it, but it soon dissipated, and I went on through the living room and upstairs to go through things in my old bedroom.

About three hours later, I was still going through material bags of things Mother had saved. Every dress she had ever owned, she had taken off the lace and rolled up. She couldn't have kept the dresses themselves, but had saved the decorations. There were bags and bags of them. It was a hot humid day and sweat was pouring down my face.

"Mother," I cried, "Why? Why did you do this?" I felt a strong overpowering smell of her, and I felt as if she were there watching and trying to explain. I sobbed and sobbed sitting there on my old bed going through those bags which could tell of old wonderful stories. How I wished she could be there telling me all about them.

I saved the nicest ones and threw the others in a garbage bag to be thrown away. We couldn't take all of them with us. The farm house was three times bigger than our home in Naples, even with the Ted's Sheds in the yard.

When we were about to leave the farm for the last time, George and I were sitting on the sofa in the living room. We had taken or given away everything we could, and now the time had just about come to leave everything but memories. I reached out to the coffee table and picked up an album. George and I started going through, it and talking about the past. I became very still as if I were in another world. I stared out the open window nearby. As I sat there, feeling in a transfixed state, I felt a gentle wafting of my Mother's spirit, along with a gentle smell she had. I felt it linger over me, then gradually float towards the window, where it went through and left me forever.

Three times she had come to me and three times I cried for my Mother. I pray, my dear Mother, that I have served you well and you are proud of me. I am very proud of you. You were a wonderful Mother. You held me close with love, but you always let me have my wings. That's a perfect Mother.

Chapter 30

Cruising Through the Caribbean

I will be satisfied to have gone to every continental state. What a wonderful country this is! And we've seen it all! We love it all! We thank God that we live here in this fabulous country.

"We're going to take a trip to the Islands," my good friend, Phyllis, said to me one day. "Want to come along"?

"Sure!" I said, without missing a beat. She was surprised! I had taken her aback, at my quick response.

"We're going on a second honeymoon. We're going on the Royal Norwegian Lines, Song of Norway, the same ship we went on ten years ago, when we were first married. They had each lost their spouses, and they later married one another.

There was nothing we would like better. It had been so long since we had traveled because of looking after Mother. George and I really needed a "relaxing cruise down the river." It was just what we needed!

In 1983 we took a fabulous cruise down to the Carribean Islands with our good friends Don and Phyllis Powless, who were celebrating their tenth wedding anniversary, along with Don's brother and wife. The trip was so relaxing and wonderful.

As George and I strode across the parking lot to the port of embarkation area, I held onto my wide brimmed straw hat, and hurried over to Don and Phyl, who had miraculously arrived at the area a couple of minutes earlier.

"You're dressed like I usually dress she said, as I walked up to them, clutching my hat in the strong wind. I had a summer tweed casual suit on. It was new, and I knew I looked good in it, so I was happy to get the nice compliment. Phyl owned a dress shop in Vandalia, Ohio, and knew good style and taste.

George and I were taken to our teensy quarters in the lower deck. The others were on an upper deck. Since we had bought our tickets late, we had to take what we could get. We didn't mind. It was adequate, really quite nice, if you didn't need to stretch out too much. Anyway, we weren't there too often, mostly to get resuscitated before the next bout of activity.

It was a swirl of exercise, lounging, and eating, always eating. The most fabulous dinners, night snacks, (hah! these were no snacks!) and I wanted to try everything, at least once! Time went so fast, there were so many things to do, and to eat, sometimes we were able to do things only once during our trip. Of course, their lunches and dinners were out of this world. Everyone ate and ate, and ate.

Sundaes are a great thing in our lives, and they had fantastic sundaes every afternoon on the upper deck near the swimming pool. But only once in the nine days did we get to enjoy the afternoon sundaes.

The midnight snack was so huge and delectable, with new concoctions. George and I always went there. At the last one, there was the most scrumptious of all meals! Also, on display there were fabulous, fantastic ice sculptures done that day and kept in the coolers. The doors of the dining area were kept locked until everything was in place and the executive chef came and opened the double doors. We all swarmed in at once. We oh'd and ah'd, many of us taking pictures of their handiwork. The food was extra super and delectable that last night.

There were lots of activities on board, as well as our stopovers at Ports o' Call. The first one was Puerto Plata, Dominican Republic. We boarded a bus early in the morning, and drove through the hubbub of the poor, worldly, hectic town of Puerto Plata, driving out into the beautiful countryside where the more affluent people lived. We were served a great lunch of barbecued chicken under the grass roofed shelters, where the musicians played island music for dancing and games to entertain us.

George and I took a walk on the beaches, where some natives drove near us in their big jeep, all hollering and stopped right in front of us. They put on a hilarious show for us and a few other beachcombers. They were delightful, laughing and acting up.

Then George and I walked down the country road, towards the area that belonged to the governor, which was guarded by soldiers on horseback. It was a lovely place.

"Peep! Peep!" we heard, and it seemed to get closer. When we turned to see what it was, an islander was walking behind us, carrying a paper bag.

"What do you have in there?" I asked.

"Oh, I'll show you. Do you want to see?" he said, in his broken English. Before he could get it opened, he accidently dropped it on the cement. The peeping stopped. I thought whatever it was, was no more.

"Oh, they're all right!" he said, as he opened and peeked into the paper bag containing tiny baby chicks. Then he had us look in the bag, and, sure enough, those little beauties were still alive, shaken but still living.

As he walked on down the road with his paper bag, we heard the chirps of little chickens going with him, as they went off into the distance.

Our next Port O' Call was San Juan, Puerto Rico, where we debarked and visited Old San Juan, with its carts of fruits and flowers along the curbing to catch the tourists. The fruit vendor had a gadget, mounted on his cart, that peeled a whole orange as he cranked. It looked so inviting that George and I had to have one, standing in the middle of the street, eating our dripping oranges.

We took a side trip, on an open rickety bus up into the mountains to see a beautiful rain forest. Near the top of the mountain, we climbed up and looked out at the gorgeous view at each window, as we wound around and up the huge stone tower. Once on top we could look over the whole rain forest.

The third and last Port O' Call was the beautiful, and wonderful, island of St. Thomas, Virgin Islands. We shopped extensively, as they had duty free shops of jewelry, art work, beachwear and island souvenirs.

I wanted desperately to get an elephant that I saw for Larry, but it was made of glass, and I thought it would be broken before I could get it home. It was made of crystal eight inches tall, but only two inches thick, but appeared to be a whole elephant. In the front seemed to be the head and long trunk, and front feet, but when turned around one saw the rump, tail and hind legs, making it appear to be a full sized elephant. I still regret that I passed it up as I was afraid it would break getting it home.

During the tour of St. Thomas, we wound up mountain roads towards Bluebeard's castle, stopping to talk to a native who was riding a little donkey, with a big head and long ears. The man was almost as big as the donkey, and dangling his legs, he was able to touch the ground. From Bluebeard's castle, we could see our cruise ship far below in the harbor. It was a beautiful sight.

On this trip, we crossed the Tropic of Cancer after leaving Miami, just north of Cuba. It is the northern most latitude reached by the overhead sun, and is the northern boundary between the temperate and tropical zones.

It was a fabulous, fast paced, yet relaxing, trip of such a variety of activities that we all enjoyed to the fullest. We were so happy that Don and Phyl had included us in their tenth year celebration.

Chapter 31
A Little Girl and a New Home

George and I signed for our new house in Yacht Club Colony, North Fort Myers, Florida, 23 Sept 1983. That afternoon, we went to the hospital to see our lovely little Lollipop, just born.

Thank you, God, for this most precious little newborn girl you have given to all of us. After three generations of all boys, albeit wonderful boys, that would never be traded in for any girl, I suggested to Judy to try for a girl for our family to enjoy. She wasn't sure she wanted to have another child, but soon planned for one, and in a few months she was pregnant again. I was elated! No one could be happier than I!

"Judy, you did it! You had a little girl this time!" I said, when I went into her hospital room.

"Did you pray before I got pregnant?" she wanted to know.

"I certainly did!" I said.

That cinches it. God gave us all a beautiful, darling girl, feisty, and with a personality all her own, whom we all adore. She is a great boost to all of us and has a legacy to fulfill, as we will always look towards her as a special person.

Boys are very dear in the Massing family as they should be. But, it was time, I thought, we should have our own little girl. Girls are different than boys! Good or bad, they are different! I am so thankful God agreed it was time for us to have a girl amongst all our boys.

Thank you God. Thank you!

I had prayed so fervently for a little girl in our lives.

Her name is Jennifer Michelle Massing. I had picked Mellisa and was planning to call her Missie. I love that name and nickname. But Jennifer was chosen. It is the most popular name given to children born today. I call her Jenna, which I think goes real well for her. Sometimes, I call her Missie.

Jenna has straight golden, almost white hair, as does Devon, but where Devon has blue eyes, Jenna has her Mother's hazel eyes, as does Joshua. Devon has the fairest skin, and reminds me of a picture of my father when he was a little boy. Jenna and Joshua have a more light olive skin.

We came to see how the work was progressing on the remodelling of our new home, to find it full of water. Four inches of water made it look like a lake. Some stupid workman forgot to turn off the water over the weekend, even though he knew water was leaking underneath the kitchen sink. It ran all weekend. The guys just laughed about it. We thought there was nothing funny about it. The following Monday they had to bring in a machine to remove the water before they could do anymore work. Later the newly painted walls peeled from the moisture from the flooded area.

In the garage they had hammered so hard they made a three inch round hole in the dining room area wall. The repair work was very noticeable so we have to always keep the china cabinet in front of it.

We had the closet in the master bedroom enlarged double its size which they built out into the garage. Even then, it was about one third the size of my walk in closet in Naples which I had always loved. When I tried to close the sliding door we found a workman had nailed it open.

I asked the workman how long he had worked for the contractor and he said he had been there the longest, three months and the other workers were hired off the street.

When our new carpet was being put down, we were told there was one hundred less square feet in our new house than we had been told by the realtor, when we bought the house. There was no way we wanted to go through another hassle about our new home. We didn't even call and let the real estate office know we knew. We had such a time deciding on this home, and decided to take what we got, without raising more problems. We were tired of problems.

It took us one year and two months to sell our Naples home, but we had good people to buy it, and for two and a half times what we paid for the house itself, ten years before, due to inflation. So all was well, at last.

After our friends, neighbors in the real estate business, had our home listed for one year and two months, we changed to another large real estate group.

"You'll probably sell it in two weeks," our lady real estate friend said to us.

"Why would she say that to us now? If she thought that, why didn't she let us go to another real estate office before, instead of talking us into staying with her?" I said to George.

It was only nine days when our lovely Casa Masbu was sold. It had been hard keeping up both houses, especially when we had a hurricane scare. It fortunately did not materialize.

Chapter 32
Twenty-Nine Palms
North Fort Myers, Florida

On the morning of November tenth in the year of nineteen hundred eighty-three, Larry brought his crew from Ted's Sheds of Fort Myers to Naples in their delivery truck, towing the eight by twenty-four foot trailer. He had loaded an eight by twenty foot shed, with double three foot doors, on the trailer to use in the move. They packed our furniture into the long shed professionally and neatly. It was a job well done.

To get to Twenty-nine Palms from Naples, one has to travel straight up Route 75 in Southwest Florida to exit 26 to the right, then left under Route 75, west on Bayshore, which has absolutely no bay or shore, showing the incongruity of old timers in Florida. Turn left onto Coon Road, where we did see a coon once, left for a mile or so on Donald Road and as you round a curve in the road, the name magically turns to Bonita. After traveling a short distance, turn right on Winston which will take you into Yacht Club Colony, a group of homes, a colony if you will, neither having a yacht or a club anywhere. There are many lovely homes, all with wonderful, friendly people. Winston dead ends in Clubhouse Road.

After jogging to the left, make a quick right turn onto Cobia Way, where you will find on the corner, our Twenty-nine Palms, so named by the Massings after living here for eleven years. Not being able to come up with a wanted German name or French, or at least, an exotic name of some kind, today I have decided our lovely home has to have a name, to be consistent with all our other homes.

George and I followed the truck and trailer with all our belongings down our road to Ridgefarm Road, then to I-75, over the Caloosahatchee, and to our newly remodeled home, in Yacht Club Colony, in North Fort Myers. The guys backed the huge trailer in our driveway and unloaded our furniture. It went like clockwork. All of the neighbors came out to inspect us in all of our commotion. We made an impression!

"We thought you were bringing in Ted's Sheds to sell!" one man said. He heaved a sigh of relief when told we were merely moving into the house.

Yacht Club Colony is a lovely community made up of all ages, babies and youth, parents, and the older generation like us. We couldn't have chosen a better place to live! And the best part of it all is we are living a mile and a half from our son and his loving, little family.

A year after we were settled in, we remodeled, enhancing our family room, and building on a large lanai, with a sidewalk and steps down to the dock. The dock was rebuilt with a wooden floor and sides, right over the old cement dock. We installed a "Dolphin" boat lift.

Our seventeen foot, center console fisherman boat is at the dock, on its boat lift, and is ready to go whenever we are. Larry named it Kestrel after that member of the hawk family. Larry and Judy, Joshua, Devon, and Jenna come over often, and we go fishing, swimming, or just cruising along to the Caloosahatchee and up and down it, west under the bridges to Pine Island Sound, Sanibel area, and on to the open waters of the Gulf of Mexico. Cruising east through the locks we investigate byways around islands and past Labelle. It is a grand life! We love it!

Monte came down on his vacation from Ohio and changed the aqua shutters and door to my favorite color, yellow, and painted our lamp post and trellis a pleasant yellow green.

We took down the metal horses and carriage from above the garage doors, expecting to put the name of our house there. But, oh, what to call our house! Years went by and we could not think of a perfect name. It was over ten years before I could, one day, realize, with the palms we brought up from Naples, we had added palms to our yard, until they amounted to twenty-nine palms. Twenty-nine Palms, a perfect name for our house.

Most of my paintings I have done over the years, that I still have, are relegated to the garage, however, there are three on the walls of our home.

One of my abstracts, twelve by forty, entitled, Horses in the Wheat Field, was given second award at Fairborn Art Association, Fairborn, Ohio. It is above our music center in the dining room. The size twenty-four by thirty-six, five bottle picture, "the family portrait," is above the sofa. I was in my bottle period when I did this picture, in the mid- sixties.

"That looks like people," a young Lieutenant, Dave Davis, from WPAFB, friend of ours said as we sat staring at it. I was amazed. He was very intuitive.

"In what way? How do you mean?" I asked, nonplused.

"Well, the first one looks like a fat rich dowager."

"Well, that could be my mother," I said, unsure of myself.

"The next one is strong-willed, with a bossy personality," he continued.

"Maybe me?" I laughed.

"The next one," he said, "is a tall sedate person standing in the center of things."

"Well, maybe that's George," I said.

"Go on. What about the next ones?" I asked.

"The next one is back there, doesn't want to cause any trouble, wants to keep out of everyone's way!" he continued.

"And the last one?" I asked.

"Well, that one is a strong willed, sassy one, sure of herself, somewhat like the first one," he said.

"Okay," I said, "The first one is Mother, the orange one is my sister, Ann, and the middle one is her husband, Connie." I was excited now. I laughed and continued quickly.

"The next one, in the background, is George, and I'm the sassy, bold one."

That picture has remained our Family Portrait all these years.

Then there is one more painting of mine in the dining room, twenty by twenty-six. It is the second ink painting I did that Easter summer of 1962 after I went to work. It has remained a favorite of mine. An art salesperson wanted me to let her have it to sell.

"I can get you four-hundred dollars for that picture," she said.

"No way!" I said, "I'm keeping that one! I have too few of my paintings left!"

The first picture I painted during that Easter break in 1962, was taken down off our walls in the family room, to make a place for two large, gorgeous shell pictures of Larry's. Larry has done such wonderful work with his photography that our walls are replete with his work. His pictures of palms, shells and birds are gorgeous, with extreme detail. Amongst them are many pictures of the southwest Florida area by Monte and George.

Two fascinating pictures by Larry are of palms at either side of our four glass, sliding door opening, leading to the lanai. Each one is of a single palm dissected by individually matted small pictures. One is seven inches by twenty-four, made up of four seven by six, matted pictures, the other one is four inches by sixty-two, made up of twelve, four by five, matted pictures with the upper half Royal Palm standing erect and the other half reversed, being reflected in water. Both are quite unique.

In our dining room are two pictures of Larry's, one being of the Ridgefarm Feed Mill, where my father used to trade. The other a cottage, is an example of Larry's work with various styles of architecture.

A grouping of four of Monte's pictures are hanging on the left side of the china cabinet in the dining area. They consist of the famous huge banyan tree at Edison's home in Fort Myers, the underside of the Naples Pier with its pilings and oyster beds, a large cypress stand surrounded by water, with lily pads, an Indian Chickee, filmed with infra red film. The later two were filmed at Corkscrew Swamp Sanctuary between Naples and Immokalee, Florida.

When we first moved here, George planted three little Phoenix Roebelenii, palm trees, in front of our twelve foot wide bedroom window. They have grown now to the roof edge, casting a lacy shadow on the drawn venetian blinds, and etching a beautiful design, when the sun comes up in the morning. It reminds me of the first time we drove to Florida in our car, and I looked out the motel bathroom window, that first morning, to see palm trees etched on the drawn venetian blinds.

George started learning plants and vegetables at his Mother's knees. She taught him to like and work with all vegetation, and he has always been very knowledgeable about trees, shrubs, plants, etc. If he doesn't know the answer to a question, he runs to his horticulture books, of which he has many in his library, to find the answer.

When we moved to Twenty-nine Palms, we realized it was barren of living plants. After planting so much at Casa Masbu, we had to get busy and start planting again.

After leaving Casa Masbu, which had been built in a clearing, our Realtor added $7000.00 to the cost of the house to accommodate all the planting we had done. We were amazed! We had no idea we had done so much. We had had so much fun planning and planting our lovely green and flowering surroundings, not realizing we were adding to the value of our home.

Twenty-nine Palms, being vacant for three years, meant that there were no flowers, very little greenery of any kind. The house had been in the hands of a banker who had engaged a young man to maintain the lawn. He took upon himself to eliminate a beautiful rock garden near the dock and all other plants and flowers in raised stone edged beds and everywhere else, leaving only a few Ixora bushes against the house. That made it easier for him to ride his exceedingly loud mower. He rode around with earmuffs to deaden the noise for himself.

He had chopped off the lower branches of all trees, making them unsightly, in order to sail around them without obstacles of any kind. Our Norfolk Island Pine ten years later was still in the process of recovery. It wasn't long before we told that young man his services were no longer needed. Following our decision, several of the neighbors did the same thing. They had put up with him and his eccentricities long enough, too. We began immediately to restore the yard to a place of beauty.

We brought up from Naples some of our banana plants, seven small cabbage palms, one of the large ponytails, and one or two of our

Phoenix Roebeleniis, Pigmy Date Palms. We sorted out our planting area in our Naples lanai and other areas outside, setting them aside so that our Realtor knew they didn't go with the house, but it was just a drop in the bucket. We had lots of work to do to Twenty-nine Palms, the kind of work we like to do.

I like to help George, telling him where things should go, and which should be changed. We make a good team. I like to do the arranging and he likes to do the work.

The croton is the world's most colorful and variable shrub. It can be used anywhere in shade or hot sun. The leaves of various crotons are long, thin, broad, jagged, twisted, each plant different one from the other. Every time I see a beautiful croton for sale, I have to have it, even though we have so many. And yet, there are so many gorgeous and beautiful plants and flowers that we do not stop at just crotons. We are fortunate to live in the land of lovely, lush, semi-tropical foliage and spectacular floral displays.

In our eleven years here, we have planted five Queen palms across the front of our house and three at the side. Today, they are all healthy, happy huge palms, giving us much pleasure. There are five Sables bunched together in the front corner with one Queen Palm on the edge of the clump.

On the canal side there are planted two or three Pony-tails which we brought from our Casa Masbu home in Naples. A clump of banana plants line up along the canal, with an arrangement of Philodendron dripping with colorful bromeliads nearer the house. At the dock are more bromeliads and a Silk Oak tree for shade, over my swing. A new and only coconut palm has been planted hanging over the dock near the water. No coconuts will fall on us! Sometimes people have been hurt badly with fallen coconuts.

The story is told that while snow birds from the north jump out of their cars and hurriedly grab coconuts off the ground in peoples front yards, the homeowner is running from the back to front with more coconuts for them to pick up! Coconut palms are so prolific, it is a big concern of getting rid of the coconuts.

Around the edge of our property line next to Bill and Margaret Lang is a row of huge Melaleucas and a very large bottle brush under which are many colorful bromeliads. Our citrus trees are lined up next to the Melaleucas. These Melaleucas were later removed by the Langs, as they were so huge they were becoming a nuisance.

Under our master bedroom windows are three beautiful Pigmy Date Palms George planted for me when I wanted to be reminded of our first trip to Florida. No, there are four now, a baby popped up so we have a little one. We never cut a tree down. Across the back of my swing, which faces the canal, four baby Queen Palms have begun to grow. I want to leave them exactly where they are. I think they will look neat and give me some shade as they grow a little higher.

Pony-tails are sometimes thought of as palms. But they seem to thrive at our house. The first triple Pony-tail I ever saw was on the grounds of Edison's winter home where we have visited quite often, always at Christmas time when the grounds and the home are fully decorated and having carols and activities there. It is always lovely, but I always look for the gorgeous pony-tails.

Our pony-tails are large and growing beautifully, liking their surroundings. We were told they were persnickety and were hard to grow. We have not found that to be true. Every pony-tail I see for sale, I scrutinize and usually want to add to our collection of six.

George's bromeliads and hibiscus are all over our yard, both front and back, and, of course the sides, too. They multiply so fast and give us so much pleasure, we continue buying and trading for more.

There are also Pentas that bring the lovely Monarch butterflies, and the low bushes, feeders and apparently night sounds about the house that bring the Mocking Bird with his hearty notes.

Our driveway on the Cobia side has a large green Sable Palm near the road, with a large golden red bromeliad against it, then two Pony-tails, against the garage on each side of the door brought from Naples, with many bromeliads under them. Then of the right side is a lovely huge golden yellow Tabebuia, with typical gnarled trunk and cork like bark.

Bromeliads are in a round raised bed and down the sidewalk to the front door, with a huge Bottlebrush tree right outside our kitchen window, that wants to die but keeps living because we love it so much. We need it to hang bromeliads, air plants and orchids on the broken, overloaded limbs which George has propped up with fence posts, in order that we can expose plants to filtered sun, which is what they need.

The Monstera Deliciosa we brought home from my nephew Terry's home in Kissemmee, Florida, has grown enormously under the bottle brush, crawling up around the trunk. The huge leaves have cutout edges and spaces that makes them beautiful. The leaves are three feet long and the plant produces an edible fruit similar in appearance to an ear of corn. We also have a Night- blooming Cereus which takes your breath away when it blooms. The blossom reaches its peak fully opened about four o'clock in the morning, and is about six inches across, and is pure white with a yellow center.

When I got out of our parked car, at First United Methodist Church, downtown Fort Myers, and went through the canopy, towards our Sunday School Classroom, I met six or eight women crossing over to their classroom at the Life Enrichment Center. Each one oh'd and ah'd over my ten-inch Evelyn Howard yellow and orange hybrid hibiscus, and two others I was carrying in my hands.

I was wearing a two piece hibiscus flowered dress with a subdued light colored yellow coat over the dress, and held the three hibiscus out in front of me, hurrying to our class.

"They're gorgeous! They're so huge! I've never seen such beautiful flowers!" Was the essence of remarks by each lady I passed. Some stopped to talk about them, asking how we grew them so large, what fertilizer we used, etc., etc.

As I arrived outside our classroom there were Sara Johnson and Lois Kurtz to greet us. Sara has to kiss us, as my hands were full of hibiscus blooms, and as we continued down the hall I threw my elbows forward to shake hands with the inside greeters, as I couldn't get my hands available. On each side of me, the wife on my left and the husband on my right each grabbed my elbows and arms, with a laughing hug and a new kiss, as I continued with my huge blossoms down the aisle to the podium and arranged them on each side of the lectern, as I did each time I had blossoms. Today they were the largest ever, and were greeted with loving exclamations. We are so glad everyone loves our blossoms. They give us so much pleasure and we love to share them with everyone.

After a good exciting class led by Rev. A. Waldo Farabee, we give our lovely hibiscus blossoms to anyone who wants them. Some take them to a sick friend, some keep them and take them home, some put them downstairs in their entrance halls to their condominium for all who enter to share and enjoy. George and I are so happy to have the wonderful opportunity to share in our lovely flowers that bloom so profusely outside our windows.

During the week, George brings in the gorgeous blossoms every day, and I arrange them on my round glass topped table in holders or just on the glass without holders where they will give us a great deal of pleasure all day, sometimes lasting two or three days, for some strong blossoms like Evelyn Howard. If I remember to refrigerate them over night, or during the day, if we are gone from the house, they will last up to three days.

People are always asking how we grow them so large and beautiful. First, we buy hybrids from Wally's Garden Center, (since made away with for progress, and torn down for a road), then fertilize them often, watch them and love them. They please us by blooming their heads off. It's a cinch!

The Hibiscus Society meeting is held once a month. If there is any problem, we can ask our fellow members what is wrong and how to correct it. Professional hibiscus growers make up a large part of our membership, and they give us programs of their expertise, and invite us to their homes. We have yearly picnics at one of the professional hibiscus growers, where we have a great time as well as obtain lots of information. There are always hundreds of blossoms everywhere, on our picnic tables, along the walls, on bushes, just everywhere. We are overwhelmed with gorgeous perfect blossoms! We never want to miss our yearly hibiscus picnics. They are great fun, lots of good eats, and wonderful friendship, surrounded by the most gorgeous, beautiful, fantastic blossoms ever seen. Florida is prime hibiscus country in America, with Fort Myers the very best!

After the yearly show is over, the cleaning up is done just before the beautiful hibiscus blossoms, with all the gorgeous hibiscus ribbon winners, are gathered together and taken outside where they are ceremoniously thrown into the Caloosahatchee river and all watch the river pick up the blooms and gradually take them gliding down into its current, pleasing to everyone. It's a gorgeous sight!

The plants have tantalizingly colorful blooms. There are many varieties, and more being created all the time through cross pollination, even lovlier and more pleasing than the next.

Bromeliads are another favorite beautiful prolific group of fantastic colorful plants that are highly respected and gloriously pleasing to everyone. The plants have tantalizing colorful leaves. There are many varieties, one lovelier and more pleasing than the next.

The Caloosahatchee Bromeliad Society is made up of professionals and just plain folks like us who love beautiful unusual plants. We have bought hundreds, and each one produces colorful inflorescence, followed by one or more pups, as we call the new young offshoots. They grow at the base of the mother plant until they are about one third the size of the mother, then may be taken off to form large new beautiful plants by themselves. The mother will continue to try to produce pups, as a matter of survival, until she eventually dies and dries up, and should be removed. This process can take several months to a year or more. As a matter of preference, pups can be left attached to the mother plant to clump.

To keep plants at their best and to grow them best, it is wise to remove the pup from the mother when ready to go out on their own. Just like human beings! They will grow better, stronger, straighter, and form another lovely plant.

Many have beautiful vibrant colorful leaves. They have huge colorful spikes, inflorescence, while others have little delicate flowers. There are all kinds, huge plants, little tiny plants, all with interesting formal unpronounceable names, which only the best growers can pronounce intelligently.

Our house, lanai, and yard are overflowing with our gorgeous bromeliads. They just keep pupping, and we keep on buying and acquiring new ones we don't have. We also win new ones at raffles held at our monthly meetings.

Southwest Florida has a prolific amount of bromeliads here, with the professionals and neophytes working together to make this area a stronghold of beauty and pleasure.

When our neighbors Bill and Margaret Lang moved to the east coast to be near their son. They sold their house to a lovely artist/gardener named Cheryl Lamm from Minnesota where she retired from Ma Bell, Lucent Technologies. She became a wonderful neighbor and a close friend.

George's first encounter with her was when she was on top of a step ladder in front of the house trimming up the Phoenix Roebelenii which grew there.

She proceeded to redo that whole house and yard and turned it into to a beautiful home doing all the work herself, even displaying some of her magnificent eagle paintings, in which she specializes, outside on the walls at the front entrance.

Inside she brightened up everything into a true Florida style, decorating with her numerous art objects, in all media, and all her paintings displaying all her original creations to great advantage.

One bedroom was turned into a complete computer room and office.

At Christmas season she set up a display of miniature lighted houses and buildings of a small town in a corner of the living room.

Outside she renovated all the flower beds and created a new look with gravel in front of the house where she planted many specimen palm trees and plants.

Sometime, in all this flurry of activity, she found time to marry John Jones and help him with his A to Z Roofing business in Minnesota.

Once she completed all this hard work she placed this home up for sale and purchased an excellent new home at Matlacha Isles on the way to Pine Island on an excellent wide waterway.

She then proceeded with her wonderful artistic talents to make this into a beautiful home resplendent with a new dock and boat lift and new plantings of trees and shrubs.

She then built a workshop into her garage to ply her skills as an artist and became an active member of the Pine Island Art Association and Charlotte County Art Guild.

We asked her to do a painting of a beach scene of Kay at Sanibel with a view of the Gulf and birds. We provided her with about four of George's photographs, and she did herself proud painting a very realistic scene of the water lapping at the shore and Kay walking among the gulls and sandpipers with a great white Egret standing by. This gal is quite an artist.

We were expecting a hurricane - the first time we had ever had one come so close. We were to evacuate our homes, taking only the most important things with us, food and water (one half a gallon per person per day).

"What shall we take?" George asked when it was ominous, that we should be packing the car soon to be on our way away from our beloved home. The car had been filled with gas the night before, so we had a full tank, a must in ominous expectation of a hurricane.

"Well, I have the car packed!" George came in the house and said.

"What do you mean?" I couldn't understand. I was still thinking of what to take.

"I'm all packed!" he said.

"Well, you know we are to take the most important things!" I said.

"Yes, I know!" He said.

"What did you pack in the car?" I asked suspiciously "What is it you packed?"

"Our Genealogy!" George said, brightly.

I thought a minute, then laughed. He was right. That was the most important thing we had. It is a legacy which we can pass on to all our younger people, our children and our nephews and nieces, and to all now and our future generations. It seems we have spent millions of hours on gathering and thousands of dollars on what we have gathered together, years we have worked at libraries, gone to grave yards and looked at wills, marriage and land records at the court houses, both here and abroad. We have bought and perused books which would teach us and help us to gather hundreds, perhaps thousands of pages of genealogy to give us ideas of how our people have lived. It has been a very wonderful, exciting and rewarding hobby of ours for many years. It was promulgated by my mother who started the whole process. The first writing we found of hers was in 1930. When Anna Rose, my oldest sister, went to live with Mother after Dad died in 1951, she and Mother continued the research, traveling all over the Midwest. That was the beginning of our interest. Ann had copied many sheets of interest laboriously by hand before they had copiers, which has made it so much easier.

We were very fortunate to be able to copy by machine. Copiers were the boon to our lucrative experiences.

I think George and I have traveled to all our ancestors homes and areas where they had lived. It has been a most rewarding experience.

I went looking for George this morning when I got out of bed. I found him in his computer room. He stood up, holding a 9 x 11 piece of paper.

"What's that?" I asked.

"It's for the garbage men" he explained. "I thought it would keep them from getting stuck with the sharp pointed thorns."

The sign said: "Handle with care. These three bags have thorns inside."

"That's really nice of you to do that! Most people wouldn't think of it!" I said. That is really being thoughtful.

As he walked ahead of me through the kitchen, I watched his bent over body going fast in order to beat the garbage man.

All of a sudden, there was the sign hanging on the refrigerator, along with a lot of other signs and pictures, etc., I had on it. I'm a great saver of things my grand kids do and have all kinds of magnetic gadgets.

There hung his sign along with them. We howled! It looked as if it belonged there. He had attached scotch tape to the edges of his sign and, as he went by the refrigerator, the tape had reached out and touched and stuck to the refrigerator.

"Well, we started the day off right, laughing!" George said through his guffaws.

"Yeah, we did," I barely managed to say through my laughter.

He attached the signs to one of the three black plastic garbage bags waiting to be picked up.

George and I went to court on an early Monday morning. We had always been interested in the court system, and were glad to have the opportunity to see the due process in action, one part of which is to see the jury in action, one part of which is jury selection.

THEN AND NOW

One time years previously I was called up to serve but had to decline, because I am handicapped with my low vision.

Now, George had received a letter telling him to report to the Circuit and County Court Complex on the second floor of the court house.

Entering a waiting room, we went to the center of a room large enough for about a hundred people, and sat in comfortable straight chairs. People came dragging in one at a time.

At five minutes after eight o'clock, the woman in front of us in the office had everyone come forward and show their summons. She proceeded to tell everyone rules and regulations as to what would happen. George asked if I could go along with everyone. It was arranged with the baliff for me to go with the group.

The prospective jurors were not allowed to talk to anyone except among themselves, because unknown to us, someone interested in the case, a relative witness or others could have come among us. This could very well cause the case to be thrown out. The prospective jurors seemed to be a wide cross section of our community, all looked and sounded like good, solid citizens of the United States.

We followed the bailiff, in a single file, to the elevator into which we pushed ourselves like sardines. We got out on the fifth floor where the bailiff walked us rapidly down the winding corridors until we came to our assigned courtroom.

He lined us up again by juror number then marched us into the courtroom, through the swinging gate of the railing, where the prospective jurors were seated in the jury box, to the right of the courtroom. As they went through the swinging gate I was told to sit back of the railing. It was a modern courtroom, unlike any we had ever seen, with light wood curving around the center where the judge sat, and the curved railing separating the spectators from the participants in the court of law proceedings. The jurors were over to the right side, facing the judge and attorneys.

The defendant and his female attorney were on the left, the Assistant District Attorney (D.A.) on the right with the court recorder in front of the witness box.

When the Judge entered from his chambers the bailiff said, "Please rise!" I knew what that meant! I had seen it so many times on TV.

The judge walked in and after he sat in his chair on the judge's bench in front of the courtroom we all sat down. He was too far away for me to see him, but I liked what he said, and how he said it. He impressed me as a very good judge. I was surprised when George told me later that he was black, perhaps that is the reason I couldn't see him very well.

The two lawyers sat at their tables, a man who told the jurors he was the prosecuting Assistant D.A. and a young lady lawyer who was the defendant's attorney, who was seated beside her.

The Assistant D. A. explained to the jurors what was expected of them, then proceeded to ask individually and collectively questions of the jurors.

Then the pretty little defense attorney for the defendant came from her table to the left, walking to the small speakers stand, from which she talked to the jurors, making a big flamboyant show of her questioning. Perhaps, she has watched attorneys in theatrical action on TV which I have seen so many times.

The Assistant D. A. objected several times at her prolonged antics, but was always overruled by the judge. It was quite a show! This was only the preliminaries! I was hoping George would be chosen as a juror, so I could catch her full capabilities.

The time was getting near a break, and when the judge called for it, I was ready. I saw the prospective jurors going out towards the jurors room, the back door, as the Judge said to do, and, although I couldn't make George out, I knew he was going with them.

"I better go with him! I won't know where to go, or what to do!" I thought to myself. I jumped up and started forward, pushing on the swinging gate.

"Who is that woman? Where is that woman going? You can't come in here!" I heard the judge say loudly.

"Do you mean me?" I said, hardly audible, pointing to my chest with my right hand.

"Yes, I mean you" the judge bellowed. "Where are you going?" I'm sure I looked surprised, but failed to say anything immediately, so he continued. "Where you going to the restroom?" He asked, a little less menacing.

"Well, I thought I would!" I managed to say.

By now all the hubbub of all the noises had completely stopped and everyone was staring at me.

The darling judge let out an infectious laugh at the ludicrousness of action by everyone, including me. We then started laughing all together.

"You go on out that way," he said through his laughing.

While they were still laughing, I said, "I don't have to." That made everyone laugh uproariously again. Then the judge called a clerk and said, "Take that woman to the restroom."

The cute black deputy sheriff took both me and the only other woman in the room near me, who turned out to be the defendant's mother, down the long hallways to the restroom and back. The mother was not too upset over her son's being in the courtroom.

"It was a matter of complete self defense," she said when she talked about her son. "If it weren't I wouldn't be here."

I felt so sorry for her. But now I understood better the questions the lawyer, especially the defense lawyer, much better after talking to the defendants mother.

It was a homicide which should never have been.

"My son has lost so much weight since this happened!" she told me.

I gave her my sympathy and wanted to ask a lot of questions, but the jurors were told not to talk to anyone, and I felt I should respect that ruling, too.

After the break was over, the Judge read the names of those not accepted, there were only the six and George left. I thought for sure, he was to be a juror, but then the Judge saw him sitting there all by himself.

"Oh, Mr. Massing I missed you. You, too are excused," the Judge said.

I was sorry, in a way, that I would not get to see the rest of the process of the court function, but I really was glad George hadn't been chosen. I don't think I could have handled it if that young man had not been innocent.

I stood up as George came through the swinging gate and stepped out beside him. We walked out in the corridors, went down the escalator, and out into the beautiful sunny day.

I sit at the end of my 4 x 8 table, where I have written most of this book, looking out the four, three foot wide, sliding glass doors, onto our large Lanai, to our boat dock where sets our 21 foot boat, an Aquasport bowrider, waiting for us to take it out. The ponytails, the Queen palm trees, the split leaf Philodendrons are growing so large now that we can hardly see the canal and boat, but we know they are there.

To my left are two of the original four foot wide windows. Outside the windows is the Bougainvillea that we brought from Naples. George has formed it into a "Standard." It blooms profusely, gorgeous red loose blossoms spring and fall during the cooler months. The windows are set twenty-four inches from the floor, so the blossoms are fully visible all the time. At the left of the front room windows, is George's computer and library room which juts further out from the house. In front of his window is our bed of hybrid hibiscus, of which we have about thirty-six.

Beyond the edge of the house, are banana plants in a clump, at the edge of the water.

The lanai has a great variety of bromeliads, a few orchids, and other plants which cover the tables and set on the floor.

Our yellow, seven piece, aluminum patio set, was bought from a factory in Hallendale, Florida, when we were staying with Mother, while our house was being built in Naples. It still looks like new. Judy loves it so much, maybe even more than George and I. Someday she will have it. There are also some fiberglass round table and chairs, with other bamboo pieces.

From the lanai, a four foot wide walk curves around and down steps to the dock. I can't imagine a nicer place to live. Of course, I've seen nicer ones, more expensive ones, but I am always very happy to come back to my home and stay. For awhile, at least! I still like to go! Anywhere! This is a wonderful world in which we live!

Making bread is a very rewarding experience. Years ago my sister Ann, gave us a bread kneading bucket which became our source of enjoyment.

A friend and co-worker of George's at Wright-Patterson Air Force Base, Dayton, Ohio, Ed Campbell had been a baker on a Navy ship before he came to work at WPAFB, and soon George was enthused as anyone could be. Ed gave him bread recipes which he had used when he was a baker in the Navy, which, of course had to be cut down to a four person family.

Throughout the years, George has exercised his authority on bread making, and recently we bought one of the newfangled bread makers at Sam's shopping warehouse.

Larry has been enthused about bread making lately, so when we were visiting Spud and Freda from Ridgefarm, who come to Ruskin, Florida, we got more enthused also. (they are the ones who got us enthralled with the Coffee Cup Restaurant in Ruskin, the restaurant has since been closed.)

"Want to go to the Coffee Cup for supper?" Spud asked.

"Sure!" We said. "We always want to go there."

They had a fabulous cheeseburger, all fresh pure ground beef from the meat market in the grocery area of their establishment, with all the trimmings, that would practically melt in your mouth, and the best homemade pies of many varieties.

Freda and I brushed our hair a little, put on lipstick, and gathered up our purses. As we went through their kitchen to leave via the back door, an alarm sounded.

"Oh," Freda said. "Our bread machine finish signal just went off! Do you want to try it before we go to supper?"

"Sure!" I said. "We are thinking of buying a bread maker."

There we stood, eating a hot piece of newly baked bread in the middle of the kitchen.

"Do you want some butter on it?" Freda asked.

"No. This is great just like it is," I said. "We might spoil our supper if we ate butter on it!"

The next day after we returned home we went to Sam's and bought the best bread maker they had. It has been a complete source of fun and satisfaction to us.

George has made Mango bread, raisin pumpernickel, Whole wheat and of course white, all delicious, especially when toasted. After making bread off and on for weeks, he decided to make a large loaf of whole wheat, which called for 3 teaspoons of yeast instead of two.

"Do you think that's all right?" He asked me.

When George popped open the top of the bread maker, he yelled to me.

"Come look at this! Isn't that awful!" He said in a loud disgruntled voice.

I looked and looked. Finally I started laughing. Then George let loose, and we had us a good uproarious laugh.

When he had opened the lid and looked into the rounded center of the bread maker, it was the strangest sight we had ever seen.

When George finally extricated that loaf of bread, we laughed even more. It looked just like a man or probably a big boy, with a full head of blonde hair all over the top of his head.

"Should we throw it away?" George asked.

"Heavens, no! Why would we throw it away? Let's eat it and see what it tastes like!" I exclaimed.

That bread was the best bread we ever tasted! I want George to put 3 teaspoons of yeast in every loaf he makes from now on! With Lorraine Collins raspberry jam, or Aunt Dovie's rhubarb jam over the melted butter on the hot toast, it is fit for a king. We've been having it practically every meal.

"It's never going to last very long!" George said.

"Who cares?" I retaliated. "Then you can make some more just like it!"

Chapter 33
A Bit of Florida

When we moved here, there was a four foot wide cluster of plants, which had a tip of red on each leaf. When asking about it at the nursery, we were told it was a bromeliad. A mother plant of a bromeliad produces several pups, all of which produce several of their own pups, each continuing to produce if left alone. Each pup has to be cut off from the mother, when it is about one third of her size, if you want an individual plant.

This particular huge cluster is the most common of all bromeliads. No bromeliad collectors want them, but we think they are beautiful. Later, we were to find many more gorgeous and colorful bromeliads. We still love our Fingernail bromeliad and have broken it down into several smaller clusters which we have planted throughout our yard.

When we lived in Naples, we had found huge Haden mango trees in a Bonita Springs Trailer Park. They were the most delicious fruit we have ever eaten. A mango is to the south as the apple is to the north and the peach is to Georgia.

We bought our first mango tree in Naples, but it died the first year in a freeze. One of the first things we did, when we came to North Fort Myers, was to buy another mango tree. It froze, too.

"The third time is a charm," I said. "Let's try one more time." The next year it froze, too!

"I really want my own mango tree in my back yard!" I said. "So, do you think we should try again?"

We planted a larger, very healthy tree, and kept it alive for several years. It flourished, growing taller than the house. We had been putting sheets over each of the mango trees, using a frame of woven plastic covered wire with a light bulb inside, to provide a little heat during a freeze. This last tree had grown so large, and having an eight-inch trunk, we thought it would survive. It had outgrown the sheets, growing too tall for George to reach the top. But it also froze, clear to the ground, in a severe bitter cold, freezing night, even with all this pampering. It takes only a few freezing morning hours, in southwest Florida, to kill tender plants and young trees.

"I give up," I said. "I guess we're not to have our own tree. We'll have to buy our mangos out at Pine Island." They have a lot of commercial groves out there with trees protected by the warmer Gulf waters.

We now buy mangos by the 1/2 bushel. We eat fresh, frozen, and dried mangos until they come out of our ears. We peel, then slice pieces off the large flat center seed. They are put in a baggie and frozen for future use. Any recipe with peaches or pineapple can be made with mango as the fruit.

Devon's Delight is mango ice. One day when they came off the boat, I walked down to the dock, with a 10 x 10 glass dish of mango ice, cut into two inch squares. Everyone was so dry, especially Judy's mother, who was visiting from Bermuda. The others were so busy unloading and cleaning the boat, they each had only one piece, leaving Delores eating the rest.

"It's just wonderful!" she kept saying.

"Eat all you want!" I said. She was so dry from the strong winds and no water to drink out in the boat. "Eat it all, if you want!"

She ate one piece after another. The cold mango was soothing to her dry lips and mouth. She did continue to eat it all, as the others were too busy to eat. We sat in the swing at the dock, watching them do the boat cleanup.

We make Mango Ice and call it Devon's Delight as he is crazy about it. We have to make it for him ever once in awhile, as long as there are fresh mangos, or frozen mangos in the freezer, we whip him up a batch. Sometimes I send what's left in a baggie home with him. One time I sent the whole dish, as it hadn't frozen enough. He does love that Mango Ice! Joshua's Delight is a concoction of Jello, fruit, cottage cheese and cool whip, which I make.

"Jenna, what's your delight?" I asked her one day.

She thought a minute. "Could my delight be the same as Joshua's Delight?" she asked.

"No!" I laughed. "You will have to figure out a Jenna's Delight!" She hasn't come up with anything yet, unless it would be oat flake raisin cookies, which she and her mother love so much.

We chopped down an old, gnarled, hideous looking lime tree that was in the backyard when we moved here. It produced scrawny little nubbins as limes. Since we like limes less than any other fruit, we decided not to plant a lime tree again.

We planted a Thompson Pink Grapefruit tree, which is heavily loaded every year with fat juicy grapefruit. One wonders how the limbs stay intact with five to ten huge grapefruit hanging down at the tip, sometimes touching the ground. The flesh and juice of the grapefruit are frozen in baggies and will keep for months. Sometimes, we have to hurry to finish eating them before the next crop.

One time, I sent several baggies full of the frozen grapefruit to Larry and Judy's, as we try to finish them before the next season's crops. They didn't get to eat them as one little boy didn't get the freezer plug put back in its outlet properly, right after he and Dad were using the outlet for another purpose.

Then they left for soccer camp in Brandon, Florida. Upon their return, the fruit was thawed and stinking along with the whole freezer of food. What a mess!

We planted a Minneola Tangelo (Honeybell), my favorite of all citrus, and an Orlando Tangelo, to help pollinate. The Tangelos produce better when they can cross pollinate with another tree in its own variety. A couple of years later we had to plant a Temple Orange in place of the Orlando Tangelo which died.

We went to a nursery and bought seven Queen Palms planting them around the front and side of our yard. There was a cluster of three large Sable Palms about thirty feet in from the corner of Clubhouse Road and Cobia Way. They tower about thirty feet in the air, and need trimming of dead fronds, and seed clusters about once a year. Below these palms are several Carissa bushes which surround the palms. We are trimming these bushes into small standards by removing all lower branches and saving one single main stem. The palms also provide a spot of shade to plant bromeliads, which must be protected from the full hot rays of the sun.

This is a lush area, and with George's green thumb, we can do fabulous things within the growing arena.

I love the delicately cool mornings, after a long, hot summer, when the house can be opened to let the breezes blow through.

When the dinner dishes are removed from the dishwasher, I purposely make lots of loud noises clinking them against one another, to attract the birds. The jangling of the silverware has a cacophony of sound which delights the birds even more. It gets all the song birds excited, particularly the Mockingbirds, and they trill their heads off! It is a regular musicale, of which I am a background participant.

The birds love loud T V and loud conversations. They may be asleep in the trees, but they love to wake up and warble melodiously for the whole world to hear.

When a comedy show is on TV, like Frasier or Home Improvement, the birds try to outdo the hilarious activities and my subsequent laughter.

"I haven't heard my mockingbird lately, Susette, our neighbor said, one day.

"Your Mockingbird!" I retorted. That is my Mockingbird!"

We laughed delightedly, as we realized she flitted from home to home, and spread her cheer everywhere.

Chapter 34
The Middle East

In February, 1985, George and I went with our church group and others, with Dr. Waldo and his wife, Marion Farabee, to the Holy Land, and a side trip to Egypt. It was Waldo and Marion's ninth trip there as hosts of a traveling party to the Holy Land. They were as fabulous as hosts as they are as Sunday School teachers, and just good people. They were the best as traveling hosts! George and I have continued going on many trips with the Farabees, as have many of our church group.

We left Fort Myers and traveled the coast to New York City landing at La Guardia Airport then were shuttled by helicopter to John F Kennedy International Airport, then off to Amsterdam Holland where we refueled. We flew high over the Alps and finally landed at Tel Aviv, Israel Airport for the beginning of our tour.

We left by bus with a driver commentator, I believe an Arab, however very well knowledgeable of our Christian religion and bible. We journeyed to Cesarea where we sat on the restored stone seats of the amphitheater, from which we could see out into the Mediterranean. As we left in the bus we saw the great aqueducts which brought water to the city from the mountains, several miles away.

We visited Megiddo entering by way of the great long tunnel under the earth connecting to the spring, the water supply for the whole area. It was a great fortress between Syria and Egypt and was the sight of many battles by opposing forces of many different nations. It is located in the Jezreel Valley where it is envisioned by Christians that the Battle of Armegeddon will be fought. We saw troughs made of stone which were for feeding and watering Solomon's horses, as he maintained stables here. Excavations beginning in 1929 revealed many different civilizations have existed here, layer upon layer, over centuries. A cold fierce wind blew across this plateau while we were there making it difficult to keep warm.

We passed through Nazareth where Jesus lived to manhood and worked with Joseph as a carpenter. He grew up here to the age of 30, when he left to live in Capernaum. We also saw His mother Mary's well, still the water supply for the local people.

Haifa, on the Mediterranean coast has a very fine seaport for their many and varied industries. It is also a very busy diamond market. We toured one of the establishments and saw first hand where the diamond cutters were at work. We weren't in the market for a diamond, but later our Arab tour guide arranged for us to look at some sample finished rings in Bethlehem, and sold at a great price.

Each evening after a full day's excursion, we were expected to attend a fascinating Holy Land, Biblical, historical lecture, in a large room big enough for several busloads of weary travelers.

The speakers were very knowledgeable, professors of religion and philosophy. We would all drag ourselves in from our buses, plop in our seats with all our heavy, hot clothes. Most of the people promptly went to sleep, from a combination of the cold, crisp, outside air and the hectic day touring vast areas. It was almost more than a body can stand.

It was almost impossible for me to keep awake, but I usually managed, as I was so interested in the lectures given by the professors. These men were selected as they were top educators in their field, some serving in local universities. I looked forward to these classes and learned a lot that I had never heard before in all my bible reading and studying.

"Wake up, George!" I would hit him time after time, but he could not keep awake. "This is wonderful! You will really enjoy it!" I knew he would be interested in the professor's knowledge and presentation, but his body would soon succumb to the elements of cold and heat.

THEN AND NOW

The professors would go into depths of religion, history, and geography of Bible times. I looked forward to these gatherings although most of the travelers, including me sometimes, could not keep themselves awake enough to enjoy them.

After the classes were over, we gathered up all our heavy belongings, and went to our hotel rooms, to get ready for our dinner, after which we went back to our rooms and flopped, preparing our bodies with more energy for the next day. We didn't want to miss a thing!

We walked where Jesus walked and saw where He was born and lived and worked His miracles. It was so wonderful to be there, seeing the land and areas we had read about so much. It brought our faith so clear to us. Every Christian should visit the Holy Land on a tour like this. It strengthens one's religion to the utmost.

We went to areas where the other people in the bible lived and worshiped. If I could make only one trip in my life, it would be to the Holy Land.

We stayed on the banks of the Sea of Galilee at Tiberias, a Holy Jewish city, where many of their famous Jewish scholars are buried. Some of us ladies on the tour attempted to visit a Jewish Synagogue service, but we found we weren't really welcome. We were not permitted to sit among the other worshipers who were all men. We had to go to the balcony upstairs.

We also had and unfortunate happening while we were in Tiberias. On the edge of the huge grounds surrounding the place we were staying was an overlook to the Sea of Galilee. Frank and Mabel Nickolson were touring with us, but Frank was taking pictures and not watching too closely what he was doing and got too close to the edge of the overlook and slid under the railing and down he went and broke his leg. So he was on crutches and in misery the rest of our tour.

We boarded a boat at Tiberias and proceeded to cross the Sea of Galilee, which is 13 miles long and 7 miles wide. We must have traveled about 5 to 6 miles as Tiberias is about half way up the west coast and we crossed to Capernaum on the north bank. On the way we passed Magdala, the birthplace of Mary Magdalene, whom Jesus healed and who became one of His most faithful followers. We also stopped for a short visit at Tabgha where Jesus fed the five thousand with five loaves and two fishes.

Waldo and Marion held a service for us as we crossed The Sea of Galilee. We pulled in alongside a dock to debark, and went ashore immediately. We walked about, where Jesus had walked and saw the ruins of the temple that stood on the site where the original temple stood where He taught. Jesus performed many of his miracles here in Capernaum. We saw where the ruins was excavated that had been Peter's home. A stone nearby was carved in likeness of the Ark of the Covenant. There was also a plaque mounted on a post with the prayer of St. Francis of Assissi.

The Mount of the Beatitudes, the site where Jesus spoke the words of the Beatitudes, is well up on a hill above the Sea of Galilee. We sat there at the porch rail of the Church of the Beatitudes, built by the Franciscans, overlooking the area, as we contemplated The Beatitudes.

Our Arab tour guide took our bus on a long stretch of hills and grasslands passing shepherds with their flocks along the way. The bus finally stopped atop one of the grassy knolls where we could see into the distance, where he said we dare not proceed farther into the hills, as we could see apparently military encampments of Syria across the border. We could see a Syrian flag flying from its staff at the foot of the hill where we were. Some of us stepped off the bus to take a few pictures and smile and make signs with a shepherd who of course could not understand us. His sheep were grazing peacefully on the hillside.

We proceeded further north to Caesarea Philipi where we walked about spillways of the River Jordan where it is much closer to its origin off Mount Hermon. Here the waters are much clearer and cleaner, so it was here that Reverend Bill Pethrick, our 91 year old retired minister, founder and former teacher of the First United Methodist Church Welcome Sunday school class, said he would get his sample of the Holy waters of the Jordan River. I took a picture of him bending over the spillway to collect his water in a little bottle he had ready. The rest of us collected our samples far down the river in the area where Christians are still Baptized in these waters.

In Jerusalem we visited the Wailing Wall, after having entered by the Dung Gate, I even went inside the little entrance at the back and talked to some Rabbis. It was very impressive to see so many in worship here. Behind the wall we could see the Dome of the Rock which we visited next. We had to remove our shoes to make entrance to this shrine of the Moslem world. It was a beautiful sight. Inside, beneath the dome of this wonderful building, is the rock of Mount Moriah, where Abraham made ready to sacrifice his son Isaac, but since it appeared they would complete the sacrifice, due to their faith, the act was prevented by an angel who appeared. Just before we exited Jerusalem through Stephen's gate we saw the Pool of Bethesda where Christ healed the man who had been crippled for many years.

We saw the site at Gallicantu where it is believed the house of Caiphas, the high priest stood, where Jesus spent the night awaiting His first trial, also when Peter denied the Lord three times before the cock crowed twice on this site. We descended from the area by steps in the hillside believed even to have been used by Jesus.

We visited the Garden of Gethsemane, getting to view the ancient, old, gnarled olive trees, still bearing fruit, which are believed to be over 3000 years old. Jesus was arrested here and taken to the house of the high priest Caiphas.

The day we visited the Garden Tomb we had rain, then sleet and snow, not a pleasant day. We entered the tomb where there was a shelf, on which a body would rest, and there were sheets of white cloth as if Christ had just risen from them.

Jericho is an ancient city, and it was called the city of Palms like our home Fort Myers, Florida, has been called for some years. It lies in the hot sub-tropical Jordan Valley and citrus, dates, bananas are raised there. Jericho is considered the oldest city in the world, dating back to several thousand years before Christ. We remained on the outskirts of the city and were allowed to explore a "Tell" or mound quite high in the air from which we could look down over the city. At the Tell we saw the results of archaeological exploration of the area leading to many great discoveries which provided evidence of the history of the area.

We followed along the Jordan River and saw an actual group of pilgrims being baptized in the Holy waters of the Jordan. Here we stopped to dip our little bottles to obtain our sample of the Holy Water to take back home. It was not as clear as the sample Reverend Pethrick obtained at Caesarea Philipi.

We explored Qumran where the Essenes, a religious sect, breaking away from society in Jerusalem, settled in the desert on the shores of the Dead Sea and proceeded to write the Dead Sea Scrolls and stored them in huge jars to hide them from the approaching Roman Legions in many nearby caves. We could see the cave entrances up on the sides of the cliffs. We walked among the ruins that had been the Essenes' place of work and worship. They had workshops to provide for their every need. They lived in tents, huts and the nearby caves. Their secret storage places remained as such until 1947 when a Bedouin shepherd boy discovered the first jars of scrolls.

In Bethlehem we visited a business of shops and souvenirs, with workshops creating olive wood articles to sell to the pilgrims. The proprietors of this business are good friends of our tour hosts Dr. A. Waldo Farabee and his wife Marion. They saw to it we were treated well and allowed to tour their creative workshops. We saw camels of olive wood being made on computerized equipment that duplicated, for example, seven identical camels to be turned out at one time. Needless to say camels are what we bought to take home.

We toured about Bethlehem visiting the Church of the Nativity built over the site where Christ was born. We descended a flight of stairs to a lower level where the place Christ was born is marked by a silver star. The Holy Manger is there also. A German group was there singing hymns we knew in German, so we joined in with our English and sang with them.

The Shepherd's Field was nearby where the shepherd's watched over their flocks and an angel appeared to them and announced the coming of Christ. Reverend Farabee and Reverend Pethrick served communion to us in tiny olive wood communion cups at a place near the shepherd's field. We were allowed to take the little cups home.

We stopped at a site along the Dead Sea where we walked along the shore of this so unusual body of water some 1300 feet below sea level. It is quite a large body of water being about 47 miles long and 10 miles wide. Kathryn waded in the water along the shore so she could say she had that experience. We could see salt crystals clinging to objects in the water. The sea has no outlet so all the minerals are trapped as they are poured in from the River Jordan.

Massada is an unusual place as it is on a 2000 foot high plateau. There is a foot trail to the top but we ascended by way of a cable car. It was a great fortress built by Herod the Great and later used by those patriots to wage warfare against the Romans. We explored the area where those 960 Jewish patriots lived and worshiped and died at their own hand rather than surrender to the Roman army which had laid siege to the place and were building a ramp to get to those on top.

We left Jerusalem early in the crisp morning air and traveled all day south through the Sinai Desert, seeing the colorful Bedouins and their camels, and their living quarters of tents and huts as we headed for Egypt.

When the bus turned left at a crossroad, I saw a sign pointing to the right that said Gaza.

"Stop!" I yelled, "I want to go down the Gaza Strip! Turn right!"

The bus driver turned in his seat toward me about three rows back.

"We can't go there. It is not safe. They would stone us!" he said. "We are not permitted to travel through that area, we must turn here!"

We crossed from Israel into Egypt at a checkpoint, where we were subjected to an inspection.

When we were leaving Israel and crossing over into Egypt, we were told we couldn't buy drinking water in bottles in Egypt, so a lot of us bought bottles of water in Israel, and carried them over into Egypt with us. This was not true, that we couldn't buy bottles of water in Egypt, but we didn't know that then.

Checking through our luggage at the border, we had to place our bottles, as well as everything else, on the surveillance conveyor belt. With all our luggage, carry ons, plus the water and camera bags, etc., George and I had a little trouble. One bottle kept falling off the belt and George grabbed it and put it back, as the lady in front of us accused him of trying to take her water.

"I didn't try to take your water bottles. I have two of my own!" George said to her, rather crossly, I thought, but continuing to get our stuff on the counter.

We were rushed as our bus to Egypt was waiting. Then they chose our suitcase to go through a special open bag check, why we'll never know! They check a few. Some young kids' suitcases were being checked, along with ours.

"Why are you checking them?" I asked one of the workers, standing nearby.

"For drugs," he said. I looked at the kids and thought, "Yes, they looked like they could be carrying drugs."

"Why are you checking us?" I then asked the man.

"I don't know," he said. "We check every few people."

Could it have been because George was floundering around at the surveillance belt?

Just ahead of us a woman had been having trouble going through the Egyptian checkpoint. I was tired so, seeing a bench, I walked over to it and sat down. The lady who was having trouble, came over and sat down beside me.

"That man was trying to take my water!" she said to me emphatically. I turned and looked at her.

"What man?" I asked, in amazement?

"That man," she said, pointing to George. "He tried to take my water!"

"That man did not try to take your water!" I said heatedly. "He was trying to help you! That's my husband, and he wouldn't hurt a flea!"

We crossed the Suez Canal, which connects to the Gulf of Suez and the Red Sea, passed Cairo, Egypt, University on to Giza on Cairo's doorstep.

Our busload of people arrived at a Holiday Inn, in Giza, Egypt with exhausted people, too tired to do anything but to go to our hotel rooms, to relax a bit and ready ourselves for dinner downstairs.

George headed for the bathroom after we entered our room and threw our luggage down. I started towards the bed, in order to relax a bit, but I looked out the window as I passed it.

"George," I screamed. "Look here! Come quick!" George came running.

"What is it?" he cried. "What's the matter?"

I stood entranced, unable to speak.

"Look! Look out the window," I said, excitedly.

We had a perfect view of the three ancient pyramids of Giza, resplendent in all their glory, looking like pictures I had seen in my school books and other places, all my life.

We stood, looking in amazement out of our window, at that beautiful sight. If we hadn't realized we were in the beautiful land of Egypt, we knew we were now!

The next day, the bus took us to see the pyramids up close.

"Are you going to ride a camel?" Maribelle Hollis asked me on the bus.

"Sure aren't you?" I retorted, laughing.

"Are you really?" George asked in surprise.

"Of course! I can't wait! It will be fun!" I said excitedly.

As we got off the bus, I walked behind the first people from our bus who were heading towards the camels, all stretched out on the ground, waiting for customers to come and go for a ride. Their handlers were standing at the front of each camel, holding their reins.

I started towards the first camel, with trepidation, but with great anticipation. Some one rushed past me and took the first camel. I had to move on to the next. George was staying behind me, so I felt all alone, really hanging back, too. A bit afraid!

As I was almost to the second camel, I felt a swish and saw Waldo and Marion rushing past me, to take the next two camels. They had been on them many, many times, and knew what to do. Which one shall I take?" I timidly asked George. It seemed to me all the camels were being taken.

"Take this one!" he said, giving me a push, which made me run forward towards the head of the camel and the camel handler. I ended up right in front of the grinning handler, and turning, realized I was four inches from the big camel lying on the ground.

Without another step, I slung my right leg over the saddle, trying to get situated, as the camel immediately started to get up. The strange movements of his front legs caused me to go forward and side to side.

"Go back, go back!" the handler screamed at me. I forced my body backward, trying to get my wobbling feet into the two long stirrups.

As the camel got up on his hind legs, he started to get up on his front legs. It caused me to go backwards leaning against his rump.

"Go forward! Go forward," the handler yelled at me.

The camel was heading out immediately while I was being shaken from side to side, and trying to keep straight, when I saw George gliding by, sitting up straight and perfect on his huge camel.

"Here, take our picture!" I heard him say, and saw he was handing his camera, his pride and joy, to an Egyptian camel handler, a thing I never expected to see. Aside from immense surprise at George, handing his camera he never let anyone touch to a mere nomad, I was trying to get myself into a decent position and arrange myself into a picture taking pose!

As I saw one of the men nearby take the picture, I managed to stay upright and sit still long enough for a good picture. I continued getting myself organized as we came out of the camel yard. We turned left where our bus was parked going single file down the road towards those wonderful pyramids.

It all happened so fast, and I had been so busy, that now was the time to enjoy our surroundings. The camel began to walk in such a way that seemed to relax me and allow me to look around. It was a marvelous, rolling, very comfortable ride. I loved it!

When we got off our camels close to the pyramids, I stood entranced as a camel was coming straight at me, hell-bent, with a colorful, young, Egyptian flapping in the wind. With an enormous grin on his young face, he stopped right in front of me. I could have reached out and touched the camels big nose and the side of his neck. It was a glorious sight, one I will never forget! I had not flinched at all, I was so interested in the event happening in front of me.

The young fellow slid off the camel's back, and took three or four steps quickly towards me. I had been smiling all the time. It was such a glorious sight! He literally swept me off my feet.

He wanted to kiss me, but I wasn't brassy enough for that, so we stood with our arms around each other. He was such a gorgeous specimen of Egypt. He kept his arm around me, while George took our picture in front of the camel. George gave him some money, then George and I walked the short distance to those fabulous Giza pyramids. When we got back to our bus later, our guide told us those young camel riders and flashing horseback riders made sixty thousand dollars a year.

The three great pyramids were a grand sight to behold. Gazing up at them near the base, we saw the people, dwarfed like ants, climbing the side to gain entrance. Mere humans built these colossal, immense pyramids of stone, requiring the labors of thousands of slaves many years to build. They were even more impressive close up than when we looked out our bedroom window.

Egypt was fantastic! So alive with history! We enjoyed it as much as we had Israel, except in a different way. The Egyptian people fascinated us with their flowing robes and different headpieces. The man-made monuments of Egypt were so bold and beautiful!

All my life, I have had an inner clock in me that lets me know what time it is, no matter what I'm doing. When I wake up in the night, I guess at what time it is, and when I look at the clock, which I always do, to be sure, I am almost always within five or ten minutes difference, whether it be a few minutes or several hours from the last time I looked.

This morning, August 24, 1994, when I was writing this book, I guessed the time at 9:15, then changed it to be 9:30, when I looked at my big clock on the wall, it was 9:27. I smiled, as it always elates me to be able to do this. I had been sleeping since 12:30.

How do I do it? I have no idea. Perhaps I have the same internal clock in me that was in my father, who always awakened at four o'clock, when he needed to shuck the corn in order to get two loads of corn out of the field before dark. That's the only explanation I can give. But I do think of my dad when I hit the time right.

One time at our hotel in Giza, Egypt, George got me up an hour too early. My body rebelled.

"It can't be time to get up!" I mumbled.

"Yes, it is!" he exclaimed. "My watch says four o'clock."

So we got up, cleaned up and dressed, stepping outside to find no one in the hall. People had been told to put their luggage out by their door by three in order that it could be packed by the time we were to leave at four or five.

We continued on our way and got on an empty elevator.

"Do you suppose they went off without us?" I asked. This was unthinkable. What were we to do?

When we came out of the elevator, there was absolutely no one in sight. We wandered around, then spied a clerk lurking in the back of the lobby. When George asked him, they together figured out George's watch had got us up an hour early. Everyone else was asleep.

My body had rebelled every minute of the time. I knew I was to get up at four and my body knew it. But we forced ourselves to do what George insisted.

We went back upstairs and I flopped on the bed, with all my clothes on, including my hat, heavy coat, and gloves.

"You're not going back to bed?" George asked in amazement.

"No, I can sleep just as well like this. We only have a little time."

My inner clock had been working then, but we hadn't recognized it. It knew it wasn't time to get up!

When the right time came, I awoke, went to the bathroom, then we went outside our door, to find the hallways, elevator, and hotel lobby teeming with activity. So, we were back on schedule.

We arrived at the Cairo train station after an hours bus ride from our hotel in Giza to a bustling, whirling, atmosphere. Full long colorful robed Egyptians were scurrying to and fro in the dark earthen floored smelly station. It was so dark, I had to be very careful to keep from being run down.

I looked up to see a gorgeous sight of a very tall, handsome Egyptian with his high fez on his head and his full colorful green robe whipping about his boots from his long stride. I stopped in my tracks, just to watch him. I could have reached out and touched him as he passed me by. Oh, how I wished I could hear his story. He had to be someone very high up and special in the beautiful land of Egypt!

Our day long ride from Cairo to the Valley of the Kings was so very interesting. The countryside is beautiful. When we arrived at Luxor we found our hotel to be beautiful. We rode in small horse-carts through the main part of the old city.

Using the hotel at Luxor as our base, we visited the tomb of King Tutankhamon where we descended into the deep earth by way of crude stairs. We were required to leave our cameras at the mouth of the underground tomb, as no photography was permitted. The walls of the corridors were lined with hieroglyphics telling the story of the young king who died at the age of eighteen. We reached the burial chamber where his mummified body was found, but his body and its sarcophagus had long before been removed for safekeeping in the great museum at Cairo. George got to visit that museum later, while I was laid up with a severe bout with my arthritis.

It was so different than anyplace else we had ever been. It was lovely in the morning when the local citizens were putting clothes, food and whatever outside their ancient buildings, preparing for another day. We saw a man sitting in the sun, smoking a Turkish water pipe, dreaming away. It was so all out in the open, free living. Our horse drawn carriage passed rapidly amongst the activities on the dirt street, while our Egyptian driver laughed and turned toward us and talked to us in fractured English. There were four of us in the carriage, with one of the women sitting on the front seat with the driver. She kept him busy explaining things to us. It was a wonderful trip. He took us downtown through the center part of Luxor, where most of the other members of our tour didn't go. The area was teaming with pedestrians, bicycles and push-carts. It was the influence of the woman who sat beside him that we were given that special ride.

This same carriage driver took us from the Hotel in Luxor, the approximate three miles to the great temples of Karnak in a horse and buggy caravan. These temples were immense in size and each had huge supporting pillars with inscriptions and hieroglyphics carved in the sides. All figures of gods and goddesses were of immense proportions. One looked in wonderment to imagine how they could have been built without modern equipment.

Our group took a ride down the Nile River. An Egyptian tried to sell me a scarab on the huge boat, as he and some other young men were soliciting sales. This one acted differently than his fellow workers, as he sat down beside me, just holding out his scarab in his outstretched hand, never saying a word, hardly looking at me. I kept shaking my head, finally pushing his hand away. He didn't leave. I ignored him, as Waldo had said to do. He continued to sit beside me, looking forlorn and anxious. I felt sorry for him, I really would have liked to buy something from him as he was the only one in his group not selling anything. He definitely played on my sympathy, but I have always hated scarabs. There was no beauty in scarabs, as far as I could see, even though they were the religious symbol of their country.

We arrived at our destination on the opposite bank of the famous Nile. We disembarked at the bottom of a thousand rock steps, at least it appeared to me at the bottom, looking upwards, that there were a thousand.

As I started going up the steps, I found it quite difficult with my bad leg. I leaned forward, and using my Nefretitti cane George had bought for me, I was laboriously managing the steps. (We found out later the cane was a head of Ramses II instead.)

A hand came out in front of my downcast eyes, to reveal a gorgeous gray and white bird. The bird had an alabaster body with an oxidized solid copper head, neck, and long beak, with long bent legs of the same material. It was exquisite! It measured ten inches long and six inches high, weighing almost two pounds. My steps faltered, as I looked up at the colorfully dressed "brother" of the fellow with the scarab. I shook my head negatively, and smiled, continuing up the steps. I shouldn't have smiled! That was a mistake! Waldo had said ignore them, pay no attention to them whatsoever.

After taking two or three more steps, I looked down into the dancing eyes and delightful grin of this same character. He had doubled over looking back up at me, he held out this gorgeous bird in his hand. I laughed! It really was a delightful sight!

I stopped, and, taking the bird in my hand, I looked at it more carefully.

"It really is gorgeous, George! It's very well made. Let's buy it!" I said, as I looked it over. The Egyptian was all smiles, I couldn't help smiling and laughing back! Who took who? He'll never know I cherish that beautiful specimen of a wading bird to this day, giving it a prominent spot on my parsons table.

The worst thing was hand carrying it the rest of the long day in my purse. It was heavy! It had to be protected the rest of the trip, especially going through five baggage inspectors. I carried it all the rest of the trip in a little handbag until we arrived home many days later. But the memory of it and the adorable salesman was worth it.

Chapter 35
The British Isles

In the summer of 1985 I talked George into going on our own, all by ourselves, to look up genealogy in England where I had twenty-five ancestors and he had five, and also to Germany to see if we could find his ancestors. He was afraid to go, but I was so persistent. I knew we could do it!

Larry and Judy and their three children took us to Miami where we were all invited to John and Sue Gunning's new home. He was one of Larry's best friends in Crystal Lakes, Ohio, where we lived when they were growing up.

They had a delicious cookout at pool side, after which Larry, Judy and Jenna took us to the airport for our trip to Europe.

The large carry on bag I had to carry was full of our eight weeks long supply of vitamins and a few medicines. The bag was unwieldy, and kept falling off my shoulder, until I learned to push it back and hold it with an elbow and hand grip.

I looked at my little family with bright eyes. I hated to leave them, but I really wanted to go on this fabulous vacation we had planned. Larry and Judy were standing side by side, and Larry was holding this gorgeous little girl high up in his arms. It was a lovely sight. One I have carried with me forever. The boys wanted to stay and play in the pool with John and Sue's children.

"Say good-bye to Grandma and Grandpa," Larry said to Jenna.

"Bye, Gamma, bye, Ganpa! she said, bright and clear.

She was all eyes, not really understanding. In her favorite pink dress she looked like an angel.

We kissed and hugged them all and started to the entrance of the plane. I turned and looked back at them and waved. It was eight wonderful weeks before we saw them again.

When we were able to get on the plane we waved goodbye at every turn in the airport where we could still see them, then headed on down the aisles and turns to the plane where we discovered our seats were filled. They had double booked in Orlando and Atlanta and there were twenty to forty people standing in the aisles trying to understand. Finally we were told to go both front and back-we were personally told to go front for which we were thankful. We were in 6A and B, so we had excellent seats, albeit small. Too small and cramped. It was a Tri Star wide body jet-cruising at 620 miles per hour at 3700 feet.

I had asked for a window seat which I got, 6A. Larry had wanted to know why I wanted a window seat as I couldn't see anything, and especially at night. How wrong he was. It was fabulous! So beautiful! I peered out the window most of the time.

I never slept any that night. It was dark by the time we were in the air. I watched the shoreline all the way from Miami to Maine. I was amazed we went up our coast, but we were to get refueled in Bangor, Maine. The plane left at 9:40 P.M. Miami and arrived in London 12:40 P.M. The night view from Miami to Bangor Maine was gorgeous-just beautiful. Then after stopping for fuel from 45 to 60 minutes we left for London. I watched out my window until I figured we were over water. It had been a three hour ride to Bangor and would be a five hour ride from there to London. I never got up once except to go to the bathroom.

In the dark I could see we were above clouds which were very strange looking-blackish with lighter color in spots. They changed constantly. Then the most gorgeous sunrise started. We flew towards it, of course, and I never really saw the sun but what I did see was thoroughly fascinating. At first there was this very delicate light at the horizon with a larger orangish color suffused above it. The white light grew larger as did the orange light all glowing and shining on the clouds. The clouds changed constantly. Sometimes clouds would be above us too, and we seemed to be in between them in a clear area. As the light got lighter the clouds appeared gradually to be all white until they looked like snow. Some would appear to be swept snow as the wind had blown it in huge mounds, some seemed like little puffy areas of snow. It seemed to glisten. Gorgeous! It then appeared to all be together as one big sweep of snow. It was changing constantly.

When we left Bangor, we went due east into the morning sun. It was a glorious sight. The sun was never seen except by the pilots I'm sure, but the way that bright sun shone on the clouds below us was one of the most beautiful sights I have ever seen. It changed constantly. The play of the sunlight and the shadows upon the clouds was something to behold.

It was daylight when we flew over Ireland (the Captain told us) and saw their lovely squares of fields below. It was a patchwork of deep greens and yellows. This was the only way we saw beautiful Ireland, as when we could have gone, there had been some bombing where we were to visit. We decided not to go as our rented car had to be left in England, and we would have had to take a ferry, an eight hour ride, then travel by bus. I'm sorry we did not get to Ireland, but it was the wrong time to go.

We landed at Gatwick Airport and commuted by train, a forty minute ride to Victoria Station, where a very amiable taxi driver put us and our luggage in an extra spacious, black London cab. As he drove down the street, we were so excited at being in London for the first time, that the taxi driver became excited, too!

"Is this your first time in London?" he asked.

"Yes!" We said. "Could you go past some interesting landmarks on the way to our hotel?"

"Which one's do you want to see?" he asked.

"Oh, anything!" I said excitedly. "We want to see everything!"

We had a mini guided tour complete with exciting narrative. He drove us past Buckingham Palace and pointed out the route for changing of the guard. We saw fabulous Westminster Abbey which was undergoing renovation, the House of Parliament and Big Ben overlooking the Thames, The Stock Exchange and government

Buildings, also many monuments, including one of Winston Churchill.

When we drove up to our hotel, the Great Eastern in downtown London, we had all become great friends. After getting the luggage out of the trunk and into the hotel, the taxi driver shook hands with us as if we were long lost buddies!

I have learned since then that the London Taxi drivers are the most courteous in the world. I believe it! Not like the French. But that is another story! The two are as different as night and day!

The old City of London is only one square mile in size, which was a big surprise to us, as we had always thought of London as a very large Metropolitan area. However the London of today is actually composed of many boroughs and parts of shires. The population is in excess of eight million.

When we were shown about our hotel, we found it to be enormously large, and well heated. Since it was extremely warm outside, heat was the last thing we wanted. I tried to raise the window but to no avail!

Looking around for where the heat was originating, I found the pipes in the bathroom were emitting heat you wouldn't want in the dead of winter.

George tried to find a place to turn the heat off, but there was none. We found quickly that in England heat was turned on and turned off centrally. One burned up or one froze, and it was not your choice when you wanted to do either. We shut the door into the bathroom when we first arrived, and kept it closed most of the time we were there. Some places turned the heat on from eight to ten of an evening. You froze the rest of the time, that is, if it were cold outside which was the case most of the time we were there, because of the high humidity.

We had been traveling on American time, now we were in London which was five hours difference. It was five o'clock and we were starved. The hotel dining room was not opened yet and we were getting hungry.

We walked outside and strode down the street to see what we could find. We saw some wild looking girls, with orange hair standing on end, with impish faces and wild dress. They were in their teens or early twenties, ganged up on the street corner, probably soliciting.

This was the first look at English punks. We were to see others later. Boys came by and the two groups were so loud and noisy, we turned around and went the other way.

A number of times we asked someone how many blocks it would be to get somewhere. "We don't have blocks here," more than one man told us when we asked. At the end of one long street, we looked down at the crossroads and, voila! There was a Kentucky Fried Chicken.

"I would never have chosen K F C if I had been asked," I said, "but that is all that is around. Do you see any other eating place down the street?"

"No I don't!" George said. "That seems to be all there is."

"Let's go then, and see how good they are in London!" I said. "I'm too tired to look any farther, aren't you?"

"Yes, I really am!" George said. "Maybe we'll feel better if we eat."

That was a delightful K F C, the best one in which we ever ate! They cooked it so delicately, just the way the old Colonel had made the recipe. It was delicious! Everything that went with it was superb, too. The very best we had ever eaten!

It was six o'clock by the time we walked back to our hotel. We were so tired and completely exhausted!

"Let's go to bed!" I said.

"What? Now? This early?" George asked.

"Well, aren't you as tired as I am?" I asked. He acquiesced. "Well let's go to bed and sleep! Maybe we'll feel better!"

We both slept until late the next morning, and found we were ready to get up and go. Our exhaustion was over.

We walked through the Banking District and on to the Guildhall, where we looked through records for genealogy, without success.

One day, we were going down the street in the banking district after working at a genealogy library, when we heard what sounded like a heard of elephants or at least horses behind us.

"What in the world is that noise?" I asked George.

"I don't know!" he exclaimed. "Strange, isn't it?"

We stopped walking, turned around, and saw the strangest sight! Every one of the huge banks had stopped work at five o'clock, and every employee was bursting out the double doors, and clomping down the street, and going in every direction. It was an avalanche of people bearing down on us! We had been the only people, now there were hundreds. We pushed ourselves up against the side of one of the banks, and watched.

They were all men, all in black or grey suits, bowler hats, and carrying a large black umbrella. The sun was shining, but the rain came at the drop of a hat, so they were all prepared. They were all intent on getting home after five o'clock. I wish we had had our camera with us, but that sight and sound has left an impression on my very soul, so I will never forget it!

After three days at the Great Eastern Hotel, working on Genealogy each day, everyone told us the Latter Day Saints had been there and microfilmed everything, all over England. They advised us we should go to our own Salt Lake City Archives, as they have it all. We told them we had been there and spent several days searching their records.

The British people love us Americans, and we certainly did love all of them, everyone trying to help us. We fell in love with one another everywhere we went.

We spent four weeks in England, driving twenty-seven hundred miles, and staying mostly in Bed and Breakfast places and some hotels. In all that time we found only one motel, similar to ours. We visited all the ancestral homes we could find to see where and how they lived. Most of the people without fail, were charming. We were served full English breakfasts until we could eat no more. This breakfast consisted of warm grapefruit juice, tea, cold un-buttered toast, two inch wide exceedingly salty bacon, very thick, sunny side up eggs,(we asked for scrambled), one sausage, two hot slices of tomatoes.

Our trip around the British Isles started with our renting a car for two weeks. We were staying on London's west side at the Kensington Hotel on Kensington Close. The rental agency was in the foyer of our hotel.

As we drove the little Nissan away, George found it a little difficult to stay on the left side of the road. Actually he drove too closely on the left side. Thump, thump, thump was loud and clear. I looked over at George. He was gripping the wheel staring straight ahead.

Thump, thump, thump there it was again! "What is that, George? What are you doing?" I yelled at him.

"I don't know!" he yelled back at me.

Thump, thump, thump. There it was again. I tried to figure it out as he wasn't doing anything about it. When it didn't happen again I figured it out to be that our leather mirrors were hitting the mirrors of three parked cars.

"Get over! You are too close to the cars! You are hitting our mirrors against their mirrors!" I yelled at him.

When he moved out in the lane a little we were all right. When we arrived at the end of the street he turned left and kept going.

"Aren't you going back to see if you did any damage?" I asked George.

"No, I might never get back," he said, "besides, I do not believe there was any damage."

We left London by way of the M4 Motor way comparable to our Interstate Highway system. For the next three days I was worried about George's driving. He kept hitting the left curbing. Going to the left was getting away from the oncoming cars that went lickety split down the highway.

"We better go back home," I finally said. "You are going to have to buy the rental agency new tires when we check in." Fortunately George became better at British driving.

We did lots of sightseeing and visited many of my ancestors areas. We did not find anyone still alive as my ancestors had come over to America in the sixteen hundreds and seventeen hundreds. I have twenty-five Grandparents from those many generations, who lived in Great Britain and George has five.

We had stopped at a Pub along our way for lunch and during our time there were advised of the nearness of Windsor castle, so it became the object of our first visit. We drove about Windsor until we found a parking place along a small lake where there were water birds and all manner of boats with people in a holiday mood. We walked back to the castle taking pictures. We took many pictures of the castle from different angles, from far and near. A magnificent sight.

We drove to Winchester and viewed the glorious Winchester Cathedral, of Norman architecture, built in 1067 and redone along simpler lines 300 years later. We also saw the round table of King

Arthur's knights with the name of the knight whose place it was to sit.

Near Amesbury we found the wonderful exhibition of Stonehenge, the towering stones standing on end leaving one dumfounded as to how these great stones could have been placed there by mortal man. These stand on the Salisbury Plain of Wiltshire.

Marlborough, Wiltshire is the location in all of England where my mother's Family Mildenhall, a corruption of Minel, originated. It was changed to Mendenhall upon settling in the United States. We stayed in the town and visited the surrounding areas where my family had resided. It's a beautiful, beautiful town all full of flowers and interesting streets, houses, and cottages.

In front of our lodgings right on High Street was an interesting open-air market down through the middle of the street. People were flocking in with their baskets and carts, and all sorts of produce and farm products were for sale in the market. It was late August, but before we arrived, their summer had been a disaster with much wet weather. Crops had rotted in the fields without being harvested.

We found Mildenhall Manor House, where my ancestors lived at Maridge Hill, Wiltshire, near Mildenhall Royal Air Force Base of World War II fame. As we sat on the front porch and had tea with the present owners of stately, elegant, Mildenhall Manor House, I thought of my Grandmother and Grandfather Mendenhall and my Mother. How they would have loved visiting this gorgeous old home of their ancestors. I was visiting it for myself and all generations to come.

Visiting ancestor's areas was interspersed with castles, E.G. Windsor Castle, and the Queen's country estate, Sandringham, and many beautiful cathedrals. The greatest thing of all was meeting the English people who loved us, and we in return loved them. I wrote a journal of our entire twelve weeks in the British Isles and Europe, which I hope to have published some day.

On the following Sunday we searched for a Quaker church, as most of both mine and George's English ancestors were Quakers. We found a church in Swindon just a few miles north of Marlborough. We attended the service, which we found to be much like the eastern U. S. services we attended in New Jersey, and met the young church

Warden Elspeth Woller afterwards, who lived in an apartment on the premises. She was a very gracious hostess and had us stay for lunch with her.

From the church we drove a few miles to Avebury where we saw other stones planted in the earth much like Stonehenge, yet these stones had more normal shapes just like great big rocks.

We then journeyed to Little Bedwyn, Wiltshire where we found lovely old St. Michael's church where Francis Mildenhall is buried. He is the grandfather of John Mildenhall, my immigrant great grandfather, several generations removed, who came to America in 1683 with William Penn.

We continued on through Wiltshire and its rolling hills of wheat and maize, thatched roof houses and red brick houses everywhere. Many manor houses, each with many tenant houses, had red brick walls.

We visited the records offices in Trowbridge, where we were allowed to research old, old records on parchment paper 300 years old, which were sort of crumbly, for genealogical purposes. I thought they should be filmed and the originals filed away, but they were in use. They did stipulate no pens of any kind were to be used in the records office, only pencils without erasers. The book George was using was approximately one foot by two foot and only about ten pages, dated 1560 to1623, of births, marriages and burials of Mildenhall Parish, Church of England. We could not read it as it was in old English script. So if Francis Mildenhall, born c.1600 had a father or he himself is in there we cannot tell.

Just a few miles before Bath the houses became completely different. No more red brick, all the houses now became a yellowish tan cement, huge, huge, huge! It is the Roman influence.

In Bath, founded by the Romans in 44 A.D., named for baths they built, originally carried Roman names relative to the baths. Waters from warm mineral springs feed the baths at thousands of gallons per day.

Dudley Moore, and his camera crew, who were filming a picture commemorating British railroads, were staying at our bed and breakfast. When I arose from my table in the dining room I purposely bumped his arm to get him to speak to me. It worked!

The other notable things we did in Bath, was one day to walk nineteen miles, as registered on our pedometer. In Bath I found a lovely cloisonne perfume bottle that I cherish. It stayed on my dresser until I was afraid I might break it. I put it in my large china cabinet, where I keep all my antique dishes from my Mother's and Grandmother's eras.

After Bath we drove into Wales, visiting Cardiff where Larry's friend John Gunning's father was born. Marcus and Doris Gunning were very good friends of ours. We had left for England from John Gunning's home in Miami.

The day we spent in Cardiff, it was raining every moment. It was amazing to see all these people, with their colorful umbrellas, running around continuing doing everything in the rain. So we did, too. It was fun! We don't want to do it every day, as the Welsh people do, but it wasn't too bad. It really was fun! We even photographed the capitol buildings, with their beautiful beds of blooming flowers, in the rain, which turned out very well. Here we searched for records of my Elmore family.

After we crossed the Severn River, back into England, the sun came out and we headed towards Scotland, after George again got his bearings. Coming off the bridge he saw a sign saying, "The Midlands", so he decided that wasn't where we were headed, he was looking for the exit to our next town Gloucester. So he proceeded along following M4 Motor way, to the next exit eleven miles away, realizing we were headed back to London. So we drove twenty-two miles out of our way, finding out the sign was right. The Midlands is merely middle England and that way leads to Gloucester.

Once in Gloucester, at last, at the county records office, we searched for Edward Keasby, from whom I am a descendent on my mother's side, who lived here, leaving for America in 1694, settling in Salem, New Jersey from whence many of my Quaker ancestors settled. This we already knew, so nothing new was found. We stayed the night at a fine B & B and had a great sendoff for Worcester with a full English breakfast.

My ancestor, George Maris, came from the Worcester area, Grafton Flyford, Worcestershire. We saw the beautiful church and surrounding graveyard, with ancient stones, where my Maris ancestors

THEN AND NOW

are buried. George Maris was my Huguenot ancestor, and lived in Inksborough, Worcestershire just prior to leaving for America.

At Stratford on Avon we saw and toured Shakespear's home. We also visited Anne Hathaway's cottage, in a lovely setting complete with a thatched roof.

We visited the Cadbury chocolate factory in Bournville. One could not buy their products on site but had to find a nearby dealer in candies.

We traveled on up the M6 motor way to Preston, bypassing Manchester as they were having problems with riots and fires. We also bypassed going on a side trip to Liverpool. Had we gone to Ireland we were to leave our rental car there and take a ferry over to Dublin which we understood would be and eight hour trip. We were sorry we did not visit Ireland and look for ancestral homes there. Also George's Cook family, Peter and Elinor, had resided in Tarvin, England, near Liverpool.

At Preston we branched off to Clitheroe, Lancashire, where just outside nearby is Waddington, in the Moors. This is the ancestral home of my Waddington family, on my mother's side.

The Waddington family was founded in the eighth century by Duke Wada who was a great Saxon chief, one of the combatants at the battle of Lagho in 798 A.D.

A beautiful babbling brook splashes through the length of the village, it's a delightful place where Waddington Old Hall commands a large area. When we explained to the person who answered the door to our knock, that this was an ancestral home, we were invited inside and shown around by the head nurse, as it has been a private nursing home since 1935.

The Hall is a stately medieval building dating back to the days when King Henry VI took refuge there in 1464. We saw the beautiful massive solid oak dining room furniture, the massive chair with its lion's head arms, being the seat in which King Henry sat. The head nurse served us English tea and crumpets at the table while I sat in his chair. When she went out of the room, George and I switched chairs, so that he could sit in the chair for awhile.

Old Hall was the scene of Henry VI's betrayal and capture in 1464. The Hall was surrounded by his enemies, but the King was

335

forewarned and managed to escape. He was captured in the nearby fields, however, and taken to the Tower of London.

My ancestor William Waddington left here and emigrated to America in 1695.

Following a tour of the whole building, we spent a good deal of time in the back in the lovely garden, while the head nurse explained everything to us. She was most gracious, and very happy to talk to a descendent of the Waddingtons.

Leaving Waddington behind we drove on following motor way M6 entering the Lake District where we took pictures of Lake Windermere and surroundings. It appeared to be quite a resort area for vacationers and tourists.

Returning to M6 we took a side trip to Cumrew where my ancestor Christopher White was born in 1642 and emigrated to America in 1677 on the ship Kent. We visited with a man, in the village, whose name was White but had no idea if he was related to Christopher. Cumrew is just a small village, a farming community. A very nice farm couple had just started a bed and breakfast. We were the 14th to stay with them. They were very gracious hosts. The following morning as we were leaving we looked out our upstairs window and saw twenty or thirty cows, black and white Holsteins, walking through town milling about our car, and here we were without our cameras. We had asked our hostess what the wire was strung across the front of the house, and she told us it was to keep the cows from eating her flowers.

When we left Cumrew we went to see the ruins of Hadrian's wall, built in 122-128 A.D. to protect England from invaders. Most of it is in ruins and extends seventy seven miles across Northumberland from Bowness to Wallsend. Parts of it were 15 feet high and another section 12 feet high.

We went through Carlisle on the way to Moffat, Scotland. It is noted for its woolen Mills. We stopped in an outlet but found no woolens to our liking so moved on.

It was a miserable day as it was raining or misting all the way to Edinborough. We by-passed Glasgow as it required us to travel west on M8 then return to go to Edinborough. The foul weather helped us with that decision. We saw some sights but the weather interfered. After staying in Scotland two nights, the day we were to return to

England the sun finally came out. We had taken all pictures in the rain to this point, so with nice sunshine we took the guided tour of the Palace of Holyroodhouse. This made the trip into Scotland worthwhile.

Our first stop back in England was at York where we saw the beautiful, York Minster, the largest Gothic medieval cathedral in Britain and walked atop the ancient wall which had surrounded the Medieval City, seeing and hearing all the sights and sounds of yesteryear.

We went to the Guildhall to search for records of my Thompson, Marshall and John Hyatt families. George's Peter Prudden, a minister, emigrated from York to Milford, CT, where he established the first Congregational church in the U. S. As it turned out the research center was closed for two weeks.

From York we drove over to Scarborough, about fifty miles. Another one of my family names being researched. We saw a spectacular sight, a view of the North Sea. We could look over at Norway and Sweden, so far away. Huge roller waves were coming up on the beach, and high on a hill above us was what appeared to be a castle. We returned to York and proceeded south toward London, about twelve miles to Selby. My ancestor Humphrey Marshall was from here.

In Nottingham we visited Sherwood Forest, famous for its great Oak trees and the exploits of Robin Hood and his Merry Men. We saw the great oak where Robin Hood lived. It is believed to be 4 or 500 years old with another 200 years life expectancy. This is all marvelous agricultural country. This county, Nottinghamshire, is covered with immense fields of wheat which were being harvested while we were there during the month of September. The countryside reminds us very much of our homeland in the mid-west.

We drove about seventy miles to King's Lynn and stayed in a bed and breakfast to be near Sandringham, the Country Estate of the royal family. We had toured the house and grounds; and as we finished, we found that church services were beginning. So we had communion where the queen goes when she is in residence here. We sat with a very nice local lady who assisted us and prevented us from sitting in the Duke and Duchess of Kent's pews. We just missed them in attendance by about one week. Some of their family was there for a competition, not races, with coach horses. We wish we could have seen it.

In Norwich we searched in their library to find a link between my immigrant grandfather Isaac Busby, (my father Milton Busby's line) and Nicholas and John Busby. I had hoped we would find one of them to be Isaac's father. No such luck.

We traveled all day through the most beautiful country. The wheat fields are all in different stages of harvest, some thrashing wheat, some already baled in huge round rolls, bales?, some being burned especially the ones where the wheat has been harvested. There are a few beautiful windmills around.

In Leicester there were 47 Busby's in the current telephone book. We had no luck with phone calls, so we gave up and drove on to Northampton.

We have both been deeply involved with ceramics and pottery for much of our adult lives, so we were told to go to Stokes-On-Trent, the ceramics/pottery capital of Britain, and go to Staffordshire Pottery and ask for the Chairman of the Board, Bill Bowers. He assigned a young lady to give us a complete tour of the pottery and later, after a meeting, joined us for tea. The young lady sent us home with a mug decorated with elephants when she learned our son Larry collects elephants.

We returned to Northampton arriving so late we found no bed and breakfast available. We did find a motel where we could park right in front of our unit, so we took advantage of this stroke of luck to relax and catch up on things we had to do. We washed clothes, took showers, straightened up the car, and took time to sort out and pack gifts for home we had been gathering.

We moved on to Bedford, Bedfordshire, where at the records hall we found a will (dated Feb. 28, 1618) of Thomas Grubb, my great grandfather, born in 1581, graduate of Oxford, who served as Rector of Cranfield Parish, St. Peter and St. Paul Church of England, Cranfield, Bedfordshire for 33 years. The present Rector, Derek Hunt, showed us all around the church and was very nice to us. We took many pictures.

George found records of his great grandfather Henry Botsford, (baptized 15 Jun 1608), from Sundon, Bedfordshire. He is the father

THEN AND NOW

of George's John Baldwin, Jr's wife, residents of Milford, Connecticut. He found other records too.

We proceeded to the Priory, a hotel near Aston Clinton and Aylesbury, where George's Baldwins lived at Dundridge Manor from 1500's through at least 1638 the date John immigrated to the U. S. aboard the ship Martin, to Milford Connecticut. John was George's great grandfather seven generations removed.

At the Priory we woke up to rain again and drove to the Baldwin's church, St. Michaels in Aston Clinton where we found a wedding was to take place shortly and all the beautiful floral arrangements and decorations were in place for the ceremony. It was a beautiful sight, so we took lots of pictures.

As it tuned out, the artist who had done the Baldwin stained glass window was in the church, so we were able to visit with him. It was apparently done as a commission by Baldwin family descendants from the states.

From the church we drove to Dundridge, the beautiful Manor of John Baldwin, and four, generations of his forebears. We spent time with the wife of the present occupants, and her sister-in-law, having an opportunity to see and copy lots of Baldwin records, in their possession.

Our next stop was Aldbury where it was reputed they threw "Witches" into the small body of water, and if they sank immediately they had not been witches, but if they stayed on top before drowning they had been witches. Many movies have been made here, one of note starred Robert Wagner.

In Oxford, Oxfordshire, we drove about taking pictures of that famous old college of colleges, of which there were fifty-three. They are situated all over the town. As we walked taking pictures the college kids looked just like college kids everywhere. I kept telling myself we were in the land of the smarts!

We left to go on the motor way to Canterbury, taking the ring road around London. We stopped in a pull over place along the highway and ate cheese, bread and bananas. George got lost, of course, as according to our maps, he had to get on A40, M40, M25, M26, M20, A249, M2, and A2. Now how could anyone keep all that straight? One road, M25, was not completed although it was on the map. This is where George got lost. It took us over four hours to come from Oxford to Canterbury, a distance of 107 miles. After we got here it took two more hours to find a place to stay. Everything was full up! We had driven 161 miles in 6 hours! That was discouraging!

We also found it difficult to get near the Canterbury Cathedral because of the one way streets that take you into town and back out without your being able to get anywhere, for one unfamiliar with the traffic flow. So we decided to walk to the Cathedral the following morning as we could see the steeple tower.

A man we saw at breakfast went with us to the cathedral and walked us in. He said most people would not even go around to the back so they miss the glory of the cloisters. They were gorgeous and huge and ancient! We walked all around and took some excellent pictures of the cathedral and downtown Canterbury. This man who befriended us had come from London to a cricket match. More evidence of the friendliness of the British people.

We headed for Dover to see the chalk cliffs. We had been told by several people to drive to St. Catherine's by the Cliffe. If we hadn't asked we would have never known how to get to the bottom of the cliffs. We had to descend a very steep winding drive. When we arrived at the bottom, the tide must have been in as the water was surging hard and blowing way way up in the air as it broke on the sea wall. It was beautiful! It took your breath away!

The only thing our son Monte had asked us to bring him was some chalk from the Chalk cliffs of Dover. He had always been collecting rocks. There were loose chunks of chalk at the base of the cliffs near where we parked so there was no problem in getting several specimens.

We then drove on down to Dover and took pictures along the way. With George's telephoto lense he could take some pretty nice views of the "Chalk cliffs of Dover." We would return to Dover later by train where we would board a ship bound for Calais, France, crossing France on a 600 mile, over night train ride to the Cote d' Azur and Antibes, France for a week on the French Riviera. But that's another story.

We had to turn the car in the next day in London, where we had leased it, so we started back. George only got lost two or thee times.

He's doing better. The times were when the main highways were not finished, and the highway signs were not too clear. We retraced our route back to London. At least we tried.

We had extended our original two week car rental time twice to get back to London. It was a fabulous trip, among the wonderfully friendly British people, in their fantastic countryside. This was the culmination of our 2700 mile motor trip through the British Isles ending back at the Kensington Hotel in west London where it all started. We would gladly do it over again!

Chapter 36
Cote d' Azur

Leaving London, we crossed the English Channel from Dover to Calais, France, where we boarded a train for the overnight 600 mile trip to the Cote d' Azur, the fabulous French Riviera where we had a time share exchange apartment waiting for us, to spend a week in Antibes, France.

France was a different story from the friendly, loving British. Some French people were nice, but some were horrible to us, mainly, I'm sure, because we could speak no French.

On the Cote d' Azur, there was everything I had ever read about, lovely city centers, sail boats docked in yacht basins, sailing ships out in the bay, naked sun worshipers on pebble beaches. We loved it all!

Our resort, Les Jardins D'Ulysse, Antibes, on the French Riviera, was within walking distance of a bus line. It was a large, spacious, four room apartment with a fully equipped kitchen, and a very nice covered patio with a great view of the surrounding areas.

When we went into the large bathroom, there was another bidet!

"Please figure out how to work this one and try to get it to work. I want to use it. I have read about them for years, but I never understood what they do," I said to George.

He worked at it but could never figure it out.

"It must be broken!" he placated me.

"Ask the manager how it works. Please, George I want to see what it does and how it works," I said. It stood out in the way of everything. There was no lid so it was just an elongated area of water sticking out towards the middle of the room. When I washed clothes, or took a bath it always was in the way. Alas, I was never to have the privilege of using a bidet!

The first time we went to the downtown area, we walked to the corner where the bus stopped. We boarded and had a nice ride to town. As we arrived at what we considered the center of town, which was a beautiful park in a downtown area. We stood up and started towards the front door.

The busman said something in French which, of course, we didn't understand. We continued on towards the front. As he stopped, he did not open the door. We were at a bus stop, we thought.

"We want out here," I needlessly said to the driver, who was by now getting quite huffy. We said a few words, back and forth, he in French, we in English. We had no idea where we would go, probably get lost, as he had turned the opposite way from the area where we wanted to go, to the left where the downtown activity seemed to be.

A man behind the bus driver said something in a gruff voice, as we stood our ground, pointing to the opposite direction he was turning, but finally we turned to go back to our seats.

By now several people in the full bus were yelling to the bus driver, with him yelling back. He finally jerked the door open and motioned us out. Thank God, we thought.

After we could find no bus stop sign at this particular corner, we watched the bus leaving, to see it turn left at a street half way down the park, then watched it turn left again.

"Let's see if it comes back left again, then that would be what he was trying to tell us - that the bus did not stop where we wanted to get off, but if we had gone on, we would have ended up to the left of where we wanted to go, but that we had to go around a complete block to get there.

We walked left towards where we wanted to go and there was a bus station, with lots of buses arriving, ours included, with everyone getting out there. We surmised then that the man behind the bus driver had told him to let us out.

"Let them out!" he probably said. "They're crazy Americans! They don't know what they're doing!"

This was the old section of Antibes. It became our favorite spot in Antibes. The old parts of towns and cities have always been our favorites.

There was a wonderful Italian outdoor restful garden where we often ate. They had the best pizza we have ever eaten. It was a simple pizza with a perfect crust and a most delicious cheese, with four anchovies crisscrossed and four large black olives in between. I wanted to know what kind of cheese it was, but it was so difficult to get our message of pizza and coke across to the Italian waiters and waitresses. They might have spoken French, but they sure didn't know English! So, we were satisfied with our plain, delicious pizza and let it go at that. We later learned the cheese was goat cheese.

We walked miles in that beautiful little town, taking in all the art and beauty of the area.

Picasso's museum had once been his home for four months. It was a large beautiful castle-like structure of stone built high on the rocks overlooking the Mediterranean.

A guided tour enabled us to enjoy the vast collection of Picasso's works under one roof, and to hear of his personal life.

As we walked on the outside of the museum, we looked across the road to the waterfront where we saw a beautiful nude woman, with flowing blonde hair, sunning herself on the high elevation of rocks along the shore of the Mediterranean.

At the end of a busy day, it was all we could do to walk up and down the hills from the bus line to enter our large hallway, that led to our apartment, and flop in our big bed.

But it was fabulous! I want very much to go back to the beautiful, gorgeous, fantastic Cote d' Azur!!

One day, we sat on one of the benches, that lined the street, which overlooked the cove that was anchorage for the sailboats. Hundreds of sailboats were moored, with their tall masts reaching skyward, from each lovely boat. The shadows in the water reflected the beauty of the colorful sails. It was a gorgeous sight. We sat on the bench for hours, watching the wind blow the boats back and forth, causing the colorful ripples to flourish. The sun was going down with its fantastic change of yellow to orange to deep red as it finally settled in beyond the horizon.

We hated to gather up our camera equipment and head for home. The air was so crisp and cool, but the view so vibrant and moving, we had just bundled up more and sat to watch the gorgeous view. We had had it all to ourselves. It was as if a magnificent show had been put on just for us. Where had all those magnificent boats been? Where were all their navigators gone now? There was no one in sight anywhere. Just us and the boats.

There were many times in our travels that we ran across a bunch of sailboats docked for the night. It always conjured up our late afternoon experience in the Cote D' Azur. Nothing ever equaled the beauty of that night.

One time in Antibes, one clerk jabbered at me so much and got me flustered that when she screamed at me, "Do you speak English?" I didn't recognize that as English at all and only realized it when she flew out of my dressing room to yell at George.

"She said she didn't speak English!" she yelled at him in her horrible way of talking.

"She speaks English," I heard George saying quietly.

That was the first time I knew what she had said. She came back to my drape-drawn room and slung back the drapes to expose an astonished Kay to the whole world. There I stood in nothing but my panties and money belt hanging loosely around my hips. I stared at her in amazement, then I reached up and, looking out the front door at the complete outside world, I slowly pulled the curtain back. I didn't leave there as I was determined she was not going to intimidate me. I thought, I like the dresses I brought in here to try on, and I'm going to try them on. To heck with her.

Not one dress fit me so I went out to get George and hurry out of the store. She was on the phone yelling at some one, I thought maybe the police.

"Let's get out of here!" I grabbed George and pulled him along until we got through the door and out on the sidewalk.

I finally found my Parisian dress in downtown Nice. A very nice person waited on me, but a big dog kept George at bay by standing and growling every time he tried to help me find a dress. So I had to do it by myself.

I was very happy when I walked out of that store with my package in my hot little grasp.

France is a wonderfully happy, beautiful country, except for some of the Frenchmen, and women, who I do believe do not like Americans. Maybe just us older generation.

One of the hardest things we had to suffer in England and Europe was trying to find a rest room.

We had been traveling on the high road above Monte Carlo, when we came to an interesting outdoor - indoor restaurant. George and I hurried inside to find a restroom. On the mirror behind the counter I saw the word Toilette, so I assumed that is what rest room was in French.

Where is your toilette? I asked the man behind the counter. I pronounced toilette with the accent on the lette, as they seemed to do with other words. He looked confused.

"Toilette? Toilette?" Then he pointed to a door which looked as if it were a rest room. I gingerly pushed the door in, and looking back at the man at the counter, to see if I were right, saw he had become very busy.

When I entered the room it seemed to be very large and with nothing in it except a hole in the floor. I was so in need of relieving myself I entertained the idea of going back outside for further instructions, but remembered how confused the man had been.

There was a lower level of a ledge on which I thought my feet would fit. I stepped inside the hole and pulled up my dress. I had to go in a hurry. My urine splashed all over my shoes and feet, so I hurriedly brought them outside the lower level and placed them on the top level. My legs were stretched uncomfortably wide, but I proceeded until I finished. It was not a very nice way to go to the bath room but when necessity calls, one does most anything. I've often wondered if it were the men's room, and the women's room was around the corner. George couldn't find the men's room, so he went in the same room I had gone in, while I stood guard for him outside. We didn't see anywhere to wash up. I wonder if we were right? At least we were relieved.

The next day we were to take another bus trip to Monte Carlo, but after waiting an hour or two the bus never came. We did not have time to reschedule that trip. So we were so sorry to miss Monte Carlo, but we had seen it the day before from the hillside above it.

Chapter 37
To Germany,
Then Back to Paree

The following day we had to leave lovely Antibes and its surroundings for our sojourn into Germany. Going through the center of France on a high speed train, we stopped at Metz, east of Paris for transfer to a two car inter-urban train for Saarbrucken, Germany, on a quest for George's family genealogy.

We rode the train to Germany in the first class section which we got into by mistake. When we got on the train, there were many seats available in the first car, but the conductor looked at our tickets and forced us to go to the second car which was overflowing with loud, sweaty people. I backed up and turned around going back to the first car. George, of course followed. The conductor was probably telling us in his German, which we could not understand, that we had to sit in the second class section.

"We want to sit here," I said in my pure English. "There is room here, not in there." After awhile, the conductor walked away, after several people got into the act, presumably telling him to let us stay. We had a cool, pleasant ride the several hours to Germany with only one other person in our car.

At the old stone figure decorated Rathaus in Saarbrucken, no one could understand us until they brought in a gorgeous black haired beauty from Berlin who had absolutely perfect English.

George's idea was that St. Wendel, which was a few miles from Saarbrucken, would have been Sanwintle, given on their naturalization papers, as their birthplace, for his immigrant Nicholas, and son Peter Massing in March, 1844. The young lady told us there was no way that could be possible, as the German pronunciation of St. Wendel is Sanct Vendel, which she thought didn't sound a thing like Sanwintle. So, thoroughly discouraged we headed back towards our hotel room.

Walking along the street we saw an interesting entrance to a Ratskeller. "Let's go down there and get us a real German dessert," I said. "I've heard all my life about the delicious desserts the Germans make." We went down the steps and seated ourselves in a completely empty room. The chef and the waitress came from the back to tell us that they were closed but would open up in a couple of hours.

"We thought we'd get a good German dessert. We've been told how great they are," George and I were both saying.

They wanted to know more about us, and we laughed and talked.

"You want a good German dessert?" the chef said finally, excitedly standing there with his white hat rakishly perched on his head. "I'll make you a great dessert! It'll be a surprise for you." He stressed how wonderful it was but wouldn't tell us what it was.

"You'll have to go back outside, give me one half hour, then come back," he said. We went back up the steep stairs to the sidewalk and wandered down the street, window shopping.

When we returned, with great anticipation we were served a gorgeous cherry crepe with aplomb. The chef waited as we tasted it, to get our anticipated reactions. We thrilled him with our exclamations of delight over the beauty and the taste of his creation. After he left us to finish our dessert I screwed up my face.

"I can't eat another bite of this!" I exclaimed. I thought he'd never leave, and I had to keep eating it. "It's so sour! These are the sourest cherries I've ever eaten! There is not any sugar whatsoever on this!"

George valiantly kept eating with a slightly less pursed look on his face than mine. Bless his heart! He even reached over and took mine and ate it too!

"Should we look in the telephone book for Massing names?" George asked.

"Of course!" I exclaimed. "I never even thought of that! We always do wherever we go!"

There were forty-four Massing names in the telephone book! It covered Saarbrucken and all surrounding towns. We were amazed! Each one answered George all the same.

"Sprecken Si Englische?" George would ask.

"Nein, Nein," they would say, then laugh and continue talking in Deutsch. George knew no other Deutsch so they had a short conversation. George would say Auf Weidesein, and close off. We broke to go to dinner late, leaving three names uncalled.

"Shall we just forget them?" George asked when we got back from dinner. It was nine o'clock.

"No," I said, after thinking a bit. "We will probably never be back here again. We've come all this way just to see if we can find from where the Massing's came, so call those three names, then we'll go back to Paris tomorrow." We had not been to Paris yet, and I was not going to leave for England and home without going to see Paree!

The first of the three names said, "Nein, Nein!" as had the others.

"But Voila! the second name was Peter Massing the same name as George's immigrant great grandfather, who came to Ripley County, Indiana, in about 1844 from Germany. He spoke some English. I jumped in and out of the conversation, helping him when he needed me.

Peter told us to take the train from Saarbrucken to Saint Wendel where we were to leave our luggage in the train depot locker, and walk three blocks to the police station where he worked. He was the Kommissar se Polizei(Commissioner of Police) of Saint Wendel.

When we walked into the police station, we were ushered into a room where we were kept waiting a long time. When Peter came in, we found him to be a handsome forty year old young man. He was quiet but smiling as we shook hands. He seemed surprised to see me, as we found out later, because he thought George had meant I was in Paris, and that George had to go back there for me in a few days.

Peter had trouble understanding us, so he excused himself and came back with a man who could speak much better English than

Peter. After that, he and George used little pocket dictionaries and we all got along pretty well.

Peter took us to a hotel outside of town where we could catch the bus to go into town, the times he couldn't get off work to be with us.

In the four days we were there Peter took us to his beautiful home in Theley several times, first to meet his lovely family, his wife Margret and their daughter Iris. Their home was a very beautiful picturesque three story with Margret's parents, whom we met, living on the top floor. We were entertained and fed a fine dessert Margret prepared with rows of fresh plums on top and special candies of chocolate covered caramel, and served an excellent wine made of apples off trees on their land.

We were invited and accompanied them to look at caravans as they wished to buy one for their travels.

One of the times Peter could not be with us we visited downtown St. Wendel. I found a beautiful red skirt which I bought that had to be altered for me. They did a beautiful job. While waiting for the skirt we strolled about St. Wendel taking pictures and had some pastries and beverages on the little circle at a small interesting café.

Peter made arrangements for us to go to the Namborn Rathaus to check on George's ancestry. He came in his uniform which he said would command attention and respect, and perhaps help. It must have, as many times we heard "Nein, Nein!" from the clerk, but she kept going back in the archives as Peter kept talking and making suggestions.

George and I kept on the far side of the room, listening intently but not understanding.

"Why doesn't he give up?" I finally said to George. It's obvious nothing is here about your people.

Then voila! Out she came with old, old papers, the original civil and church diocese records of births, marriages and deaths of George's immigrants, as well as three more generations. We were so excited and poured over these papers and were given copies to take home with us.

Without Peter Massing, the police commissioner, we would never in a million years have found George's ancestry. Thank you, Peter, for your perseverence. You and Percy did it! Just as George and his Percy do things. George has always said, "Me and Percy (personifying perseverance) did it again."

After this fabulous find, Peter took us the next day back to Namborn where he knew of a Massing home, with the name Elizabeth Massing and the date 1891 on the lintel above the door. She had the home remodeled at that time. Mr. Hoffman, the new owner told us he remembered Elizabeth Massing, who had lived there until 1975, telling him she had two uncles in the family who had gone to America. These are believed to have been Nicklaus and his son Peter, George's great, great grandfather and great grandfather. The house used to have a blacksmith shop at the rear.

The whole front yard was full of huge peach, pink, and red roses, which reminded me of George's deep interest in flowers and plants, including red roses.

The next day we were at the train station to board our train to Paris. The train did not come to a stop, it merely slowed down, and a young man, standing in a large opening in the side of the train, reached from the moving car for my hand and luggage. I flew up into the car so quickly I bowled him over and landed on top of him on the floor. He recovered quickly and then reached down and pulled George and his luggage into the car. We don't know how he did it but we made it and continued on to Paris, following a wonderful trip to Germany.

There were no hotel rooms that came up on the computer at our hotel in Saint Wendel, just as there were none that came up on the computer when we were in Antibes, France, which caused us to go to Germany before going to Paris. When we arrived in the train station in Paris George got in a long line at the traveler's aid station to see about a hotel room. Rooms were available just as I knew they would be. The room we chose was less money, but in a good area where we wanted to be.

After securing our hotel room we were met by an old crusty, short, sour taxi man who gathered up our suitcases, and piled us in his old dilapidated black car. As we jerked away, George and I almost lost our heads.

"Ooh, gosh, that was awful!" I said.

But that was only the beginning. It was a far cry from the time our gentleman, Englishman, met us at Victoria Station in London, and took us on our wonderful sightseeing tour before arriving at our hotel there.

This Frenchman was dour, ugly, hateful! He would step on the gas and the old car would lurch forward, then the driver would slam on the brakes. I was sure he had just learned to drive. It was beyond a doubt, the worst car ride I ever had. By the time we went through the third circle, I was as sick as I ever was in my life. He was probably taking us a round about way to our destination, to run up the meter but how did we know?.

"I can't stand this, George!" I kept saying. We were being thrown from side to side, forward and backward. I was ready to throw up constantly.

When we finally arrived at the hotel on a side street, the driver hit the curbing forcing the cab to come up on the sidewalk and bound back to it. Then he slammed on his brakes. I was never so glad of anything as I was to get out of that awful cab. Then I looked around. " Where is it?" I said loudly. "I don't see it, where is the hotel? I don't see it!"

"There!" the driver pointed. "It's right there." It was a very narrow sidewalk with the walls of the building flush at the edge. There were some double glass doors that opened up into the rather small, but lovely, hotel lobby.

When we were taken to our hotel room, we found it hot and without air conditioning; but, by now, anything looked good to us. Our room was nice, but very small. The bathroom was as big as the bedroom, with the inevitable bidot, which George never learned how to use. I wanted to use it! But, try as we did, we couldn't figure it out!

The bedroom had a wonderful, stocked refrigerator, which we used quite a bit. It had new eats in there that we found delightful. When we tried to get more of course, they were out of them, so it was a delight only one time! Every night we came home from our sightseeing to a cold pop and a delectable tidbit.

We found the only way we could use our suitcases was to put them on the bed and open them, as there was no room anywhere else.

To sleep we closed them and put them in front of the door. To leave, we had to move them away from the door, and put them on top of the bed, or in the nice big bathroom.

One window could be forced open to a rooftop where we envisioned a burglar could come in from the roof which was right outside the window.

The humidity was such, and there was no way to get a breeze through the open window, that when we came home, always late on purpose, we could hardly catch our breath!

George insisted we never go to sleep with the window open, so when we felt we were sleepy enough, one of us got up and closed the window for the night.

Paree, however, was lovely. All my expectations were fulfilled! This hotel was in a wonderful spot for us to walk to the Arc de Triomphe, Champs-Elysees, and the Eiffel Tower, and other wonderful areas.

The first evening we walked down the street about a mile to Champs-Elysees to see the sights. When we crossed one of the streets, we passed four or five people going the other way.

"There she is!" Some one said. As we walked further down the street, I noticed people walking out into the street, looking towards something.

"Let's go back and see where she is," I said to George. As we came closer and looked down the side street, my pulse jumped and I caught my breath.

There in all its glory, was the one thing that has always made me straighten up and take notice, the fabulous Eiffel Tower!

When I see it at the end of the French Pavilion's movie, at EPCOT, in Disney World, my heart pounds, as the tower is flashed upon the screen with a myriad of lights, with Debussy's music playing in the background, reminding me of that first time I saw it in Paris.

One day after we had been on a day tour, we decided to have a light afternoon tea, as we used to have every day in England. As we were sitting eating French pastries and drinking their tea, I looked to my right and there was the back of a huge, huge building, very nondescript, so I was not able to make it out. The building ran far down the street beyond my limited vision.

"I wonder what that building is?" I asked George. He looked it over carefully.

"I don't have any idea," he said.

The Louvre Museum was a must for us to see. The next day when our tour arrived at the Louvre, there was the beautiful front of the building, the back of which was the long nondescript building we had seen from the sidewalk café the night before where we had our afternoon tea and French pastries.

It was larger than I expected. Too far to walk to find something of which I knew. I believe we should have stayed days trying to find the things we wanted to see. The best picture we saw of my interest was the Mona Lisa. It was surprising as it was so old. The Mona Lisas I had seen all my life had been all so fresh and new. I studied it for a long time. It didn't give me the great happiness I thought I would feel. It left me with great sadness. Mona Lisa didn't seem to smile at me.

The following day we were on an all day tour which was a long trip. When we arrived back at the bus terminal near the Louvre, we decided to eat in an Italian restaurant down the alley. It took forever, and was dark, before we were seated. After we were finished eating, we saw a shop open, and decided to do some browsing. It took us a long time to make our purchases, then we wandered around looking at a monument of Joan of Arc outside in the square, and other things.

We were completely exhausted when we stood at the corner to be picked up near the sign that said taxis stop here.

We waited and waited. There came a taxi finally. It swerved over away from us and went on. The next taxi did the same. A couple of young girls walked out into the line of traffic, the farthest from the taxi sign, and caught a taxi going by real fast.

"Look, George, he stopped for them! Let's do that," I said, "We'll never get a taxi." Of course, he wouldn't. He was sure we would get run over. After watching taxi after taxi go by real fast, one pulled up in front of us.

"Where are you going?" he asked, through the lowered window. I told him and he mumbled something, then jammed his foot on the accelerator. Gone was the taxi.

"We probably weren't going far enough!" George said.

Then another taxi came running past us but stopped out in the square, near the Joan of Arc statue. There were two young girls wanting a taxi and they had a man from the hotel nearby with them. The taxi man got out of his car hurriedly and opened the door, at which time I passed the girls and the driver and got inside the taxi.

"We've been waiting a lot longer than they. No one will stop for us!" I said. They stood in amazement. I suppose this was a first for them. It sure was for me!

"You can't do this!" the hotel man said.

There was an impasse. I crawled out of the taxi and let the girls in. I berated that hotel man so loudly and strongly, I'm sure no one had ever talked to him that way.

The hotel man told us there was another place to catch a taxi over there and down the street. So we went over there and down the street, and over there and then some, realizing that the jerk had just told us to get us away from his hotel I imagine.

I was crying so much George told me to go in a corner store which seemed to be a travel agency. While I sat in the corner crying George told the man about our plight. He was extremely sympathetic and seeing a taxi coming, ran out his door to flag it down. In a few minutes, he was back and telling us this taxi man would take us to our hotel. It was about midnight and we were completely exhausted.

The following day we took a long and enjoyable boat ride on the Seine, returning, and docking near the Eiffel Tower. It just takes one's breath away. To walk towards it and see the majestic steel structure that Mr.Eiffel built, between 1887 and 1889, for the Worlds Fair Exposition, is overwhelming. To think they almost tore it down after the fair was over. That would have been a sacrilegious feat! Incomprehensible!

People came and went, while we stood at the top looking and walking all around, picking out landmarks in the large arena that was gathered before our eyes.

It was dark when we finally came down, and crossed the bridge over the Seine to walk back to our hotel, about two miles. We cut through the Palace de Chaillot, (museums), expecting it to be a short cut. It had about a million steps. We were very tired, when we stopped at a little restaurant, on the way. We relished the stop, trying to use up some of our Francs, as we were leaving tomorrow for London. A couple from near Dallas, Texas, came in and sat across from us. They were leaving the next day also, for home. We enjoyed a short visit with them and then walked on to our hotel.

Chapter 38

Back to London

The hovercraft, Princess Margaret, from Boulogne, France seemed to beckon us for our trip back across the English Channel to Dover. We were so excited, but not for long. My excitement turned to anticipation of getting off the blasted carrier. I will never take another ride on that thing! It shivered and shook as it hurried all over the place. The weather was raunchy perhaps causing us a rough ride, never again will I go on that ride! I found no pleasure in any one given moment.

The Penn's Club in Bedford Place, was our home for the next five days, after which we would fly back to America.

I am at home! This is a Quaker bed and breakfast where the Quakers go for a nice quiet place. We slept here for the five days back in London and had our breakfast and evening meals here in a very friendly atmosphere, like being with family. We shared a table and visited with other guests during each meal.

We attempted to go to Kensington Hotel via the Metro Station and underground tubes, to check on our extra luggage we stored there during our visit to France and Germany. We found it over-whelming for strangers to the system. You descended via large lifts, (elevators) to the lower level, with people who knew what they were doing, rushing all over the place. So we finally gave up the idea and with considerable difficulty returned to the surface with lots of help from the British individuals traveling there.

We made a visit to the Friends House, where we checked their records for Isaac Busby ad John Mildenhall, my great grand fathers who were immigrants to America, with no results.

We rode the bus the next day to Kensington Hotel to pick up our luggage we stored there.

We took a taxi for our return to the Penn Club with our recovered luggage.

We took a tour boat down the Thames River seeing many beautiful sights, The Tower of London, Big Ben, The House of Parliament, Westminster Abbey, Cleopatra's Needle, lots of things.

We got off the boat at Greenwich, to see Wren's Royal Observatory, (Christopher Wren designed this as well as St. Paul's Cathedral and the majestic west towers of Westminster Abbey.) We were able to put one foot in the western hemisphere and eastern hemisphere at the same time. We were able to see the ball on top the observatory go up slowly and drop fast at exactly one o'clock. It tells ships in the Thames River exactly what time it is. This is the source of Greenwich Solar Mean Time for the world.

After lunch we visited the Maritime Museum and rode the bus to the Thames Barrier which is considered one of the eighth wonders of the world. After several devastating floods, these barriers were designed to prevent the flooding of London. They apparently do what they were designed for as there is no more flooding.

We visited Harrods, the famous huge department store, finding little to buy as gifts due to their high prices. We did find a beautiful dolly with a puffed hat that I fell in love with. So, we bought it for me. She was dressed in an adorable gray corduroy skirt with white lace. It was decorated with pink ribbons. I'll keep it for awhile then Jennifer will get it.

Harrods even had a wonderful market including a complete meat market.

We then boarded a bus to go to Oxford Street where all the other department stores are located. Here we bought some things for gifts for home, beautiful jackets for Larry and Monte, pearls for me by Christian Dior and a pretty string of blue stones for Mother Massing.

On our last day in London we witnessed the changing of the guards at Buckingham Palace. We were fortunate to have only five or six tour buses in lieu of the usual forty five, so our tour guide took us where the huge crowds would not be, so we saw the wonderful horsemen and band at close range and head on. The Royal Air Force was first in line marching with the band.

The guardsmen were an impressive sight with their furrish-covered busby's (hat) adding to their height. An additional group of horsemen were then coming toward us with body armor, shiny helmets, shields and leg covering. They were quite spectacular! Our tour guide was not sure who they were. He did say they were not part of the guardsmen. So we got to see something a little extra.

We then toured the Tower of London with their beefeater guards on duty everywhere. The first thing we saw was the British Crown Jewels on display under heavy security.

Inside the courtyard we saw first hand where Anne Bolyn was housed and the very spot where the guillotine stood that was used to behead her, on the order of her husband, Henry the Eighth. My husband George is related to her through his Wells family line.

We then toured Westminster Abbey which is a gorgeous place. It took us an hour to go through at a pretty brisk pace. A great number of famous people are buried there, Isaac Walton, Stanley Livingston, Charles Darwin, Elizabeth Ist and her sister, several kings and queens, Alfred Lord Tennyson, Robert Browning among others. It is a huge fabulous, gorgeous building. It has been added to for years since the original was built starting in 1050.

We then went around the corner from Victoria Station and ate lunch at a pub. We wanted one last meal at a pub. It was loud and jumping, the largest and noisiest we have been in, also lower class, with rougher characters there.

We boarded another double decker bus for Trafalgar Square, first floor standing room only. We asked someone next to us to tell us when to get off for Trafalgar Square. A young lady said, it's the next stop to where she gets off so she'll take us there, and so she did, having to backtrack to her stop. This is another example of how the wonderful British treated us.

At Trafalgar Square we watched the thousands of pigeons and people watching and feeding the pigeons.

We bought a few gifts for the family nearby and returned to the Penn Club in time for supper.

This has been a fabulous, wonderful trip. We don't want to go home! We have had a fabulous time. It has all been so fantastic! It has been beyond our greatest expectations and dreams, almost beyond comprehension that we could have had such a beautiful experience. Thank you my Heavenly Father, for this wonderful trip!

America here we come!

At the end of our five days in London we were so exhausted we debated whether to get a taxi to take us from our hotel to Gatwick Airport. The taxi won out so we ensconced ourselves in a black luxurious taxi with enormous room and we were so glad we did. It cost fifty dollars to take us fifty miles but it was worth every minute. It was the most relaxing ride we had had just cruising at a nice speed, with the exuberant young driver elucidating on all questions or comments we came up with. He made us feel as if he were our best friend. He got a big tip!

The taxi driver who had taken us to our first hotel had driven by Westminster Abbey, Big Ben, Stock Exchange, Government Buildings and Buckingham Palace, to name a few, when we told him to take us around to see some of the sights. He was great, too, and shook George's hand with a firm grip when he let us out. We've heard the taxi drivers in London are the most polite taxi drivers in the world. We attest to this whole heartedly.

Not so in France. Our first ride in a taxi in France was a hair raising experience of which I've never heard. He wouldn't talk to us acting as if he knew no English, as a lot of people did, then we heard them speak some English. This taxi driver would push his foot down on the accelerator which made us jerk back and forth, then he would slam on his brakes, all across town. I don't know if it were him or the car. Both I imagine. We had to take him as he was next in line, but after this ride we walked. I was physically ill when we arrived at our hotel. We were just glad to get away from him.

When our plane arrived in Miami, Larry, Judy and our three grandchildren were waiting for us. We were both happy and sad. Happy to be home, sad it was all over.

"Well," I said to Judy as we pulled out of the airport in our car, "We made it!"

"I didn't think you'd make it out of the airport," she said.

The shoulder bag I wore had been so heavy with vitamins and a few medicines that it took a long time to get used to it, and it kept falling off my shoulder. I guess we didn't exactly look like seasoned travelers.

Chapter 39

Ted's Sheds at Southwest Florida Fair

The people who came to the Southwest Florida Fair had to go right past Ted's Sheds setup. It was cold and windy and we were bundled up against the terrible cold that seeped in our bodies. I had a stocking cap on, and knitted gloves, and a heavy coat.

The wind was so brisk, it stung my face, so I kept back inside a 12 x 16 shed, sitting on a stool, while waiting for fair goers to show interest in Ted's Sheds, and stop by to talk.

One woman looked in at me, while George had an interested customer outside, talking to him in the wind. He was yelling at him in order to be heard.

"Come in!" I said to the lady who was peeking inside the shed. "It's warmer in here! We even have a little heater!"

She came in, looking back at a man standing stock still in the middle of the roadway.

"He's my father. He won't move when I leave him," she said.

I looked and there he stood, looking so dejected! "What's wrong with him?" I yelled above the wind. "Tell him to come in out of the wind and get warm."

"Oh, that doesn't bother him," she said. "He just won't do anything when I leave him. He just found out he has macular degeneration, and it has changed his life. He won't move, just stands or sits when I'm not there to help him."

I have macular degeneration," I said, "and I move around all the time! Try to get him to come over here, and I'll talk to him."

There were no other people around at all. There he stood in an empty street at the fair. She called to him, but he ignored her. She went over to him and tried to bring him back. Finally, he came very slowly, like an old decrepit man. I felt so sorry for him! He wouldn't come in the shed where it was warm, so I stood outside in the whistling wind, screaming at him to be heard. He was so dejected it seemed to me he could never get himself back on track.

"You can learn to use a cane and then you will be able to go anywhere by yourself," I said, telling him all about the school for the blind where I had been. I knew how he was feeling, and tried to help him. It was all so new to him, not being able to see. He felt his life was over, just as I had.

But it's not! It takes time to learn to function without eyesight, or with low vision, but when we accept the fact we will never see as well as we used to see, we can change our lives a bit to accommodate our infirmity, and get back into life.

I seldom think of being partially blind anymore. I hardly remember how I used to see. I hunt for a lot of things, mostly my glasses, which do help a little, and my shoes. But life goes on, and we have to adapt to it. It can be done. I hate the fact I have no eye contact with people. So I touch a lot. I like to get closer to people than I used to do.

I have often thought of this woman's father and wondered how they have managed. Hopefully he can get around better now, and she knows he'll be all right. It is a strain on all concerned, for both the one who is losing his\her eyesight and for his\her loved ones who care for the one who is losing the eyesight. But, hey! Life goes on! Be happy, you people with low vision. I love you!

George was selling Ted's Sheds at a large arena, and I was standing at the edge of the crowd that was milling about the sheds, looking them over. I looked away from that crowd to see what was going on elsewhere and saw there were few people there. There was a large area where there was no one.

As I looked, a wonder horse, I presume a clown, passed me slowly. As my gaze followed the only moving thing in sight, I watched mesmerized. The horse was moving along quietly, as I stared at its painted backside, all swirled in vivid colors, a wooden horse like a beautiful German plaything. I wondered how it was moving along. Then I saw two big floppy feet with a khaki looking sloppy pant-legs coming way down over the old shoes.

As I watched, the feet began to pick up a little momentum, finally going a very high speed. It looked so interesting, I couldn't take my eyes off the horse and feet. The pants leg rose higher and higher, until they were almost out of sight, up into the rump of the horse.

Then I saw a man coming towards the horse, looking to his side at another display. They came head on. The horses head and feet collided with the man, throwing the horse fully on the cement, all flattened out.

The horse and feet got back up on their course, and started on with slow momentum. The man slid sideways and went on. I looked around at the people, but no one had seen this happen except one person, a woman at whom I smiled and said, "That was one bad collision." She hardly looked at me, and went right by, going to her destination of the next exhibit. I thought, "Probably a foreigner who doesn't know any English!" We have so many of them. Sometimes they shake their heads, and mumble some foreign language, sometimes they just look quizzically at you, then go their way with a smile. This woman did neither, just glanced at me and then went her own way.

I looked past her to see the horse and legs were picking up a little speed, going on down the open aisle formed by no people being around.

There was a terrible clatter, as I looked beyond the horse's rump, to see a large piece of equipment of some kind coming towards the rump and feet. It was falling apart, falling towards the horse. As it fell breaking up, with pieces falling forward and sideways. A young girl, who had been walking towards the horse, fell from flying parts of the big machine. She started falling, and trying to save herself from injury, she was all sprawled out on the pavement, sliding furiously towards the horse and feet.

The horse and feet had picked up a lot of momentum and was now going very fast. The girl and the horse collided with a big bang.

I looked back at where George was selling Ted's Sheds, only to see he wasn't there. He had gone back into a shed, I suppose. I ran out into the open corridor, to get a better look. The girl fell into the feet of the horse, knocking the whole contraption over on its side. It was a horrendous collision, with everything going everywhere!

Then I woke up! It was all a dream!

Chapter 40
Kid Stuff

George never liked the water. He never liked to get wet. He never liked to get his big toe wet. So, after fighting and trying to help him and have friends or relatives help him I now have given up. I don't even think he likes to shower. He just does not like water. He drinks very little water, takes a pill with a teaspoon of water.

When the children were small he tried to get them to be careful, don't do this, don't do that!

"Let me handle the children in the water, George. Don't scare them, or they'll be afraid of the water like you!" I implored.

George's mother raised him to be afraid of water as she had a bad experience in a boat in a storm on the Wabash River in Indiana when a girl.

Both of our boys learned to swim very well. Larry would get high scores in Scouts and anywhere he was. He also earned his swimming merit badge and was a qualified life guard. Monte loved swimming but not for scoring. He was a loner in swimming as in most things.

"Don't tell our kids what to do," Larry once said to the two of us when we cautioned them about something they were doing. "I'll do that. Judy and I'll do that."

So now we have three free spirits doing everything. It is delightful. They do what they want to do when they want to do it. They have to ask Mother or Dad if they can do some things, but they are free to think, ponder and manage on their own. They are much smarter than we were and living much more interesting lives than we ever did. More power to them and to their parents who decided their lives should be open to their needs and wishes.

Fortunately they are all good kids getting into very little trouble and none which can't be straightened out more or less easily. I'm rooting for them.

Once we took Jenna to a worship service, at Grace United Methodist Church in Cape Coral, to hear Doctor David G. Kelley, Minister. He is also a practicing psychologist, doing marriage and family counseling, and helping blind people cope with their afflictions.

While we were in line to shake the ministers hand after the service, Jenna saw a huge empty area, and could not restrain herself. The large entrance of the church was so huge and empty that Jenna seized the moment to do cartwheels. I was so surprised it was a shock until I heard several people being so thrilled at her doing this, that I forgot where we were for a few cartwheels. Then I asked her not to do them, and told her this was not the place. But, I have to admit, that was a beautiful sight. A little four year old doing cartwheels, over and over.

When all three were doing cartwheels and physical activity in our home, it was wonderful! They outgrew it, of course, and have gone to better things. They play children's card games and ones they've invented, not following Hoyle. They like to listen to loud music, their favorites, Jazz numbers for Devon, while Joshua prefers Regge, and Jennifer likes what she calls oldies. Her ideas of oldies and what I'm used to are not the same. I personally prefer classical and semi-classical, and easy listening.

There is this beautiful bottlebrush tree right outside our kitchen window which is often covered with fancy bright red bottle brushes all over the tree, with outstretched limbs that were so heavily loaded they became too heavy and had to be propped up with large posts. We hung beautiful bromeliads on the nearly horizontal limbs. This tree looks out towards the road and is a favorite spot for our mocking birds.

Devon had been helping his grandpa cut his pups (babies) off the bromeliad mother plants, starting them in another pot.

I was looking out the window, doing my dishes at the sink, when I saw a body fall out of the tree, onto the ground with a big thud! I grabbed a dishtowel, to wipe my hands, and ran out the front door.

"Devon are you hurt?" I yelled at our grandson, who was ten years old at the time. He lumbered up gradually, walking off slowly, going away from me.

"How did you do that? What happened? Are you okay, Sweetie?" I kept asking him, alarmed at what I had seen and heard.

"I'm okay, Grandma!" he said as he walked around. He had fallen with such a thud and let out such a horrible yell, that I was very alarmed.

He had fallen flat on his back from the high branches of the tree, but he began to get his breath back, and seemed all right. I never saw him climbing a tree again!

My nine year old granddaughter, Jenna, and I love to play cards. Our grandsons Joshua and Devon used to love to play cards but their thoughts are elsewhere now with flying airplanes, building models, baseball, soccer, fishing, boating, bows and arrows.

When I was a little girl, my sister Mary Ellen, and I would pester Dad to play cards with us as the boys, our brothers, soon lost interest playing with younger kids.

"Ask Dad if he will play," Mary Ellen used to say to me.

"Pop, play cards with us please. Pretty please!" I would whine. I knew just how to do it.

Pop would liven up our game tremendously. He would slap the cards down on the table and talk loud. He was so much fun.

After a period of time, which was never long enough for me, Pop would get to acting a little strange and I would become quiet watching him. I knew what I would finally find out. I just wasn't certain when it would happen.

"You cheated, Pop!" I would yell when I thought he had done something sneaky.

"No, I didn't," he would tease. It would go on a little longer and I would see him do something funny again. I never quite saw it happen but that was what he wanted. He would tease us several times before he would let us find him out for sure.

"You cheated, Pop! I saw you!" I or Mary would scream. He would laugh uproariously and knew he had actually won what he had set out to win. The conclusion of the game!

"I'm not going to play with you! You cheated!" Mary and I would yell in unison.

Jenna and I play well together, never fighting or cheating. She is so alive wanting to do everything. I truly hope she and all four grandsons will always want to do things and learn something all the time. The process of learning never stops. I hope it never stops for me or my grandchildren.

Chapter 41
The End of Monte's Dream

Monte was a crew chief for Engineering Companies having surveying jobs in Dayton and surrounding areas. He showed us many streets he laid out and construction sites he surveyed for buildings, many of them large plants, even one for General Motors.

As jobs became harder to find for these engineering firms, Monte traveled to Cincinnati and Kentucky to do survey jobs.

After years of working in the cold winters and hot summers, and extensive constant travel to work sites, Monte decided he wanted to make a change.

"I think I'll go back to school," he said to us one day when we were in Dayton, Ohio visiting him.

He quit working and went to Sinclair College in Dayton. Education is the best commodity we have. To educate a mind is the best insurance of a good life.

Monte was ready for college. He hadn't been in high school, where he had taken two years of vocational schooling, which was the basis of his construction and surveying life. Monte took up the hard classes like calculus and trigonometry with a vengeance.

"Do I have to take English?" he asked me several times.

"Yes, you do if you want to graduate!" I would say. "English is wonderful! You will like it once you start to take it. It will help you in your studies of other subjects, too."

We gave him a Handbook of the Third International Dictionary and a Roget's Thesaurus, two main tools of smart minds.

Monte received glowing reports from all his studies, being on the Dean's List. When he had taken all the courses he could in Sinclair, he went to the new Wright State University on the east side of Dayton near WPAFB. He kept taking his subjects he wanted and loved, leaving English for last. He had over two hundred credit hours which would give him at least two majors after he had taken his four English courses.

"I'm really enjoying the English," he said, after attending a few classes.

"I knew you would!" I said!

But it was too late for the diploma.

"What makes the difference if I don't get the diploma? I have all that education. I know all these things," he said.

Monte applied for a job at National Cash Register Company (NCR). He made an excellent impression on the interviewer with all his knowledge, and they created a new job for him. He was assigned to a large laboratory where there were thirteen different models of computers on which he tested software for compatibility between computers. Monte was delighted with his new assignment knowing he was on his way in the computer world. He had big plans for his future.

In November we received a phone call in Florida saying he was going to have an operation the next day. We packed quickly and got the first flight out. He had been taken into surgery when we arrived.

We sat in the waiting room facing the hallway and the elevator.

"I never saw such sad faces," a social worker said to us as she came out of the elevator and walked towards us.

"Our son is being operated on, and we thought he might have been the one coming on the elevator," I said.

She spoke gently to us and later talked to us after Monte was brought down.

"I'm glad you came, Mom and Dad! were his first words to us. It meant so much to us to have him say those words. The last time we had spoken his life had been so happy and going so well. Now it was a complete turn around. Our hearts were breaking. He was rolled to his room, but we were told to remain in the waiting room in order to talk to the doctor, who would be down shortly. It was torture waiting for the doctor to come. When he did arrive, he talked to us out in the hall. He still had on his green surgical clothes, with his mask hanging under his chin.

"Monte had a severe blockage," he said. "I had to take out two feet of his intestines. I never saw anything like it! I didn't expect him to pull through the operation."

We were speechless. We stared at him as he continued to tell us what he did. We were numb. After he left us I started walking slowly down the hallway. I started to sob as I could not control myself any longer. George had followed me and we leaned together sobbing.

A neighbor's daughter, Shirley Roe, who grew up with Monte, when we lived at Pinecrest, came walking to us and threw her arms around us and we all cried together.

We stayed in Dayton while he recuperated.

Monte went on his new job in April. He absolutely loved it. He made lots of friends there. It was perfect for him.

March 17, 1989, was our Fiftieth Wedding Anniversary. We wanted to have a party and invite our many friends and relatives. Monte didn't want to come to Florida but when we suggested we get a place in New Orleans for a week he said that would really be great.

We got the reservations and had plans all made when we received a call from him saying he had trouble with his head and had to have more surgery.

We flew up to be there with him. The cancer cells had progressed, passing though the base of his brain in the cerebellum, and were growing in his head. We knew he hadn't been well but he never complained.

Our son was dying. There was nothing we could do except to keep him from thinking about it.

When he got well enough we took him driving to movies, festivals, and a trip to the Ohio Amish Country. When Monte was well enough we took him anywhere he wanted to go.

We took Monte to his therapy and we ate out a lot. We had a great rapport with our son.

When Monte was too ill to go outside he would tell us to get out and have fun.

"Have fun!" he would say as we went out of the door. To this day whenever I say to anyone or hear someone say "Have fun" I think of our beloved Monte.

We went back to Florida about a month later.

We kept in touch with Monte by calling on the phone every day. So, Larry would call if we couldn't. We would talk about an hour each time. So we did keep in close contact. We talked of everything under the sun except his sickness. He never wanted to talk much about that.

Later in September, we had a time share week in St. Augustine to spend, when during one of our calls to Monte, I said what I oftentimes did to him on the telephone.

"Why don't you come down and spend a little time with us?" I said, "We would love to have you."

"I'll call you back," he said after a bit more conversation.

"I'm coming down," he called back in a few minutes. "I called for a ticket but I'm not sure just what flight I'll be on! I'll call you back to let you know!"

We were elated! But we received no phone call. We called to see when he might arrive. No one had any information. We asked when the next two or three planes would come in.

"We'll go to each plane and wait to see if he gets off," I said. "Did you ever wait for someone you did not know would arrive?" We waited and waited, standing back away from the gate to allow people to get off. The crowd became thinner and thinner until no one came out. We still waited. Finally, I turned to go. George looked back one more time, as we started to leave.

"There he is!" George said, excitedly.

As I turned around and looked back, I saw a sad, heartrending sight. My beautiful son was standing in the doorway, leaning on a cane. His hair was starting to come back after the loss of it to cancer therapy. He was wearing deep red suspenders over a gray shirt. He was not smiling, he was exhausted! It had been too much for him.

I ran towards him and as he took three or four more steps, I grabbed him. He was thrown backwards and I had to steady him. I pulled back and we looked at one another. His beautiful big brown eyes were dull and pale.

"How did you know I was coming?" he asked incredulously.

The next couple of days we stayed at home for him to rest, but went a little, as he felt like it. He always thirsted for new places and new things to do.

We left it up to him whether we should go or not go to St. Augustine that weekend. He thought it would be all right. If we had not gone things would certainly have been different. He had planned on staying with us for the rest of his life.

When we arrived at St. Augustine, we were late in getting into our apartment, it was dark, about nine at night. He was worn out. That night he had a bad attack and we had to call his doctor in Dayton, who had us get more medicine. He also told us about Interferon, which was a new medicine, which might help him with his cancer. It was very expensive and the patient had to pay for the first thousand dollar treatments. We said we would gladly! We would do anything to help our child live and get well!

Monte wasn't sure. He didn't want to go back to Dayton! He wanted to stay with us.

"Why, why, oh why," he kept saying over and over. My heart broke!

That small glimmer of hope of the Interferon therapy got us on our way back to Dayton the following day.

As we went farther into the north I knew I had to have more warm clothes. For a late September vacation in Florida, white clothes and all shorts were enough. We stopped in South or North Carolina at our favorite store, Wal-Mart, where George had to get some film.

"God please help me find something quickly so we won't lose any time!" He was with me! I never found anything so fast in my life before or after.

I went over to the women's area, grabbed up a large loose dark blue pair of jeans, that were the exact length for me. I couldn't believe it.

Then I saw a dark gray, two toned gorgeous sweater. It looked too fancy but I grabbed it and ran to George at the checkout. These two pieces are still in my wardrobe. They were given to me by God, and I will never part with them. They are still perfect for me.

We took Monte home.

The next day we found a darling apartment, which we fixed up expecting to stay the winter.

The Interferon therapy took a long time to get started. We had hurried up there to get it going, but doctors don't see emergencies the same as we do.

Monte was on steroids, interferon and other medications. We took him to therapy every day.

The home care worker came on Wednesday, finding Monte's vital signs necessitated his going back to the hospital. This would be his last time. Monte's doctor, Dayton's most prestigious oncologist, was at an out-of-state conference, and his substitute doctor told us he would not live through the weekend. We called Larry and he flew up getting there early in the morning, so he went to our apartment to sleep after staying with Monte for awhile.

When Monte's regular doctor returned to see Monte on Saturday, he was a bit miffed at the substitute doctor. "He will live three or four months longer," he said.

George and I had been staying with Monte day and night. Since Larry had slept late Sunday, he said he would stay Sunday night with Monte, letting us go home and rest.

Monday morning, when we relieved Larry, he went back to the apartment to sleep awhile before catching his plane to go back home in Florida.

Later, but before noon, Monte took a turn for the worse. We'd better call Larry and have him come back. We woke Larry up and he said he'd be right there. He rushed back to the hospital but was just a bit too late.

George and I stepped outside Monte's door in order to let the nurse take care of him and walked down the hallway. When we returned, we came back to a very still room.

"I think he just died," she said.

George and I ran to his right side, and I put my hands on his face. He heaved a big sigh, and he was gone. I said, "I love you Monte," just before he gently breathed his last breath. I feel he heard me.

The funeral was well attended. We had a beautiful obituary put in the newspaper, so all his friends could see it. Many came from Crystal Lakes and a lot from NCR.

Visiting hours the night before the funeral was full of old friends, his and ours.

"He seems so tall," Rita said.

They had him laid out with his arms and hands extended into his groin. He looked so handsome in his best Italian Conte Roma suit. His favorite rock hammer, which he used so often to find special rock specimens, was placed in his casket with him.

At the grave-site, Shane and Seth and George and I sat in chairs, with Larry standing behind us. Larry's outstretched arms, his left hand on my left shoulder and his right hand on George's right shoulder, gave us great comfort. His arms held us together. It was a wonderful feeling I had, thinking we four are together. We had been such a wonderful little foursome, always sharing everything. One time we went mushrooming together. When we found only one mushroom, I fried that one and cut it in four small pieces. We always shared everything.

Monte was born August 13, 1950, and passed away November 13, 1989. He was buried in the Woodland Cemetery, 118 Woodland Avenue, Dayton, Ohio, on a beautiful hilly knob, under stately oak trees, easily seen, close to the drive, where people could visit him, like he wanted. Squirrels play and frolic amongst the fallen leaves as the sun beams through the branches.

His large, professionally marked and identified rock collection was given in his memory to Sinclair College, for a display in the Geology Department, with some to be used for "hands on" examination by the Geology students.

A beautiful monument was erected for him with a computer and his favorite tool, a rock hammer, etched in the granite. His two great loves of his life were his computer and his rocks.

As we drove back to Florida we stopped at an historical park in Kentucky. We visited the museum viewing artifacts in which Monte would have been very interested. I found a perfect little rock which reminded me of Monte and his love of rocks. It had a smooth indentation in the center in which my thumb fit and moved around. I bought it and slipped it in my pocketbook. I carry it with me always. It is my Monte rock.

Chapter 42

A Eulogy to Mother Massing

Mother Massing was a talker. She talked mostly about people she knew and what they did or said. Nothing of interest to anyone. Joe used to say "Who cares?" which would get a laugh from everyone but Mother. She would go blithely on talking. Joe would finally interject another "Who cares?" which would illicit another laugh. Sometimes she would continue and she we would go another round of her talking with us listening until Joe would again say, "Who cares?" Then she would finally get the message.

After we fixed up our Fort Myers home I told her the third bedroom was hers.

"Is this really my bedroom?" she asked as we stood in it with her suitcase after bringing her up to stay a few days with us.

"Yes it is!" I said. "It is your bedroom. Anytime you come up to visit us from Naples, it is your bedroom. We fixed it up for you."

She seemed pleased but I have wondered if she thought I meant for her to come stay with us. She had always been so close with Joe and his family it had not entered my mind she would come so far away from them.

During her visit with us she seemed to be unable to let us out of her sight. Even when Sunday came and it was time to go out in our boat she would not stay at our house alone. She had always been afraid of the water so we did not even entertain the idea of her going with us. Some one had to stay at the house with her. It naturally had to be me although no one looked forward to our Sunday afternoon on the water more than me.

When we took her home, she asked every conceivable question of no interest one could imagine. All through her life she has asked these same kinds of questions to get us to respond, I guess. After counting twenty questions she asked by the time we arrived at the Route 75 highway, which was only three and a half miles from our house, I scrunched down in my seat and whispered to George, "You have to answer from now on."

"Look at the clouds. Aren't they beautiful?" Mother asked.

George took over and answered the next thirty questions. She asked fifty questions during our usually quietly pleasant trip to Naples, which was less than forty miles from our house to her house. She must have been a very lonesome person. It wasn't as if she didn't want to go home. She was ready. We let her decide when she wanted to go. I never quite understood my Mother-in-law, although I did like her and knew she had the best heart in the world. She never quarreled with anyone, but she surely did have a mind of her own.

She worried about everything. The word worry was said by her three or four times every day. She wouldn't go places. She missed out on so much, because she wouldn't do things. She was a very negative person, and yet she wanted to be with someone all the time. Once in a great while she would laugh a hearty laugh that was beautiful, but this did not happen very often.

Mother Massing was a beautiful seamstress doing everything just right. She taught me how to do everything right in making clothes. It is a good thing, as I became unable to sew when my eyes became worse. Since 1979 I have not been able to see to sew.

George was the only one who could do anything correctly with my clothes. I took new clothes to be hemmed or changed to people who ruined them. They would get them too short or too tight, or some other unsuitable, unwearable way. When I lost weight and had to have my things made smaller, several things were ruined. So I taught George, who was willing, the things his Mother had taught me. He does a terrific job on everything. He still asks me what to do and how to do it, but he can get everything just right.

THEN AND NOW

When we go shopping, George acts like a seamstress and checks out the clothes I am looking at to see if they are made right and tells me what the labels say.

We have our favorite shopping areas, mostly Penney's and Burdines Department stores, and a few others, where we are known and helped. George and I talk constantly about what I am thinking of buying. Sometimes he goes off on his own looking for something I might like. Several of the clerks know us and help him as much as they help me if not more so. They are so helpful and nice to us.

When I go inside the fitting room, George will continue to look at the clothing racks to see if he can find anything else. I never see another man in the women's clothes helping his wife. They usually stand at the edge of the clothes in the aisles, if any man is man enough to go shopping with his wife. I have a great husband! Not just anyone could or would do this for his wife.

Then the hard part comes. George has to make my waistline larger and shorten the skirts and slacks. He also has to shorten sleeves on jackets. There are very few pieces I can wear right off the rack. Usually the blouses are all right. I could easily lose thirty pounds and probably get down to wearing the kind of clothes they make now, but I have tried for years to lose weight with very little success. Even the doctor tells me I should and that doesn't help! I'm made like my Mother and have fought the battle of the bulge all my life being very successful until we went to Naples. There we had no friends for awhile and so what did we do? Ate. And ate. It was fun, but my weight became overweight.

When we moved to Fort Myers, I continued gaining gradually until I couldn't take it off enough to fit in the clothes I wanted to wear. Now I am making a concentrated effort and losing a little once in awhile. I have given up my most delectable edible, ice cream with hot fudge poured over it. I never thought I could do it!

Once in a while George and I have a pecan ice cream cone at the food court at Edison Mall, or an even better one, if there is such a thing, at Disney World at the corner of Main Street at Magic Kingdom. When we go to Disney World we always agree, when the time comes, when either one of us feels like getting on the monorail ride to the Magic Kingdom and get a fabulous huge, butter pecan cone. Nothing tastes better than a cone from there. It is well worth the trip from Epcot, our favorite place or MGM which we really do like a lot also to go to the Magic Kingdom, if for no other reason than to get a cone!

Mother talked a lot about everyone but she never said anything derogatory about anyone. She told everything she knew about anyone but she never gave an opinion, whether it was right or wrong, or how they could better their lives. I found it, as I'm sure most people did, that her talking had no merit and thus could be useless in even conversation of any kind. So, I learned to let her talk and only answered when asked a question. I believe most people felt the same way. If one gives any information whatsoever to a person like this, he should realize that information will be passed on to someone else.

I love a good give and take of a conversation. It was hard for me to realize some people do not think that way.

Mother Massing was good as gold and loved her family to the utmost. She did an awfully lot of things for us all.

Mother Massing helped raise Joe and Ginny's children and they loved her dearly. She would have helped us more, if we had lived closer. She spent a lot of time with Joe's family, all during her life, up to the time she had to go to a nursing home-

One day she called from Naples. "I can't turn off the stove. It is so hot in here. I am awfully hot."

I was frantic!

"Call Joe and Ginny," I said. "They will come over and help you."

"I tried calling them but they don't answer. It is so hot in here. I have opened the door to the hall but it is not relieving the heat much!" she said.

"How many burners do you have on? How did you happen to do it? Why can't you get them shut off?" I kept asking questions

"I had one burner on and was frying chicken, but somehow all, the burners got on. I couldn't remember how to turn them off! They are so hot all over," she explained.

I was so afraid for her.

"Mother, keep the door wide open to let the heat out into the hall. Don't open the windows as that will cause a draft. Go to a neighbor for help!" I said.

"I went across the hall, but the neighbors were gone, and I don't know the other neighbors. They are new," she said.

"Take it easy then and watch nothing gets on fire. We'll be down there right away," I said.

"Oh, I hate for you to do that. I didn't call you to get you to come down," she said.

"Of course, we'll come down. It will take us about forty or fifty minutes. Just watch so no fire starts. If it does, throw soda on it, or towels, but don't let it get started. We'll hurry," I said.

I ran to tell George who came in from the yard. He had been weeding and working with his flower beds.

We ran around grabbing things to wear changing our work clothes, and were in the car in the shortest time possible. George never moved so fast nor did he drive down the highway so fast. We Prayed all the way!

Quickly stepping out of the elevator, we hurried down the hall. feeling the heat almost immediately. As we walked into her excessively hot apartment, we found Mother standing four or five feet from the stove, far enough away she wouldn't get scorched.

"I didn't know what to do!" she said crying.

"You did right!" I said, as I ran over to the stove and switched off the four burners, which were all red hot.

Perhaps we should have called the fire department, but we didn't. We have always taken care of our own problems. We were very fortunate that there was no fire and Mother was all right.

We knew now Mother could not live alone. We hated the thought of this, because she had done a fantastic job of taking care of herself. We had gone down to Naples to visit her a lot more lately, as we knew she was getting so she couldn't do everything she used to do. She was still boiling chicken and making her own meals. She set lemon Jello with pears in it all the time and always had cottage cheese. This was a good meal. She loved peas and angel food cake, and ham. She ate well. We would take her to Long John Silver's or Morrison's Cafeteria or some new place she loved to eat. Sometimes she would have chicken ready. We always ate it when she asked us to do so. This made her feel as if she was helping. She was a great person. Never wanted to feel a burden on us.

The time had come that all older people face. They can't live alone anymore. We discussed it with Joe and Ginny and we all decided to try to get her into the Greater Naples Care Center, where my mother had been. We thought that nursing home was a very good one. Ginny said she would take care of it since she lived in Naples. She called the next day and said they were full up and wouldn't be able to take her for a couple of months.

"Let us see what we can do up here" I said. Fortunately there was an opening at Pine's Village Care Center on Pondella Road which was only seven miles from our house. This was perfect.

George and I drove down to Naples and picked Mother up. This was so reminiscent of when we picked my Mother up at Hollywood for the last time and drove her across the Alligator Alley to the home in Naples. Both trips were very sad and heart wrenching.

Mother did not like the home and took many mouths to adjust. We visited her there a lot and Larry and Judy and the children went to see her quite a bit. We attended the social activities and musicals just as we did for my mother.

Mother lived there for about three and a half years, the last year being very poorly. It was a blessing when she breathed her last breath.

Sometimes you have to tell them it's all right to go on. They cling to life thinking that is what you want them to do. A holistic head nurse told us this in a meeting at the care center.

This is what they told us about Monte. When I released him he died in three or four hours. It is a hard thing to do. But I did it again with Mother.

"Mother we love you. You've been a wonderful Mother but it's your time to get your rest now. You can go on to heaven and we'll get along all right." I was crying, so had to move away from her bedside. It seemed I was losing everyone. My circle of loved ones was getting smaller.

George had stood beside me not uttering a word. I looked at him. He was crying too.

"Mother," he said, "Kay is right. You have been a wonderful Mother to all of us and a wonderful grandmother to Joe and Ginny's and our children. Now it's time for you to go on and be with Jesus."

We called Joe and Ginny when we got home and when we went back after dinner they and their daughter Gina were there.

"She hasn't much longer to live," Gina, who was a nurse, told her Mother on the way home.

That night we received a telephone call from the care center. Mother had died peacefully in her sleep.

Joe and Ginny and George and I went on the same airplane that took Mother back home to Illinois. She was buried in the Georgetown Cemetery beside her beloved Mother Delana Daisy Parker. We visit their graves every year when we go home for a visit.

Mother war buried in a gorgeous deep pink, long sleeved dress with sequins on the front, a dress George an I looked for, for days when Gina was about to be married. It was perfect for both the wedding and perfect for her funeral. She looked beautiful with her white hair and beautiful white clear skin.

Chapter 43
Sanibel and Captiva Islands

In my opinion, Sanibel is one of the most wonderful places in the world. Everyone who lives there thinks that is so, every one who owns and operates a business there thinks that is so. At least, everyone I have met there thinks there is no place like Sanibel. And I am inclined to think that is true.

Crossing the big beautiful bridge and causeway that curves from the mainland to the island itself is an experience everyone should enjoy. It is a drawbridge and sometimes one is caught when it is opened for a sailboat or two, a large cruiser or a yacht. No one minds waiting as the view is so terrific. We dream of being on that vessel coming through.

Turn left at Periwinkle Way after coming off the bridge, and one comes to the end of the island, passing one of our Time Share Resorts of one week a year at Shell Island Beach Club.

We bought this time share in 1980. Actually, we bought two, but traded the one on top as the sun shone too intensely through the skylight all day. We sold this one and bought a lovely floor level at Sanibel Beach Club, also on the beach, due west from the bridge and a little north. We like this one best of all our time shares. Sunrise Bay on Marco Island is our third time share, which we often exchange, mostly for traveling.

THEN AND NOW

We have heard bad things about time shares but we are very satisfied with ours. Never in our years of ownership have we ever had problems. I think when we hear about problems in ownership of time shares, the owner's have not really understood what they are all about and expected more. We know what we bought, how to use it, and are extremely happy with the whole situation. We give it a five star status.

From our apartment, at Sanibel Beach Club, we have a lovely beach on which we can lounge or walk down to the beautiful lighthouse at the far end. There is a flat area near there where the fourth grade teacher brought her students on a picnic and beach combing outing when Joshua was in the fourth grade in November 1988. We took a sack full of assorted candy bars to the children to eat after their lunches. The teacher was very appreciative to have us do that. She was teaching them how to collect things on the seashore, and constantly helping, and explaining to them about our sensitive environment properly.

The first time we were ever on Sanibel, in about 1953, Mother and Ann took George and me, Larry and Monte, there on a picnic. We were with them on a short vacation, so, even though the weather was bad, we prepared a picnic in Hollywood and crossed Alligator Alley a little after sunrise in Mother's Cadillac. Huge flocks of beautiful white Egrets and other birds were out in full force. They were awakening from their long night's sleep, and preparing to leave the rookery for their feeding grounds.

When we arrived on Sanibel, it was cold and windy but the sun was shining, and it was glorious. We stood and watched the surf pounding against the shore, and listening to the frolicking waves. We were entranced. We threw our blankets on the beach, having the boys sit on the corners to keep the wind from blowing it away. The food was laid out on top of the blanket. We ate, talked, and laughed, as the wind blew unmercifully against us. It was a most memorable picnic.

About forty years later, George and I are at our Time Share, Sanibel Beach Club. It is a lovely two bedroom condominium which overlooks a large, rolling, well landscaped lawn, with full view of the beach. We carry breakfast in our little Igloo Lunchmate to the beach, along with our chairs, eight ribbed, four colored, umbrella, and camera. George twists the umbrella support into the hard wet sand.

We watch the people in the water, walking into the morning sun, which causes a reflection and silhouette effect, and eat away at our breakfast. I had packed in our igloo a half a green Honeydew melon, a huge Golden Delicious apple, (the best apple after Grimes Golden), a knife, lots of paper towels, and a bottle of root beer.

We sit, and eat, and take pictures of interesting people who obviously love Sanibel as much as we do. George took people who had waded (at high tide they would have had to swim), out to the sand bars looking for shells and sand dollars, people walking up and down the shoreline, and the Sanibel Stoopers! He missed a picture of three bicycle riders who came along too fast, and engrossed us in their beauty until it was too late for a picture. The Sanibel stoop is nationally known as it is when a person, more often a woman, who finds and bends over stiff legged to pick up a beautiful shell. It's an engrossing and timely position which gets into a lot of magazines. So, if you are an avid reader, you have seen the Sanibel Stoop!

After hours of watching and walking, we come back to our Condo to view the beach from our screened in open lanai. We will go out again in the evening, and view the plentiful gulls that come flying in and around, the food that people throw up in the air for them to catch. It's a beautiful sight and a great pleasure in which to participate.

Morning and evening, shore birds are everywhere and are beautiful to watch. There are willets, gulls, sandpipers and pelicans galore.

If we have company, we take our mats and extra chairs and umbrellas to the beach. Larry and Judy, and the children come out each time we go and are with us at least a day. We want them more but they work, and the kids are in school and involved in soccer. If they come out on week days they would almost have to start back when they arrive. I keep thinking, someday it will be different, but when? Not in our lifetime!

We are always happy to have friends during the week. Then we do what they want and go where they want to go. Sometimes they just want to go to the beach, which is fine by us.

There are so many wonderful shops, dining areas, both expensive and inexpensive (they even have a Dairy Queen, but no other fast food.)

My favorite place to eat is at the The Mucky Duck, internationally known, which is near the end of Captiva Island, at the end of Andy Rosse Lane. The Sanibel Captiva Islander says, "It's located deep in the heart of downtown Captiva directly on the Gulf." It is very popular and frequented by many world travelers. We can, while eating there, hear the patrons mentioning their home port, and they come from many far away places.

The Mucky Duck opened for business on January 29, 1976, having been purchased in 1975 by the Mayerons and the Webbs, who turned the property into a restaurant. It became an English type pub, completing a dream of Webb, who had been a bobby in London for 20 years. He and his wife remembered and old English pub in Stratford-On-Avon called the Black Swan which they used to frequent. It was known to the locals as the Mucky Duck.

So was born the Captiva Mucky Duck. When first opened, it boasted a dart board and game room. The Duck was a true local spot to savor cold beers, play darts, enjoy beautiful sunsets and sing along with the old player piano till the wee hours of the morning. The menu was limited to English dishes and fresh seafood.

From this beginning evolved a wonderful full service restaurant of world renown.

It has a lot of British paraphernalia hanging on the walls and Mucky Duck Shirts, Caps and Mugs and other items for sale.

The magnificent view from the dining area enhances the food that is served. My favorite food is barbequed prawns wrapped in bacon, which are served with steamed vegetables and garlic new potatoes. The best desert is the Mucky Duck Surprise, the homemade walnut brownie sundae. Be sure to ask for both chocolate and red raspberry toppings. George and I share one after a hearty meal.

Victor and Memo keep you in a happy mood. Anyone can have a window seat, just ask either of them. Be sure to ask Victor where the birds are if you don't hear them.

Many people gather on the beach in front of The Mucky Duck each evening, to watch the sun go down. If you watch carefully at sunset, you might see the green flash. It happens so seldom one needs to be alert to see it. The last time we were there I heard two women talking, one said she thought she saw it. I had not seen it that night. George and I have seen it when at a Naples beach. As the sun goes down over the horizon, there will be a quick flash of green light, when the atmosphere, and the elements, are just right. It is beautiful and happens a mere moment.

The first place we go, and sometimes again it's the last place we go, is The Mucky Duck at the end of Captiva Island, which I consider and extension of Sanibel. It really is, because one cannot get there without going across the toll bridge to Sanibel, then at the end of Sanibel, crossing Blind Pass bridge to Captiva. The South Seas Plantation is really at the end of Captiva, but it is a private area not open to the public. So, I always say The Mucky Duck is at the end of Captiva, as it really is for us, although it's on Andy Rosse Lane, just before the fire station. If you pass here you have gone too far.

The hot rays of the sun have to be watched nowadays. All that sunbathing and tanning I have done all my life have been bad for me, the doctors say, so now I am paying for it. Gone is the delight of the hot sun's rays on my body and the rush of happiness of just being out in the sun.

We still go to the beach a lot, but we take umbrellas and chairs, and wear lots of SPF15 or SPF 48 sun lotion.

Sam's Club has been selling compact disks on relaxing music of rolling waves, which are fabulous and are selling like hot cakes.

I can lie in my bed, close my eyes, and envision myself lying on the sand near the lapping waves, with gentle bells and xylophone coming in at intervals. It's enough to satisfy my longing for truly lying on the beach in the hot sun. It brings back many memories of the sun, surf, crying birds above, and just plain sun. It transforms my whole demeanor and allows my subconscious to take over.

Imagine what happiness we have when we truly get to the beach and loll around, not in the hot sun anymore, but in the cool of the evening, or the early morning brightness. We leave the hot, sunny midday to the ones who don't know better. With a wide brim hat and sun screen and being fully clothed with shorts and top, George and I cruise the beaches up and down, watching the shellers, doing the

"Sanibel Stoop," viewing the birds hunting for a morsel, fully enjoying the beach and its environs. Shelling used to be a great activity of our outings, but we leave that activity to others now, taking our camera along with us on our walks. A lot of pictures are taken of birds and people, as we sit in our chairs under our multicolored umbrella. Oh, what a life! There is none better!

We wanted to go outside to see the sun set, so we started out our back door.

"Wait, I want to take some bread to the birds," I said, and hurried back into our downstairs apartment. There were only three or four pieces of Italian bread left from our Sunday evening sandwiches, when Larry, Judy and the kids were here. I was surprised as that meant the seven of us had eaten two loaves of bread. Joshua had said he had eaten four sandwiches himself, and the others probably ate about that many. Big eaters!

I hurried outside, dangling my bread wrapper with its few pieces of bread in it, as I hurried down the rolling lawn and onto the wooden slatted walkway, up and over the bridge to the beach. As I hurried after George, the Gulf was silently lapping at the edges of the sand.

As I walked along the beach, I soon missed George walking beside me. I turned to see where he was, to find him with his ever present camera at his eyes, focusing on some distant sea view. He has this long lense which has to be focused just so, to get the best picture. As I looked backward, I saw a beautiful sea gull following me in my own footsteps. I turned completely around and walked backward.

"Hey, look, George," I yelled to him, as I was getting further and further away from him. "This little guy is following in my footsteps!"

I was walking too fast to go very far backward, so I finally turned around, going forward again. I kept looking back, and that little guy kept following me, right behind me in my own footsteps, running fast to keep up with me. It reminded me of our duck we had when we were little, when it would follow my sister Mary and me down the street, to go from Grandma's to downtown Ridgefarm.

"Oh," I finally got it! "He sees my bread hanging from my left hand!" The long bread wrapper was dangling from my right hand, and evidently shining, as I swung it in the sun.

"Okay, you!" I said aloud. "I'll give you some bread!" I was headed towards the area where we always saw people feeding, which was about a mile down the beach.

I opened up the long sack, reached way down in it, broke off a piece of bread, and tossed it to him, walking backwards again. He caught it in his beak, then looked at me again, expectantly. I tossed another, laughing at him. To my surprise, two more gulls came out of nowhere, so I tossed them some pieces of bread. Then a whole flock of gulls rushed in, engulfing me. I laughed at all of them, tossing bread at them as fast as I could. The bread was Italian and mostly crust, so it was hard to tear off, but I did it as fast as I could. I thought the birds were going to eat me up!

They became wild and ferocious, and I knew I should have brought a whole loaf of bread. There were so many of them! Where had they come from? I had seen only this one little fellow who was following me, and yet, before I knew it, there were hundreds. At least it seemed that there were that many.

The next day, I had planned on buying another loaf of bread, but we forgot it, and it was evening, time to walk out on the beach to see a lovely sunset. I rummaged through our snacks, coming across a sack of popcorn, which I thought would be good for the birds.

As we walked down the beach, there was no sign of any bird! I started eating the popcorn, myself, as I walked beside George, who was looking through his lens to find a good picture. As usual, he stopped to take a picture, so I continued walking and eating the popcorn.

There were quite a few birds but they didn't hover. Finally, I started throwing popcorn up in the air. One gull came, then another, but where was the group? I tossed a handful of popcorn in the air.

That brought them! Here they came flying in, surrounding me. I would toss a handful in the air. Some of those lucky birds would catch a fat, white kernel from the air, some tried but couldn't catch any, some just stood on the sand, waiting for the kernels to fall, then they would chirp and feed on what they could find.

Bread was much better for them to catch, evidently they couldn't see the popcorn in the hot setting sun. So back to the grocery store to get another loaf of bread for the next night!

We love Sanibel in the springtime, but mostly we love it in the fall after a hot summer. It's fantastic to go to our Sanibel Beach Club for a week and visit all our old haunts.

One time, we used our Time Share to stay at the South Seas Plantation for a week. It was great! We loved it, and especially the delicious rack of lamb for two served at the Royal Crown, their excellent on premises restaurant. It was cooked and served to perfection! But what a price, seventy-five dollars. It was the most we ever paid for one meal. We must go back there, when we hit it rich, like win the Florida lottery! (Which we don't play.)

There are many interesting and diversified shops on Sanibel and Captiva, such as Bailey's General Store, gorgeous shell shops, intriguing clothing shops, beautiful beach wear, and many specialty shops for gifts and island souvenirs.

My favorite of all shops is The Sandpiper. It is located in Palm Ridge Place, as we turn off Periwinkle to go to Captiva. It is owned and operated by Nola Shehorn Francis, a lovely and readily helpful shopkeeper.

She meets us each time with a broad smile, salutations, and a big hug! She is one sweet angel, perfect as an owner of a fabulous gift shop.

"I love your hat!" She expostulated, when we first walked in the other day, and she came around the counter, to hug us. "Oh, you look so good in it!" Now I thought so, but no one had ever said so. Now, you wonder why I like this gal?

She'll help you find anything or come up with something else, as good or better. She has a great inventory of unusual and practical gift items from all over the world. There is something for everyone.

Listen to the music she plays in her shop. It is available on both compact disc and cassette tape.

This last time we bought a couple of CD's from the wonderful talented fingers of Newell Oler, a fantastic pianist. In the past we bought several tapes of his from Nola, but now we have a CD player, which is much better, of course!

When we arrived at the Lighthouse Shops I walked right over to the clothes rack hanging in the sales area, which are summer stocks that they are trying to sell to make room for the new winter merchandise.

We have so little winter down here in southwest Florida, that I seldom buy any winter clothes anymore. That's mostly for tourists to take back up north or to their homes in Europe.

"Where in the world have you been?" I heard a lady saying. I turned to see Sally, my favorite saleslady in this store. "Don't you usually come before this? I was just thinking about you the other day!"

So, I guess I am thought of by my salesladies in my favorite haunts.

Of course, I always buy something! What is the business for? I never go just to look! I go to buy something. And I usually do. Not often do I leave my favorite stores without buying something!

This day, I bought a beautiful two piece slack set of coral poly/cotton, my favorite blend, made by Jantzen, for half price. I love this material, and am a sucker for half price sales!

There was a relatively new restaurant which we had never visited before. The write up in the Sanibel newspaper made it sound so enticing. It was patterned after some of the sidewalk cafes we visited while in Paris, France. The ambiance was with a definite Parisian flair like no other cafe we have visited here. The decor, the food, the waiters, all made one feel he was on the left bank, in Paris, France.

It was opposite the fire station on Captiva Island, and once we were interrupted with the loud sirens coming out of the station and going past. That we could have done without! I'm sure they never had this problem on the Left Bank in Paris!

The tables were set up along the wooden railing, of a long narrow porch, so we found us a spot, and ordered. The food was delicious! George had a grouper sandwich and I had a huge, humongous, fabulously delicious, catfish like none other I had ever eaten, with very tasty fruit.

"Are you ready for your other half?" The cute young waiter asked.

"I'm giving that to my husband! I can't eat it all!" I answered, as I was still eating on my first part of a huge hard roll half, the like of which you've never seen.

"I mean your other half!" He yelled back at me, as he went on down the narrow porch to another table. "I just gave you half a sandwich" he said. Then I realized what he meant. The sandwich was made of a long hard roll, a special new bread made in Fort Myers, and he had used only half the roll for my sandwich. Here I couldn't even eat half of that. It was a fantastic sandwich. We have to go to that baker, who is new in town, and try some of his bread and rolls. This was hard and crusty, with a marvelous texture and flavor.

Then we got desert! It was fabulous! They called it a strawberry sandwich, as it had a bottom and a top square piece of puff pastry, crisscrossed for beauty. In between it had Haagen Dazs ice cream, with sliced strawberries on top, then a sauce over all and a decoration on top. Voila! We hit the jackpot! Fabulous! Just like Paris!

It is nice at Marco Island too, where we have another Time Share but there are not as many things to do there. It is more sedate, with large condominiums and millionaire homes. One of the homes, belonging to a famous ball player was built to include his parents and parents-in-law, each with their own apartments. It was valued at seven million dollars when it was first built a few years ago.

We use our Marco time share for our trips away from home usually. We used it to go to the French Riviera in 1985 in conjunction with our trip to the British Isles and Europe. We stayed at Antibes, France, on the French Riviera, a wonderful, gorgeous area. We didn't want to leave when our week was up. The French Riviera and Cote d' Azur are all it's cracked up to be. Just fabulous! And it cost us twenty-five dollars only! That is, twenty-five dollars after our regular maintenance fee we pay each year, and a small exchange fee. Can't beat that!

How far we have come from that first picnic on Sanibel beach in 1953!

Chapter 44
Family Fun

George and I had to hurry the last minute, because the VCR failed to work when he set it for my afternoon soaps. We rushed out to pick up Devon and Jenna to chauffeur Devon to his special learning class in the southwest part of town. Since we lived fifteen miles north and east, it would take us twenty or thirty minutes to go through the heavy in season winter traffic.

Our car turned into Bayshore Estates, just as the Junior High kids had been delivered by their bus and were walking towards their individual homes. We stopped near Devon and his friends.

"Hop in! We have to hurry," Grandpa said.

Devon quickly said goodbye to his friends, and jumped in the back seat of our new car with his soccer bag which was serving as a book bag today.

After we pulled in the driveway, being careful not to hit the camping trailer on one side and the large boat from our water way, which was setting on its trailer until cleaning and shining before putting it back in our canal. Devon jumped out of the back seat, ran in the house to clean up a bit, and get Jenna, whose piano lesson had been canceled as the teacher had the flu.

I quickly crawled into the back seat, so Devon could have the honored front seat, and I could sit with Jenna in the back seat. This is our favored seat when we four go places together, usually such as just now.

"Devon do you need these books?" I yelled to him, as he was already out of earshot.

"What?" He called back, he came running back. "What did you say Grandma?"

"Do you need to take these books tonight, or don't you need them?" Sometimes he did, sometimes he didn't, in the past.

"No, I don't need them tonight," he said, starting to walk away.

"Well, here, then take them to the house. No need to take them with us!" I said, a little crossly. They leave things everywhere! Always a mess, everywhere they go!

I started to lift the bag of books, to give to him, but they weighed like bricks! I pulled and dragged the bag up and over my knees, trying to get them to his reached out hand.

"They're so heavy!" I mumbled. "What on earth do you have in there?" I asked, as I pulled and tugged it across my other knee.

"Its not heavy!" He countered. He proceeded to lift that ton of books up and out the door as if it were a bag of marbles. I had to laugh, as I marveled at the strength of this little thirteen year old boy! He was growing up! Had the strength of Samson! Or was it that I was growing old and weak? Both, I guess!

After going across that terrible traffic, we arrived there in time (sometimes we were late), and George, Jenna, and I settled down to talk and whatever. Sometimes we window shopped at the Royal Palm Square where there were lovely shops. Sometimes we actually shopped buying lovely clothes, eating ice cream cones, or something. There were lovely areas where there were feisty ducks and babies. We hadn't seen the ducks for so long. It was a great deal of pleasure to lean over railings and follow the ducks in the numerous waterways. It was something to see the reaction of the mama when one or another of her babies went the wrong way and they would get separated. One could be fascinated at the interaction of those darling little families.

But not today. George passed a dogeared old book back to us in the back seat.

"So you want to read this?" he asked. It was "The Good Crop," by Elizabeth H. Emerson, a story of Quaker migration of a family, who ended up in the eastern part of Illinois, the family of William Rees. It was so similar to my people that it was like reading about my own families, who went to Vermilion Grove, Illinois.

George read for awhile, until he became sleepy, which was always the case. He can't read without going to sleep. When his actions slow down, everything in him says, "Hey let's give up! Let's go to sleep!"

So Jenna took over, and read until she was tired. I would stop her once in awhile to tell her how it was with my people. So between talking and reading, the time flew by. It was soon time for Devon to come out of his classroom at Sylvan Learning Center, a private school engaged in tutoring students needing special attention in specific subjects.

"Let's go into the mall and meet Devon," I said. "Maybe we'll see the ducks." No ducks were seen, but we walked around, leaning on the railings, and saw the new water lilies in the waterways. I told Jenna about Claude Monet, the fabulous artist whose water lilies were so lovely. I had stood looking at his huge paintings of water lilies in the Chrysler Exhibit in Cincinnati, Ohio, for a long time. I couldn't take it all in. They were so lovely and quieting; it seemed as if I were searching my soul. There was one whole room of Monet and his water lilies. It was the most quiet room of art work I have ever studied. So peaceful, so uplifting, so great! Now here were these little patches of water lilies, just beginning, and out of these would come huge gorgeous water lilies that would heal the heart of everyone who took the time to look.

In later years our good friends Doctor A. Waldo Farabee and his wife Marion, would come to spend summer vacations at the property next door to Claude Monet's country home and ponds at Giverny, France, where he painted his famous series of water lilies. The Farabees daughter Judy married the Ambassador for Art under President Reagan who established a museum for American Art at Giverny and took up residence there.

Devon came bounding out the door, and almost ran into us. We hurried to the car, woke up Grandpa, and thought of where we would eat supper. Pizza Hut won, but when we arrived there, the lot was jammed with cars and people were standing in line outside the door.

THEN AND NOW

It takes a long time at Pizza Hut on a slow night, so we opted to go next door, to Taco Bell, one of our other favorites.

When we arrived home, the kids raided the refrigerator for ice cream bars, and desserts.

We ensconced ourselves in front of the TV, eating our desserts, watching this years awards ceremony and playing cards. Devon won everything he played. He was really lucky! Sometimes just Jenna and I played, while Devon lay in front of the TV to watch more closely the ceremonies and ice skating.

Jenna and I were playing Gin Rummy when we had a perfect game! She asked me for a certain card, I said no.

I drew from the deck, put it in my hand, discarded a card. Jenna picked it up, discarding a card from her hand. I picked up her discard, put it in my hand, and discarded an unwanted card, which she picked up. It went on like this for every card. At the end, I said "Gin!" and laid down my perfect hand, discarding my extra card. It fell on empty space, as there were no unwanted cards that had been discarded. It was a perfect game! Never in any of our lives have we ever had a perfect game like this! We couldn't believe it. I wonder if we could get into Guinness book of Records? We had never picked a card from the deck, we had never discarded a card that the other didn't want, and we came out of that perfect game, putting the extra card on an empty area, where there had never been an unused card. Who ever heard of anything like this!

About nine o'clock Jenna called home, to see if their folks should come and get them. I talked to Larry.

"Do you want to come and get them?" We usually took them home, but I thought he might want to come over for awhile.

"Yes," he said slowly. "Do you want to go over to Grandma's and get Devon and Jenna?" I heard him ask Joshua. I had forgotten Joshua had his license now, and when there was a car freed up in their household, he was allowed to use it sometimes.

Joshua came wandering in, and tried to collect the younger ones, who were reluctant to leave. Finally, after collecting health bars to take home, picking themselves up and getting out the door after a smack or two of love from grandma they all left. Such a nice group of kids! We had a wonderful time.

Joshua stands straight with shoulders back. He is unmindful of the zits gathering on his face. He has more hobbies than anyone I know. He wants to get involved in everything. This is good! As he grows older he will be able to sort out his wants and wishes to better advantage and become a well adjusted young man. He is starting second year of high school with good grades behind him. He has a lot of great friends both his age and older. He has a good rapport with people and is an even keeled, kind and just person with a lot on the ball. He will be able to do anything he wants to do in life. Keep your mind on high, Joshua, you will make it to the top!

Devon is a beautiful gorgeous light blue eyed young man with blonde hair which is kept in a contemporary cut. He is wiry and strong.

Devon is slow and easy going, but with a strong desire to please, a good worker if you can get him started. He has strong likes and dislikes and complete dislikes. He knows what he wants and what he doesn't want. He is beginning to pick up his room which was always utter chaos.

He looks like an angel walking down the aisle in church, as an acolyte, to light the candles. When he sits beside me in church he sometimes likes to hold my diamond ring up to his beautiful eye and see the sparkles. I know my diamond does not sparkle near as greatly as his eyes.

Last night ten of us went to The Red Lobster in Fort Myers to have a birthday dinner for Larry who is forty-six May 28, 1993.

We had to go before or after Joshua's band concert in North Fort Myers High School where he is finishing his freshman year. We opted to go after the concert. The concert was beautifully done. His music teacher gets top performances out of his students.

Larry, Judy, Joshua, Devon, Jenna, Jacob, the exchange student from Germany, Judy's nephew and his girl friend from Bermuda, Michael and Janine, and George and I were seated at a ten-foot table where we proceeded to have a fabulous dinner.

Of course we all had ordered our favorite dinners.

Michael who says he can't get good shrimp in Bermuda ordered a shrimp cocktail, a shrimp salad and a shrimp dinner. The desert was a chocolate layer cake with a candle on it for Larry.

THEN AND NOW

This morning fairly early Michael, none the worse for his shrimp dinner, Joshua and Devon were over to go out fishing in the John boat Larry keeps over here at our dock which is on a canal which goes out to the Caloosahatchee, name of which means Calusa River for the Calusa Indians former residents of this area. I sent them off with a large baggie with zipped lock top full of watermelon pieces.

"Get me a snook!" I said. Snook is a protected fish that can be fished this time of year. It is said to be the best fish there is but we have never tasted it!

"Never go to bed without saying I'm sorry, if you have had an argument or disagreement with your husband." I have followed that throughout my life. Many are the nighttimes I've said, "I'm, sorry." I never say I'm wrong. It works!

Jenna and Robert were over two days after Memorial Day and they helped George severely prune some of our overgrown plants, banana plants and philodendron. (Robert was the German exchange student living with Larry and Judy for a year.) The banana leaves are up to six feet long and get split and unsightly and brown in the sun and wind and require pruning to control their size.

The Century Plant is green with a white edge, with long graceful bending shafts about 4 feet long and 8 inches wide, and long sharp barbs on the ends, with sharp spines along the edges. We had brought one plant up from Casa Masbu in Naples when we moved here in Yacht Club Colony in North Fort Myers. Century Plants grow pups through underground root systems, and one day will produce a large white blossom high in the air and then die. Our mother plant is at least 15 years old and hasn't bloomed yet. It just gets bigger and bigger.

Robert used George's ten foot, long handled pruning saw with a ten-inch blade one and half inch wide to cut the shafts from the mother plant Robert held the shafts while George used a small pruning saw to cut them into shorter, more manageable pieces, which were put into plastic bags for the lawn trash pickup.

Jenna raked and picked up the long banana leaves and piled on the wheelbarrow ready for bagging. She raked and swept and bagged the Silk Oak leaves covering the dock and sidewalk. With all the yard trimmings and litter we had thirteen bags.

Two days later, Joshua and Robert came over to help again. Joshua did a bang up job of mowing and trimming the whole lawn while Robert cleaned out all the lead troughs and down spouts which were so full of leaves and debris and stopped up, water was overflowing during the rains.

We had Tombstone Pizza, frozen melon balls, and sliced peaches for lunch. It was hot, the temperature being in the 90's and very humid. Everybody was ready to break for lunch and get something cold.

As long as we have wonderful grandchildren, and a willing German exchange student, we will be very happy.

We stopped early for everybody to get baths, eat more candy and ice cream bars, and get dressed up for Devon's eighth grade graduation ceremonies.

Joshua went to the Civic Center to play in his school band for the graduation exercises for the North Fort Myers High School.

The rest of us would be attending Devon's graduation at the Lee County Exhibition Hall.

George and I picked up Devon at his house to take him to his graduation ceremonies as Larry and Judy were arriving late.

"Who's this handsome guy?" I asked, as he got in the back seat of the car.

"I'm not handsome!" he said.

Yes, you are! You look great!" He is such a beautiful boy with his gorgeous blue eyes and golden hair cut in the latest style.

Jenna ran out before we pulled out.

"I'm going with you!" Jenna cried.

After arriving at the hall, Jenna, George and I sat in the chairs, saving three chairs for Larry, Judy, and Robert, our German Exchange Student.

"You look nice Robert!" I said, as he had told me that afternoon he didn't want to go because of his suit. "Judy always makes me wear it, but I hate it! The coat is too short, and the pants legs are too wide."

But he looked fine to me.

"Judy are you a leopard?" I asked her.

She mumbled something about having trouble getting into her leopard dress.

"You look great!" I said. Her waist line was drawn in so tightly that she looked fantastic. She has a beautiful body, but lately is eating too many sweets, she thinks. Wish I had a body like hers!

Larry looked handsome in his suit as usual, and Jenna had on her Easter dress and locket.

The main speaker told the 170 graduating students to try to be true to themselves and not follow the crowd. He said they can do anything they try to do.

All the young ladies and young men were dressed in gorgeous, mostly dark clothes, many of the girls in formals and the boys in tuxedos. We left Devon, having fun with all his friends. Later, he went to an after graduation dance also held at the same hall.

The next day after Devon's graduation the school was scheduled for renovation and remodeling.

"I love this house, more than any place in the world," Jenna said, the other day.

How pleased I was hearing her say this! I knew what she meant! I also loved my grandmother's house. It was a haven.

"Why do you say that, Sweetie?" I asked her as we sat watching TV.

"I don't know." She thought long and hard. Then, "I guess it's because there aren't any brothers here to fight with me!"

'Would you ever move from here?" she then asked.

Again, I knew what she meant! She would be lost, knowing she could not come here, to get away, to just be quiet and relax sometimes. I thought for a moment.

"Yes," I finally said, then went on quickly to a stunned little girl. "If we could find a larger place that I loved, I might. But it would have to be bigger and better than this."

We looked at one another, thinking our own thoughts. What could be better than this, I'm sure we both were thinking. She loves this big beautiful home with its large rooms where the children have turned handsprings, played ball, etc.

I knew how she felt! Had not I felt the same way with my grandmother's lovely old home in Ridgefarm, Illinois? There is a bond between grandchildren and grandparents, and between parents and children. I remember going back to the farm when Mother was not there. It wasn't the same. I loved the old farm house; but without Mother there, it just wasn't the same. It isn't the house that makes a place a home, it is the people in it. Wherever the people are that you love, is home. That's the place you want to be.

This is stabilization to my grandchildren. This is the only Grandma's and Grandpa's house they've known. I know they love it as much as we do. I guess we better stay here, if only for them!

Jenna was lying with her head in my lap, as we sat in the back seat of the car going towards home after a shopping spree.

"Grandma," she said, raising her hands to my face. "I'm not going to read your book."

"Why not!" I expostulated. "I'm writing it for you!"

"Well, it's going to be this big!" she said, as she held her two hands up in the air about twenty inches apart.

"That's my girl! You better read it, young lady! It is for you and your siblings, and all my relatives, all of whom I love dearly and want to know of their ancestry." I told her.

My dad used to tell wonderful tales of his former relatives, but I didn't listen enough to remember. I loved them at the time. I hung on every word, but they have gone from my memory. I wish he and Mother and my Grandpa and Grandma had written their life's history all down in a book. I would get it out ever so often and read.

What pleasure! What information, what delightful stories I would be reading now. And so I leave my legacy to you, Dear little Jenna, and to your siblings and relatives to garner the essence of living we all had. I pray that each and everyone of you will enjoy my book and it won't be twenty inches wide! I promise!

One day Jenna told me about talking to her father about right and wrong.

"You've been around your grandmother too long!!" she said he told her.

Jenna isn't perfect, but she's about as perfect as they come. She's definitely a keeper! We'll not throw her back!

She's a delight, adorable, and a little wacky. At ten years of age, she's about as wonderful as anyone. She's definitely my kind of girl!

THEN AND NOW

As Jenna grew from a toddler when she would come to visit, she always liked to sit in my lounge chair with me. There was just enough room for her to sit at my side. For years, and as she grew older, the space became smaller and smaller until she could no longer fit there. We were jammed in like sardines. "Somebody is getting too big!" I said.

"It's you, grandma!" Jenna retorted.

"No, it's you!" I said, laughing.

There came a day when we could no longer sit in my lounge chair together. I wish I could take off weight, but such is not the case. With less exercise and a hearty appetite, my hips don't get any smaller. Also, Jenna is growing up, and we can't stop her from growing.

Jenna unwound her long-limbed legs from her grandpa's big lounge chair and straightened up as she walked across the floor. She looked so grown up. The little sweet-faced blonde doll was growing up. She is now only ten years old going on eighteen.

She loves to lollygag all over the place, be it my king-sized bed or Grandpa's huge lounge chair, as if she is a rag doll. But when she extricates her bod from her lounging curling ball, she becomes a beautiful gorgeous young lady. One never knows whether she will be the little girl or the gorgeous delightful young lady.

The following is an adorable little essay written by Jenna when she was in 8th grade.

Soccer Field
by Jennifer Massing

The soccer fields at Bayshore Elementary are big and there are four of them. Some are being made on someone's yard because he said we could.

I've been playing soccer since I was one year old. I know you might think that you can't be on a soccer team that young, and you are right, but my family had a special team. We played against each other, my youngest brother, Devon, was on my team and my oldest brother Josh, switched sides to be the goalie on both sides at different times. Devon and I were against my Mom and Dad.

Whenever I got the ball I would go through my mom and dad's legs and when I got to the goal Josh would say, "Watch out she's got a strong kick," and he'd move out of the way and I would score. At other times my mom would come after me and I would fall over the ball and cover it so no one could get it. Then my mom and dad would tickle me and that didn't work sometimes so they picked me up and I would still have the ball in my hands.

Then my mom would say, "Get her favorite baby doll, from when she was born." When my dad came out with it I knew I shouldn't look because it would catch my attention, so my dad would get a blanket and put it on the ground and he would put my baby doll on it. Then I would drop the ball and crawl over by my baby doll, but when my mom kicked the soccer ball by me it would catch my attention and it would start all over again.

I keep thinking of writing but I can't seem to get started. Who is going to read this? George just read the former day I wrote which we both found very interesting. It brought back the memories.

I am writing today as I sit at the desk with which we started Ted's Sheds in 1977 or maybe it was bought when we came to Charlotte County, first to Punta Gorda, then to Charlotte Harbor and now to Port Charlotte which is really Murdock. It is close to Port Charlotte and is operated as Ted's Sheds of Charlotte County. Larry found this area and it is the best place we've ever been. Larry is staying home today and yesterday as Judy's Aunt Marguerite and Uncle Chick from Orlando were here for the Fourth. George worked yesterday and today. I came up today, as I like to do, as he works only a half day on Saturday then we go to eat out and a show.

When George stopped at Larry and Judy's house at night after work as he usually does as he has papers to drop off he found a strange predicament. I thought it worthy to write down for future readers.

Judy was in the yard really going to it which Judy doesn't often do with Jenna who was cowering and blubbering in front of her. When George could get it out, he found that Jenna had picked five grapefruit off their small grapefruit tree we gave them a few years ago and said when Judy asked her why she did it that she wanted to take a grapefruit to Daddy. She wanted Daddy to have a grapefruit each morning for breakfast. Daddy, by the way, is the only one who eats the grapefruit. The grapefruit are green now and small as an orange as they will not be ripe and ready until November.

As Judy and George went through the living room Judy whispered that Marguerite and Chick were leaving. As they went into the kitchen

THEN AND NOW

the two were packing their car refrigerator (Marguerite always brings great food when she comes down). Judy had told George that they had all gone somewhere except Chick who wanted to stay home. But when they got home they found him encased in a picture frame. The glass had broken all over him. The picture itself was safe, undamaged. He had to tell them a picture (one of my hand painted pictures done by my Aunt Florence), had fallen off the wall and he couldn't get the frame off his head. It was tight around his neck! Well, I laughed so hard when George told me about it I thought it's a good thing I wasn't there.

Chick insisted on going home right away.

George asked, "Where is Larry?" He was in the front room (George had passed him but had not seen him). He was sitting near the mantel piece with his mail in his lap. When George went through there to leave Larry gave him a weak smile - probably wanted to laugh.

There are so many great movies today we don't know which one to see. So, I guess we will have to cut it to two movies and eat in between. "Robinhood" is first choice, then an R rated Julia Roberts show, "Dying Young." In a way I don't want to see it as it is about a young man who has cancer, but I think the character has a wonderful life with Julia after he is ill. Monte didn't have such a wonderful life after he became ill. I know I will cry all the way through it. I sure hope Sharon goes to see it. Maybe she will cry too.

Joshua and Devon are at Horse Camp together. Two other boys from our church, as well as boys from other churches, have gone for a week to ride and care for horses. They got new boots and washed out jeans and new long sleeved shirts (to wear in the sun). Joshua wore a denim shirt of Larry's. It looked great on him. Way too big, but that's the style and it will be cooler. It's been in the 90's all week but it has rained every day sometimes most of the day and that keeps the temperature down.

Jenna has been going to a County Summer School Camp. Devon has been going too. They love it! Joshua will be going to a soccer camp in Orlando.

Yesterday, 26 June 1993, George and I parked the car at the shopping center, North Fort Myers, and proceeded to go to Publix our best grocery in the area.

"Let's go in the hardware first," George said. "I want to get some steeples."

"What are steeples?" I asked. I thought of steeples on top of churches.

"Steeples!" George said a little crossly. "I want to hang those new bromeliads we just got at our meeting Sunday. I need steeples to put them on the tree."

We entered the hardware store and walked real fast between the aisles going to find the steeples.

"Can I help you?" We heard a woman on our left which slowed us down as we tried to see past the shelves and bins between us in the aisles.

"Let me help you," a man came running from our right.

Where had he come from? He must have been beside the entrance door putting up stock when we came rushing through the door.

"What do you want?" he asked.

"Steeples," George said. "I want steeples."

"Steeples the man asked in surprise? I don't have steeples. I don't know what steeples are. What do you want to do with them?"

"I use them to attach bromeliads in our trees," George said.

"Oh, you mean staples!" the man said.

"No, I mean steeples. My dad used them all the time on the farm. He definitely called them steeples. He fastened barbed wire to fence posts with them," George insisted.

The two men went down the aisle and turned to the next aisle. At the far end were rows of boxes full of little things. One box was holding big staples.

George stared at the side of the box at the label with his hands in the box fishing out staples.

"Staples," he said quietly. "These are what I want and they are called staples, I'm sure Dad always called them steeples.

Dad lived on the farm when George was one through seven. I am sure George has used "staples" before. But George is a very stubborn Dutchman, as we call him sometimes. He knows what he knows for sure!

"Maybe that's what your father did call them," the clerk was kind enough to say! "In different parts of the country people call things different words."

Like my Dad who would run into the house when the threshing machine had broken down and yell at everyone in the house wherever they were, "I have to go to Purie!" So we rushed around and hurriedly got ready and jumped in the car so we could go to Peoria, Illinois, to get the broken parts replaced. And sometimes Dad had to go to Terry Hut! I never knew how to pronounce or spell Peoria, Illinois, or Terre Haute, Indiana, until I grew up.

Chapter 45
Going Home in 1993

George's cousin, Betty Parker Walsh, had a birthday June 12, 1993. Her daughters Karen and Jamie had been planning a surprise party on her for two years. George and I drove up from Florida from 100 degree, hot, humid weather to arrive at Aunt Dovie's home in Georgetown, Illinois, where we stay each year when we come north for a visit to our Illinois and Ohio relatives.

Yesterday, before we arrived at Aunt Dovie's, we drove up through Scotland past our farm where I and all my sisters and brothers lived for so many years. We went so slow in order to look at, and talk about the crops, the land, the buildings and the family.

A truck came barreling up behind us, and he started to go around us. The driver slammed on his brakes and yelled, "Are you looking for someone?"

Amazed, we laughed and told him who we were, at which time he said, "I recognize you! You did look familiar! I live just down the road." As we continued talking he said,"We have been having a lot of vandalism in the area."

Driving on, we turned at the Harrison schoolhouse corner, where all of us kids went through the eighth grade before we attended Ridgefarm High School, turned right instead of left towards Ridgefarm, and continued a mile down the road, where we turned in going down a long lane to my great grandfather Silas Milton Busby's former home.

The wild colorful flowers and flowing high grasses, were so beautiful where the lane curved into the drive towards the huge old barn.

The old homestead had been torn down years ago. I remembered when the house was at the end of the lane before the curve in the road took one to the barnyard and to the barn. The house was a tall, gray wooden building with square wooden columns at the front of the full length porch. As one entered in the center door there was an entrance hall which held a curving stairway to the upstairs. Downstairs on the main floor on the right was the kitchen and dining room and on the left was the parlor and living room. There were several bedrooms on the second floor, with a small steep stairway leading to the third level at the top of the house where there was a lookout for Indians.

George got out his camera and was taking pictures of the colorful meadows and barn, as I walked around enjoying it all.

I heard a horrible sound of a truck coming closer and closer, wildly furious sounding as if it were a wild animal mad at the world. It came across the plowed fields from the nearby farmhouse where my best friend, Jean Mills, used to live. I continued walking quietly and leaning over the yellow goldenrod and bluish pink clover, and other things I saw.

Since I cannot see very far I completely ignored the truck and its antics until it got closer. As I glanced up all of a sudden, the horrible sound stopped and the truck turned and quietly drove away leaving us alone to continue enjoying the wondrous feeling, smells and memories of days gone by. I guess he realized we were just enjoying the beauty about us.

This farm was bought by Loran "Spud" Spesard. He also bought Mother's farm after she passed away. Spud's grandson now farms the old family farmlands as Spud is retired from farming, living with his wife Freida, in Georgetown. They spend several winter months in Ruskin, Florida, a two hour drive from us.

We drove out of the lane feeling so good, and continued down another long county gravel road going north to another stop where we knew our ancestors had lived and died and knew one of George's great grandfathers is buried there. The Pilot Grove Cemetery was across the road where we stopped to visit the old burial grounds. We were hesitating as to where to park the car as we were at a crossroads, when we heard a commotion of feet pounding and scuffing running towards us. A young man had come out of the large farmhouse on the corner and stood staring at us belligerently.

"Hello," we said, quietly. "We are checking our ancestors in this graveyard."

He quieted down and became quite friendly as we talked of mutual friends and relatives.

Isn't it a shame that these young people have to guard their lands this way, instead of running out to meet us with open arms and happy smiles, the way we used to do when George and I were young and gay and full of life, for friendship and neighborliness.

The Pilot Grove Cemetery monuments were so old and vandalized that we were unable to find Robert Parker, Co G, 125th Illinois Infantry, Civil War Veteran, a great grandfather of George's, although DAR records indicate this is where he is buried. A rubbing of stones by DAR members showed what appeared to be Robert Parks in the cemetery listing. It is assumed by genealogist, Jackie Haworth, to be the grave of Robert Parker.

George and I continued on the back country roads to Danville, Illinois, the County Clerk's Office in the Vermilion County Courthouse, where we worked on the Lands our ancestors bought and sold. Between the Busby and the Jones families there are numerous transactions of land.

After lunch, we went to the Illiana Genealogical Society Library, where all books and materials have been taken from the Danville Public Library, and merged with their records and catalogued, for use by their membership and visitors in their research for their genealogies.

This Illiana Genealogical Society occupies the same area where Ginny Massing's father and mother, A. L. and Anne Ross. had a restaurant, The Duchess, and where Ginny herself sometimes worked.

THEN AND NOW

It was strange to sit there at the table, working on genealogy, knowing that many times we sat in the same spot, eating good chicken and noodles.

After spending a couple of hours there doing research on genealogy, we joined the Illiana Genealogical and Historical society.

Arriving at Aunt Dovie's in Georgetown, we had a wonderful swiss steak dinner, after which we settled down in the living room to visit. We usually stayed with Aunt Dovie while we visited Illinois family and friends, and toured the graveyards.

George carries a key chain with thirteen keys on it that open our house, our car, and our two offices. It is so heavy it weights him down but he insists on carrying all of them. When we arrived at Aunt Dovie's, she gave him two more keys, a key to her house and one to the garage, etc. George hauls all those keys everywhere we go. He attached them to his large set so now there is an even larger bulge in his pocket.

We suffered more with the heat and humidity this year than we had in our 100 degree temperature and high humidity we left behind in Florida. Aunt Dovie has an air conditioner which she does not use unless she thinks it absolutely necessary, so I sat around with a fan that went a mile a minute.

"Kay, are you hot?" Aunt Dovie asked.

"Aren't you? I answered. "I'm burning up."

"Well," Aunt Dovie said, "I'll turn on the air conditioner then. I didn't think it was too hot, myself."

We sweltered from the heat that year in the north. Perhaps it is because we always have air conditioning in the south which cools us down.

The surprise party on Betty was not a surprise, after all. Betty surmised that something was being done, as she usually does. From the time she was a child and continuing until now, she has always ferreted out her Christmas and birthday gifts, in the closets where they had been hid. But she was surprised when she saw us there. She had expected all her family that lived nearby and as far away as Louisville, but she had not expected George and me to come from as far away as Florida.

KATHRYN BUSBY MASSING

There was plentiful sumptuous food, beautiful delicious birthday cakes, and wonderful comradery among about forty relatives and friends.

It was a lovely day of celebration in a screened in pavilion at Forest Glenn Park, in Indiana, a few miles from Danville, Illinois.

On the way back to Aunt Dovie's after the party was over, we stopped to see Aunt Dovie's, Aunt Sudie's, and Mother Massing's half sister and husband, Shirley and Leon Korb. They have a quaint, sprawling country home just outside of Georgetown.

After we left Illinois, we made our usual trek to visit our grandsons, Shane and Seth, in Ohio before returning to Florida. We had to hurry home this year in order that Larry and Judy and family could go on their summer vacation to the Washington, D.C. area and so George could manage the Massing's Ted's Sheds business.

Chapter 46

Daytona Beach

After a super week in St. Augustine, we drove south on the fascinating A1A, the route that is closest to the Atlantic Ocean.

We came to Daytona Beach, which is one of my favorite beaches, not as quiet and serene as Sanibel Beach, but more alive and spirited than any other beach on which we've ever been. It is teeming with activities at the busiest times, but quieter on blustery days. Any day of the year is the ideal time to go to Daytona Beach. Some days, one can drive along the shore in rain or in fog with few people in sight. Sometimes, the people on the shore are huddling against the blustery wind, and from the white caps billowing high and rumbling towards shore. But the beach is overcrowded on hot, humid days, more than other days, as everyone is anxious to get cooled off. Today was a hot, humid day.

We drove down the crowded Daytona Beach in our car, stopping to take pictures of the activities. There were lots of interesting sights. Most of the three wheel bikes, and two wheeled scooters lay inactive, a sight which made great pictures. We came to a quiet area and parked our car, took out our chairs and placed them on the beach, then I went into the water, which was fabulous. Daytona Beach is the best beach in the world. Everyone should go there at least once.

The ocean was too rough for me today, so we sat in our chairs with the sun to our backs, and we watched the huge, splendid waves billowing up and crashing down to a ripple, spreading out as they came up on the wide, wide beach.

The few people who were brave enough to venture out into the breakers were soon hurled back to the flat, watery shore.

I spit and it came right hack and landed on my tongue. I was one surprised woman!

"Whoever heard of such a thing?" George asked. "That's what you get for spitting into the wind!"

As I leaned back in my chair and sat quietly for awhile, I felt a strong presence of God. My mind wandered to Monte, and I was soon crying. Why did he have to die? He had had a rough time in his life, and then his life was just beginning to open up and become exciting. My poor baby! I loved him so much. If only I could have gone to heaven instead of him. But we never know how life will turn, and all I have of my darling Monte are memories and some mementos. It has to be enough for now.

The myriad of beach goers was striking and fascinating, as we drove along the beach again. Fast motor bikes and scooters, each with 2 or 3 riders, were rushing past us with streaks of colorful clothing flying in the wind, the delighted young riders holding on tightly as though they were one entity.

When we left the beach, we were starved, and we decided to look for a restaurant. There had been a great dining room, where we had eaten several years before. As we traveled towards New Smyrna Beach. where we thought it might be, we discussed the area, and thinking we had to go further south, we decided to cross the Intercostal Waterway at the first crossover, just in case it was there. We expected to have to cross back over to Route AlA and travel further south to the next crossover. But, there it was, Aunt Catfish's Restaurant!

It was a little different, as they had remodeled since we had been there. We couldn't find the front door! There was a long porch with several blue doors all alike. We tried to enter some, finding them to be stationary. We then saw the menu on the outside, and stopped to read it.

"Are you looking for the way in," a man asked holding one door open from within.

When we were seated, a big buxom German woman came over to serve us. She was ample all over, and never smiled, but had a cheery voice. She took us into the next room to an old fashioned, black, hot, iron stove on which were stewed apples, grits and cheese, and baked beans. We then moved to the salad bar where there was everything imaginable, where we loaded up and ate and ate.

We were full when our main course was brought hot from the kitchen. George had fried catfish and I had ordered a half a chicken baked in a cranberry and fruit sauce with more on the side. George found he could eat all his dinner but half the fish, but I had hardly begun my huge plate of food when I was full. The huge baked potato needed salt which we don't use anymore so I tried putting pepper on it as I do sometimes. The pepper would not come out then I noticed it was almost empty and had very large holes.

"Would you help me George? I'll probably get too much pepper on," I said, giving him the shaker.

"You just do it like this," he said, and turned the container almost upside down. With one shake, he had poured out about a teaspoon full on my potato. We gasped!

"I could have done that!" I said. It was hot! It was fully ground large pepper, and hot! That was the end of the potato eating.

"Look, George! I like this," I said, "Our plates revolve!" I turned it for the potato to be on the upper side and the chicken in front of me, the proper way to be served. I whipped it around again. It was marvelous! "We've never been served a meal on a lazy Susan before." George was nonplused as he tried to revolve his plate. Then he looked closer at mine.

"It's not on a lazy Susan it's just the way she sat it down on the plastic place mat." We laughed so hard as I turned my plate around and around. I wonder why they don't serve big meals on a lazy Susan? It sure would be easier to eat!

After I had eaten all I could, I asked the big, buxom beauty, if she could bring me a box to take the rest of the food home.

"You want a bag?" she asked, staring at me unsmiling.

"Yes, that would be all right," I said as I stared back at her.

All the time, looking at me, she slowly put her hand on her ample breast, and pushed her two first fingers in between her apron top and her dress and started to pull out something. As she did it very ceremoniously and slowly, she continued to lock eyes with me. She tugged and pulled until presto, she popped out a little bag from her bosom.

"Oh, that's why you are way out there in front!" I exclaimed.

"Do you want another?" she asked, half smiling as we were laughing so hard. She looked at my full plate when I said "We probably do." She then pulled and tugged from her left side of her bosom, extracting another baggie.

"I'm just full of bags," she said as she could see we got a big kick out of her.

Chapter 47
Washington D. C. and Philadelphia
By George C. Massing
Washington D. C. and Environs

The Travel Ministry of First United Methodist Church spring tour for 1991 was a long planned trip to Washington, D. C. and environs. It was led by our very capable tour guides Dr. and Mrs. A. Waldo Farabee (Marion). The trip was scheduled for April 16-24, 1991.

We departed Southwest Florida Regional Airport, on April 16 and flew to National Airport Washington, D. C.

Upon arrival we immediately boarded a tour bus and proceeded to the Vietnam Veteran's Memorial where we walked the length, searching the names and noting in awe the flowers, mementoes, letters and all sorts of things left for lost loved ones and friends. At one point a beautiful reflection of the distant Washington Monument reaching skyward into the fluffy clouds is very apparent. The Vietnam Monument gave us a first hand glimpse of the magnitude of the great losses in that conflict.

Someone was kind enough to take our picture in front of the reflecting pool with the magnificent Washington Monument in the background. We easily fit the description of a couple of happy tourists.

It was a happy sight to visit the monument of Honest Abe. The great marble structure consists of thirty-six columns with a likeness of Mr. Lincoln perched upon an armchair in the center of it all. The Gettysburg Address and the Second Inaugural Address are carved on the walls. Across the way is the Arlington Memorial Bridge, the approach to the Arlington National Cemetery.

Across the Tidal Basin we visited the Thomas Jefferson Memorial. It's a huge dome surrounded with Greek columns. It houses a large bronze statue of Thomas Jefferson, visible from many angles through the columns. Panels surround his statue containing inscriptions of Jefferson's writings.

We descended to the Tidal Basin via a marvelous wide set of stairs, where a young woman, who was studying photography in college, approached us. She thought we would make a good picture for one of her projects for photography class.

After an exchange of a few moments finding out about her and relating òur family's interest in photography, we agreed to pose for her. She took several shots of us with the Memorial as a background. We were surrounded with other visitors and members of our party.

We boarded our tour bus and headed for Vienna, VA. Wolf Trap Hotel, which would be our home for the next eight nights.

On our second day we visited Hanes Point, or East Potomac Park, on a peninsula created by Washington Channel, where we viewed a most interesting sight. An immense sculpture of bronze was imbedded in the earth, entitled, "The Awakening," created by artist J. Seward Johnson, Jr. and installed in 1980 as part of a citywide sculpture show. It is a half-buried giant figure of a man breaking through the earth. At one point is his left hand, barely protruding, opened as if to grasp something. Then his head and right shoulder appear with his arm extended, with and object clutched in his hand raised heavenward. At another point are his leg and knee partially protruding. Waldo and Marion posed for a picture with the giant protruding hand. Some of the more than 1200 cherry trees in this park were in full bloom and were much photographed by me, and Lois Brown.

We had a guided tour of the U. S. State Department and Diplomatic Reception Rooms with its elegant furnishings and formal rooms with deep carpeting, and immense decorative chandeliers everywhere, for

THEN AND NOW

entertainment of foreign diplomats and other heads of state. Beautiful fresh bouquets of flowers were everywhere. Cabinets lined the walls displaying very old and precious silver keepsakes of years gone by.

At the Library of Congress a guided tour and film covered the highlights of this magnificent library. We saw a beautiful display of fine paintings, sculpture, mosaics, and murals. It houses millions of volumes of books, manuscripts and myriads of other records. It has genealogical records and reading room. I took a picture of the Gutenberg Bible on display. Many of the presidents have their papers on file here. We lunched in their sixth floor café.

We received a guided tour, an excellent IMAX film, on a five-story screen and then roamed about looking at all the marvelous displays at the National Air and Space Museum. Tom Crouch, from Crystal Lakes, Ohio, our former home, a good friend of our son Larry's, is the Curator of the museum. They also were together in Scoutmaster Harry Stuck's Boy Scout troop 27, Crystal Lakes, Ohio. The first thing we saw during the walking tour was the Wright Brother's plane they flew at Kittyhawk. Charles Lindberg's "Spirit of St. Louis" was also nearby. We saw Air Force drones, experimental aircraft, space capsules, and the early Ford tri-motor in which the U. S. mail was flown. The museum covers a complete history of flight, from the earliest to the latest in air and space travel. There is a large exhibit of paintings done to portray planes and pilots in actual combat during our wars.

We spent and hour at The Methodist Building where we relaxed and sat in pews for a very interesting talk by a young black man. We about filled up the small chapel. We all congregated on the walk in front of the building and discussed the everyday life of the police in Washington, D. C. with a very young police officer patrolling by bike.

Union Station is an immense building with beautiful columns at the entrance reaching for the sky. The interior has a huge vaulted tunnel like dome constructed of framed glass panels emitting the light of day. Other parts of the dome are made up of round golden skylights. The whole roof structure seems to be supported by great columns. One room is a complete atrium with palms and other fabulous semi-tropical plants. We ascended to the Mezzanine where we had a very nice lunch for our whole group. After lunch we took an escalator to a very high point where we could look down upon the tracks and see the trains arriving and departing.

We visited The Supreme Court Building, where the Supreme Court Justices hold their deliberations of cases referred to the highest court in the land, for a final decision. We were shown a film explaining the functions of the court. A guided tour allowed us to see first hand the surroundings where the justices ply their craft. We were allowed some time in the gift shop to buy mementos.

At the National Gallery of Art we had a guided tour and visited their gift shop. We saw paintings and sculpture from the thirteenth century Europe to present day America. It covered all the media of art. Examples of works by many of the great masters were on display.

For a half hour we toured Georgetown, seeing where many socialites live as well as other less prominent, with many quaint and elegant shops. There is a rich assortment of restored townhouses.

We proceeded to one of these beautiful townhouses, where Ambassador and Mrs. Daniel J. Terra resided. Mrs. Terra, Judy, is the daughter of Dr. and Mrs. A. Waldo Farabee, our tour hosts. Their daughter and husband had invited the whole tour bus to high tea. Their three-story home was elegantly furnished throughout, the beautiful living room including a grand piano. We were all invited to roam freely. The Ambassador and Judy were gracious hosts. They had a most wonderful collection of art objects. Mr. Terra was the Ambassador for Art under President Reagan.

The lovely High Tea consisted of a very sumptuous, large table of elegant sandwiches, cheeses, fruits, cookies and cakes. The tea was served by some of Judy's many lovely lady friends from the Washington, D. C. scene. Following the Tea, we all gathered in the central area of the home to listen to Ambassador Terra, who gave an excellent talk on his art and cultural activities, here and abroad.

At the U. S. Capitol none other than Senator Porter Goss greeted us and hosted our tour throughout our magnificent center of government. He took us throughout the Capitol, visiting Congressional chambers, and allowing us a peek in on a Senate session. Following our tour he assembled all of us on the Capitol steps for a group photograph, and a farewell speech.

On the way to The Kennedy Center for the Performing Arts we passed Watergate, President Richard Nixon's nemesis, which was pointed out to us by Rev. Farabee with some appropriate remarks. We toured the Kennedy Center, with its beautiful chandeliers, objects of art everywhere, and the suite of The President of the United States. We had lunch at the center.

In the afternoon we toured the National Museum of Natural History, a part of the Smithsonian Institution, where we saw some of our favorite characters, the beautiful penguins. There were exhibits of wildlife from all parts of our nation, such as the majestic moose, lesser deer, the Elk, bison, and displays depicting early man. There was a magnificent full size African elephant in the rotunda, complete with his huge ivory tusks. On display also was a beautiful gem collection, which included the Hope diamond.

To finish this day we had dinner at an elegant restaurant, we then returned to the Kennedy Center where we had toured in the morning, for a fabulous concert by the National Symphony Orchestra, rounding out a full day.

Our visit to the National Arboretum was very interesting as well as rewarding in seeing so many beautiful plants of all types and varieties, actually horticultural wonders, well planned for the best possible display to the best advantage. The bonsai display was very beautiful, with well-formed, graceful, unusual plants, many of which were in full bloom. Of particular note were specimens of pines and firs. We toured the grounds where the azaleas were also in full bloom, as were many trees responding to April showers, such as dogwoods, redbud, and fruit trees.

We spent two hours touring the National Zoological Park, first having our lunch along side our bus at the concession stand. There was the usual display of animals, but the two giant Pandas, of Chinese origin, were special. Of note, there was a two-hump dromedary, humongous hippos, and a beautiful tree with all kinds of animals and children carved from its trunk and branches.

Arlington National Cemetery, across the Potomac from Washington, D. C., was an impressive sight with its row upon row of our fallen countrymen marked by white head stones. We sat on bleachers to view the endless marching of the guards at the tomb of the Unknown Soldier and the changing of the guard ceremony. Although the original soldier was from World War I, remains of a soldier from World War II, the Korean War and remains of a service man from the Vietnam War are interred there. We viewed the grave of President John F. Kennedy, marked with the eternal flame. It covers a considerable area and contains large irregular shaped stones imbedded in the grass. On a large bronze tablet, also imbedded, are parts of his inaugural address. His brother Sen. Robert F. Kennedy lies nearby.

Our last stop for this day was at the Iwo Jima Statue. We all took photographs of this famous memorial commemorating that erection of the American flag at the summit of the mountain our Marines stormed during fierce fighting with the Japanese. There were enormous casualties on both sides before our valiant Marines were victorious.

On Sunday we attended church services at Foundry United Methodist Church. Worship services were conducted by Dr. Ed Bauman, Senior Minister.

Immediately following the services we left for Lovely Lane Chapel, American Methodism's birthplace, where we received a guided tour of the chapel and museum. The building is of stone with a tall bell tower. We were seated in the chapel where we were told of some of the rich history of our Methodist church. A beautiful recital was given us on the wonderful old chapel organ, by our speaker. We then proceeded with the rest of our tour. We were shown where many of the early meetings took place where Francis Asbury was elected Superintendent of Methodists in America. There were pictures and other memorabilia of the time.

Old Otterbein Church was our next stop being the historic church of the former Evangelical United Brethern, which merged with the Methodist Church in 1968, becoming The United Methodist Church. Lovely Lane Chapel, "Mother Church of American Methodism" organized on this site in 1779.

We had dinner at Inner Harbor before returning to Wolf Trap Motel for the night.

On the following day, Mon April 22, we spent six hours on a guided tour of Williamsburg, V. A. I took lots of pictures of horse drawn carts on the streets and shopkeepers in their shops. We ate lunch and snacks at various little wayside shops and Inns. We visited a shop of handmade pottery and baskets. We walked the streets among people in the garb of yesteryear, all looking very authentic. We viewed several backyard gardens, one quite formal, then a nearby apothecary shop. We came upon the governor's mansion, quite an outstanding piece of architecture for the day. We saw a blacksmith at his forge. There was a nearby encampment of early militiamen in neat rows of tents, and we were given a demonstration of the firing of the cap and ball rifle in use at the time. The final demonstration was a fife and drum corps performing for us, and the firing of a cannon.

The ship, the "Spirit of MT. Vernon," took us on a cruise down the Potomac, past Hanes Point, with the sculpture "The Awakening," protruding from the ground. Passing the home of George Washington, Mount Vernon, high on the hill, was a beautiful sight nestled amidst the trees on the grounds in a gorgeous setting. We docked and went ashore up a winding path passing beautiful wisteria growing wild on the hillside. The path led us through the marvelous old trees to the circle drive before the entrance to the house. We toured the mansion, each room perfectly preserved and picturesque. The dining room table was set as if to expect the family to be ready for dinner. Everything was as if the family was still in residence. After we toured the house we spent some time on the veranda, where the view of the Potomac was spectacular. We toured the grounds, the stables and slave quarters.

During that afternoon we toured The Washington National Cathedral, what an impressive sight! The towers, the architecture inside and out are magnificent. Our group sat together in the pews. The alter, the pulpit were beautiful beyond description except for seeing for one's self.

This evening we celebrated Dorothy Thompson's birthday with a party, down the street from our motel, complete with a cake and candles. She and her husband Burton have been longtime members of our Sunday school class, the Welcome Class.

On the final morning the day of our departure we did get to take a short tour of the White House. We entered through security at a side visitors entrance. We saw parts of the ground and first floors including the state dining room and the east rooms. We actually didn't see much of the White House.

We flew home in the early afternoon, from a very eventful trip! In review we could not see how we covered so many wonderful sights in the allotted time. "Everything went like clockwork." Our tour hosts, Dr. Waldo and Marion Farabee are to be commended for a job well done!

Birthplace of a Nation Tour

Philadelphia Area

On April 28, 1991, we departed Fort Myers non-stop for Philadelphia International Airport for a nine day tour of Philadelphia and the surrounding area led by tour hosts Dr. and Mrs. A. Waldo Farabee (Marion).

Our first stop was at the Franklin Mint Museum where we saw fine collectibles created by the Franklin Mint such as antique cars, exquisite jewelry, metallic weathervanes of yesteryear, fine dolls, sculpture, items of bygone days, works of art, limited edition creations.

We were headed for the Brandywine Valley and on the way we stopped off at Chadds Ford Inn for lunch. It was in a beautiful rustic house of stone, which was the home of the original owner and builder, Francis Chadsey, a Quaker from Wiltshire England, who purchased his land from William Penn's commissioner for land grants. Many famous people have passed through here, including Martha Washington on the way to join her husband at Valley Forge. On the walls are works of art by three generations of the Wyeth family.

The Brandywine River Museum is located in Chadds Ford, Pennsylvania on the banks of Brandywine River. It was a Civil War era grist mill that was converted into a fine museum of American art. Some of the outstanding artists are three generations of the Wyeth family, displaying fine collections of American illustration, still life and landscape painting. Outside along the river trail are wildflower gardens of plants native to the area.

Longwood Gardens are located at Kennet Square, Pennsylvania, thirty miles west of Philadelphia in Brandywine Valley. It was the former Country estate of the Pierre S. Du Pont family and consists of 1050 acres. The conservatory is immense with beautiful arrays of massed beds of colorful lupines, calla lilies and a solid white border of flowers with full heads like hydrangeas along the walkway.

We stepped outside to view a spectacular display of fountains performing to beautiful music. We then resumed our tour of the conservatory with a fine display of indoor rose gardens in full bloom. Then we visited the orchid house full of wonderful blooms. There were many more flowers too numerous to mention, many of them unknown to me. We visited the Pierre S Du Pont mansion on the grounds. It was a wonderful example of the well to do gentry. The grounds were covered with gardens, ponds, fountains, topiaries, walkways and floral displays requiring 65 gardeners to keep the gardens beautiful year around.

We visited the home and grounds of Green Hills Farm the 60 acre homestead of Pearl S. Buck viewing all her memorabilia and received a set of her book "The Good Earth" to commemorate her 100th birthday.

In Doylestown, Bucks county seat, we visited the former home of Henry Chapman Mercer. According to Waldo Farabee, our tour host, he was an eccentric historian, architect, anthropologist, archeologist and tile maker. We visited his home Fontahill resembling a Tudor castle that was designed and built to exhibit his collection of tiles and prints from around the world. His Mercer museum is a collection of 50000 objects of Early American Tools and other items that document the lives and tasks of early Americans prior to the industrial revolution. We viewed several floors of all sorts of tools and all kinds of relics from yesteryear.

After a visit to Peddlers Village, a considerable group of unique shops with merchandise from all over the world, we continued on to New Hope, quite a cosmopolitan village where artists hang out. We continued on and had quite a unique ride up the Delaware Canal on a mule drawn barge. Mules were hitched by a special harness to the bow of the barge and tread along a path on the bank to pull us along. The barge was apparently of the type used on the canal from about one hundred and fifty years ago.

We also attended a short service in the church, the birthplace of The Episcopal church in the United States. Benjamin Franklin,

KATHRYN BUSBY MASSING

George Washington and Betsy Ross also worshiped here. We rode past Betsy Ross's house where she sewed the first flag of the USA.

Several places we visited were Fairmount Park, Strawberry Mansion in the park, Rittenhouse Square, Washington Square, and the Norman Rockwell Museum. This museum was very unique in that it had on display the Norman Rockwell illustrations which we knew so well, often being displayed on the front cover of our most popular magazines.

We visited Lancaster County and saw all the very well kept Amish farms and all their quaint ways and their horse and buggy conveyances. Our best time was at an Amish Homestead occupied by an Amish family and still using horses and mules to till the soil and tend the crops. We had our lunch at a traditional Amish farm restaurant in the Pennsylvania Dutch tradition, being served family style.

Our afternoon this day was spent at Ephrata Cloister an early American communal society. Everything was in the most primitive as compared to our lifestyle of today illustrating the austere life these people lived in their faith to reach their religious goals.

Our stop at Bryn Athyn was where everyone was a member of the Swedenborogian faith, including a visit to their cathedral Glencairn, the home of the architect for the cathedral is a cultural center housing art and collectibles from around the world.

We visited Valley Forge National Historical Park, the 1777 and 1778 winter quarters of the Continental Army commanded by no other than Gen.George Washington himself. They suffered untold hardships here being poorly equipped and without adequate provisions. They threw up log huts for shelter from the riggers of the cruel winter. We saw replicas of these tiny huts. They sheltered from the elements but allowed the men little space for existence. Items required for the troops were just not available. They were not only very short on food but their uniforms were in rags. We can only imagine what it must have been like during that fierce winter with snow on the ground. We saw Gen. Washington's Headquarters; he fared a bit better than his troops.

My Revolutionary War ancestor, Guion McKee, served three years with Captain James Montgomery's Company, Colonels Mackay, Broadhead, and Bayard in the 8th Pennsylvania Regiment. This regiment is listed as being present at Valley Forge during that winter. No proof has been found that Guion McKee was there. The beautiful memorial at the entrance to the grounds lists a McKee, Hugh. We believe that since the regiment was there so also should be Guion.

We later visited the home of Mr. and Mrs Molesworth to share in their collection of memorabilia from years gone by, all sorts of antique musical instruments, a huge collection of dolls of every type imaginable, and an old movie theater. Every room was packed with all these collectibles, with every inch of space in use.

We took a historical tour of old downtown Philadelphia where we saw The Liberty Bell and were able to be within inches of it. Looking past the bell, we saw Independence Hall where we visited Congress Hall. We saw Benjamin Franklin's grave just inside the wrought iron fence at Christ Church Cemetery.

At Mill Grove, The Audubon Wildlife Sanctuary we saw first hand the results of his early renditions of wildlife as he observed it. He hunted, observed, and collected and did many of his sketches along the Perkiomen Creek and Schulykill River areas. We toured the farm and the rooms of his home where lots of mounted specimens were on display and many of his life like drawings and paintings of bird life as he observed it were on display.

Wharton Esherick's Museum Studio and Collection was a sight to behold. He created every object he needed to redo the old farmhouse and make it liveable and a place for him to work and create. To me the most remarkable object was his staircase leading in two different directions from a common support. It appears that a whole tree trunk or limb was used for the main support. The one selected was just right with a twist to give the final spiral effect. Each step was carved from a solid block then notched or morticed into the support, bolted and standing alone, only attached on the one end. The other stairs, to another level, was also free standing to a point, as it was attached on one end notched in the wall, the other supported by a freeform support with the lower step part of that support.

He was a carver, an artist, a craftsman. Everything in the house had his indescribable artistic touch. Even the exterior had the same definite design.

On Sunday May 6 we had our worship services at St. George's United Methodist Church following a guided tour of the historic church. It is the oldest Methodist Church in the U.S. used continuously for worship services.

We also visited Philadelphia Museum of Art, seeing the works of the early masters.

Rodin Museum, among the works of Auguste Rodin, the French sculptor, displayed his well known sculpture, The Thinker.

At Franklin Institute Science Museum we learned how science and technology are instrumental in our lives.

We had a guided tour through Gettysburg National Military Park outlining the movements of the battles seeing where gun positions were and viewing the row after row of monuments depicting what took place at the site.

At the Eisenhower national Historical Site we had free rein to rove about the farm viewing what life must have been like when occupied by the Eisenhowers. It is a neat, well kept farm, complete with windmill, reflecting the great pride and industry of the Eisenhowers. Inside all was set up as if the family still was in residence. Everywhere was an indication of waiting for foreign visitors and other notable people to arrive, all was in readiness.

We attended a performance of the Philly Pops, Peter Nero conductor, at the Academy of Music. It was a beautiful evening of a mixture of the best of music forms.

Our last day in the area we spent visiting DuPont homes in Delaware, namely Nemours, the 300 acre estate of Alfred I. duPont. We traveled through a winding road of woodlands to reach any signs of habitation. The mansion was furnished throughout with rare antiques dating back to the 15th century. We visited the extensive French gardens with all kinds of beautifuul specimens in full bloom.

The second duPont home visited was Winterthur Museum and Gardens. This wonderful museum, "Winterthur, houses Henry Francis duPont's collection of more than 89,000 examples of furniture, ceramics, textiles, metals, paintings and prints made or used in America between 1640 and 1840."

On our last evening in the Philadelphia area we had dinner at Mendenhall Inn, Mendenhall, Pennsylvania.

THEN AND NOW

Mendenhall is named for the Mildenhall brothers, Benjamin and John and a sister Mary, who emigrated from England in 1683 from Mildenhall, in Wiltshire. Mary did not stay but returned to England. Mildenhall was originally the family name which dates back to 1275, during the reign of Edward I. The Mendenhall Inn is situated on a part of 1000 acres purchased by Benjamin Mendenhall in 1703, from the heirs of William Penn. The Mendenhalls had a fine reputation as barn builders and constructed many barns in old Chester County and throughout Southeastern Pennsylvania. The large barn, which is yet a part of Mendenhall Inn, probably housed a mill for cutting and shaping lumber for barns. According to an old property plan the present lobby of the Inn was one of the original barn buildings; the lower floor of the mill is now the Main dining room, where the old beams are still intact. And in the mill room, on the second floor, practically all of the original framing can be seen. (The above is extracted in part from the Mendenhall Inn's menu which carries a "History of the Mendenhall Inn.")

My wife Kathryn Busby Massing, the author of this book, is a maternal Granddaughter, eight generations removed, of the above-mentioned John and Elizabeth Maris Mendenhall. We and our family visited the Inn many years ago. This time we returned with our Church Family, First United Methodist Church, Fort Myers, Florida, for dinner the final night of our nine day tour of Philadelphia and environs. Our tour group was shepherded into the upper level mill room, and what a lovely sight and evening we had. We were served baked stuffed flounder and the vegetables and desert of the day. The dining room was elegant, with candlelight and fresh flower arrangements for centerpieces on each table. The service was splendid and everyone enjoyed the evening, some saying it was a highlight of our trip.

We flew from Philadelphia direct to Fort Myers the following day.

Chapter 48
Edison Parade, Ridgefarm Reunion, Disney World and Church

Thomas A Edison first came to Fort Myers in 1885, coming back here to Fort Myers every winter until his death in 1931. Mr. Edison held over one thousand patents, more than anyone in history. His most notable, the light bulb, the Edison Phonograph and the first sound recording motion picture system. He was given the title of Wizard. It was in his hometown of Menlo Park New Jersey that the first commercially successful lamp was lighted in 1879. His inventions basically brought us into the beginning of the computer age. The Edison Festival of Lights Parade, held annually in Fort Myers, honors his memory.

In February 1994 at the time of the writing of this article a quarter million spectators were expected to line the 1.6 mile route of the 56th year of the parade. Champion performing bands and floats come from all over the United States to participate in this spectacular parade. Each band periodically sounds off and is "put through its paces," as well as many performing acts, during the march.

There has never been a rain during the parade, sometimes prior to the parade, and after, but never during the parade. It is the only night parade in the state of Florida. Every spectator was given two bags, one white bag for recyclables, one brown bag for garbage, etc.

THEN AND NOW

The finale takes place at Fort Myers High School stadium with a show.

During the Christmas season the Edison and Ford Estates are the center of attraction. Constant guided tours are made from the ticket office area through the estate grounds which are decorated with a Christmas theme and thousands of colorful lights. Among the colorful plants of the grounds are lighted groups of angels, reindeer, and all sorts of magic of Christmas. Constant Christmas music fills the air and choirs sing on schedules.

The two homes are lighted and decorated for Christmas and displayed in all their glory. Throngs of people pour past the lighted, decorated rooms. Everyone is taking pictures of the glorious sights.

The First Annual Ridgefarm High School, Ridgefarm, Illinois, graduates Alumni, who are in Florida, was held Sunday, January 16, 1994, at Emerald Pointe Clubhouse, 25188 Marion Avenue, Punta Gorda, Florida, 33950, from 1:00 to 6:00 P.M., hosted by the Brewer family of furniture store and mortuary descendants of Ridgefarm, Illinois. There were interesting stories of the life as a morticians family. One such story was the teller's showing off the caskets to her friends, at the end of which she crawled into the casket and settled down amongst the puffy pillows. Another story was the time she came home from school with a very important story that could not wait to be told. She ran into the room where they were working on a cadaver, preparing it for burial. She pulled up a stool nearby and watched the proceedings.

Ridgefarm has had a huge effect on the education, happiness and success on all of its graduates. Many continued on to secondary education, many getting their masters degree and doctorate degree. We all feel a strong sense of well being and pride for having lived in and near Ridgefarm, and being able to attend such a high caliber school.

There were about thirty present including spouses or friends of the Alumni.

A great time of reminiscing, recollection, and conversation of things of the past filled the room in little groups of re-acquaintances.

There was and air of joviality and fond memories without exception by all in attendance.

There was a buffet luncheon of ham, hot dishes, cold dishes, and desserts, after which each spoke of their lives in Ridgefarm and after.

One of the graduates alumni and her husband had a career in the army and had three different times of three years each in Germany. How could you be so lucky! That's what I wanted to do, remember? I found two unexpected cousins. My favorite aunt, Lois Busby, had a sister, Vera Hutchinson, who married a Wathal. Their son was there. Then a woman said her grandmother was Louisa Mendenhall. I became so excited! My great grandmother, Louisa Mendenhall, nicknamed Louizy, was the mother of my mother. Her grandmother had to be the namesake of my great grandmother, Louisa. It is exciting to meet your long lost cousins, even if it is on down the line many years later!

Jean Strubinger and I were talking.

"You lived north of us," I said. "Do you remember when you come down south to the Harrison School road? If you would turn left there, there was a tall house at the end of a long lane. That was my great grandfather's home."

"Oh, did she have seashells?" Jean asked me.

"My mother did," I said, surprised. She had in her mind turned right, then left again at Harrison School. I was talking about my great grandfather's house. You turn left on to the Harrison School road, and then the house is on the right after a short distance. But yes, my mother did live in the house you mean.

"It was a big white house," Jean said. "She had our class when I was going to Harrison School, come to see her seashells!"

What a small world! Mother had a whole room of shells, she and Dad had collected in Florida, some huge ones, some little teensy ones, some in groups. They were all in the bedroom downstairs to the right of the entrance. Mother had collected and gathered so many shells, she had cleared out the bedroom, and bought cabinets and a glass topped table, arranging her collection beautifully.

I remembered then of Mother telling me of the school children coming to see her collections. She was so knowledgeable about each and every one of them, displaying them perfectly.

It's a small world after all!

For years we bought Florida resident tickets for admission to Disney World called Three Season Salutes and a later version Four Season Salutes. This allowed us to visit all areas of Disney World, all year long, as many times as we cared to go. Epcot is great! It is our favorite. We love to go there.

My favorites at Epcot are, The Land and France. The singing before The American Show is absolutely fabulous. There are so many wonderful areas to go at Epcot!

We also enjoy MGM very much, and occasionally go to The Magic Kingdom, but it has so many baby strollers, it's hard to get around there sometimes. My favorite there is "It's a Small World" It also seems to be the favorite of all the baby stroller activity too, naturally, so the lines seem too long sometimes. It is an attraction for the wee children of all ages!

Our church affiliation has varied over the years with my maternal ancestors, mine beginning with the Anglican Church of England, one Grandfather, Rev. Thomas Grubb II, ten generations removed, a graduate of Oxford University, became Rector for 33 years, of the church at Cranfield, Bedfordshire, England. There is a plaque, which we saw on the wall of the church, that attests to this fact.

My Grandfather, John Mildenhall, (later Mendenhall), (eight generations removed), came to America in 1683 with William Penn, on his second voyage. He belonged to the Society of Friends (Quakers), his father Thomas having joined that movement before him. The Society of Friends was founded in England in about1652 by George Fox. The following generations were all Quakers, and I was raised a Quaker by my mother Georgia Mendenhall Busby. My father Milton Busby was a Presbyterian.

Upon my Marriage I became a Methodist, the religion of my husband, George Massing. Two of his grandfathers, Peter Prudden (ten generations removed), and his son, John Prudden (nine generations removed), were ministers. Peter was the first pastor of the Congregational church of Milford, Connecticut and John, a graduate of Harvard in 1668, followed in his father's footsteps.

George's maternal church ancestors were also Quakers from England and followed that faith until George's mother married his father who was a Methodist. His father, George's grandfather,

KATHRYN BUSBY MASSING

Joseph C. Massing was Catholic, being raised in the parochial German settlement of St. Magdalene, Indiana, and served by the St Magdalene Catholic Church, later living in Danville, Illinois, where he married Flora Ellen Roderick, a Baptist. They actually attended each others church, in Danville, his being St. Joseph's a German Catholic Church, a practice unheard of in those years. George and I attended his grandmother's Baptist Church for about a year then became affiliated with St James Methodist Episcopal Church where his mother was a member.

When we moved to Ohio, we looked for a Quaker church, but it was six miles away, and held infrequent meetings. So, we settled for Medway United Methodist Church which became our church home for thirty years.

Moving to Florida, we attended Hollywood Hills United Methodist Church for about one year while our home was being built in Naples, Florida, staying with my mother who had moved full time to Hollywood. This church had a marvelous bell choir which was invited to Europe where they performed.

Once we settled into our home in Naples in 1974 we joined the Golden Gate United Methodist Church, where we became close friends with Rev. Alfred Jodie and his wife Nancy until his transfer to a church at Cleveland, Florida. We then transferred our membership to North Naples United Methodist Church, with George's brother Joseph and wife Virginia and George's mother. We remained there until 1983 at which time we moved to Yacht Club Colony, North Fort Myers and transferred our membership to First United Methodist Church in downtown Fort Myers, Rev. Donald Padgett, Pastor. He was a wonderful down-to-earth pastor, speaking without notes and doing the entire scripture lesson from memory. He hailed from Pahokee, Florida, and was proud of it, later retiring there.

At First church we attended the Welcome Sunday School class began by, and taught by, retired minister, Rev William "Bill" Pethrick, who was excellent, and in his 90's. When he could no longer handle the class he was replaced by Doctor A.Waldo Farabee, a native Floridian from Fort Myers, a wonderful, excellent minister. The class was built up to one hundred members. He teaches the class well and with aplomb. When he has to be away, he has his wife, Marion, fill in for him, as well as other retired ministers and lay persons, such as Gary Snyder, an excellent choice. He is also the travel minister for the entire church, arranging many fabulous trips both in the United States and abroad. His wife, Marion, accompanies him on all these functions adding her touch and expertise to the success of each one. He also arranges with Broadway Palm Dinner Theater for church members to have the opportunity to attend the top theatrical shows brought there.

When they spend their summers in France and take other leave Rev. Farabee arranges for Charge ministers to handle the class in his absence.

One such minister was retired Dr. Willard Fetter, a minister for 27 years in Dayton, Ohio, a former Evangelical United Brethren, which church merged with us and caused us to become United Methodist.

The Welcome Class is always very receptive to his manner of teaching, and his witty remarks. The lesson was on Abraham and Sarah, who had the baby Isaac when they were somewhere around 100 years old.

Dr. Fetter ended the lesson by saying he saw a great white egret, perched on the top peak of his house this morning before he left for church. "I stretched and looked very carefully to be sure it was a great whit egret, and not a stork!"

The very thought of a stork bringing a baby to their house made us all laugh.

Reverend Padgett was followed by Reverend Kenneth Blitch, then Reverend Walter Edwards.

Rev. Edwards always opens his prayer with a statement, "You pray for me, while I pray for you."

Reverend Archie Buie served the church as the next minister. He was a mild mannered man.

Our present minister Reverend James Rosenburg has high aspirations. He guided the church with the sale and move of the Kingston-Langford home to its new location across Fowler Street.

He holds the River of Life Service in the Life Enrichment Center on Sunday morning before he conducts the traditional service in the Sanctuary at 11:00 A.M.

He teaches bible classes following the potluck suppers.

His latest effort is an ongoing 3 year plan for a "Downtown Spiritual Awakening Campaign" based upon the need to revitalize our church and meet the demands of a great influx of people to the downtown area from the growth of new condominiums such as the Beau Rivage, High Point Place and others. This creates the possibility of the arrival of 3000 to 5000 new residents in our area in the next few years. Reverend Rosenburg is ready, hoping, and planning for this new challenge.

Reverend Phil White serves as an excellent Assistant Pastor, lending his expertise to all services.

Chapter 49
The Last Trip to the North - 1994

The summer of 1994 was a big one for the Massings.

Robert, Larry and Judy's German exchange student, packed up most of his belongings, mostly American by now, and went back to Germany. He and his fellow exchange students had a last fling in New York City, amongst tears of regret for having to leave America, and happiness of returning to their loved ones back home.

George and I left Florida, to travel up I-75, turning off onto I-24 at Chattanooga to go to Illinois to visit our old, beloved home towns, and on to Ohio to attend the Eagle Scout Award ceremony of our Grandson Seth Massing, and to visit family and friends there.

Joshua was to leave for Germany, to visit Robert Rochele, the German exchange student, to visit with him for four weeks. Larry and Devon were to go to Holland for Devon to play soccer there, traveling on through Holland, sightseeing, then on to Germany to visit with Robert's family along with Joshua. The three then traveled on to Theley, Germany, to visit our German friends, Peter and Margret Massing, whom George and I visited in 1985 and we call our German cousins.

Jennifer accompanied her soccer team to England where they played soccer with British teams.

We planned our trip to the North in July 1994 to coincide with an Eagle Scout award ceremony for our grandson Seth Massing to be held near Yellow Springs, Ohio, on July 24. We traveled through Alabama, Tennessee, and Indiana to Illinois first, on routes familiar to us.

We stopped in Lawrenceville, Illinois, and spent three hours looking for my cousin, Merle Jones, who was the great grandson of Ira Grover Jones, also my great grandfather. We could not find him there so our trail led us to Chrisman, Illinois.

Merle and his first wife, Magdalene, were the ones we visited, with Mother and Dad, the first time we came to Florida, as they lived in North Naples. She was one of the first school teachers on Marco Island and she took us there to show us her school.

We enjoyed that day very much, visiting that lovely little schoolhouse among the trees and foliage. We have loved Marco ever since. It seemed wild and wooly compared to now, with its huge condominiums on the beach and multi-millionaire homes, where the elite live.

From Lawrenceville we drove north, through Paris, to Chrisman.

"I got that in Paris!" I said one day to Jenna.

"Paris!" she said excitedly. "Have you been there again?"

It was a nice little present we had bought for her.

"No!" I laughed at her reaction, which I hoped to get.

"Illinois!" I said. "Just Paris, Illinois! I wish it could have been Paris, France. I would dearly love to go back there."

Now, in 1994, with his wife of fifteen years, Merle is living in the most coveted spot for older people to live in the eastern Illinois area. His second wife, Gertrude and he had been school-day sweethearts who had married other loves, and now had found their way back together!

They are very happy in their home in Shady Rest, a care center at Chrisman, Illinois. There they have a cottage for couples with all the rest of the care center facilities available to them.

Merle Jones is a great grandson of Ira Grover Jones. He is the last in his generation. His expectation of a long life is continuing, as he is only 91, and his father and uncle lived to be 95. Both he and Gertrude, who is 91 also, have a keen sense of living and are a wonderful, beautiful, and alert couple. It was a pleasure to talk with them.

"You are just young people!" They told us.

To them we were! Isn't age relevant, after all?

That's not what Larry and Judy, our son and wife think! And our grandchildren think we're positively ancient!

"What are we going to do with Grandpa and Grandma?" Jenna asked her mother one day. "How are we going to help them when they get too old to take care of themselves?"

"We'll just have to take care of them!" our Judy said.

That was nice to hear. We have never worried about the future, planning it the best we can, but enjoying the present to the fullest!

After we left Chrisman, we continued north, going through my birthplace Ridgefarm, Illinois, as we turned west at the center of town and slowly went past Grandma's old Victorian home, I choked up, as usual. It was still beautiful, albeit crumbling, but it held so many marvelous memories.

As we approached the front of the house, there was a young man at the top of a tall light, a new light that had never been there.

"Do you want to stop?" George asked me.

"Of course! Yes! Let's do!" I hadn't thought of stopping, but why not?

We unhitched ourselves from our seatbelts and things around us and tumbled out of our car.

As I stood below the young man and looked up at him, he made a beautiful picture leaning himself against the post, working on the light itself, with the house in the background.

Steve Metz, the owner of the house disentangled himself, and came down to talk to us. He was and extremely pleasant man in his late thirties or early forties, handsomely blonde and lean.

"This used to be my Grandma's house," I said. "We have visited you before. Do you remember? It was when my Mother died in 1981."

"Yes, I remember," he said.

We continued talking, mostly about the house, and what he had done with it, getting it back in shape.

"The inside is mostly finished. I'm going to do the outside last," he said.

"May I see it?" I asked hesitantly, I couldn't wait any longer!

"Sure," he said. "Come in!"

As we went past the side of the house, to the side entrance, which entered through the kitchen, I noticed the brick on the house looked beautifully pointed, neat and new.

"Yes," he answered when I asked about them. I had those pointed. They do look nice, don't they. He had done marvels with the inside of the house. Lots of changes, to make it more livable in the "now" time, but it still had the feel of Grandma's house.

When we walked into the parlor and he pointed out the original look of the fireplace, I was ecstatic! It was back to the original state of heavy walnut instead of the white painted fireplace we saw in 1981, which, of course, had left me completely cold and hurt. This fireplace was gorgeous! Back to Grandma's time. The way it should be.

I imagined Grandma's beautiful Victorian furniture and oriental rug there, instead of the new modern contemporary furnishings and the heavy plush rug.

It brought back a flood of memories.

The winding staircase was there, painted, but soon to be stripped by Steve's wife. As I stood looking at the lovely winding bannister that I flew down so many times, I told Steve about it.

"Yes, my kids have tried that a few times!" he said.

"You have to jump off at the end!" I said. It had been so much fun.

"How much have you done upstairs? I asked. "Could we see that?"

We went up the stairs, and turned right, right into Grandma's bedroom. He had put a beautiful wooden wall between her old bedroom and the next bedroom, to give more privacy, and had put in a bathroom where there had been a closet.

After we had seen the bedroom Aunt Florence always used, or I did if there were more than one girl visiting Grandma at a time. I told Steve how I used to climb out of the window onto the flat top of the porch. He plans to fix the flat top into a porch where they can sit and read or just enjoy the outdoors. I can't wait to see that finished, and hopefully sit there myself and reminisce.

We went upstairs to the full attic where we kids used to play and try on Grandma's beautiful clothes she had bought to use in Europe.

There was another steep stairway that had a trap door, which we went up, and crawled out onto the top of the roof, fourth story.

What a sight! You could almost see the world from there! I had never done that. For some reason, as a youngster, I had never tried it, but I'll bet my bottom dollar my twin ornery brothers had done it!

It was a physical ordeal for George's and my old bones, but it was a fantastic visit down my memory lane!

As I rounded the side walkway, and viewed the front of the house to leave, I thought of that wonderful swing I sat in so many nights and thought of the world and where I would go in it.

"Are you going to put up the swing that used to go in the curve of the porch?" I asked.

"Yes, I am," Steve said. "That's the last thing I'm going to do. When that goes up, I am through!"

Well, Steve, I can't wait! I want to swing in that spot again, and reminisce of all the marvelous old times, and the fantastic new times that have happened to this old girl!

Steve Metz is a highway contractor.

He bought the house fourteen years ago at an auction. The guy who was bidding against him wanted to demolish the house! I am so glad Steve bought it and is restoring it.

When we left Grandma's house we continued west out of town on the Indianola road on to Sidell. We reached a dead end where we would turn left into Sidell or turn right to go to my cousin Irene Pugh Knight's home just north a short distance on the right. She is a twin to Eileen Pugh Weathers who lives in Ridgefarm on the way east to my farm home.

Irene welcomed us with great delight and showed us all around her lovely home inside and outside. She showed us furniture very well made by her late husband.

Outside she showed us her beautiful flowers of which she is very proud. George took numerous pictures of her flower beds.

She sent us home with several plants and an Allium bulb for George to try to raise, as well as seeds from many of her beautiful plants, such as Bachelor's Button, Marigolds and Hollyhocks. Somehow the Allium bulb she gave us got into our compost heap at our home where it bloomed and produced about a dozen or so new bulbs.

We returned to Ridgefarm and drove out to the farm, and looked at it as we went by. In my memory, I saw and loved our old hundred year old house, where now is a very nice mobile home, but one which supplants my wonderful thirteen room house, and leaves me cold. We drove on down the road and turning at the corner, went to see Bill Busby, my cousin.

Bill was in his garden, working in the cool of the evening. He came towards us with pleasure on his face. It was good to see Bill, and reminisce a little, as we always do.

We drove the open byroads up to Georgetown, George's birthplace, where we reminisced as we passed George's home where he lived at Meeks Station, (also called Essaw). We went by his old school, Wingard, where he and his cousins attended and their Grandmother Parker, long before them when it was a log cabin. We then drove on to Lickskillet, where his great grandparents, Ma and Pa Schooler, Marinda and Charles, had a grocery and general store with one gas pump. Later his Grandparents, Mom and Dad Parker, Daisy and Lon (for Alonzo), resided and operated the grocery in Lickskillet, and where so much of their lives happened. George told me again about his family and their escapades. They included a most tragic event after the family was returning from an outing. All of the family had alighted their buggy except for Pearl (George's mother's sister, and Betty's, Albert's, and Donald's mother), when the team of horses hitched to the buggy became agitated and ran away down the hill to the barn and beyond into the creek. Pearl was killed in the wreck of the buggy.

We waxed silent as we drove into Danville where George grew up and was graduated from Danville High School.

"Let's go up and get one of those fantastic sundaes we used to get!" I said.

We did, and it was just as we remembered it, the best in the world. The Turtle Sundae, as it is called, is made from buttered pecan ice cream, covered with delicious caramel with a big glob of thick hot fudge in the center , and covered completely, and then some, with crisp fantastic special buttered pecans. As I said, the best sundae in the world!

As we entered Danville, Illinois, we were looking for a hotel or motel room where we could stay for several days. There was no hotel or motel room available anywhere, until we had to go miles east, to get one. It was the Redwood Inn, where we arrived and stayed for several days.

Our room is huge, and reminds us of our first home after our marriage in Danville.

The next morning our delicious breakfast consisted of a Kent (the best!) Mango brought from Florida, bought on Pine Island, ripening on the way, delicious, juicy peaches bought along the highway coming through Georgia, and a beautiful ribbed yellow muskmelon, from Sandtown, Indiana, where we always bought delicious melons when I was a kid. We bought it in Lawrenceville, Illinois. A meal fit for a king!

We ate on our round table under a lamp hanging above us in our pre-fabricated spacious motel room at Redwood Inn, east of Danville.

Saturday we drove to Eugene, Newport, and Cayuga, Indiana, and visited George's cousin Donald Hawkins and his wife Winifred, who showed her huge doll collection to us. She has every doll ever made, I think! The collection was bigger than my sister, Anne's doll collection. Donald farms 2000 acres of Indiana bottom land.

We went to Eugene cemetery and looked for the grave of William Conner, the father of Ruth Conner, who married Ira Grover Jones, and who were my great grandparents.

I love to go to cemeteries, thinking of all those people who have lived before me. I try to envision their lives and how they looked. Ruth is buried in old Hopewell Cemetery, a Quaker Cemetery nearby in Indiana, as she died young.

The Cayuga, Indiana, Fair was going on, so after the best catfish dinner we ever ate at the Covered Bridge Restaurant in Eugene, we went to the fair. Cayuga Fair was always a favorite fair of my dad's and, of course, us kids, too. It took me back to the olden days of my youth to go there. George and I went to the cow barns, the fowl and poultry, saw the art work and beautiful quilts. After checking out the midway, we left, happy and venerated. We had had a good time at the fair! George's dad, who raised saddle and light harness horses, used to have his horses race at this fair as well as other fairs. George's Uncle Alman Hess drove the race sulky in the races. He stayed at the farm with George and his family each year during fair season and traveled the fair racing circuits.

When George was seven in 1925, he rode and showed his Shetland pony at the Edgar County Fair, Paris, Illinois, winning a red ribbon for second prize, competing against 12-year old youths.

The next day, we went to Target Discount Department Store (Danville doesn't have a Wal-mart which is our favorite) and bought one hundred dollars worth of work clothes, just perfect for George in his yard work at home. It was lunch time so we had a delicious grilled chicken sandwich with a coke, there.

As we drove down the street, we decided to have another delicious turtle sundae at The Custard Cup, which was established in 1949. We have been going there ever since, buying this fabulous turtle Sundae. No one else in the world makes one like The Custard Cup!

We stopped by Aunt Sudie and Uncle Nig's on the east side of town. Sudie is George's mother's youngest sister. We enjoyed talking about old times, and new times, too. Aunt Sudie and Uncle Nig have been married fifty years. She is 88 and he will be 95.

We then left Danville and made our way to Ohio to arrive there in time for our son Monte's youngest son, Seth to be awarded his Eagle Scout award in a special ceremony.

One of my fondest wishes was that each of our sons would get his Eagle Scout award. It was not to be. Monte fizzled out when he was still in the first part of Boy Scouts.

Larry continued with his scouting until he became a Life Scout. He received the Order of the Arrow. As he grew older he became an Explorer Scout. I thought for sure he would get his Eagle. But not so.

Therefore, when Monte's second son, Seth, was nearing his Eagle Scout Award, I was ecstatic. Finally I had a son, nay, a grandson, who became and Eagle Scout. What a joy it was to know through all the

THEN AND NOW

perseverence of scout training and work we finally had a boy who attained his Eagle Rank in scouting.

On Sunday, July 24, 1994, it was a perfect day when Seth Matthew Massing and his friend, Charles Baker, received their Eagle Scout Award.

The sun shone brightly as we drove to Yellow Springs and entered the John Bryan State Park, where the award ceremony was to be held.

As we got out of the car and walked towards all the activity of preparation, we met Shane and his beautiful girl friend. I kissed both her and him, as had Shane's Aunt Connie, before me.

There was a commotion behind us, and, to my surprise it was Seth driving his car, close to us as we stood along the drive.

"Hello, Grandma!" Seth said.

"Hi, Sugar!" I answered. "You're driving!" I knew he had a car, but I had never seen him behind the wheel.

"This is my friend, Charles," as he introduced his buddie, who leaned over closer to the window.

"I met you one day!" Charles said.

I looked closer at him. I remembered him!

"Yes, I remember!" I said, with enthusiasm. "You were in the kitchen one day when we came to see Seth!"

They had been eating snacks and drinking Cokes. It had been several years ago. Now he was all grown up and handsome!

"I have to park the car, then we'll be over," said Seth.

We turned back to Shane and his friend, and wandered over to the activities.

Shane and Seth's grandfather and grandmother, on Cindy's side, talked to us, saying how glad they were that we could come.

"We wouldn't miss it!" We said, "It is great to receive an Eagle Scout Award!" Cindy had told me only one percent of all scouts receive their Eagle Scout Award. We were so proud of our Seth, and Charles, too, to think they had persevered to finally be able to receive the award.

Tables were set up with cold drinks and food for after the ceremony. Fifty chairs were strewn under the shade of the tree shadows, with the head table across the front. On it were their awards, merit badges, medals and certificates that both boys had earned.

We found the best spot for us to see, the front row on the left side. People milled around until they found seats amongst friends.

Cindy and Dave Long, Shane and Seth's stepfather, managed the group until the presentation started.

Several former Eagle Scouts participated in the ceremonies as they progressed with the scoutmaster leading.

The president of the United States, and the governor of Ohio, both of whom became Eagle Scouts, had been invited to the ceremony, both declining to come but sending beautiful letters which were read. The United States Congress sent a beautiful letter also which was duly read.

The Eagle Scout awards were presented to each young man in turn, each standing tall with their parents and repeating his vows of anticipation of helping "my God and my Country" at every opportunity he has.

It was a beautiful, impressive ceremony held in the most wonderful setting of huge northern trees in the shadows of millions of leaves.

After the ceremony, George and I congratulated both boys, handsome and resplendent in their uniforms, for their efforts well done and wished them a bright and great future.

We got in the long line and served ourselves to fried chicken, potato salad, baked beans, and other goodies. The cake decorated with its Eagle Scout emblem, was a devil's food.

It was time to go! We said our goodbyes telling both boys there were presents for them on a table. They were tired, but both perked up at that.

We left, driving through Yellow Springs, where we had gone for art lessons so often. George took classes on the potter's wheel from Cindy Metcalf who taught at Antioch College. She had her degree from Alfred University, one of the most famous schools for pottery in the United States. George also took sculpturing from Alan MacBeth who had an art studio and restaurant there.

Yellow Springs has changed quite a bit. It is larger, teeming with more activities, with art being the biggest.

THEN AND NOW

We drove to Dayton to visit Monte's grave for the last time before we started home the next day.

Nearby was Monte's favorite place to eat, Joe's Pizzeria, which is still there, making the same pizza we went to get for years, many many times with Monte and several times each time we go back up north.

Even though we had eaten heartily at the Eagle Scout Ceremony, we had another supper at our and Monte's favorite, Joe's Pizzeria. The girl who always waited on us gave George a blue bag with their name on it from their 40th anniversary celebration in 1999.

The next morning, we packed and left for our beloved Florida, the best place in the whole world.

At Cincinnati, we stopped at the now renamed, The Mill, Watertower Square, in Newport, Kentucky, the Palm Beach Outlet Store, were we have shopped over the years. The minute we walked inside, I saw a beautiful subdued red and yellow plaid jacket, trimmed in yellow satin. I tried one on, bought it, within five minutes after entering the store.

Two more hours were spent finding three silk sport coats for George.

"Now, Kay, we're not going to spend much time in here!" George had said, rather sharply, as we got out of the car.

"George, don't say that! You know we never spend anytime anywhere where we aren't interested. If we see nothing we want, we'll leave right away, otherwise, we'll stay and look things over!" I admonished.

We continued on our journey south towards our home in Florida. We looked for barbeques all through Kentucky and Tennessee. There used to be big signs on the highway, but since small signs or no signs were politically correct, we do have problems finding what we want.

Finally, a barbeque! It was awful! But the nicest couple sat next to us. They were from Idaho, and after making a couple of jokes about Idaho and Iowa, we became quite friendly. He gave me a recipe for how to make perfect barbeque. I can't wait to try it out.

They were going to Northport, Florida, to finalize his father's estate, so we told them to come see us at Ted's Sheds. We work every Saturday at Ted's Sheds near Northport.

"Do you want to know where you can get the best barbeque around Northport?" I asked.

"Well, I make my own," he said hesitantly, "but yes, where is it?"

"It's at Labelle, in a little log cabin. It is delicious! Everything they have there is delicious!" I was getting hungry! This barbeque didn't compare!

As we paid our bill, a couple of women from Ohio, heading for Florida, were paying their bill.

"Wasn't it delicious?" One of them said. I hid my face near the canned preserves. The other lady was very upset.

"It can't be that! You've charged me twice!" I heard her say. "That's twice as much as it should be."

"Oh, yes, I have charged you twice!" the waitress said. "I'm so sorry!" It was an honest mistake, you could tell, but who ever heard of charging double the bill?

As we went out the door, the four of us together, I looked back at the waitress and saw she was busy trying to understand the terrible mistake she had made. "Do you want to know where you can get really delicious barbeque?" I tried to be subtle! But I threw all caution to the wind. " It's at Labelle, Florida, in a little log cabin. It is delicious!" I said.

Upon our arrival back home, after a trip of 3000 miles of driving, I entered our home, and yelled, "Hello House,"as I usually did after a long trip. It is so good to be home! I love to travel but I'm always glad to be home!

The next morning, as I stood at the kitchen window looking out at our beautiful lawn, I saw a gorgeous white egret with its long curled neck, stepping gingerly and delicately, the way they do, and it was such a beautiful sight, yes, we were home! That was a sure sign of it! The next day when we went to get groceries to fill our refrigerator which was empty, we were driving along, coming to a red light, when another gorgeous, white egret flew quietly and gently through traffic, above and across our car, to get on the other side of the road. He flew right across our windshield, as if to say, "Hello, welcome home!" We laughed happily as he glided past another car and to the side of the road. It was such a beautiful sight.

THEN AND NOW

For five years, I have prayed for Monte, our second son, that he was in heaven and would be the first person I would see, coming towards me as I walk, or glide, through the pearly gates of heaven.

Lately, I have been asking for a sign from God that Monte is with Him now and that I would be given a sign.

Yesterday, George and I picked up our pictures we took on our trip, when we visited Monte's grave in Dayton. For five years I've been praying for Monte's soul; now I have prayed for a sign that God has him in his arms. I got that sign.

I found George bent over the pictures from Ohio, clearly sad and touched.

"Did you see the light at the top of Monte's tombstone?" he asked me.

"No, I didn't!" I said. "What light?"

As I sifted through the pictures, I came to the ones George took at the cemetery. We always take pictures when we go there to be closer to Monte and to mourn him. Although we know his spirit isn't there, we feel his presence strongly when we are near his grave-site, thinking he knows we are there and that we still love him.

One of the pictures George took had a very bright light in the center of the tombstone at the top where I always stand and hold my hand, thinking so strongly of my son and how much I love him and pray he is safe with God.

This is the sign I have been praying for! I feel God has told me he has Monte, and he is all right. Thank Thee, my Father, for this fantastic sign that our beloved son is with you! I know now that Monte will be the first person coming towards me as I walk into my heavenly home.

Chapter 50
Now

For a while we discussed just what we should do, since we were approaching old age, and just what kind of plans we should make toward a solution. We decided it would be best to live out our old age with our children. So, when a beautiful house with an acre and a half area of land came up for sale, we dropped by to see it. It was about 5\8 mile from our home in Yacht Club Colony on the way to town.

We were anxious for Larry and Judy to see it, but they thought it was too early to think of all our living together. Joshua, their eldest, had a home himself, which had been a home he and Devon lived in the last few years of their high school education so they could be near to their school. That left only Jenna at home so there was plenty of room for all of us if we bought this new home in which we could all live together.

It was some time before Larry and Judy decided to go to see this new place, but they finally arranged with a realtor to see and examine the home. When they did see it, they fell in love with it, too. So we bought it together and immediately sold our two homes. It was absolutely the best thing we ever did!

Our home has two bedrooms upstairs, with a living room, an alcove, and a bath room, all for Jenna and Devon, who remained at home. Downstairs below this area, with a lot of open space outstanding, is a family room which is George's and my living room, with a utility room and hallway that has become George's computer room with a closet for him under the staircase. The hall opens into our bathroom and our bedroom and a huge walk in closet. In the center of the house is the kitchen and dining room with the living room at the side of the large entrance hallway and in front of the dining room. At the side of the dining room, there is a hallway that has Larry and Judy's bedroom and large walk in closet at one end and their large beautiful bathroom at the other end, after which there is a door that opens out to their office room. It used to be an Jacuzzi room. They needed an office more than an indoor Jacuzzi. They later installed another Jacuzzi outside next to the pool cage.

Front porches are across the front and back runways at the side between the house and a two car garage that we turned into a recreation room. The runway was enclosed to house the freezer and a second refrigerator and to become the laundry room. There is a lovely back area the full length of the house with a beautiful swimming pool and lanai area. To the back is a large double plus garage or barn for cars and overflow storage. A 10 by 10 room at one side has become a pottery room. Larry has installed a large Ted's Shed, to become a photographic darkroom.

We have lived here three years and love it more and more each day. George has grown all kinds of flowers and trees besides the twenty one live oak trees, twenty one sable palms, three queen palms, six citrus trees plus a "million" flowers and shrubs. It keeps everyone, especially George and Judy busy! But they thrive on it. Larry has since become very involved.

George is a Master Gardener now. He took the course about the same time we moved here, the Class of 2000, under the outstanding teaching ability of Stephen Brown, The University of Florida, Lee County Agent for Horticulture. So he loves all these plants and trees with a passion and goes to the continuing classes and meetings to keep up in education through classes and field trips. Larry and Judy are almost as crazy over everything as George, and amongst them, they keep everything looking great all the time.

George started a butterfly garden, perennial garden, rose garden bromeliad garden and Larry has built an elevated vegetable garden providing us with a continuous flow of fresh vegetables for the table.

KATHRYN BUSBY MASSING

This butterfly garden has been established as a site for reporting species of butterflies present each Tuesday. A "Butterfly Patrol" has been established with 20 some reporting sites to gain a feeling for what species are located throughout Lee County, Florida. This area reports as Site 8. We have Zebras, the state butterfly. One week there were 10 present, 7 on passion flowers, and 3 on the fire bush. We also have Cassius Blues, Cloudless Sulphurs, Florida Dusky Wing, Gold Rim Swallowtails, Great Southern Whites, Gulf Fritillary, Long Tailed Skippers, Orange Barred Sulphur, and White Peacocks.

We are located off Bayshore between Business U.S. 41 and I-75 and can be in downtown areas in about 20 minutes.

Chapter 51

Observations

There is much beauty in this world, but America is the tops! Traveling as much as we have, we have enjoyed every moment, have loved our wanderings, have been delighted in our travels in other countries, but America takes the cake! America has everything!

From the quaint little towns of the East, to the open fields of waving, fully ripened grain and long green rows of the corn fields, to the rolling hills, and straight highways, to the hominess of the quiet small towns, to the huge seething cities, America is full of life, love and the pursuit of happiness. The people are the catalyst, holding it all together, with their versatilities and thoughtfulness of one another. Woe to the man (and woman) who stays home all the time and lives in his\her little shell, never seeing God's gift to all of us. Life is as we make it, the riches for what we do with it.

God gives his people the ability to do fabulous things, from the farmer, to the artistic, to build houses, and all the other wonderful things we have, to the ones who enjoy the ability of his fellow man. We should appreciate all the wonders man has accomplished, be it large or small. Mankind, through the help of God, has given so much to this world of ours. I am sure God is well pleased with this old world, especially with America. God Bless America! But there seems to be a destructive element seeping into our beautiful land.

When she smiles, she can light up a room. When she scowls she can cause a person to want to take a step backward.

She is the heart of America, the inner self of a large country, the soul of America.

She hates what is happening to America. Where it was all easy and gentle living is now utter chaos and complete disillusionment. The drugs, the morals, the inability to get along with one another, all seems to be prevalent except in a certain section, and that is a small section. It is not whole as they creep in towards the lives of all in the center.

Can't this destruction be stopped? There have been bad times in the world before now, but people stepped in to correct the outcome of unscrupulous lives and thoughtlessness of others. Let there be gentle kindness toward each and every one to pervade the inner souls of all Americans. Humans must learn to love and live with one another. Give your love and thoughts beyond yourself, America, then we will have the Promised Land and welcome all newcomers to our perfect world.

All my life I have been given the freedom to make my own decisions. As a child I was molded into a free open Christian who was allowed unrestricted choices. Love of one another, correctness of living and my own developed thoughts and reasoning were allowed to nourish.

"I am either a personality" I said one day to my good friend Thelma Wolters at Crystal Lakes, "or a character!" She guffawed so loudly and long I had to join her.

There were times things didn't go right and I was forced to change directions, but after awhile I would get back on track and life would be good again. Time marches on, it never stops for anyone or anything. We have to seize the moment and make of that moment the best we can. My life has been good, great, fantastic. I would like to live it all over again, mistakes and all.

My husband encouraged me in all I endeavored to accomplish. He has always been there to help and become interested in everything I wanted to do, and yet keep me on the ground instead of flying too high at times. He and I make one. We give ninety percent of each other to one another. Not fifty percent as some people think they should. That stops too quickly with repercussions. He is now and always has been my best friend.

I'd like to believe I glided through life like a soaring pelican through the throes of life, gliding down to a slower and slower arena to land on the last edge of my life, onto my awaiting ground which will forever hold my wasted body, only to let my spirit soar again into the air and beyond into eternity, to be remembered and loved by all who knew me as one of the people in their lives who made a difference, I love you all.

> I've had my ups and downs.
> Life has been both hard and sweet
> I don't expect either garlands or crowns
> But my life has been hard to beat.

George thinks I am a complicated person. I think I am a very simple person. Freedom to do what I want, love of God and humanity has given me respect for right and wrong, and the purity of life have led me to activities and growth which have kept me moving towards a satisfied life. I think I am a very dedicated person to the idea my English teacher in high school taught me to be concise and to the point. I do not like to talk when I have nothing to say. It is very difficult for me to make small talk. I have known people who have made small talk a dedicated art. It is beautiful. They know exactly what to say to make people feel good. I wish I could do this. When I say things sometimes I think of my coming across as insincere.

One has to be oneself. One time I had won at my bridge club at Crystal Lakes over and over.

"I hate winning all the time I am very embarrassed to win every time we play," I said to my best friend Rita.

"Why don't you just throw the wrong card or something so you will loose?" Rita said.

"I can't do that! That would be like cheating! Everyone would know!" I was amazed that she would suggest it.

I kept playing as well as I could with no pleasure. I was just getting the right cards.

Finally the day came when the winning streak was broken and I lost. No one was happier than I. I had won ten months straight in a two table bridge club.

Joe, George's brother, said, "You can take the girl out of the farm, but you can't take the farm out of the girl." If this be true, and I hope it is, each part of my life has progressed because of the former part or parts. Put them all together, and I think my life has been pretty darned interesting.

I'm all for entering a new phase each and every day!

I want to go forward, and yet I want to reminisce and wonder about my past. I do not want to stand still. That is the most boring thing to do.

So, I want to keep moving on to bigger and better things, always remembering the old. I don't want to stand still, I don't want to "hide my light under a bushel," I want to go and do and learn and live!

George can never admit he is wrong. It just isn't in his makeup. That's why he has "Percy" at his elbow. Through perseverance he does accomplish much more than he would by just giving up. It is sometimes very difficult living with someone who can't admit he is wrong as nothing is accomplished. If one can admit he doesn't know it all, one can get on and accomplish more than being a "stubborn Dutchman" as George calls himself.

Many is the time I have to leave his side in order to save my sanity. The boys used to say we argued a lot. I agree. It's because of that darned stubborn Dutchman, isn't it?

What has happened to our quiet restaurants? Even our favorite places to get food are so noisy sometimes with customers talking and yelling at each other, and the waitresses, waiters, or cleanup crew throwing dishes together in a large container, that it is impossible to not having indigestion and broken eardrums.

The most wonderful place to eat for peace and quiet, gentle consumption of delicious food, is the King's Crown at South Seas Plantation, at the end of Captiva Island. It was so quiet there that we thoroughly enjoyed a marvelous meal of my favorite food, Rack of Lamb. The lamb was succulent and delicious, cooked perfectly, served beautifully, and joy of all, we had a quiet relaxing two hour meal.

This reminds me of a meal we had in England where we ate at a country inn on the Moors near Waddington, where everyone was so quiet, I was afraid to speak to George and I talked so quietly, we could hardly hear one another. It was fantastic! Everyone was talking so quietly we could not hear what they said to one another. Usually, I hear what everyone says to everyone. My hearing is so astute, a doctor told me, "It's almost a curse!"

I said, "Yes, I believe it is a curse!"

My sensitivity to smells is also a curse. My sister, Anne, had such a nose. She smelled everything! It really irritated the rest of us! From her smelling dirty socks to later years of smelling everything, no one else did, was really a bore for the rest of us.

Realizing that my nose and hearing are exceptionally sharp, all I ask is to have normal noise and smells around me. Please!

To me, and many people like me, they are too loud!

Do you remember, "Children should be seen and not heard?" That was an old axiom when I was growing up. I don't believe it. I love children of all ages, and I love to be around them. They are so wonderful with their learning and accepting new ideas and thoughts. Their growth is such a pleasure to see. But when they are fighting and squabbling, screaming and having tantrums, come to the forefront, I would rather be somewhere else for awhile.

My Mother was always at us to be kind and quiet. She wanted peace at all levels. No arguing at all. We were allowed to disagree with one another, but when we became loud and argumentative, she broke in to get peace back! She was the peace maker from the first time there was an argument, and was the peacemaker when she was in her nineties. She couldn't stand it when I raised my voice at George. She thought he was perfect. I knew he wasn't, but I did know that I shouldn't yell at him. Not when Mother was around, anyway!

One day I was watching the best TV show, voted nationally to be the best, and my favorite of all TV Shows, Home Improvement, and was laughing hilariously about everything that happened on it.

Wanting George to enjoy it too, I called to him, as he was working on his computer, actually typing a part of this book.

When he came to the family room, I ran the tape back to the beginning, as I did not want him to miss anything. The show was on the differences of their activities in the home. It pitted her non ability when it came time to fix the sink, etc., to his learning about sorting and washing clothes. It was the funniest Home Improvement I ever saw.

As we sat together, watching the funniest TV show on TV, I laughed hilariously at everything. George sat mute.

Finally, after the funniest part was over, I looked over at George to see why he hadn't laughed when the audience was going wild, and I along with them.

George had gone to sleep!

George's sense of humor is just about nil. I have often told people, "It's the German in him."

People used to say, "What's the matter with George?" When everyone else was having a good time.

"Nothing!" I would say. "That's just George!"

George goes at one speed: Slow. "Are you going to get on the computer?" I ask many times. "Shall we edit today? Or now?" I thought we would never get this book written.

"Come on, George, let's work! I said, many times. "I'm going to forget everything! My head is hurting, I need to get this out of my head!"

Now it's out of my head, on paper, I never have to think of it again!

I have two regrets in my life. Number one, I did not go to an academic college, and number two, I did not have more children.

I could have gone to the moon if I had had more education. Education is the greatest deliverer from a dull life that there is. One must be one's self to do what one wants in life, but education makes one freer and helps him/her to know just what he/she wants out of life, and, more importantly how to do the things he/she wants out of life.

THEN AND NOW

Children are a complete blessing to a family, the love a family needs. Without my children I would have been far less a woman. And, of course, it goes without saying, grand children are the icing on the cake. Great grandchildren, of which I hope I have many and varied, will be the decoration on top of the icing.

Life is good. Life is wonderful. I pity the poor pitiful people who don't want to do anything. There are so many wonderful things to do in this wonderful world! I can't imagine getting them all done. If we had the wherewithal, I could easily have become a jet setter. Go everywhere, do everything! With class! I read about them, and envied them, wished I could have been one of them. But since I couldn't I did the next best thing. I was alert to everything and, tried to do everything I could. I dragged or pulled George. Sometimes it did some doing, but together we made things happen. We've had a good life, one that is not over by any means. We will continue living a full and fruitful life as long as we can. Then we leave it all to our children and our children's children. I pray they all have full and happy lives. Never say it can't be done! It can, were there is a will, there is a way. It only takes the finding of that way! Keep trying, and you will have as full and happy life as we have had!

If one way won't work, look for another. Be open for suggestions, change plans in midair, if necessary. Press on to better things! Always press on! Don't become stagnant! That is the bane of all survivors! Push on, change direction sometimes, get started again. You'll be glad you did!

Do you laugh a lot?
A Laugher lives a lot longer!
Laugh and live!!

Lift your heart and be gay,
Traveling briskly on your way,
To better things and happier days,
Today, forever, and always!

For every moment we are unhappy or mad at something or somebody, we lose a precious moment we could have had in this wonderful, wonderful world. It is lost, gone forever, never to be relived again. So it behooves us to be happy and grasp every moment, make it the best moment we can. Savor the moment, and enjoy life!

What ever happened to my beautiful teeth, my snappy brown eyes, my beautiful blonde hair, my gorgeous legs, and my small waistline? Gone, gone, gone! But I still have spirit! I still want to go places and do things! I like my lounging chair, but I like to get out of it and go and do! I pray there are many more years of happy happenings in this old body of mine.

Here comes George. He's all spiffed up. He's taking me out on the town. It's a surprise. I like surprises.

What on earth has happened to our economy? I just bought a two piece gauze outfit with the price tag of $32.95 each.

When I was a little girl going through the depression, feed corn for the chickens was put up in some kind of bag. Since people had so little money, the makers of these bags tried something new and wonderful. Instead of putting the chicken feed in a brown gunny sack, they made a new design and put the feed in beautiful flowered bags of the same material. It was a new improvisation. How the women loved it. They could hardly wait until the feed bags were empty! They used the material to make beautiful new skirts, blouses and dresses. Everyone wanted them, mostly because they cost nothing.

George and I are growing old. Ah, I said it! I used to say "We are growing older." I was 39, and then 50 plus. Today. We are old! George is 85 and I am right behind him at 84.

"I don't want to grow old" Mother Massing used to say. "I'm not going to grow old."

"What's the alternative?" I said one day when I got really fed up with hearing her.

She looked at me intently. I could see her wheels turning.

"Well what is?" she finally said!

I laughed and told her.

"We die. We are sure to die." She never said she didn't want to grow old again.

As we grow older, we become feisty and yet we mellow out. Things don't seem so important as they used to, yet, try to cross us, and we put up a good fight. Our minds are made up as to how things should be, but when things are different, we accept them as they are. We have found out, there is no reason to fight against the flow of life so we appear to accept things the way they are. We let things go on around us without a fight. We mellow out! Let the younger generation take up the fight. We want to grow old peaceably. It's like a train going down a track. We see things coming, making lots of noise, but if we stand still and let the commotion come and go, we are still here when the commotion is all gone and everything turns back to quietness, and we realize it didn't matter, after all. Why stir up trouble? Things are going to happen, no matter what we do. Things will get done by those who want them done, then after it's all over we can all get back to the matter of living.

That's growing old. It really is nice. We can live and love without all the commotion and upheaval of younger folk. It really is great to be of the older generation. Voila! We've made it through the fast hurly-burly of life, now it's time for the glorious sunset of life, knowing we have fought the good fight and are on the smooth road to eternity. Next stop, Heaven!

The American Dream is to have more than your parents. Our children, we are told, is the first generation that will never make more than our parents. Is this true? What has happened to our amicable America, the place we love?

I'm not giving up on America and its dream! It still exists! Keep your head up high. Keep forging ahead and doing your best, and you will have that American dream! This is still the best of all worlds! Why do so many people want to come to our America? Because it is a dream to live freely and, if we persevere, we will have that dream of ours, to be happier and more affluent than we would have been somewhere else! America is still the best! Hurray for America!

About The Author

Kathryn Busby Massing was born into the Quaker faith on a 152 acre farm in mid-central Illinois, two miles from the Indiana line, in the area known as the Harrison Purchase. Ridgefarm, her hometown, has one of the public libraries built by funds donated by Andrew Carnegie, and is known as the Carnegie Library. Needless to say this library was a great influence on Kathryn being a continuous user of the library throughout all her years in the area. Her love of books led her to become a junior high school librarian in Ohio after moving there in 1943. She later became a law librarian in charge of the Judge Advocate Library (JAG) at Wright-Patterson Air Force Base, Dayton, Ohio. The library served sixty Air Force military and civilian attorneys.

She has been a mother and homemaker raising two sons to manhood, in the Methodist Church to which she had converted, with strong reminders of her Quaker heritage.

She has been an artist producing many fine works of art in all media. She was a member of Fairborn Art Association, Fairborn, Ohio, and The Dayton Art Institute, Dayton, Ohio, and has participated in art shows of those organizations.

She is widely traveled, having visited every state of the union except Alaska and Hawaii, some several times. She and her husband, George, spent eight weeks traveling in the British Isles, France, and Germany, with a brief visit to Italy. They also visited the Holy Land and Egypt on a seventeen-day travel ministry trip with the First United Methodist Church of Fort Myers, Florida.

This book is the story of her family life, art, friendship, and travels.

Printed in the United States
25551LVS00004B/34-51